Scouting with the Buffalo Soldiers

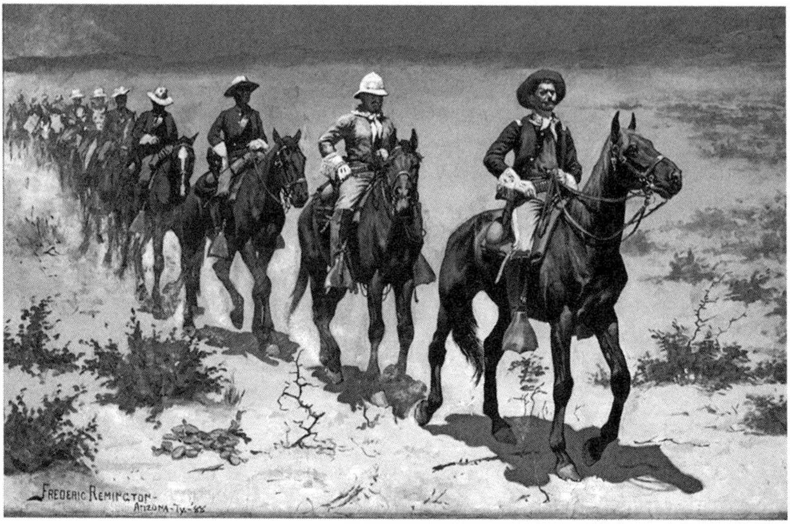

Scouting with the Buffalo Soldiers column of troops

Scouting with the Buffalo Soldiers

Lieutenant Powhatan Clarke, Frederic Remington, and the Tenth U.S. Cavalry in the Southwest

by
John P. Langellier

Number 19 in the North Texas Military Biography and Memoir Series

University of North Texas Press
Denton, Texas

Printed in the United States of America.

10 9 8 7 6 5 4 3 2 1

Permissions:
University of North Texas Press
1155 Union Circle #311336
Denton, TX 76203-5017

The paper used in this book meets the minimum requirements of the American National Standard for Permanence of Paper for Printed Library Materials, z39.48.1984. Binding materials have been chosen for durability.

Library of Congress Cataloging-in-Publication Data

Langellier, John P. (John Phillip), author.
Scouting with the Buffalo Soldiers : Lieutenant Powhatan Clarke, Frederic Remington, and the Tenth U.S. Cavalry in the Southwest / John P. Langellier.
North Texas military biography and memoir series ; no. 19.
pages cm
Includes bibliographical references and index.
ISBN-13 978-1-57441-811-8 (cloth)
ISBN-13 978-1-57441-820-0 (ebook)
1. LCSH: Clarke, Powhatan H. (Powhatan Henry), 1862–1893. 2. Remington, Frederic, 1861–1909—Themes, motives. 3. United States. Army. Cavalry Regiment, 10th (1866–1950)—Officers—Biography. 4. United States. Army—African American troops—History. 5. Indians of North America—Wars—1866–1895. 6. African American soldiers—Southwestern States—Portraits. 7. LCGFT: Biographies.

UA31 10th .L36 202
973.8 [B]–dc23

2020023995

Scouting with the Buffalo Soldiers: Lieutenant Powhatan Clarke, Frederic Remington, and the Tenth U.S. Cavalry in the Southwest is Number 19 in the North Texas Military Biography and Memoir Series

The electronic edition of this book was made possible by the support of the Vick Family Foundation. Typeset by vPrompt eServices.

Peter H. Hassrick and Thomas D. Phillips, Ph.D.
Mentors, Scholars and Colleagues

"An acquaintance formed in strange circumstances
and upon an almost unbelievable introduction
ripened into a friendship...."
Winston Churchill, My Early Life

Contents

List of Illustrations and Maps

Acknowledgments

The seeds of this project began in October of 1968, when as a senior in high school, a group of colleagues and I interviewed William Corbusier, son of the post surgeon at Fort Grant, Arizona, during the Apache campaigns. During the exchange he mentioned a visitor to the garrison, Frederic Remington, who was the house guest of a young officer named Powhatan Clarke. While the name Remington resonated, Tenth United States Cavalry Lieutenant Clarke meant nothing to me. Decades later, all that changed as a series of events and years of sporadic research, beginning at the Arizona Historical Society Library in Tucson, culminated in this publication.

Over time, search for more sources brought me to the University of Arizona Special Collections in Tucson. With the assistance of Roger Myers and Katie Young, I obtained images from the Leighton Finley Collection. In addition, in St. Louis at the Missouri History Museum Library and Research Center, Molly Kodner, Jaime Bourassa, and Lauren Sallwasser were stellar as they made the all-important Powhatan Clarke collection available to me. Clarke's cadet days brought me to West Point's Unique Resources Department of the United States Military Academy Library. Among others, Suzanne Christoff, Elaine B. McConnell, and Alicia Mauldin-Ware efficiently provided everything I requested and more. While I served as a visiting research fellow at the Buffalo Bill Center of the West, Mary Robinson, Mack Frost, Karen Roles, and Eric Rossborough guided me through the phenomenal holdings of the Harold McCracken Library.

Laura Foster, executive director of the Frederic Remington Art Museum. Ogdensburg, NY, generously carved days out of her demanding schedule to afford access to the incredible resources housed at this institution while her colleagues Laura Desmond and Shannon Ghize made certain the images were provided in a timely manner. Floyd D. Gottwald, Jr. cannot be thanked sufficiently for allowing *The Alert* to appear as the book's cover. From the Desert Caballero Western Museum,

Mary Ann Igna understood the difficult deadline I faced, and rose to the occasion with expediting my request for an impressive piece in that institution. At R. W. Norton Art Gallery in Shreveport, Louisiana, Loren Culver was most prompt and professional in providing a key painting from their many treasures.

So, too, did Catherine Tedford, director, and Carole Mathey, assistant director, at Richard F. Brush Art Gallery, St. Lawrence University, Canton, New York, respond to my request for a Remington cavalryman that often is overlooked. Similarly, The Virginia Museum of Art in Richmond granted permission for two of Remington's works thanks to Howell Perkins.

Robert Ray at *True West* assisted me with scanning images from my own collection as well as from the magazine's archives. Christopher Smith graciously shared his F.L. Palmer scrapbook and images from one of Clarke's fellow West Point Class of 1884 cadets. Art and Chris Sowin of Pahaska Books unearthed a number of fine photographs to accompany the text. Long-time colleague Stephen Gregory surprised me with an unknown candid cyanotype of Clarke at Fort Bowie, Arizona. Finally, my ever-helpful hero at Fort Concho National Landmark rushed the photo montage of Forrestine Cooper and her family in time to meet the printing deadline.

Jonathan Deiss served as my eyes at the National Archives in Washington, DC. RA Arancio-Parrain translated letters in Clarke's halting French. My youngest niece Geri Bertagnolli transcribed extensive pages of letters and diaries, along with providing preliminary proofreading.

Despairing that I would never complete this effort, Bob Boze Bell, Rick Collins, George M. Langellier, Jr., and Clark Whitehorn all urged me to persevere. So, too, did Jack Blades, who likewise enthusiastically hunted images for me as well as shared rare materials that became available just prior to publication.

All this would have been to no avail had it not been for the patience and support of Ron Chrisman, director of University of North Texas Press. The daunting final editorial process fell to Dr. Karen DeVinney, assistant director/managing editor. I can assure you that this was no easy task.

Turning to two final inspirations in every sense of the word, the late Dr. Peter H. Hassrick took time from his own scholarly pursuits at the Buffalo Bill Center of the West to offer expert guidance and assistance that enhanced the project. Finally, Thomas D. Phillips, Ph.D., labored for months reading chapter after chapter, commenting, editing, encouraging, and challenging the never-ending drafts. His sage advice, knowledge of the subject matter, as well as practical and sometimes difficult to accept but always instructional suggestions, proved indispensable. In many respects, he could be considered as the co-author of this book. Thank you to all those mentioned here, and others who made this publication possible.

Introduction

"Cadet Gray and Army Blue"

> The officers of the Old Army were a more mixed lot than any other peacetime period except after World War II. West Pointers predominated in the company ranks, but a large portion of the field ranks were held mostly by men who had served during the Civil War and were adjudged good enough to keep when the Regular Army was reorganized after the war. However the nonprofessionals as a group shared the ideals and the code that distinguished the career army officers.[1]

Two men from the post-Civil War "Old Army" shared much in common. Both attended West Point, graduating at the bottom of their respective classes as the "goat," for their low academic marks and high number of demerits for an array of infractions.[2] Despite their less than illustrious classroom performances, each earned their commissions as officers in the United States cavalry. Both went on to prove their bravery in battle as hell for leather horse soldiers.

Indeed, both of them embraced and embodied the "stylized code of conduct" of the officer class of their time, which historian Oliver Knight astutely described as: "Holding on to what was left of the values of the prewar

Army and seeing themselves in a light that was to some extent distorted by their fantasies" as living "in a miniature Arthurian court" where they played the role of "a medieval knight *sans peur et sans reproche* (one of their favorite expressions….)"[3]

This pair of Victorian-era paladins lived up to this self-image to the fullest. Finally, both died at a young age while serving in Montana, leaving behind grieving widows, who never remarried.

There the similarities ended. The older of the pair, George Armstrong Custer, fell on June 25, 1876, at Little Big Horn and passed into legend.[4] The younger of the two, Powhatan Henry Clarke, drowned accidentally while swimming in the Little Big Horn River, which ran adjacent to the post where he was serving—appropriately—Fort Custer. After his demise, Clarke would pass from the public eye.

Born during the American Civil War on October 9, 1862, to Southern gentry, Clarke enjoyed considerable privilege. He traced his lineage in the United States to at least three forebears from Virginia who fought for the Continental cause. His father, who was a medical doctor, served as a Confederate cavalry officer. Afterwards, Dr. Clarke, a family patriarch in a patriarchal society, resumed civilian life to take up a distinguished career as a college professor. In short, unlike the Custers, the Clarkes stood in the ranks of the elite.

Dr. Clarke and his wife spoiled their eldest offspring, whom they nicknamed "Powie." They provided him with a good education including study abroad in France. Through family connections, the gangly lad secured an appointment to the United States Military Academy. Upon completing four grueling years of study, Clarke barely received his commission as a second lieutenant. He did so at a time when the old guard of Civil War veterans, many of whom had been appointed from civilian life, were approaching the end of their days in uniform.

Clarke, like most of the junior officers of the last quarter of the nineteenth century, hailed from West Point. U.S. Military Academy graduates received assignments based on their status from top to bottom. Those with the highest standing could choose the best openings such as with the prestigious Corps of Engineers.

Clarke being the "goat" of his class meant his lowly ranking relegated him to an assignment not only with either an infantry or cavalry regiment, but also one comprised of black enlisted men, a posting not uncommon for the times. Because the widespread racist atmosphere during and after Reconstruction differed little from antebellum attitudes, many officers disdained an appointment to a regiment manned by African Americans. For instance, Custer's anti-black views meant he declined a lieutenant colonelcy with a regiment consisting of African American enlisted personnel, eventually to accept a similar assignment to the Seventh Cavalry.[5]

Clarke did not have the luxury of seeking another billet. So it was that he linked his martial star to the Tenth Cavalry, one of the two mounted Regular Army regiments formed in 1866 with black troopers commanded, in all but three cases, by white officers.[6]

Despite the prevailing prejudices held by most white officers and their civilian counterparts of the era, Clarke at the outset of his military career seemed ambivalent about his lot. Eventually, he evolved from accepting his situation to maintaining that he commanded some of the finest troops on the frontier regardless of skin color.

Clarke would share his experiences and enthusiasm not only privately, but also publicly, at first through the lens of an artist-author who became an unlikely comrade—Frederic Sackrider Remington. The relationship between the two youthful romantic spirits began on an adventurous road that parted barely a decade after they met.

Born on October 4, 1861, in upstate New York, young Remington grew up with the martial tales spun by his Civil War veteran father, "Pierre," and his comrades. As historian Peter Hassrick suggested, young Remington "doted on stories of his father's daring exploits in Virginia and Louisiana" as a Civil War Union officer.[7] Consequently, he must have been in his glory when as a teenager in 1876 he attended a military prep school. "Bud" Remington, as he came to be called, spent the next two years there. During his time at the Highland Military Academy in Worcester, Massachusetts, he wrestled with military drill manuals while spending "his free time committing youthful pranks" along with churning out "awkward pen sketches" depicting cadet life and other martial themes.[8]

After graduation Remington went on to a short-lived academic stint at Yale where at 180 pounds, an impressive weight for the time, he joined the football team. Athletics, horseback riding, and eventually pen and ink sketches were favorite pastimes that eventually led him on a path that he and his family could not have imagined.

In due course, the fledgling illustrator emerged as a world-renowned figure, blazing the trail for scores of artists who followed him. Arguably, the status Remington achieved blossomed from his forays in Arizona where he mingled with black troopers, Indian scouts, and dashing officers including one of his favorites—Clarke, whose name he constantly misspelled,

Clarke, like the vagabond Remington, also grew and drew from lessons learned on the demanding frontier. For one thing, his heroism during the pursuit of Geronimo, the Apache Kid, and Masai as part of the last gasps of Apache resistance would bring the lieutenant to the attention of his superiors, including former store clerk turned Union volunteer Nelson A. Miles, who would rise to the top of the U.S. Army's hierarchy.[9] Additionally, some of the American reading public, in great part because of Remington's efforts, and in small part because of Clarke's own jottings, began to take note of this up and coming frontier soldier.

Clarke's entry into the realm of writing as reporter, commentator, and military reformer experienced mixed results. Even when reaching less controversial conclusions about the American military establishment, Clarke did not rise to the stature of the brilliant Union Volunteer Major General Emory Upton, a Union "boy general" of the Civil War whose first-hand knowledge of that bloodbath inspired him to produce a new tactical manual drawn from the carnage he witnessed. Later, his experiences and observations from extensive travel abroad led to more broad-based provocative strategic studies.[10]

Yet Clarke's foray into this arena was not without merit. Indeed, he may have made larger, more significant contributions had he not died young. For instance, his temporary duty in 1891 and 1892 with German mounted forces might have offered important insights of value during World War I. That was not to be. Instead, his reports to the secretary of war about the much-vaunted Germanic martial prowess would be dutifully filed and forgotten.

Speculation aside, the fact that much of Clarke's candid writings and other documentation scattered among several repositories has survived, make it possible to reconstruct the life and times of a Victorian ideal for many men of the era.

It was a time when there was no place for other ethnic groups in their frontier pantheon.[11] Instead, among the iconic heroes for many males was "the cowboy … the last cavalier…."[12] Driven by a thirst for "western adventure" they "journeyed west to stake a claim" and to test and prove their "manhood on the battlefield," albeit one that was imagined rather than real, at least until the Spanish American War.[13] For Clarke, the West was not a make-believe "giant theme park" as it was for these dudes. It was a dangerous place where hardship, privation, and the threat of death required determination, fortitude, and courage.[14] Despite this critical difference and others, Clarke and Remington formed a fast friendship against the stunning backdrop of Arizona and Sonora.

In some respects, their relationship helped launch Remington's career, propelling him on to the national and indeed the international stage. To a certain degree, the New Yorker lived vicariously through Clarke's actual exploits and those of the frontiersmen in blue—the army in the West—capturing many nuances like a latter-day ethnographer although heavily romanticizing these military men in the process.[15]

While filtered through a particular perspective, as historian Thomas Phillips argues, Remington would move on from his chance meeting with Clarke and cursory introduction to the "buffalo soldiers" (a term he helped popularize) to a rapid:

> ascent into the ranks of one of the most celebrated American born artists [which] can be traced to his first rough renderings of black soldiers in Arizona Territory, which would play a prominent part in the approximately 2,300 outpouring of his pens and paint brushes, produced between 1886 and 1897, nearly all of which were published. Of these, approximately twelve percent (270 images) represented the frontier army with some fifty or more of these capturing black soldiers. As such, a sizeable audience was shown a fairly faithful face

> of military in the West including African American troops. In this latter category, Remington presented the black frontier regulars as soldiers—uniformed, armed and equipped as their white counterparts. His art recorded their martial duties and overall offered a positive image of these blacks in army blue, which made a large, important, and even influential segment of the reading public aware of their presence. In so doing, Remington might be viewed as the father of the buffalo soldier legend as it has come down to us today.[16]

In fact, Remington benefitted from his association with Clarke, but the connection was not one sided. As the artist grew in stature and gained influence, he encouraged the young officer to publish his own writing that would reach a larger audience than his personal letters to family and friends. Remington also featured his comrade in his own articles and renderings including one of his first pieces recognized by the established American art community, an oil on canvas of Clarke. Thus, Clarke gained as much as Remington did from their association.

Such exposure on a national level, Clarke's genuine valor recognized with a Medal of Honor, and notice by important superiors established Clarke as a promising officer. For instance, the *Army and Navy Journal*, must reading for all officers of the era, portrayed Clarke as "a slim, wiry six-footer, with a laughing impudent face adorned by a small black moustache. His eyes are black and his hair black and curly. He is skillful at boxing, fencing and wrestling, a dead-shot and a superb horseman."[17] With such a glowing peer review at an early age, one can only wonder what part he would have played if he had lived a longer life.

Speculating about a future that was not to be serves little purpose. Conversely, there is merit in charting the obscure, fleeting course of this young frontier soldier, based on the wealth of personal correspondence and other primary sources. Here is a nearly unprecedented, intimate, human look at the evolution of a flawed but fascinating junior officer. Rather than taken from the perspective of a senior commander's self-promoting memoirs written long after the fact, Clarke provides an oft overlooked point of view from an up and coming subaltern earning his spurs and coming to grips with the profession of arms. Clarke's unfiltered, relatively unselfconscious journals, confidential letters, and even public pronouncements, offer a provocative window to a transitional period, not only in the U.S. Army, but also in the nation as a whole as it faced racial issues, the closing of the frontier, and this one-time minor, fledgling republic's emergence as a budding international power.

Chapter 1

"In Dixie Land Whar I Was Born"

Born in Alexandria, Louisiana, on October 9, 1862, the new arrival would be christened Powhatan Henry Clarke. Newborn Powhatan Henry took his first name from the seventeenth century leader of a confederation of Virginia's early Algonquin-speaking people known as the Powhatan and their august chieftain, Wahunsenacawh, who would be referred to by the whites as Powhatan, the legendary father of Pocahontas. James Clarke, the founder of the line, arrived in early eighteenth-century America from Surrey, England, taking up residence in Powhatan County. His descendants remained there for several generations and would join the ranks of the "F.F.V." (First Families of Virginia) with several of them serving during the American Revolution and War of 1812 against the British. In fact, John Clarke held membership in the Society of the Cincinnati, a fraternal organization founded in 1783 for veteran American and French officers of the Continental Army, and was said to be "a friend of Gen'l Washington…."[1]

Prior to the arrival of the newest member of the venerable Clarke clan, his father, Dr. Clarke, had left the Virginia home of his forefathers to make his way to Rapides, Louisiana, which was near his assignment as a member of the faculty of the Louisiana State Seminary of Learning. Established in 1860 and re-designated later that year with the appended term

"Military Academy," this institution of higher learning was destined to become better known under the title adopted in 1870—Louisiana State University. There the young surgeon-scholar assumed duties as an assistant professor of chemistry and the school doctor. West Point graduate William Tecumseh Sherman, who after the war between the United States and Mexico had left the army for civilian pursuits, served as the school's first superintendent.

During Dr. Clarke's brief tenure at Louisiana State Seminary, he met Louise Frances Boyce, three years his junior, whom he wed on May 14, 1861.[2] Lore has it that Louise "was well known throughout the South and was noted for her beauty and genteel dignity." Louise was one of two children in the Boyce household. Her mother, Irene Archinard, supposedly was "a descendant of the last Spanish commandant of Louisiana before it came under control of France."[3] Tragically, Irene died at age twenty-two.

Louise's father hailed from Londonderry, Ireland, where he read law and entered the bar in 1820. Around 1824, after sailing from his familiar native land to an unknown future in Louisiana, Henry Boyce arrived in St. Martin where he soon established his legal practice in Alexandria, Louisiana, his residence for the next four years.

By 1828 Henry Boyce acquired land, dubbing his estate, near Alexandria, Louisiana, along the Red River and Bayou Rapides, "Ulster" as a nod to his homeland. These holdings grew over time, a portion of which became the town of Boyce. Typical of his region and era, Boyce was a slaveholder.[4] Beside oversight of plantation activities, Boyce divided his time as a Louisiana district judge from 1834 through 1839, the year Irene passed, possibly as a complication of childbirth. Boyce's short-lived first marriage left him a widower. Before long he wedded a second time, in this instance Octavia Delany Mullanphy of St. Louis. Octavia, one of five daughters of John Mullanphy, St. Louis's first millionaire, bore Judge Boyce's third child, Mary Elizabeth. Meanwhile, Boyce continued as a planter until being appointed as the U.S. attorney for the Western District of Louisiana followed quickly by President Zachery Taylor naming him to the bench as a judge for the U.S. District Court for the same jurisdiction. Confirmed by the United States Senate in 1850, Boyce presided for nearly a dozen years. Then, on February 19, 1861, he stepped down from the bench, as war approached, turning full time, as conditions permitted, to his cotton plantation from that date until his death.[5]

This comfortable life ended for the Boyce and Clarke families after the firing on Fort Sumter, South Carolina. By June 13, Dr. Clarke requested orders. As of April 2 of the following year, as part of the Army of the Mississippi under Albert S. Johnston, he saw action at the Battle of Shiloh as adjutant of the First Mississippi Cavalry commanded by Alabamian Andrew Jackson Lindsay, a graduate of the U.S. Military Academy who formerly was a captain in the United States Army's Regiment of Mounted Rifles during the war with Mexico. Later, in 1862, Clarke joined the staff of Brigadier General Daniel M. Frost during which period among other things he engaged in buying lumber for bridge construction to Avery Island. This return to Louisiana coincided with the doctor's impairment from rheumatism, an ailment that prompted him to seek a less demanding assignment near his kinsmen.

Meanwhile, the war forced his wife, newborn son, and in-laws to flee as Union forces neared. Heading back to see them, on May 9, 1863, Lieutenant Clarke returned to the estate only to be taken prisoner. The captivity proved short-lived. He managed to escape so that he could serve out the rest of the war.[6]

Eventually husband, wife and infant son were reunited, and the doctor turned solider indicated: "The Baby is perfectly well & certainly much better in temper." Not long after that, the war drew to a close, bringing Lieutenant Colonel Clarke (his final rank) back to Louisiana.

Returning home, he soon received word of his father's death in October. Despite the loss, Dr. Clarke concentrated on resuming civilian pursuits. Among his post-Civil War accomplishments, he became a member of the board of visitors of the Louisiana State University.

By 1872 Dr. Clarke looked to new opportunities. The ambitious physician and academic packed up Louise and their two sons, their eldest, "Powie," and Henry Boyce, who had been added to the household on March 9, 1871. The doctor had accepted the professorship of natural sciences at Baltimore City College. He also held the position of professor of chemistry for thirty years at Baltimore Medical College. In later life he would be elected as vice president of the Maryland Academy of Sciences.

On New Year's Day 1873, Judge Boyce sent a message to "Colonel" Clarke, mentioning he had received a bottle of whiskey for Christmas.[7] He conveyed other tidbits of what seemed to be a comfortable existence, perhaps more so than scores of his fellow former planters who had fallen on difficult times with the extinction of much of their wealth after the toppling of the Peculiar Institution. For many if not most whites in the South, the blow of losing the war and their slaves, combined with the follow on of Reconstruction, which among other things had denied Boyce from taking his seat in the U.S. Senate when elected in 1865, stung the onetime Southern elite.

Evidently Boyce took the new status quo post bellum in stride. At the twilight of his life, he had more emotional matters on his mind. Boyce confided to his son-in-law that he must "realize now the comforts of a wife and can comprehend something of the duality of feeling … that I am suffering under. I want to go there [to Baltimore], but I can't leave here." In short, he missed his daughter and her family in Maryland, but he must remain at home with his own wife and the others left in Louisiana. He concluded with bidding Clarke to convey his affections to Louise and little grandsons.

This seems to be the last known communiqué to his transplanted relatives in Baltimore. On March 1, 1873, at age seventy-seven, the venerable Irish attorney turned Southern gentleman died. Little Powhatan still had one living grandparent left to dote on him—his paternal grandmother Mary Clarke, who responded from her home in Milford, South Carolina, where she presumably resided with one of her children. Acknowledging a letter from her young grandson, she informed: "I was most agreeably surprised to see how well you could write."[8] Grandmother Clarke confessed she often talked about her grandson "to strangers … I have to stop for fear I weary them." She went on to recall when he had lived with them briefly, he had come to tears one day.

Later that same year, when he was barely ten years old, Clarke was off on an expensive holiday abroad with his mother. Writing from Paris in early August 1873, the dutiful son expressed his honesty, at first disliking his new surroundings, but he began to warm to the unfamiliar Parisian scenes.[9] Taking in impressive sites and sights he recounted viewing the moon through a telescope and experiencing a carriage ride under the *arc de triomphe*. The short note concluded with an early indication of his passion for things equestrian: "don't sell my horses unless you can save the money for us." Whether Clarke simply displayed a childish concern for his precious horse, or had some inkling of the value of money as well at this early age, is unclear, but even as early as his days at West Point, he would reveal a certain appreciation for finances. Even then, his spending patterns proved erratic.

The trip abroad represented more than just a tour. It served as a prelude to his embarkation on an early stage of his education. He was to attend *le Societé de Marie Institution St. Vincent* in Seplis, France. Remaining on the Continent after his mother's return to Maryland, like many children sent off to boarding school, he alternately experienced separation anxiety counterbalanced by his first taste of being away from parental controls, meeting new friends, and facing a very different world from his childhood past. Letters home, such as one of the earliest, dated March 2, 1874, sometimes contained snippets of French.[10] Later communications came increasingly in that language, although his rudimentary understanding of the tongue of his host country was only exceeded by his total disregard for punctuation. While he could be excused in both cases due to his youth, avoiding periods, commas, and the like also might be seen as his lack of interest in school and perhaps even the early marks of a free spirit. Indeed, while his academic performance tended to be above average in many cases, and he frequently made reference to his parents about grades and honors, he perhaps emphasized these factors to please his family, rather than out of any personal passion for learning. His regular pleas for letters from home also underscored his periodic loneliness, and indicated his strong bonds to his parents. These topics remained leitmotifs in his correspondence for years to come.[11]

At another time, he demonstrated a desire to remain close to his mother, but likewise disclosed a growing acceptance of his lot. "I would have written to you sooner but I have been too busy having fun and had no time to do so …" he offhandedly remarked. Then, he countered with the lack of a letter from home, having not received anything in the mail for what he felt was too long a silence. Playing the guilt card, he lamented, "I was a little troubled to know if you were well and I did not know why dad was not writing to me."

This French sojourn indicated young Clarke's developing personality. He could be competent, charming, and dutiful when it suited him, but often proved lazy or uninterested in his studies. That pattern persisted after the teenager sailed for home.

Once he reached stateside, Clarke recommenced his academic pursuits, with attendance at Georgetown as a fourteen-year-old college preparatory student. There Powhatan, like many of his friends, enjoyed a rather carefree life as opposed to a goodly number of Gilded Age children in the United States who worked from an early age and lived in squalor. While at Georgetown, Clarke's parents remained the prime recipients of his correspondence. As in the past, he pledged to "study hard this year," assuring them that he "had not missed a lesson yet…."[12]

To a certain degree his grades reflected adequate effort with a respectable 88 in English and an 82 in French.[13] Further, he strove to earn awards for top marks in mathematics, which in fact he would do at least during the forthcoming January.[14]

Diligent application to this subject may have taken on particular importance in that Powhatan had been permitted to spend the holidays at the U.S. Navy Yard in Washington, D.C. At this juncture he may have been looking toward a naval career that required proficiency in mathematics. Perhaps he likewise sought approbation from his role model father. As such, Powie strove to master arithmetic to gain paternal recognition.

After Georgetown, Clarke than moved on to the Maryland Agricultural College (now the University of Maryland). Founded in 1856 and designated a land grant school under the Morrill Act of 1862, the institution would be presided over by several former Confederate officers in the first few years after the Civil War's end. Among them, William H. Parker, a graduate of Annapolis at the head of his class in 1848, had fought for the South. Parker as a captain founded the Confederate Naval Academy located in Richmond, Virginia. He remained at the helm of the school that would become the University of Maryland until 1882.[15]

During his course of studies there, a January 1878 letter confirmed the youth's interest in the U.S. Navy.[16] In response, Dr. Clarke assured his son that he "was a boy once" and proud that his eldest offspring was "getting no demerits"–a situation that would change all too soon! The doctor lauded: "You deserve more credit than a boy who has no mischievous tendencies & it is the more gratifying as you are doing it to please us." The former commissioned officer offered that his heir had "chosen a profession in which order & obedience are essential to success & I shall always do my utmost to assist you in schooling yourself to the conditions imposed." Such heartfelt fatherly outpourings and gentle advice could have served Clarke well. Alas, they were not guiding stars.

The following month Clarke received more encouragement from his father, who wrote: "I am glad you are getting on better in your studies & hope too the demerits are less."[17] He went on to admonish: "I shall be disappointed if your next report is not in every way better." Then he sternly queried: "Why can't you read over and correct your letters?" In the future the doctor warned "if you send letters with the words left out I shall pay no attention to them. You must school yourself to some method & order." He stressed punctuation, although he himself was not always careful about that detail. Gradually letters to his father actually exhibited more care.

Words from his friend C.S. McCawley must have been more welcome as they were devoid of parental preaching.[18] McCawley's idle jottings focused on sailing with friends, an interest both teenagers found a pleasurable pastime. McCawley's next message penned a few days later disclosed more pithy information. On March 25 McCawley asked how some of their mutual acquaintances "got along with drill," referencing his speculation that "I suppose skirmish drill must be very pretty. I should like to be there and see you."[19] Clearly martial elements remained a significant part of the curriculum as McCawley's letter reflected.

Late March also induced Cadet Clarke, which he was considered under the 1862 Morrill Act, which among other things required of so-called "land grant" colleges to "without excluding other scientific and classical studies and including military tactic, to teach such branches of learning as are related to agriculture and the mechanic arts...."[20] In this instance, Clarke sought a response from his mother whom he once again complained had been neglecting him.[21] Clarke must have been a bit chagrined by her echoing the double edged comment of his father that although she was "glad that you improve in your studies" she wished her son would "reduce the number of demerits" that continued to mar his record, and remained a habit once he entered West Point.

Dr. Clarke's May 2, 1878, letter must have also stung him because he chastised Powie about an undisclosed breach of discipline at school.[22] He opened: "I have read your letter & carefully. First of all obey to the letter the terms of your punishment & have the manliness to tell" others he did "so in conformity of your father's wishes." Here Dr. Clarke evoked the inflexible ideal of Victorian masculinity, which he bolstered by challenging: "Unless you do this you are not fit to be an officer & mark me, not one of you there [his two co-perpetrators] will ever be unless you learn this lesson."

Strict but just, the colonel remonstrated: "From your own account you deserved punishment but that it is excessive for the offense committed is evident." Had Powhatan committed "repeated breeches of discipline" Clarke's father reiterated, "you deserve it," but if the penalty was meted out "in a moment of anger or annoyance I am sure Captain [William] Parker [the university's president] will mitigate the same punishment, which he certainly should not do for any other subordinating notion. Of this last I am sure so be a man, for this is the crisis in your life & take the word of a devoted & loving father it will be doing right & [you] will never regret it." The concerned parent added a post script: "Write at once when I know that you have commenced to obey orders, I promise you that the punishment shall not be fully carried out for I feel to[o] sure of Capt Parker & besides you may rely fully upon my looking zealously to your proper treatment." But he cautioned his namesake, do not "do anything at all" that would compromise his "self-respect for any earthly consideration," something his son should urge upon his two co-offenders who all "would loose [*sic*] nothing by obeying first & then they can protest."

Regrettably, Powhatan ignored these admonitions on more than one occasion in the future. It appears that he had developed new traits that would plague him, not the least of which were ignoring, or on occasion challenging, authority. He had developed a certain headstrong, self-assured yet sometimes disastrous attitude about doing what he pleased with little regard for consequences.

The doctor was not so put off by his son's arrogance and actions, as to deny some funds for Powie to attend the forthcoming school ball.[23] The doctor's conclusion was typical of other letters: "I sincerely trust you are studying hard & that your report will be a good one."

In May, Clarke acknowledged receipt of a returned earlier piece of correspondence that he would send on to his mother's spinster sister Mary Boyce in St. Louis, a well-connected relative who would play a key role in his life.[24] He further clarified the matter of funds he had requested from his father for shoes and underclothing, while he spoke of receiving uniforms from his Aunt Mary.

In turn, Dr. Clarke said he would look into the matter of shoes that had not been completed for his son and signed off: "Your Attached Father" rather than the usual more affectionate closing, perhaps demonstrating his continued annoyance with his somewhat disappointing namesake.[25]

By summer Powhatan's grades had improved to the degree that his mother found them "quite satisfactory" although she could not say the same thing in response to the continued mounting up of demerits that would "count largely against" the aspiring applicant's bid for an "Annapolis appointment…."[26] While she prayed daily for him to attain this goal, she noted "all gifts are in God's hands" and her son should not "place too much confidence in Him." In short, as in the past, her mantra for Powie continued to be "study hard."

With 1878 nearing an end, Dr. Clarke once more expressed disenchantment with his son who had elected to go to Washington, presumably to the Navy Yard, rather than coming home in spite of the fact that this "was a violation of the spirit of my order to you not to go…."[27] The doctor hoped that the next academic "report may justify me in letting you leave the College at Xmas, for as disappointing as it is … to your mother, I shall feel obliged to carry out the warning if you do not show marked improvement by the beginning of the holidays." Dr. Clarke pronounced the struggling student's marks "were only 'Tolerable' in everything" which was made worse by the fact that the lad had "only three studies – this looks badly; try hard, my dear Son, to do better." The doctor urged: "Think less of play & more of the object you have in view" which meant he should apply himself if he hoped to enter the U.S. Naval Academy.

Grades were not the only rub because demerits continued to tarnish his record then and later at the United States Military Academy. "I fully sympathize with you about demerits given by your boy officers," because his father knew well how a bit of power sometimes was abused. Nevertheless, the Victorian idealized archetype and admittedly unreal view of knighthood entered the picture when Dr. Clarke's instructed, "you must remember that in the days of chivalry, when great men did great deeds, none were thought fit to rule till they had learned how to obey & always bear in mind that on duty it is the officer you obey not the boy." What Clarke must do was use all his "forbearance & tact to keep from being demerited (for it injures none but yourself)." The elder Clarke reminded "but under no circumstances sacrifice your self-respect at & never let yourself be imposed upon. It is no disgrace to be thrashed by a boy if you do your best…."

Here Clarke told his son to stand up for himself. The doctor understood "all this advice" probably worried the cadet "as it generally does a boy but I have faith in my experience" and he shared all this freely and in a timely manner for his son's benefit. Continuing, the Confederate veteran said his wife had been to Annapolis where she learned that "many boys failed because they 'did not know it was going to be so hard.'" As such, all this advice was to prepare Clarke for what was to come. In the meantime, the doctor told his son: "Write me about your champion friends & how you spend your play time." To assure young Powhatan all these admonitions were meant to be heartfelt, the last words were: "all send you love—affectionately father."

These urgings aside, the moment of truth came when five senators from 47th Congress (all of whom but one had served in the Confederate States Army) recommended Powhatan's nomination to Annapolis. With the lobbying of his parents and others, Democrat U.S. Senator Thomas F. Bayard (Delaware) signed an endorsement to this end with counter signatures from fellow Democrats Richard Coke (Texas), Benjamin Jonas (Louisiana), and a pair of senators from South Carolina, Wade Hampton and Matthew Butler.[28] The standard political rhetoric sent to President Rutherford B. Hayes portrayed sixteen-year-old Powhatan Henry Clarke, son of the president of Baltimore City College, as a "young gentleman for appointment 'at large' as a Cadet in the U.S. Naval Academy" based on the aspirant's "intellectual, moral, and physical qualities."

Embracing Darwinist and traditional concepts such as proper breeding and bloodlines, Senator Bayard set forth: "He springs from a virtuous and patriotic ancestry, eminent for their public services, whose example and precepts will naturally induce him to follow in their footsteps." Turning to another popular theme, that of healing the nation and putting the unpleasantness of the late war to rest, the senator submitted: "I am further induced at this time to ask you to make this appointment because Mr. Clarke is of Southern birth, the son of Southern parents." For this reason the candidate appeared most appropriate because "the time has come," opined Bayard, "when the work of restoration of the natural relations of the citizens of the Southern States to the Government of the Union, cannot be prosecuted too diligently; I hold it to be an evident and pressing duty upon all who hold the Union dear, and desire its perpetuation on the only basis of justice and mutual affection."

Then the senator from Delaware played his political trump card: "Nothing it seems to me would more effectually enlist the pride and affection of a people more than to see their youth enrolled in positions of honor and trust under the flag of their country." At this juncture Bayard underscored, "For a period nearly equal to the life of a generation of men, circumstances have restricted the Presidential selection of Cadets at Annapolis and West Point to the sons of citizens of the Northern and Western States." The causes for such practices "had passed away, the reasons for such restraints have all ceased, and the restriction itself should cease." Here was a test case Bayard championed, allegedly: "As an American, having no interest or aspiration inconsistent with the honor and happiness of my Country and every portion of its inhabitants." Given the fact that several Southerners had gained entry into West Point by this time, again spoke of an attempt to use political leverage to strengthen the case for Clarke's appointment.

Indeed, despite disclaimers of an absence of sectional political motivation, efforts to promote Clarke's case smacked of Southern Democrats attempting to sway Republican President Hayes to use his prerogative as commander in chief. In that capacity he could select a certain number of candidates at large for entry into the two military academies. This effort ran into obstacles.[29]

First, Hayes labored under charges that he came to office as the result of a backroom agreement to withdraw the last federal Reconstruction troops from the South who bolstered Republican regimes in the region. But neither the so-called Compromise of 1877 nor Hayes's views about government based on meritocracy induced this former Union volunteer officer to act on the case set forth on Clarke's behalf. Besides political and other considerations, one cannot help but conclude Powhatan's poor performance at school weakened his quest to be named a midshipman at the Naval Academy.

Although time and time again he had been urged to improve academically and practice self-discipline, Clarke's constant, bordering on habitual, indifference to guidance was evident in more than one letter such as one sent during May 1879.[30] Elsewhere he mentioned that he "had only one report [offense] last week and I could not help it. I made a mistake at parade and [the] Lieut sent me to the guard room to stand during supper" and "he forgot us until 'taps' and as the officer of the day could not find him we were left to spend the night there on the floor…." He and whoever was with him passed "a very uncomfortable night." In the morning his superiors were "much astonished and told us we could go on the sick list," which he declined.

Later, Clarke indicated he "was reported for talking very loud at table several times" but he promised "to get a clean score for next month." Then, typical of many students away from home then and now, Powie asked if his papa could spare a dollar so he could have his shoes repaired. He promised he would reimburse him because he knew the family was "just able to make ends meet." A few weeks later he requested $1.50 from his father for gloves, collar buttons, and sleeve buttons.[31] In anticipation of end of term Clarke wanted to know if he should come home first or go to Washington. The welcome mat was out again after what may have been a less than cordial period.

Shifting subjects, the University of Maryland's recently arrived tactical officer, although stern at first, was being less severe with the result that all the boys began "to like him…." The new lieutenant also gained points with the rank and file to the delight of Clarke and most probably some of his comrades as he had "been giving" the cadet officers "the mischief and [he] reduced several of them which make them act a little more sociably...." Clarke clearly evidenced tendencies to eschew authority particularly when wielded by peers.

This minor triumph over lording by fellow cadets did not offset another obstacle at school. Math continued to challenge him. Aside from this, Clarke remained determined to seek assistance from his father for admission to Annapolis; in addition it appears he requested support from other family members and friends, a tactic he turned to time and time again.

Clarke's mother was among those who pressed the case. One attempt involved their St. Louis connections, in this instance Congressman Richard Graham Frost, none other than the son of Dr. Clarke's former Confederate commander early in the Civil War, who had married one of John Mullanphy's granddaughters, Catherine Jane Clemens. Given that Clarke's maternal grandfather previously had married into this same wealthy family, the interweaving of familial ties and old comrades in arms who had served with Clarke's father, helped further Powhatan's martial aspirations as proved the case in more than one future instance. A Democratic Congressman, Frost held a seat from Missouri's Third District for one term.[32] Writing to Mrs. Clarke on House of Representatives letterhead, Graham opened: "I had hoped that it would be consistent with my duty to give my appointment at the Naval Academy to your son." Much to his chagrin, Frost found "upon inquiry that under the Statute every candidate must be an actual resident of the district from which he is named and must be certified by his congressman." Given these requirements, Frost could not oblige.

The next attempt to secure a berth at Annapolis passed through Democrat Congressman J. Floyd King, who represented both Louise and aspiring Midshipman Clarke's native Rapides Parish, Louisiana. This former Confederate colonel regretted he could not call on Mrs. Clarke personally but indicated that "it was almost certain" that there would be a forthcoming competitive entry examination.[33] In that case "young Clark[e] shall have a chance" to take the test in early May of the next year and the congressman promised he would "not rest here, but will see what may further be accomplished."

Another member of the House, E. John Ellis, a graduate of Louisiana State's law school and ex-Confederate captain who served Louisiana's Second Congressional District for a decade, made Mrs. Clarke the same pledge. He swore "by the shine of her splendid eyes it shall be so," which was to say that if Powhatan passed the test "standing on his own merit … he shall have the nomination."[34] Congressman Ellis remained faithful to his word. He informed Mrs. Clarke that the next midshipman entrance exam would be held for his district "the latter part of the month in New Orleans."[35] In this way Clarke had a means to be selected for the Naval Academy, while the congressman, like many others in the House, could point to a candidate's qualifications based on competitive testing, which was not mandatory, rather than just being selected because of political connections. Louisiana's Fourth Congressional District's Joseph B. Elam likewise entered the picture. The attorney turned one two-term congressman sent Powhatan "a blank which you will please fill and return" that was required for Clarke to compete.[36]

With such stellar support, the former Rapidian, according to the May 19, 1880, edition of the Alexandria *Louisiana Democrat*, was among "ten candidates … recently examined … for appointment to the United States Naval Academy." The brief article further indicated "Master Powhatan Clarke" was "No. 1" in the selection, but inexplicably, he did not join other midshipman entering Annapolis that year.

The reasons are not clear. There apparently is no known evidence as to why Clarke's quest for a naval career ended. Proximity to nearby family, and his stated ambitions and actions to take up life at sea, were recurring themes. What abruptly ended this course without further mention in the documents that still exist? Could Clarke have thought better of life afloat, away for long periods from loved ones and the life he knew? Then, too, the excitement of Civil War tales and current campaigns in the West may have attracted the rambunctious, romantic Clarke. He possibly readjusted his sights to what he may have viewed as more adventurous career.

While the cause of this shift toward another option remains uncertain, Clarke now turned to the United States Military Academy at West Point. Clarke evidently had secured a letter of appointment to West Point from Representative Elam.

As such, he contacted an acquaintance from early school days asking what he might expect at West Point.[37] On June 1, 1880, in reply to this question, Willoughby Walke, an 1879 Academy appointee from Virginia, disclosed United States History and Geography would be of "particular importance." Walke added "arithmetic is exceedingly simple as is also English grammar … provided you are well prepared."[38] He counseled: "you need give yourself no troubles nor anxiety about being able to pass…." On the other hand, Walke made Clarke aware that he would find it to his "advantage to deposit enough [money] upon your entrance into the academy to cover immediate expenses, which are very heavy, so as to enable you" not to go into debt. He suggested around $100, no mean sum for the Clarke family to provide.[39]

Heading from Maryland to New York, Clarke arrived for his entrance examination at West Point. Clarke, like so many others, then proceeded unheralded to find his "way to the Adjutant's office in the Administration Building and reported" where he "was courteously received and handed the Instructions to Candidates to read….[40]

Once he had trudged to West Point's main gate, Clarke and his fellow appointees were required to present his letter of appointment to the Academy adjutant, register with his full name, age in years and months, names of his parents and their address, before heading to the medical board for a physical requiring him "to strip to the skin then called one at a time before three Army Surgeons in full uniform who examined the lungs eyes ears teeth and feet made the candidates hop first on one foot then on the other raise their hands high above the head cough bend over forward," and put through other paces to determine their fitness from a medical perspective.[41]

After being pronounced fit, Clarke went to the West Point treasurer to deposit the required funds brought from home to cover his immediate expenses before admission. If he passed the academic examinations, the balance would be applied to purchase of his first uniform and other associated costs.[42] Then Clarke headed to his temporary quarters, which in his day consisted of rooms with "two alcoves at the end opposite the window." On his arrival there would be "no bed, no carpet, no curtains and not even shades." The bare bone furnishings included a clothes press and shelving for two cadets although three or four were assigned to space while candidates.

In addition, "two small iron tables, a wash stand, an iron mantel, and a steam coil with a marble slab" as a heat source completed the Spartan accommodations. Moreover, "certain articles for use by all occupants of the room" consisted of a "looking glass, a wash basin, a water bucket, a cocoanut dipper, a slop bucket and a broom." Any other articles were to be issued separately "such as a chair and a pillow."[43] The "Blue Book" issued to each new cadet specified the strict room policy of placement of items, a prescription Clarke often treated cavalierly during his four years at the Academy.

Soon thereafter, Clarke faced the anticipated examination covering the spectrum of topics Walke indicated, that is, a general battery of questions designed to determine aptitude in reading, arithmetic, geography, grammar, and history.[44] After completing the tests, Clarke and others awaited the results. As they did so, at two o'clock Clarke and all the candidates gathered in formation, perhaps with some of them being dispatched for towels, then all of them were off to bathing facilities in the basement of Company D's barracks for a good scrub.[45]

Upon returning to the barracks Clarke and his compatriots would proceed to the Academy supply point, the commissary, where each of them received "the articles necessary for his own immediate use."[46] Their next stop was "to the shoeblacks" where they would have their footgear "cleaned and polished," a paid service they were to use as "often as necessary to keep" their "shoes in proper order." Those with hair deemed too long marched off to the barber to trim their locks, but not their facial hair because "the barber was not permitted to do anything but cut hair."[47]

Clarke ultimately learned the outcome of his tests, which he told of in one of the longest of his surviving letters from West Point that followed a telegram home. Both bore good news for his father and family,[48] notwithstanding a feeling "that I would be in Baltimore before the end of the week; I even had my trunk packed and the bedding ready" to return home as a failure. Instead, an excited Powhatan exclaimed: "you can imagine how agreeably disappointed I was to find that I had passed." Thrilled, it was all he could do to contain himself from "getting out of ranks and whooping." For once, however, he restrained himself from a boyish outburst, "when my name did not fall on the deficient list." He had managed along with sixty-six others to receive passing marks sufficient for his admission to the Academy.

Ever desirous of familial acceptance he disclosed having dreaded the thought of walking "in at breakfast to-morrow in Baltimore and cause the disappointment to you, mama and Aunt Mary after all the trouble I have put you to in the last few months." Striving to redeem himself from past misdeeds and the diligent pressing of his case, Clarke saw this triumph as "an opportunity of showing my gratitude…."

While he had won the prize, there was a price to be paid. Clarke would not be "allowed to leave the 'post' for the next two years." He would "have to be satisfied by writing and receiving letters from you as I would not like to come home dishonorably…." Some of these musings reflected a new bout of homesickness, which he freely admitted. Yet Clarke assured "do not think I am unhappy however for I have made up my mind to go through with it and I am contented and I am beginning to like the place very much."

Thus, after a long, circuitous route and surmounting many obstacles (not a few of which were self-imposed) Powhatan Henry Clarke had taken the first major step to achieve the dream of many a child of Civil War-era veterans and civilians alike. Fired by much touted bravery of blue and gray clad warriors, Powhatan Clarke, Frederic Remington, Theodore Roosevelt, and others from the post-Appomattox generation sought to prove themselves. Craving martial glory and fulfilling that fantasy presented a significant challenge as young Cadet Clarke soon discovered when he marched onto the Plain at West Point.

Chapter 2

"Benny Havens, Oh!"

When the just over 5 feet 7 inches tall, 127-pound Clarke was admitted in June 1880 to West Point, he numbered among the youngest applicants who survived the medical and academic examinations that year.[1] No longer considered a "candidate," Clarke and the rest of those who had passed muster marched off to the commissary responsible for issuing supplies including "plebe-skins," the temporary garb consisting of a rubber overcoat, cap, and white gloves while awaiting the tailored uniforms, which he had been measured for when once confirmed as an incoming member of the Class of 1884.[2]

Being fitted for his cadet gray represented an outward symbol of what the seventeen-year-old would face for the next four years. Self-discipline and performance in the classroom, however, would be the real measure of the teenager as he approached manhood. Regrettably, Clarke performed poorly in both arenas. Some of his near failure stemmed from persistently overlooking advice. At least Clarke paid attention to Willoughby Walke's prescription that incoming plebes (similar to freshmen in civilian colleges) should refrain from speaking to "yucks" (AKA "yearlings"), "cows," and "firsties" (roughly akin to college sophomores, juniors, and seniors) except

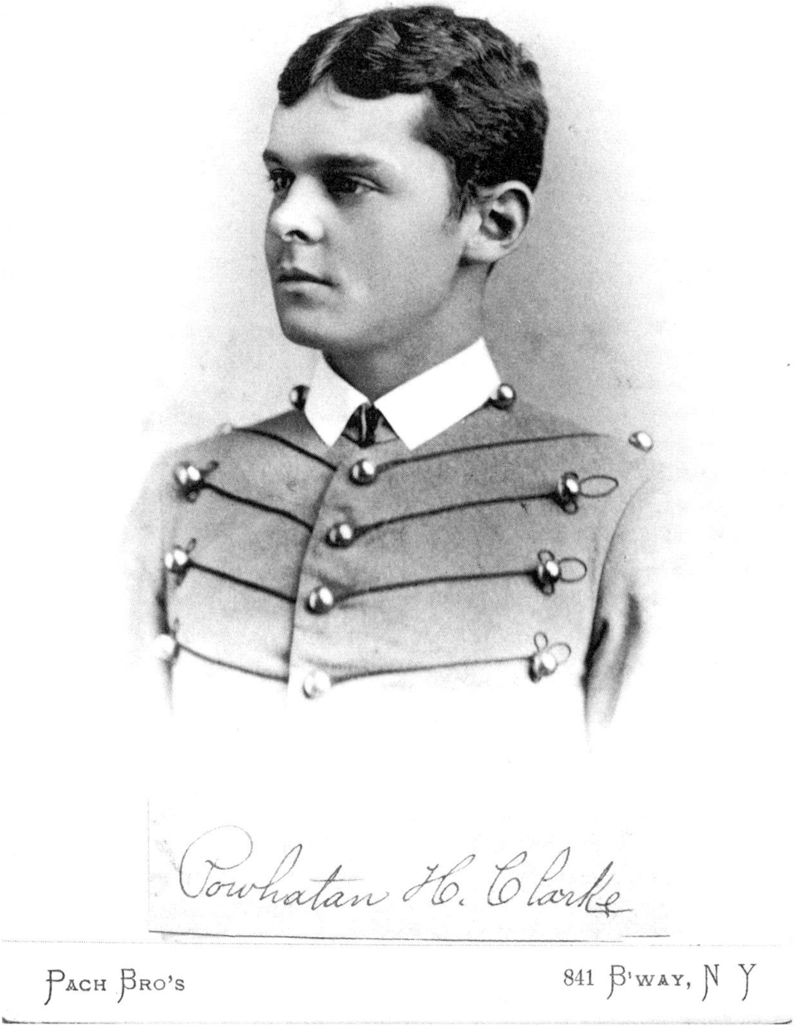

During June of 1880, Powhatan Henry Clarke and ninety-six other candidates took the entrance examination to the United States Military Academy. Of these hopefuls, thirty were rejected and sixty-seven were admitted to West Point. Although Clarke joined the Corps of Cadets, he narrowly escaped dismissal because of poor grades and high demerits for disciplinary infractions, which meant he graduated at the bottom of his Class of 1884. Author's Collection.

those directly over these first-year cadets, and then only in response to being addressed by a superior.

Further, Clarke discovered he and his fellow newcomers were subject to hazing. Here again, it appears he drew on his experiences at Maryland, and possibly his father's earlier guidance, which helped steel him against bucking this tradition. Consequently, he recounted that when "the cadet officers" entered his room "trying to get me excited" he ignored them. Wise to their antics, Clarke found these upper classmen "not even as bad as those at Md. Agr. Col. So they got disgusted and left after scattering my clothes and bedding on the floor and giving me instructions how to replace them."

Displaying another inkling of a slowly growing maturity, Clarke concluded that the negative press "about the hazing" was misconstrued, exaggerated. He opined they did "not amount to a row of pins and certainly not enough to make the reports that are usually made about" the severity of the tradition. He contended: "The reason for this is that instead of tak[ing] the word of army officers who graduated here they usually take that of those who are not able to stay …," meaning cadets who for one reason or another left.

The newcomers now packed their civilian clothes away, donning "plebe skins" supplemented and eventually replaced by uniforms "as fast as they were made…." The traditional cadet gray outfits could be traced to the founding of the Academy in the early 1800s, the most distinct of the garments being the long-outmoded, heavily padded swallowtail coattee.

This tightly tailored dress coat was to be worn habitually buttoned up to the chin with a white starched removable collar attached to a white collarless shirt underneath. The constrictive coattee had no pockets. Handkerchiefs had to be tucked into the coat's chest or caps, while a cadet typically had to carry his lead pencil hidden in between the buttons near the neck unless an unauthorized small flap of material was sewn to the underside of the tails. This prohibited modification would be "just big enough for a little pen knife and a pencil an inch and a half long …" but if discovered, would result in demerits being assigned.[3] Over the ensuing four years both demerits and costs of purchasing and repairing uniforms and clothing periodically required outlay from Clarke's pay account.

These first purchases came from the money Clarke brought from home and deposited at West Point per Willoughby Walke's suggestion. Taking heed, Clarke had deposited $108.35 to open his account.[4] This amount would be augmented from his pay of $45 per month after the administration of the oath of allegiance. He incurred other sundry expenses during his four years at the Academy.[5]

Even so, Cadet Clarke would not have direct access to the money, nor at any time were he or his fellows to exceed their balances.[6] Deductions from the cadet's account logged in an individual ledger book for each man kept track of expenditures and income.

Using this process, Clarke obtained his first tailored uniform that was to be worn properly and conforming to regulations. One of Clarke's earliest "skins" (cadet slang for demerits not to be confused with the interim clothing while a candidate) came on August 10, 1880, as a result of his collar being unhooked on the coattee. This first infraction related to the violation of regulations for the uniform was not to be the last in this category. Clarke tended to be a repeat offender in this area, and in many other categories, such as routine tardiness.[7]

With their new martial outfits provided, the Plebes joined the cadet corps, "at first to march to and from meals and then for parades," but unlike the upper classmen, they did so by carrying "disengaged hands palms to the front." When supper ended, they could "bathe in the Hudson at Gee's Point." Many of those who could swim availed themselves of the privilege.[8]

Cooling off in the river may have taken on a heightened appeal after Clarke's class left barracks for summer camp, the six weeks akin to basic training. Starting on July 1, when the academic year commenced, this phase introduced all plebes to the Academy's martial routine before they headed to the classroom after late August. Presumably, Clarke looked forward to what must have seemed like a great adventure under arms and under canvas, and the final "beast" week that wrapped up entry into military life. Stowing away everything but the bare essentials, each cadet fell in with their basic "bundles, brooms, and buckets and marched over to the camp."

After assignments of billets made according to rank, Clarke and his comrades went to their respective tents that would be their "homes till the

29th of August the day to return to Barracks." Once the Plebes reported, the Yearlings and First Classmen would "teach them how to fix up their tents" in the prescribed manner.[9]

While being exposed to the Academy's regimen, Plebes also glimpsed their life to come if they managed to survive the hurdles of the first year. Camp season was more than parades and practice for the "firsties" and "yearlings" who oversaw their recently arrived comrades. These veterans could enjoy the company of the "many ladies and other visitors under the trees near the guard tents." Besides promenading, the lordly upper classmen could attend hops (military slang for dances) three times a week during "camp" but Plebes were barred from this diversion. "However they went to the old fencing room in the Academic Building and took dancing lessons and as no ladies were admitted they danced with one another."[10]

Once this field outing ended, giving them a small taste of playing at war, it was time to face the challenge of the classroom that for the next four years would tax Clarke. Moving into his two-man room in the barracks, the time came for Clarke to study.[11]

As a fellow cadet recollected, the unrelenting routine wore out the newly arrived soldier-scholars, who until they completed their first two years experienced much the same from day to day and month to month.[12] It was at this point the "Seps" arrived to link up with the fourth class. They were "candidates who for some good reason did not report in June. They began recitations with the rest of the plebes but for weeks they attended drill in squads by themselves."[13] With the June and September Plebes now assembled, Clarke and his classmates settled into alternating formations, drills, and other military training with the rigorous demands of the classroom.[14]

Clarke struggled to make the grade and avoid being found deficient, which usually led to dismissal. While his grades ranged near if not actually at the bottom, he stayed the course. Unfortunately, despite purchasing eighteen packages of envelopes plus 435 $.03 stamps and 180 $.02 stamps during his attendance at the Academy, only a few surviving letters remain to shed light on this dark period. Here and for some periods of his later life, evidently many letters disappeared. Regardless of a lack of supporting correspondence from West Point, it was obvious that Clarke at best remained an indifferent pupil. Did inaptitude or attitude account for his low grades? Likely, both factors came into play.

At least one would assume Clarke fared better than most in his French classes. Here he likewise showed little promise, however, ranking occasionally in the middle, but usually lower in the class standings in a language his parents spoke and in which he received instruction in France. One wonders about Clarke's indifferent showing in what should have been one of his strengths, and if he even bothered to read the copies of *Le Figaro* he contributed to as a mandatory expense for a subscription along with his French texts.[15]

One of his rare pieces of correspondence from those days reflected a less than impressive grasp of the language.[16] He made this point clear when he opened: "I am certain that you did not expect a French letter but I finally gathered enough courage to try and write you one in hopes that you would not be too attentive to my numerous mistakes."[17]

He went on to recount that the new superintendent, bold Civil War Union cavalry commander Wesley Merritt, began a "new custom" by holding a holiday in honor of George Washington's birthday on February 22. Festivities included a hop that Clarke declared "a great success" although he did not attend. Clarke indicated: "I did not go because 3rd (year) is the last of the classes that permits you to assist at the ball." Given the prohibition of visitors and leave from the post during their early years at the academy Clarke relayed "it is difficult to obtain dance partners and I prefer to stay home instead of playing ornament to the back of the dance hall as do most of the time the 'yearlings.'"

Clarke at least enjoyed one element of his training, which showed a considerable capacity and passion for horsemanship. "We have been given saddles now but we are obligated to pass the stirrup. I would like to ride bareback. I learned to jump … which is great fun…."[18]

This upbeat conclusion contrasted with Clarke's earliest known letter as a cadet, which he posted toward the end of his Plebe year. Clarke confessed to his mother about being "in particularly low spirits" and apologized "for causing so much anxiety."[19] He now felt "confident that with the proper amount of application" he would "be able to get along very well." He did not "think the 90 demerit" rule being proposed to replace the 100 demerit limit per every six months, would "be adopted, for when the 'warnings' are read it is always for those only who have gotten more than 20 a month. I did very badly last month, and it was that which made me feel so very discouraged…."

Evidently Clarke experienced a wakeup call. Staying at West Point hinged on doing "as well as I can" during his remaining days as a cadet. Also, he postulated during the forthcoming "year a great many of the file-closers" would be his classmates, "and as classmates do not skin [give demerits] to one another, I will not have much of a chance of being reported at the 'formations.' I had the pleasure of receiving four demerits for the first skin in February for not reporting a classmate and was compelled to report him after all." Here Clarke exhibited a trait that seemed to border on a point of honor. He loathed causing peers to receive demerits.

Continuing, "I got a 'skin' [the] day before yesterday for not marching in section properly and as it was four demerits for me if I did not get off [reveal], the two who caused the report, thereby brought them but two apiece, besides that the officer of the day advised me to report them…." Clarke bemoaned, "such is the risk of a section marcher and such have I been since January. With the exception of three or four weeks and all the men in my section act as if they were going to a wake so that I am always on needles for fear of seeing the O.D. [officer of the day] or some other equally dangerous being coming up on me."

Despite this lackluster performance of his section and for that matter him, Clarke indicated he had "some slight hopes of making corporal next camp." He realistically followed up with the remark that the possibility of promotion was "exceedingly thin." He then admitted his "composition marks are usually deficient but not enough to affect my English marks and there is no danger of their finding me [deficient] on English for I can make it up on something else." Despite the struggles, he liked his instructors, especially his English professor, but "the 'math' instructor gets pretty mad now and then and seems to have a very high regards for the men he sends up out of his other section…." At least company drills had ceased, which was a blessing because he found it impossible "to run around in the wind for an hour and a half and then keep awake for his surveying class until 'the PM.'"

All in all, Clarke remained a free spirit. He suffered the consequences as he did when attending school in Maryland. Fellow cadets and officers cited him for infractions, which went against his record of general merit as well as could lead to expulsion "from the Academy for deficiency in discipline," if he received "more than one hundred demerits in six months."[20]

Unwilling to mend his ways, and staunchly headstrong in not reporting others, Clarke indeed accumulated many demerits, punishment tours, and occasionally was placed under arrest as indicated by Special Order No. 135 August 25, 1883, III, releasing "Cadets Clarke, P.H. and Cole, G.W ... from arrest." While not the worst offender in the Academy's history, this was one of the rare instances where Clarke ranked high, but in a negative sense. For instance, George A. Custer's (Class of 1861) infractions took up five-and three-quarter folio pages for 726 demerits in four years. Still worse, George W. Patten's (Class of 1830) 1,077 and Charles H. Larnard's (Class of 1831) 1,658 respectively topped the list before the 200 annual-limit came into being.[21]

Although Clarke did not approach Patten's and Larnard's dubious records, he did outdo Custer. Cadet Clarke's demerits covered just over eight folio pages for a four-year total of 788, or in other words approximately 166 per year. While never in danger of expulsion because of these "skins," Clarke succeeded in amassing more demerits than his predecessor the "Boy General" Custer. It is of interest that Clarke would have accumulated even more black marks except for the fact that during the early part of the Plebe year, incoming cadets received a one-third reduction from their monthly total as part of their introduction to the Academy's system.

Similarly, Clarke's grades during September 1882 through January 1883 approached disastrously low levels. The academic board, one of the functions of which was to determine if a student was deficient and thus subject to dismissal, met on January 11, 1883. They reviewed this weighty matter regarding Clarke's underperformance in drawing, tactics, and chemistry. In deliberations concerning all three subjects the thirteen members unanimously voted in Clarke's favor concluding the cadet was

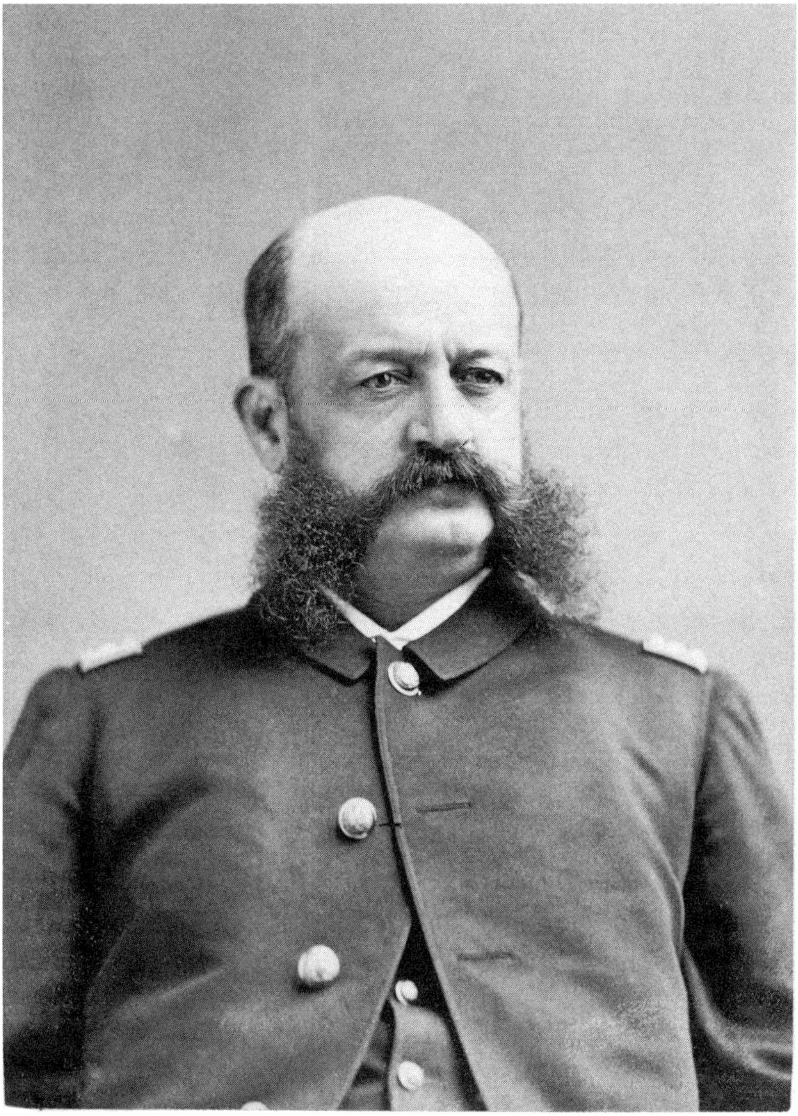

PACH BRO'S 935 B'WAY, N. Y

Chaplain William Morton Postlethwaite served in a dual capacity as the United States Military Academy's religious leader and as a professor. Clarke held the clergyman in high esteem. Author's Collection.

not deficient. Conversely, Clarke, along with a trio of other cadets, had been found to fall below the minimum in Philosophy, but based on oral and written examinations administered "for those not undoubtedly proficient" he avoided expulsion.[22] Presumably, having approached the brink of ending his military career, Clarke took heed, never to repeat this close call again except once more in June of 1883. It was then that his marks in drawing ebbed toward the lowest allowable limit. Once more, the academic committee unanimously concluded Clarke's marks were sufficient, thereby reprieving him.[23]

Avoiding mention of these brushes with possible disaster, Clarke fell back on his usual mantra to his parents about working "very hard now and each week," which forced him to stay up late studying. He let it be known that he had only been to "bed once or twice before eleven on account of Engineering as the figures and illustrations have to be drawn up in notebooks every lesson and they are the most tedious things I have yet [faced] on account of details." Given his status as a "First classman" he at least had the privilege of not having to comply with "lights out" until eleven each evening.

Fortunately practical engineering taxed him less, and the required manual labor seemed to his liking. Light artillery training also appealed. It required riding three times a week. He delighted in the fact that he had "a first rate horse" and knew "of nothing so exciting as our cavalry charge as foragers and skirmishers the horses seem to know what 'raise sabers' means and the bugle barely finishes the 'charge' before the whole platoon is bearing up the plain howling and cutting for all they are worth."

Overall, Clarke stated his class did very well with several "bright members" meaning that there would be a number of fine engineers added to that elite branch, which admitted only the top graduate or graduates each year from the Academy depending on the number of vacancies in the corps. That was all well and good, but Clarke expressed his lack of interest in this career path. He cautioned his father not to conclude this perspective sprang from "sour grapes." Far from the case, Clarke claimed his stand on not desiring a billet with the engineers or artillery, even if his grades warranted these top berths, arose from not wanting to be "bound down to the work" they had to do. Further, he insisted he did not "like the men" who strive for these branches as "they are too ambitious and show their selfishness too much." Of course, the situation would be different "if there were any chance of war," in which circumstance Clarke "would give anything to be in the artillery but if ten or fifteen years of peace have to be gone through I would rather not just sit it out in some coastal fort." Besides, because most of these posts were in the East they were "too near theater girls," an expensive temptation for a second lieutenant on $1400 a year pay. It was better to be sent West where a young officer had a better "chance for saving something instead of being continuously in debt." Clarke also claimed he knew "some officers" who "would be in debt at the north pole and that probably for ice but I hope I am not one."

What Clarke's first assignment would be may have loomed in the back of his mind, but his immediate future continued to rest on the outcome of his classroom performance. In the meantime, as his second year neared an end, he finally became eligible for his first leave in two years as a so-called "furlough man." Perhaps in anticipation Clarke of this escape from confinement, Clarke laid out $18.25 to a jeweler.[24] This may have been for a signet ring given that in one letter he had thanked his father for sharing information about the family crest. Pride in his heritage aside, Clarke claimed he "would rather be a graduate of West Point and a 2d lieutenant of U.S. cavalry" than a member of the European gentry, a group that in years to come he would become acquainted with from personal experience. He then shared that the next war probably would take place in Mexico as the people were "becoming disgusted with settlers and though civilization must conquer you know how carpetbaggers are and I do not blame the Mexicans much."

In what seems to be as his final letter from West Point to his mother, Clarke's usually respectful tone toward her at least momentarily altered. Whether actually standing on principles or simply reacting as a youthful rebel who brooked no challenge to his budding manhood, even by a doting parent, Clarke uncharacteristically criticized her. Somewhat full of himself, Clarke acknowledged that he had destroyed a recent letter from his mother per her instructions. He then launched into expressing that she irked him by her reprimands about his studies and demerits. He assured her that he would not have "been the only cadet" who would have been "piqued" by the dressing down she gave him.

He explained: "It is true that demerits are in a great way due to boyishness is in fact childishness and I frequently recognize that I have a great deal too little dignity for my age but that will come when I give orders" that others would have to obey notwithstanding his "reputation for carelessness." Stung, Clarke lashed out: "The principal point however is the idea you have of manly duty as you think it proper to rebuke a cadet who" strives "to be honorable and maintain a proper 'esprit de corps' with not having a sense of manly duty" and an unwillingness still "to save a demerit in order that they may gain a file in class standing."

In turn, Clarke admitted he had "never been ambitious for class standing and during the past two years could not have gained enough to make up what was lost without more exertion than I thought it worth and even then I probably could not have done much." Was this an excuse for his poor academic record, or did he really not care about status? It seemed all that mattered was receiving his commission as an officer where he could cease being a parade ground soldier ruled by those he probably viewed as martinets. He longed to get on to the work of a commander of men on his own terms.

Further, Clarke asserted his demerits resulted in "enough punishment … to last for months," perhaps feeling singled out by what he perceived as the stern measures instituted under Superintendent Merritt and the commandant of cadets. As long as he were not found deficient, he would not be concerned. When it came to martial matters such as parades, guard mounts, "or any formations that require care and attention and when the bearing of the corps may be criticized or when there is necessity of bracing up the general discipline and setting a good example to the lower classmen," Clarke avowed that he always rose to the occasion.

In point of fact, his parents eventually were able to breathe a sigh of relief after years of fretting over a doubtful outcome. In 1884, their son received his diploma. Cadets and their proud parents could join their offspring and take their place among other august attendees including President Chester Arthur; Secretary of War Robert Todd Lincoln, the son of the slain Great Emancipator; the army's second highest ranking office, Lieutenant General

Philip H. Sheridan; and others, not the least of whom was the commencement speaker, Brigadier General George Crook.[25]

After all the preliminaries, Crook spoke toward the end ceremony. Quickly recalling his time as a cadet thirty-two years before, he noted much had changed since those days. One thing remained constant: the inclination for new graduates "to throw off all restraint, to give up books and study, and to relapse into careless habits." He reminded them that their days as cadets had only laid the "groundwork of what was necessary to make them soldiers. They had learned to obey, and were proficient in the theories upon which the art of war is based, but the practical knowledge" had to "be gained by experience." They now had "to pay attention to details and learn to do little things well." These graduates must avoid "idleness and mental indolence. Unfortunately, these are faults to which the young graduates from West Point are especially liable to fall victim. They are too apt to consider their future as certain, to think of their years of study as years of drudgery," he observed, conclusions that described Clarke.

Crook went on to advise these "young soldiers to study geography and geology and geological formation[s] of posts where … stationed, so they could tell, from certain physical peculiarities, the general condition of the country they were not particularly familiar with." He emphatically pronounced: "There is no one branch of study more important than mastering this art," which he stressed was "one that stands higher among the requirements which make the great General. Nor is there one which will be more useful in military service on the frontier."

Nearly a decade before professor Frederick Jackson Turner espoused his provocative "frontier thesis," Crook reached a like conclusion.[26] The general prophesized: "Now the Indian question is practically solved, we have no frontier, and the unarmed emigrant may make his home and rear his family safe from harm and without need of protection…." While somewhat premature in his forecast, Crook judged the Indian to be "more ready to accept civilization, than civilization is to accept him."

In this light, the general advised the treatment of Indians included the cardinal rule not to make "promises which you cannot fulfill; make no statements you cannot verify. When difficulties arise, as they occasionally will, endeavor to be so well informed of all the circumstances of the case that your action may be powerful and convincing because just and impartial."

He cautioned not to "expect too much at once," from the Indians, and not to "lose courage or patience." Further, he warned: "You would find that the Indian has no rights which our people are compelled to respect. The benefit of laws which protect the white man are not extended to the Indian." It would take all the "intelligence, courage, and energy" of officers sent to the West to deal with these factors. "Constant thought and observation" would prove "indispensable" and while he stated "the principles of strategy" remained unaltered "since Hannibal, and Caesar," rapid, constant change meant "to the military student, except as a study of strategy, the history of ancient wars"

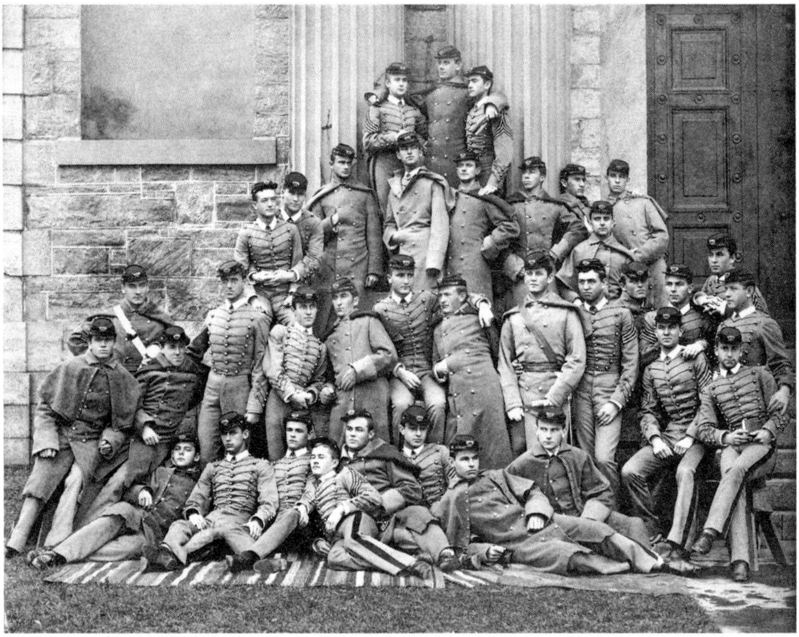

After four years of rigorous classroom requirements, those who survived West Point's demanding courses graduated in the Class of 1884 including Powhatan Clarke, who appears in the front row, far left, lounging on the ground. Author's Collection.

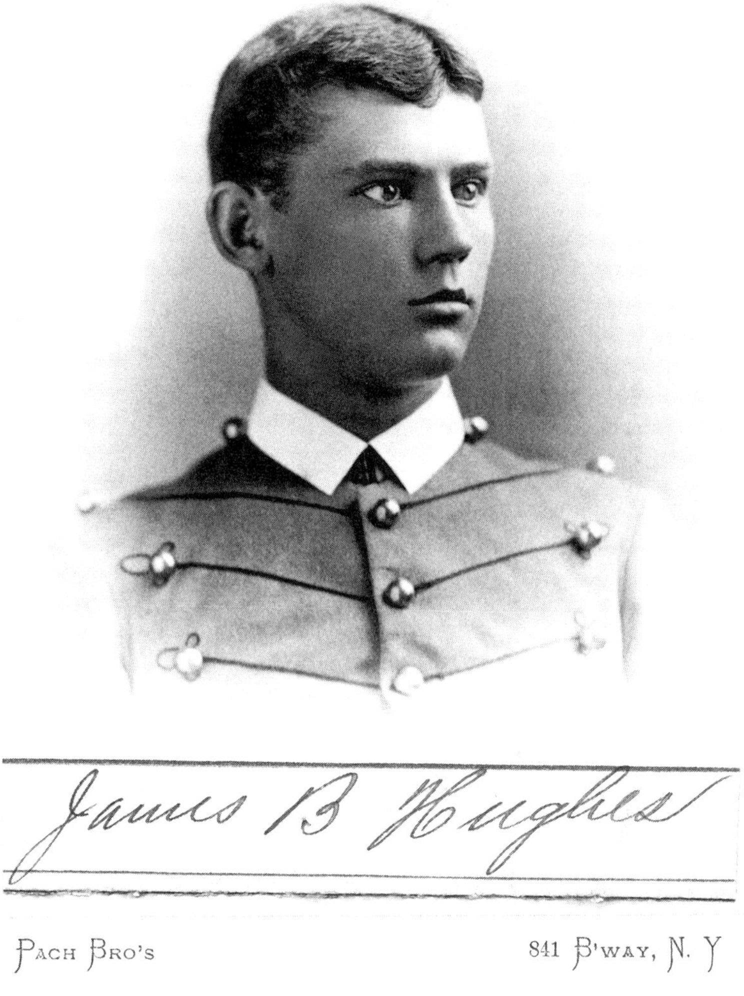

Cadet James B. Hughes graduated second to last in the Class of 1884. Clarke and Hughes shared more than dubious academic distinctions. Both performed well in combat, and served alongside each other in the Tenth U.S. Cavalry where they became life-long friends. Author's Collection.

no longer assisted the modern warrior. The time had come when brains were "fast taking the place of bullets."

Consequently, Crook found it imperative for "the graduates to keep up with current events, and think in advance of others." Crook ended with the admonishment: "Four years of your life have been passed amid scenes which recall every patriot's heart the perilous days of Revolution, when the fate of the struggling colonies hung by a thread.... Let their aims be yours, and though it may not be your fortune to take part in history which they did, you will not have lived in vain."

Did Clarke pay better attention to Crook than he did in most of his courses? It is impossible to answer. One thing was certain: against odds that were more often than not, self-imposed, barely passing many a class, and suffering a mountain of skins likely due to a number of factors from indifference, to passive aggressiveness, and downright defiance, Clarke had prevailed. Although he emerged in the "last section [which] was called 'the Immortals'," he nevertheless avoided discharge for his infractions and poor grades.[27] In the process he lived up to the nickname bestowed on him by members of the Corps—"BJ" which in cadet slang meant "fresh or lacking in respect" and was an abbreviation for " 'Bold before June' from the time when a Plebe" entered the Academy to "the day before June graduation."[28]

Now, along with his fellow Immortal, and indeed only one notch above him in general merit at graduation—James Hughes—Clarke put aside his cadet grays to wear the army blue as a second lieutenant in the Tenth U.S. Cavalry. Before reporting as a frontier officer, Clarke embarked on a last lark. Now a bit taller and with some muscle and weight added since arriving as an ungainly Plebe (now he stood a hair over 5'9", and weighed 142 pounds) this risk-taking survivor of West Point's rigors was, as announced in one of his previous letters home, looking forward to being spoiled as a carefree guest of his Aunt Mary Boyce in St. Louis.[29]

Chapter 3

"Ere the Fair Land of Texas"

After four years of treading water at West Point, he was off to his first exposure to frontier soldiering. Clarke leisurely traveled west, passing through St. Louis. where he, along with classmate James Hughes, who also was ordered to Texas, "met a great many very pretty and nice girls."[1] True to form, the pair continued to embrace the philosophy of all play and little work. Powhatan's Aunt Mary Boyce, his mother's half-sister, aided their antics, supplying them with her carriage and a driver. With stylish transportation at their beck and call, the shavetails engaged in a last fling at "all the clubs and had lots of fun playing pool and billiards and chatting with the men who are very nice. Take it altogether the St. Louis people are about [as] cultivated and hospitable as I have ever met." During September 1884, with their graduation leave concluded and orders in hand, the newly commissioned second lieutenants boarded a train and headed to Fort Davis, Texas.[2] After reaching Marfa they took a stagecoach that ran daily from this eastern terminus of the Southern Pacific Railroad, continuing on for some 180 miles to their final destination.[3] Completing this last leg of their journey, the tired travelers were "glad enough to land" on October 12.[4]

After the outbreak of the Civil War in 1861, U.S. Army forces had abandoned this seven-year-old southwestern Texas post. By 1867, federal troops reoccupied the site and began to rebuild the post adjacent to the old one. The fort was "located at the mouth of a cañon about three-fourths of a mile long, about 400 yards wide at its mouth, and gradually narrowing to its termination in a recess in the mountains," which rose on either side being "formed of metamorphic rocks …, about 250 feet high." These formations provided a dramatic "very rough and precipitous," backdrop to the garrison that was "covered with grass and small oak trees." On their way to the fort, Clarke and Hughes passed through the "wild and barren," countryside "with no trees excepting a few live oaks in the cañon in the rear of the post, and a few cottonwoods and Limpia."[5]

At this point in its existence, Fort Davis's troop garrison consisted mainly of troops from Tenth United States Cavalry. The Tenth was one of six regiments manned by African Americans and created by 1866 congressional legislation providing for a much reduced "peacetime" army.[6]

The provision for blacks in the ranks of the Regular Army was unprecedented. Heretofore official policy barred African Americans from enlisting except in volunteer units, and only then in time of war. The four years of fighting to preserve the Union eventually resulted in mustering of more than 180,000 blacks in both the army and navy. Their record did not go unnoticed, and was one of the motivations for some Radical Republicans to propose that the U.S. Army adopt the U.S. Navy's long-standing policy of integrating blacks into its enlisted force structure.[7]

This was not to be. Black soldiers would be assigned to specific infantry and cavalry regiments such as the Tenth U.S. Cavalry under the command of white officers.[8] The first regimental commander, Colonel Benjamin H. Grierson, like a number of the senior officers in the unit, owed his place in the peacetime establishment to service as a Union volunteer. Grierson's 1863 raid through Mississippi as part of the Vicksburg Campaign gained him a reputation as one of the foremost Union cavalry leaders. Moreover, this much-touted exploit, along with his credentials as a loyal Republican, paved the way for two decades as commander of the Tenth.[9]

Grierson formed the regiment at Fort Leavenworth, Kansas. After a rocky start there, he deployed his troops to other posts in the state.[10] Eventually, Grierson's men took stations at forts in Indian Territory (Oklahoma) as well as some companies reporting to Fort Dodge, Kansas.[11] During April 1873, a shift to Texas began with three companies being dispatched to Fort Richardson, two to Fort Griffin, and another pair to Fort Concho. The companies remaining in Indian Territory concentrated at Fort Sill and Camp Supply. During the summer of 1873, somewhat of a lull descended on Indian Territory, although raiding parties of Apaches, Comanches, and Kickapoos, continued to haunt to the south in Texas.[12] The black troopers spent most of the summer in the saddle, scouting for these raiders, but saw little action.[13]

After the winter of 1874–1875, the regiment gradually completed the shift to Texas.[14] Thereafter, details from the Tenth participated in extensive expeditions aimed at sweeping the Indians from the region known as the *Llano Estacado*, or Staked Plain.[15] Over the ensuing years, black troopers and their white officers engaged in numerous small campaigns against raiding, roving bands that culminated in 1880 with the campaign against the Warm Spring Apaches during the so-called "Victorio War" of 1879 and 1880. Under the adept Apache leader Victorio, they fought a two-front war against the United States and Mexico. Following his September 1879 escape from the San Carlos Indian Reservation in Arizona, Victorio led a costly guerrilla war against forces from both sides of the border until his death in 1880 at the hands of Mexican troops. Even then, the duel continued with aged Chief Nana carrying on resistance until 1881.[16]

Following the conclusion of the clash with Victorio and his followers, a long-sought peace settled over the Texas-Mexico border region. This brief tranquility allowed the Tenth Cavalry to concentrate its companies at Forts Concho, Stockton, and Davis, although the troopers continued to patrol the Rio Grande to the south and the Guadalupe Mountains to the west. Cessation of major field operations, however, did not bring about peaceful coexistence.[17]

In 1882, regimental headquarters transferred to Fort Davis. For the next three years, the regiment enjoyed a welcome rest from the constant campaigning of previous times. As more settlers arrived in west Texas, the region evolved from its former frontier violence.[18] It was this state of affairs that existed when greenhorns Powhatan Clarke and James Hughes respectively reported to Troops K and B for their first duty assignments at Fort Davis.

In a letter Clarke began on October 1, 1884, and fleshed out during his overland journey from Missouri, he noted: "Our captains immediately took us to our quarters and made us feel perfectly at home. That night we met a great many very nice fellows at the mess and the next day moved into our pleasant quarters where we will remain until the new houses are completed."[19] Clarke also shared: "The post is a beautiful one right in the mountains and so high up that the summers are perfectly delightful" or so he believed without actually having experienced the season. Without first-hand information, he likewise ventured to conclude: "The winters are very mild except when a norther happens along which is not very often and is the only time we use fires. This is said to be [the] healthiest post in the army."[20]

As for the men, his Southern bias appeared when he referred to "the nigs" as "very military and seem to take pride in being soldiers." In the same breath, Clarke delighted in the fact that Hughes and he had "two very good men detailed … from our companies to look after the horses, clean up and make themselves generally useful to 'the lieutenant' which is quite a relief to me…."[21]

Here Clarke referred to the long practice of employing enlisted men as servants, or in army jargon of the era, as "strikers" (also referred to as "dog robbers"). Oliver Knight pointed out these were soldiers "worked for an officer until 1881 when an Army regulation—citing an unenforced law of 1870—prohibited officers from employing soldiers in private service." Regulations or not, the tradition "never did disappear entirely." There were "many enlisted men" who gladly assumed the role "for the extra five dollars a month paid by an officer, to live in private quarters, to eat better than in the company messes, and to be excused from guard duty, drills, and roll calls." Given that several of the enlisted men had served as domestics, at least in the immediate post-bellum period, finding experienced servants, often a source of complaint, was not difficult in a regiment with black troops. According to Frances Roe, a frontier army officer's spouse, many candidates existed to fill such jobs when the enlisted complement included African Americans.[22]

Such tidbits of daily life filled Clarke's letters home. As was his previous practice, he regularly rotated contact with his parents, interspersing his

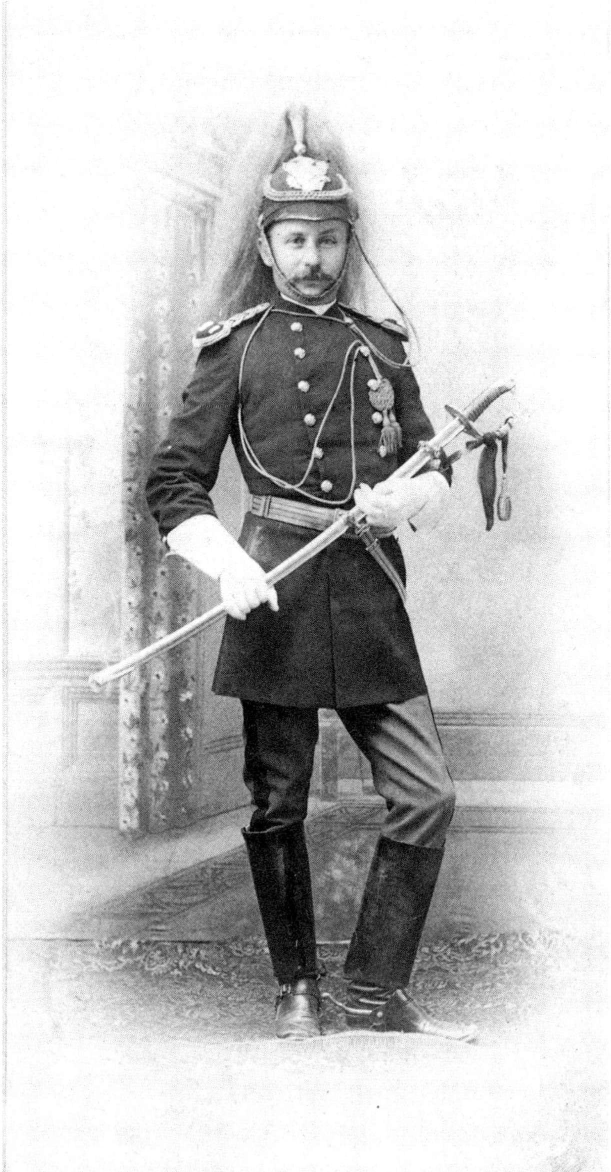

Civil War-veteran Captain Thomas Lebo became Clarke's commanding officer in Troop K, Tenth U.S. Cavalry. Library of Congress.

letters so that each parent received an individual note on alternative dates. Thus, on October 4, he informed his father: "I am perfectly delighted with our post and very agreeably surprised with the troops…."[23] Here Clarke repeated the contention of one of his senior officers who had quipped: "'a lazy worthless white man will go into the army whereas a negro of the same kind will always lounge around home and live from the hand to mouth and steal whereas those who are adventurous go into the army.'" This instance of Clarke voicing prejudicial perspectives served as a benchmark of his early attitudes about the rank and file of the army, both black and white.[24]

What is more, Clarke began to form opinions about his fellow officers. He opened with his company commander, Captain Thomas Lebo, whom he contended was "a splendid soldier who takes great pride in his troop even to this most minute detail." Born on November 17, 1842, Thomas Coverly Lebo served in the Civil War as a Union volunteer from his native state, at first as a three-month volunteer with Company B, Eleventh Pennsylvania Infantry. Afterwards, Lebo continued with other regiments throughout the conflict thereby beginning nearly forty-four years as a soldier. After the war's end, Lebo returned briefly to civilian life before being commissioned on June 12, 1867, as a first lieutenant in the Tenth United States Cavalry. His captaincy came nearly a decade later on May 17, 1876.[25]

Under this old horse soldier, Clarke asserted that Troop K was "the best mounted at the post, their equipments are new and kept as well as West Point's. He goes to afternoon stable call and tattoo giving me reveille and morning stables which immediately follows reveille and company drills the very duties I would rather have especially … as I always have prided myself on drilling and am conceited enough to say that I can handle a company." Clarke lauded his men were "as well drilled as a cadet company" performing under "most efficient non com. Officers."

Clarke added battalion drill, which involved two to three companies and took place only once a week. Ever equine minded, he originally rode a troop horse that was "very good" until he could afford to "purchase one which I am sorry to say will sink me $150 though when I get up in life I intend to get a first-class horse as I think every officer should have [one]." He remained true to this goal and would have splendid mounts to equal his considerable equestrian skills.

Clarke and Hughes continued to share a captain's quarters for the time being, but knew they would have to move at some point. Returning to the regimental makeup, it appears he found "the younger officers with whom I associate are very steady and the older ones do not in any way attempt to influence us" although he made a passing remark about the "dissipated" element in the regiment including, according to rumors, Lebo. At least Lebo did not require any one else to join in his excesses, which Clarke gathered from the rumor mill consisted of "sprees on occasion and he is not a steady drinker and confines his sprees to the night … and does not bother anyone in the day time."[26]

In spite of this situation, Clarke viewed Lebo as a first-class officer. Further, he "was surprised at" Lebo's "mess kit for the troop. All the china being made to order with [a] red border and cross sabers and 'Troop K' in the center of the plates." He declared these plates "much better than we had at the Point and the darkies ought to like a captain who fits them out with silver knives, forks, spoons ect. [*sic*]."

Not unlike his practice at the Academy, in part Clarke remained conscious of costs. Now his monthly base pay was $125, as opposed to $540 per annum as a cadet where he enjoyed free meals.[27] On active duty he had a mess bill that ran $30 a month, washing, and an enlisted servant that cost him $5 each. This meant "actual expenses do not exceed forty now though with … fuel ect [*sic*] they may be 50 or 60 and we can wear what we chose off duty." In contrast to West Point, "very rough clothes" were permitted so that a young officer could "live more economically than … anticipated." In this way, he looked to save money for his next leave. This also meant he could begin to pay off loans accumulated prior to receiving his commission, such as expenses incurred during his leave after his second year at West Point, as examples of Clarke regularly spending beyond his means.[28]

Clarke's next letter to his mother, as well as subsequent correspondence to his parents, indicated alternate states of excitement, loneliness, learning the ropes of army life at an isolated garrison, military routine, and adapting to his new, unfamiliar environment. As an example, his November 5, 1884, quickly penned update to his mother noted he had moved into new quarters as did Hughes, making them "more comfortable than ever before." Relocation to a permanent billet, and completing one of his numerous repetitive responsibilities, filling out muster rolls, kept him from replying to his mother's letter. He also gushed about the "beautiful bay" horse he just had bought and claimed it was "the finest thing that ever walked." Moreover, he referenced the new-found joys of having a striker whom he was "perfectly delighted with." His attentive "man," wrote Clarke, pampered the lieutenant to the degree that he had "gotten so aristocratic that I don't even move a collar button" when his soldier valet was present. He pronounced this enlisted assistant as having "a reputation after six years as being as honest as the day is long."

Unfortunately, Clarke somewhat ingenuously reported that the officers who employed the servant in the past gave him whiskey, "hence he necessarily gets on a tear" from time to time. Rather than send him to the guard house, Clarke simply marched him off to bed given "he had worked so faithfully...."

Ten days later, he was at his desk again churning out a message on November 15, 1884. To offset serving as the recorder for a boring "Board of Survey," Clarke had a bit of time to read, although he had "not looked at The Outline of Irish History." Nonetheless, he expressed gratitude for these gifts from his mother, especially "as I know how little you have to spare. Please do not sacrifice the little pocket money for me which you have though I would like to have the books very much."

Despite worries about his mother's finances, which was restricted as an allowance controlled by his father in keeping with Victorian mores, Clarke added that he enjoyed keeping abreast of current affairs through periodicals. Indeed, later letters listed specific requests to supplement titles available at the post library and as loans from fellow officers.[29]

He indicated a recent "bear hunt was not a success as the best dogs we had were lost the first day on the trail in the mountains." Furthermore, he contended, "those we had left were too young." At least the hunters felled "a deer and an antelope." During the outing, Clarke "had a splendid time following the dogs though it was the roughest work I have ever had of climbing mountains from sunrise to dark without any meals in between and sometimes no water."[30]

Little did Clarke realize this foray was nothing compared to the one that followed, but for the moment he relished getting back to camp to "find supper ready and a good fire in front of the tent with the blankets all made down. We lived like Princes as we had a good cook, plenty of canned vegetables, venison, and fresh milk and butter from a large ranch about a mile from camp." Indeed, roughing it was not all that rough for officers who enjoyed a brief respite from boards of surveys, court martial duties, and other mundane garrison matters that occupied most of a junior officer's time.[31]

As Douglas McChristian observed in *Garrison Tangles in the Friendless Tenth* … for officers: "More often than not the life was a rather monotonous grind at military duty, from day to day, month to month."[32] The senior lieutenant in Clarke's Troop K made this clear in a number of his diary entries, in which he describes seemingly endless repetitive rounds such as officer of the day, a recurring function for all junior officers who were required to receive "the report at retreat, tattoo, and reveille, attend the watering of horses, and inspect the Guard at discretion." Other time-draining pursuits, as Clarke indicated, involved stints as judge advocate (essentially the prosecutor) or conversely as a counsel for the defense during routine garrison courts-martial. Additionally, occasional funerals, regular inspections, overseeing schooling for non-commissioned officers, disciplining subordinates, and processing reams of paperwork gave pause to one of Clarke's comrades who considered resigning his commission, "seeing how little it is honored or appreciated in this country."[33]

Clarke's November 21, 1884, musing to his father revealed more about the typical unvaried attention to mind-numbing minutiae experienced at Fort Davis.[34] Clarke had recourse to consult military law volumes and write up proceedings of garrison courts-martial. A defendant's plea of not guilty required Clarke to fill up "five pages of foolscap" as "the unfortunate judge advocate." Previously, acting in this same capacity for his first case "took nine but between them five pleaded guilty so that it was a relief. I have only three more to try. Thank heavens for sometimes they fill up a cord of paper in one case."

Instead of legal matters, Clarke longed to join Hughes whose troop and Troop A as well as another unit "from Peña = 125 men" who "left on Tuesday for the Rio Grande after some Apaches … who have been hair cutting." Despite Clarke's volunteering for the patrol duty, two of his seniors "refused and it would have been useless. It was the first time I felt blue when I saw 'A' Troop saddling up at reveille. All the men seemed to be in excellent spirits at the idea of a scout and I hope they do something for themselves."

Longing to take to the field, Clarke added: "They say a camp with a lieu[tenant] and thirty men is to be established down near the Rio in the Davis Mts and as it is my next detail on 'Detached' Service I hope that they will overlook my inexperience and send me down as we are the only troop with 3 commissioned officers with us and they could not let me off."

Clarke's reference to the paucity of officers reflected a constant complaint related to temporary assignments: leaves of absence for a wide variety of reasons, assignments on "recruiting details" as well as "personal leaves," sometimes for extended periods, "courts-martial, and service on official boards," as well as other factors regularly "stripped companies of commissioned personnel."[35] Clarke also disclosed another common occurrence in the frontier army when he mentioned the arrival of First Lieutenant John Bigelow to fill a vacancy in another troop. He indicated Bigelow "was much worried over his prospects for quarters." This universal apprehension arose from the practice of assigning quarters by rank and seniority, meaning that the arrival of a new officer with a higher standing could "rank out" a junior who would have to move to other quarters.[36]

No stranger to the frontier, Bigelow started his military days at Fort Duncan, Texas, for his first brief taste of troop service. Barely two years passed, when a detail to return to West Point as an assistant professor of French brought welcome news. This posting left Troop E without sufficient officers. Bigelow soon appeared on the Academy's faculty rolls from January 1, 1880, to August 24, 1884. Following this assignment, he took leave through November 16 with a new member of his household, Mary Braxton Dallam, whom he had married in Baltimore, on April 28, 1883.

Another milestone occurred in 1883. Bigelow received word in October that he would move up a notch to first lieutenant. It was in this grade that

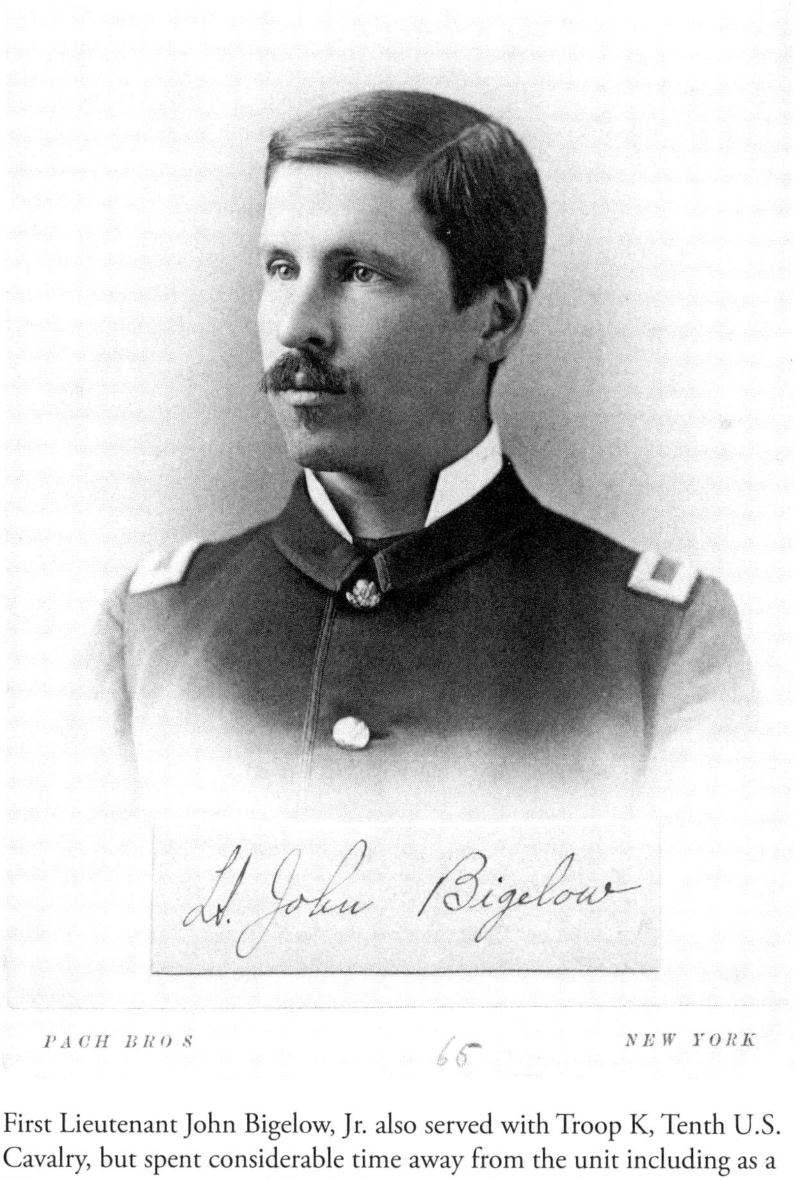

First Lieutenant John Bigelow, Jr. also served with Troop K, Tenth U.S. Cavalry, but spent considerable time away from the unit including as a West Point instructor while Clarke was a cadet. Bigelow's older brother, a friend of Frederic Remington, proved influential in furthering the artist's career. Some of Remington's first published work appeared in Lieutenant Bigelow's serialized articles, "On the Bloody Trail of Geronimo," for *Outing Magazine*. Author's Collection.

he subsequently returned to the Tenth, transferring from Troop E to become second in command of Troop K, which eventually had consequences for both Bigelow and Clarke. For the moment, however, Clarke focused on the present rather than an unforeseeable future. One of his immediate concerns was a reference to a not uncommon malady in the frontier army, one of the twin evils afflicting the military—desertion and alcoholism.[37] It was this latter ill that afflicted Clarke's company commander as he indicated in one of his earliest communications from Fort Davis. Clarke recorded that his captain had quieted down as the result of "an extensive spree which he is just getting off of. It is a pity but a thing apt to happen to a man who was a boy in the war and of wonderful activity with little knowledge outside of his profession and sent upon a garrison with nothing to do but go to the club."

Although Lebo fought his demons, he always treated Clarke very kindly and insisted his subordinate "take his scouting saddle on my hunt" because the English-style Whitman seat that the lieutenant "bought in St. Louis did not have the necessary packing arrangements." Still green and with little in the way of comparison, Clarke thought himself "very lucky in my officers…." He added that many of the officers hailed from the South. They delighted over the recent elections that brought more Democrats back to national office. This reference was to Southern Democrats who, with Reconstruction shelved over a half dozen years earlier, reemerged as a power in Congress. In many ways, the status quo ante bellum had returned to national politics. Clarke, voicing his own Southern biases, told his father "the darkies seem to think they are in … danger from the Democrats."

Closing on a personal note, Clarke regretted the absence of classmate Hughes. He lamented: "I feel lonesome without Jim and the quarters seem deserted and I have no one to play billiards with in the evening."[38] In his letter of November 30, for the first time, Clarke ventured his opinion about local affairs as they applied to the chain of command. He wrote that the "scatter-brained Lieut. who commands the leading party" (the advance force) hesitated for fear of ridicule from older officers who cautiously awaited permission to cross into Mexico rather than jumping "the boundary like Captain Lebo and several others did in so trusting to luck of not meeting Mexican regulars." This situation mirrored a long-standing frustration that existed since ratification of the 1848 Treaty of Guadalupe Hidalgo that ended the war between Mexico and the United States. Among other provisions of the international agreement, one interdicted crossing into Mexico by U.S. forces fighting fleeing Indians who headed into sanctuary below the border.

Meanwhile, Clarke read for amusement and engaged in such military requirements as "the usual Sunday mounted review and inspection which is a pretty ceremony." After that official assignment, he attended Mass "in our ugly little adobe chapel being shoved around by the Mexican señoritas … and then taking your place." The ethnocentric, chauvinistic Clarke added: "If they were very pretty I would not care but they are irrationally ugly and have their heads covered with their shawls." At least he held a higher opinion of the new "Padre" that he portrayed as "a very intelligent Jesuit who has spent 12 years in France so that we have some pleasant little chats in French." Clarke remarked that several of the officers' wives were Catholic, but were in the minority in the predominately Protestant officer corps.

Clarke delighted in the fact that one of the senior officers, Captain Alexander Scammel Keyes, "had seemingly taken a great liking" to him and "promised to try to get [me] sent down to the Davis Mts to pick out that camp I have spoken of and that he would take us so that we could have a hunt. His wife is very much like a creole her father being a rich old Mexican cattle man (originally Scotch). Her mother was a Mexican. When she and Keyes were married the old man and her brothers were at the front door with shotguns while Keyes took the back door…." He added their daughter was "at one of the Baltimore convents …" and urged his mother to call on the girl "someday as the little thing is very lonesome," a situation which he could well understand.[39]

After completing her eastern education, the young lady might return to the family. This proved the case for recently promoted Captain Charles Lawrence Cooper and his wife Flora, who brought their two daughters and son to Fort Davis. Their Philadelphia-born oldest child, who recently graduated as valedictorian in her class of 1884 from St. Joseph's College, Miss Forrestine Cooper embarked on a new and very different stage of her life. She left behind the refinements and comforts of the East for the less than genteel West.

Like Clarke, the spirited student turned pioneer gained new experiences. In the process, she added to the small garrison's cast of characters. The precocious teenager soon encountered the post's other new residents. At Fort Davis she recalled her meeting "two young lieutenants" who "were graduated from West Point the same month and year that I finished school in Philadelphia in June 1884." The three were destined to be neighbors because when the Coopers reported to Fort Davis they "learned that owing to shortage of quarters these two officers had been assigned temporarily to rooms on the second floor of our own home. My brother, then a boy of fifteen, had the other room upstairs. This left the lower part of the house for my parents, my sister, and myself."

The youthful trio became acquainted; little wonder given their proximity as they shared " a common front hall and stairway, the only exit except through our dining room, and the very informal manner of living in a frontier army post of those days." Seventeen-year-old Forrestine and the two twenty-one-year-old West Point classmates soon formed a trio.

The young officers caught Forrestine Cooper's eye, although she saw their differences in appearance. Nonetheless, she found them handsome, "and magnetic, and both were of the best type of Southern gentlemen. In a short time, they were the most popular young officers in the regiment, and though older men laughed at their boyish pranks, they agreed 'there is good timber in them for officers.'" Interestingly, Forrestine Cooper indicated that she "had never been taught to dance, so that deficiency was remedied very soon when both young officers began to teach me 'how to step' with out treading on my partner's toes. I consider they were martyrs to a sense of honor."[40]

She gained two charming companions who made her transition more pleasant including equestrian excursions with "Both Jim and Powhatan" who "were unusually fine riders, and when the three of us rode together, I was the audience while they tried new 'stunts.' It was a regular Wild West Show, plus West Point Riding Academy tricks. So life ran carefree and joyously for us all."[41]

Clarke and Hughes enjoyed a similar benefit of being thrown together in this tiny west Texas world, which Quanah Parker visited along with George Fox, an employee of the Indian agency trader at Fort Sill. Fox exhibited a facility for the Comanche language. The Quahada leader had befriended and adopted Fox into his band.[42] "On this trip, Fox acted "as secretary, interpreter, and confidential advisor" to Quanah.[43]

During the course of his stay at Fort Davis, "Quanah requested an officer and detail of soldiers." Clarke drew the assignment to accompany Quanah, Fox, and a few other Comanche men on an outing in southwest Texas. Clarke was about to perform "his first duty in connection with Indians." He hurried at once to meet Quanah and Fox, and "discuss plans for the trip with them."

When the two men met: "Quanah studied him [Clarke] quizzically, watching the impulsive, boyish mannerisms that were characteristic of the young officer. It was a delightful evening for us all, filled with laughter and jokes. After Powhatan had left, Quanah smiled" at Forrestine Cooper's parents, as he said dryly, 'Boy Clarke.'"[44] Later. he would regale the Coopers with other stories about the young horse soldier, whom he seemed to take to heart.

On December 9, 1884, Bigelow added: "Clarke is ordered to escort them with about a ½ dozen men." The next day, he recorded seeing "Clarke off this morning with the Indians." Bigelow made mixed comments about "the Chief of the Comanches in Indian Territory" who appeared to him as having "a determined, and intelligent, though not bright, look." Once clad in "a blanket and breech clout" now "he is dressed like a white man." In fact, "Quana was in a 1st Lieut's uniform" when he went out on his quest "to go about 60 miles South of here to get a certain herb they prize as medicine"—possibly peyote.[45]

Clarke offered a more-lengthy description in a telling December 6, 1884, letter to his mother.[46] He divulged how this outing tested his mettle, causing him to grasp the challenge of the rugged land, sparse food, and the unpredictable weather—all factors to be contended with during future campaigning. The green frontiersman also gained admiration for Quanah whom he referred to as "Quuia."

Further, Clarke related that two of Quanah's fellow Comanches, Tabeyutsen or Rising Sun, and Mantoes, rounded out the group. Captain Keyes recommended Clarke "to the commanding officer or as we say the 'K.O.' as a very good officer to escort them to the Chaniti Mountains."

Keyes's suggestion found favor. On Wednesday the ninth, the conglomerate party of Indians, interpreter Fox, Clarke, and a sergeant with seven men left Fort Davis at 10 AM, reaching the railroad station at Marfa at 5 PM. That night, they took shelter in a deserted two-room ranch house. Once encamped, Clarke said: "Quuia gave me a war dance or rather sang it for us during which I naturally went to sleep after our 32 mile ride in rain and sleet. The next day we broke camp at daybreak marched all morning in a very rough wind nearby messing at the spot which is where they [the Comanche] used to come down to the Rio Grande."

At sunrise the next morning, they pressed on, as Clarke reported, "a misty norther set in on us and made us all feel cold and damp. Quuia said he would go with the Indians and we could wait, but I told him that my orders were to follow him … so we continued not withstanding that we only had twelve slices of bread for nine men."

The situation did not improve as they rode. They struck a canyon which required descending "a mountain side covered with rock and nearly perpendicular." Fox cautioned they could not get down, but Clarke "took the lead with the Sergeant." Everyone dismounted at that point. In fact, Clarke "had been walking nearly all the time" given the extremely rough country that took its "toll on my horses." Then, as Clarke reported, "after advancing down half way it grew steeper and one of the horses behind and over me started a large rock which came down like an avalanche. Fox yelled for God's sake Clarke look out. It passed two feet behind me cut my poor little horse…. The rock grazed his front feet. He jerked back as he was slightly cut and got away but I easily caught him … and we finally got down into the cañon."

It was there that "Rising Sun followed the cañon for several miles during which time we eat our lunch and we struck across the mountains." Continuing for the most part on foot because of the difficult terrain, Clarke nevertheless remarked about "a hundred varieties of cactus some very beautiful. I brought Mrs. Bigelow a very pretty Turk's head cactus. It is perfectly round and has branches of four thorns each which grow all over the green surface making a perfect network." Although he appreciated the flora, he discovered the Spanish dagger lived up to its name. They are "anything but comfortable" he discovered "by running one in above the knee and Fox also … ran one through his shoe."

Undeterred, Clarke displayed grit if not downright stubbornness. The lieutenant pressed on, insisting the party follow despite the fact that "the country got so rough that the horses could go no further." Both Fox and the sergeant advised Clarke "to turn back" but, bent on displaying his fortitude, Clarke "told him that I did not propose to give Rising Sun a shade [reason or rationale] to grumble at so I started after him followed by all…." Not to be outdone, the tough sergeant, who had been left in charge of the led horses, followed hard on Rising Sun's tracks "leaving the rest of the party a mile behind as we went up and down over mountains two and three thousand feet high."

After a great deal of climbing, Clarke "reached the top of the tallest mountains I have yet been on and from the top of it I saw the Rio Grande two or three miles" in the distance. This was at about 5 PM. He headed toward a mountain to the right coming back about an hour afterward "to collect the party which was rather scattered." Not until around sunset, did they regroup. Horses and mounts "halted for water until the canteens were emptied" then the exhausted men rested. Clarke admitted: "I was the first to get back and have never been so played out in my life…. Fox wanted to make a dry camp and pull for camp [the] next day but I decided that the brutes would be too stiff so we went where we got to the steep mountain that had given us so much trouble in the morning." Once more, Fox objected it would be impossible to mount these "nearly perpendicular slabs of slippery rock with narrow footholds."

Clarke refused to halt. Adamantly the fatigued but proud subaltern informed Fox he "intended to make camp if it took till daylight." With that vow, the sergeant "started up with me on his heels." The trooper's exhausted horse gave out, twice going down to its knees with the rider in the saddle. In turn, Clarke's mount "fell once and would have rolled but that I had a good footing and threw all the weight on the bridle which swung him lengthways." When cresting the summit, the two lead riders waited for "over half an hour as Fox and the Indians were nearly played out…."

After Fox linked up with Clarke, he told the lieutenant one of the troopers evidently remained "way down the mountain" and could go no farther. Clarke "immediately started down finding him lying down. I urged him on but [he] staggered, caught the bunches of grass above him, and laid up against the mountain. I started his horse finally having to take the ammunition belt, gun sling [carbine sling], carbine and overcoat and make him catch me round the neck and carry him up the hill."

When seemingly they had faced the worst, the weather compounded their woes. As Clarke recounted, a fog rolled in "so thick that we did not dare to move any further and had to stop in a little arroyo on top of a high ridge when after a great coaxing we managed to get the fire lit."

Heat and a source for cooking their meager fare presented only one challenge. They all had scant water. Fox offered the Indians two dollars to go for a canteen of water but "they would not risk it and there we stayed the wind blowing fearfully scattering our fire over us."

As Clarke recalled: "The man who had given out was very sick and I was afraid he would not move in the morning as he acknowledged having been sick during the day but being an old soldier he did not like to own up" to his being incapacitated, which Clarke thought demonstrated the grit of troopers from the Tenth Cavalry. He added, "I think as neither he nor any man … made a single complaint." The untested lieutenant was learning his men were made of as stout or even stouter stuff than he was. Clarke confided "having left my overcoat" back at Fort Davis "I could not sleep very well; a saddle blanket and one thin old blanket one of the Indians forced me to take. About three A.M. nearly all fell asleep notwithstanding the cold…."

The ordeal continued. Clarke spun out his narrative with the capstone that the fog not only remained the next morning, but also "the ground was white with frozen rain and mist." The haggard party "reached camp at twelve, took dinner and slept all that afternoon. Fox told me the next day that in all his experiences with the Regiment he had never made a rougher march we having gone twenty-five miles right over mountains which is never done and that I was fortunate in not having lost a horse on the mountain."

No doubt Clarke delighted in hearing such praise regarding what amounted to his first field command. In the process, he had shown the Indians "how our men could hold out. When they got back they told the officers that I was a goat for climbing."

They soon would have their chance to tell this tale, because after "the evening of the fifth day" the party turned about for Fort Davis reaching the "Grande Rio where we had a big feed. I gave all the canned stuff left to the men. At daybreak we started for Marfa; reached it at 9:00." Afterwards, in the evening, Clarke presented "two antelopes to Quiia." With the game as a main course, Indian and soldier alike "had lots of fun listening to old scouting stories told in Comanche and English Fox acting as an interpreter. Quiia then thanked us and hoped we would visit him at Fort Sill."

Before departing, the legendary Comanche dined with the Coopers one more time and as Forrestine Cooper recorded he "had many jokes to tell on the young officer, one of which was his falling asleep near the campfire" and when the lieutenant's forage cap rolled near the fire, "only the patent leather visor was left, and so Powhatan rode back to the garrison with a large white silk handkerchief tied about his head like an old lady's hood." Notably, Quanah's good-natured anecdotes about "'Papoose' Clarke, who wore a baby cap, and chewed things like a baby," were revealed in the young officer's presence, "who enjoyed the jokes at his own expense."[47]

The Comanches left the next day. That afternoon Clarke gave the men of his troop "one of the roughest drills they have had since I have been here to show them" that they were "not so tired as they might expect. (I hear they called me the dude but having double timed some of them … and ridden them as hard as they know … I think they will get over their ideas."

Perhaps Clarke believed this tough treatment would gain respect. Discipline, not his personal strong suit, formed a cornerstone of command for frontier officers. Clarke needed to add this skill, which seemed to be developing because he contended now that the men under him:

> never complained, always volunteered to do anything they could for me when they got into camp. After a hard march they sit around the fires laughing and singing. The old sergeant with his fifteen years' experience proved invaluable to me being an excellent guide, tough as leather and very responsible. Fox asked him if he did not have too much to do. He said no not much. It was the lieutenant's first trip and he felt responsible for seeing that none of the property was lost as the lieutenant would have to pay.…

Clarke's isolated foray with several of his men afforded important insights about his subordinates. The trek had a maturing impact. During this experience not only had he learned some valuable lessons about his soldiers by spending time with them under extreme conditions, but also, the unseasoned newcomer began to earn some respect from his men. One thing was certain, he led by dogged example.

While Clarke did not reveal his thoughts on any of these matters, he did share some other topics in the closing passages of one of the longest letters ever sent home. Returning to Quiia he noted during the march they discovered several day-old-sign of "some Apaches whose trail we ran across near the Rio." The formerly fierce warrior expressed sorrow that they had not arrived at the spot earlier "as he hates the Apaches and with the good marksmen we had we could have cleaned up," Quanah contended.

Additionally, Clarke filled in more information about the episode that had sent his "bunkie" Jim Hughes on a hard ride "one hundred and thirty miles into Mexico" on the trail of raiders who had killed a family and run off their livestock. The perpetrators turned out to be Mexicans, but only eight ponies were recaptured while the patrol lost one mule and a pair of their mounts.

While Clarke longed to head out again, that desire took second place to his return to general courts martial assignments. This time Bigelow served as the judge advocate with a full plate of many cases including "serious desertions, disorders, ect [*sic*] frequently causing penitentiary sentences."

Somewhat offsetting these less than thrilling duties, John and Mary Bigelow were "always kind as ever" to the two bachelor roommates. As to his career, it seemed that Captain Keyes seemed "satisfied with his having detailed me for the trip" with Quanah, "which was very good for me being the youngest officer and lowest officer at the Post."

Hospitality from others proved the order of the day in December during the holiday season. The ever-observant Forrestine Cooper preserved another story about Clarke at Fort Davis, this time as they spent Christmas together with their military family. In part, her reminiscences reflected the peculiarities of a frontier army community, as well as the racial views and class consciousness prevalent at the time. A physical as well as social divide existed between the barracks side of the post, where enlisted men resided, and officers' row, separated only by a relatively small rectangular parade ground.[48]

"Christmas 1884 was celebrated at Fort Davis by everyone in the garrison," Forrestine recollected, "from the colonel of the regiment down to the smallest pickaninny on 'Suds Row,' where the wives of the colored soldiers constituted a colony of laundresses, some times depleted by excursions into kitchens of the officers' families as cooks."[49] Rivalry arose between each troop as they "vied with the others in having the most elaborate dinner, and the officers and families went from one mess room to the other inspecting the decorated feast, and deciding which one excelled." Afterwards, "on officers' row, individual celebrations gave way" to a Christmas Eve "general gathering at the library." Here each "child in the garrison had been remembered by a gift on that tree," then with gift in hand they "were to be sent home and a dance continued the festivities for the officers and their families."

Much to her chagrin, Forrestine "was considered too young to be classed as grown-up, and was not to be allowed to attend any dances until my eighteenth birthday…." Her mother set down the rules that she could attend the celebrations from "three and remain till nine o'clock, then I must go home." Some of the other officers' wives "interceded for me," as did Clarke, Hughes, and Colonel Grierson's oldest son, all of whom previously had helped teach her to dance. Her champions won out. She remained. At the appointed hour Post Chaplain Francis Weaver took center stage to distribute the presents to the little ones.

Bigelow portrayed Weaver as seemingly "an earnest energetic man" but "unpolished…." Perhaps the chaplain's former service as a Union enlisted man, and later for a short period as a soldier in the post-Civil War Regulars, tinted Bigelow's perceptions.[50] Regardless of Weaver's abilities and past, tonight he stood in for Father Christmas handing Forrestine her gift "as one of the children of the garrison." To her embarrassment "Powhatan and Jim enjoyed my confusion until they, too, heard their names announced …, and each of them also received a toy as garrison children."

With gifts distributed, all the young folk scrambled to the table. "A vacant chair on either side" of Forrestine "at once was appropriated by Lieutenant Hughes and Lieutenant [William] Shipp, who grinned at Powhatan as he realized he was ‘cut out’ by them both. He tried to ‘transfer,’ offering various inducements, but failed. A child opposite me called out, ‘You can have my place, Lieutenant Clarke.’” Clarke accepted the offer “with thanks and then announced triumphantly that he had the best place after all, as he could look straight at me all the time he was eating. Then he proceeded to make life miserable for poor Lieutenant Shipp, who did not know me as intimately as the other two.”

Dancing followed. When the merriment ended, it was time for church services. Forrestine remarked: “So we left the dancing and music and entered the ambulance [actually a multifunctional light vehicle not solely used for medical purposes] at the library door.” Although headed to Midnight Mass, the Coopers and most of those who made their way to church were Protestants unlike Clarke who “was a Catholic, as was Mrs. Keyes.” Religious affiliations aside, all rode under a beautiful moonlight sky. When they “reached the little, one-story adobe building, all windows and the wide door were opened so that rays of light from within the church lighted up figures, men with bared heads, and Mexican women draped with black shawls, who unable to get into the church, were kneeling outside in the roadway.”

Stepping “down from the ambulance” the entourage “could get no nearer than the kneeling figures. Then, the courtly Sir Walter Raleigh, Powhatan, unfastened his blue cape, lined with cavalry yellow, and lay it on the ground for me to kneel upon. So we heard that Christmas Midnight Mass.”

After church, with her three escorts in tow, the teenager returned “to the hop room to the music, bright lights, dancing, and laughter, and soon my Christmas was over. But when my parents started to walk home with me, Powhatan and Jim went along, and Lieutenant Shipp went, too.” A smitten Forrestine Cooper vowed never to forget that Christmas.

On the other hand, Lieutenant Hughes may well have wished to purge that holiday from his memory. He declined attending a meal on December 25, “through [a] temporary indisposition, consequent upon too much punch drinking in the course of the afternoon.” This binge “mortified” Bigelow, who likewise “did not like Clarke’s off hand way of apologizing” for Hughes “absence: ‘He is not well. You will have to excuse him.’”[51] Regardless of this faux pas, Hughes soon returned to duty.

Meanwhile, Clarke concocted a scheme to avoid the routine of Fort Davis, which he discussed in a February 7, 1885, letter to his mother. Drawing on his French-speaking abilities and presuming his father was capable of "pulling wires" (Victorian military parlance for "pulling strings") a not uncommon effort by "some of the West Pointers ... to secure posh jobs ... particularly if they came from influential families," he set forth a preposterous scheme.[52] Clarke must have imagined his father had sufficient clout to contact President Chester A. Arthur to pave the way for a stint in France. The brash young lieutenant hoped he could land temporary duty at the French cavalry school in Saumur.

He mentioned other topics including a spate of court-martial proceedings against fellow Tenth U.S. Cavalry officers. These actions brought Bigelow temporary command of Troop L "whose officers are awaiting trial." This necessity stemmed from the prevalent problem of a limited number of officers available for duty being compounded by the requirement that officers awaiting courts martial or in arrest were prohibited from carrying out command and other military duties.

Bigelow's temporary reassignment resulted from a series of events demonstrating the infighting, poor performance, and bad behavior of several officers at the post who tarnished their names and perhaps stained their regiment's reputation. As one example of this sorry state of affairs, a member of Grierson's inner circle and related through marriage, Lieutenant William Davis, Jr. (satirically nicknamed "Whispering Bill" because of his booming voice) did more than bellow. After Christmas, the drunken Davis came to blows with an infantry officer while the two men were at the post sutler's.

It was at this Fort Davis facility where the other officer, who evidently previously preferred charges "against Davis for speaking disrespectfully of President Lincoln and his son, the Secretary of War," reopened the dispute. According to Bigelow: "It was through some allusion to this subject that the encounter came about. Davis has a black eye." Bigelow did not know the physical state of the second officer.[53]

Adding to the situation, Bigelow set down a January 17, 1885, incident of "Another scandal" in which "Captain Keyes got drunk as Officer of the

Day and hobnobbed with a colored soldier in the same condition." Crossing both racial boundaries and class lines, Keyes's breech of decorum prompted another junior officer to press charges only to be induced by "Grierson to withdraw them" with the assertion "that they could not be substantiated…." The accusing party resented this rebuff. He informed Grierson "he would not withdraw them until he had been apologized to before the officers present—three or four" of them for Grierson's failure to take action against Keyes. He further demanded the colonel acknowledge Keyes's wrongdoing." Grierson complied. Keyes, as one of the colonel's "favored few," however, avoided any reprimand or actions related to his indiscretions.[54]

No sooner had Keyes skirted a potentially career-ending disaster than Lieutenant Davis publicly blurted that he would slap Major Anson Mills "the next time he met him," threatening to repeat his previous bad behavior. Mills dispatched a note to Davis that if the lieutenant acted on his menacing warning, he would kill him. As was Grierson's wont when it came to favorites, he intervened to protect Davis. Forcing the regimental commander's hand, Mills succeeded in not only having charges forwarded to higher headquarters, but also added fellow Tenth U.S. Cavalry Lieutenants James Jouett and Carter Johnson along with Davis as a trio he alleged went "to a local saloon operated by an ex soldier … and became drunk on duty."[55] It was the arrest and subsequent legal proceedings against two of the defendants (Davis and Johnson) that brought about Bigelow's short-lived command of Company L.

Johnson's trial especially weighed on Bigelow. He even took time to attend the closing of the court martial remarking: "I thought the argument for the defense rather weak. Johnson's main accusation is being in a disreputable place. He should have known he could not prove its respectability" but rather should have argued "he did not know what kind of place it was." Bigelow predicted that Johnson would be dismissed from the service. He was wrong. Both Johnson and Davis were reinstated. Bigelow returned to Company K.[56]

During these legal maneuvers that placed Bigelow in command Company L, Clarke had to shoulder the burden of Company K for Captain Lebo. As before, the captain claimed to be ill. Hence, Clarke oversaw the routine, from being present at Reveille, inspecting barracks, and attending drill, stables, parade, and Tattoo, all of which he found monotonous. Despite this, Clarke confessed that he was "rather glad now that I went to West Point … as my life would not be as happy as it is."[57]

Later, in a pair of undated letters to his parents, he disclosed a possible departure from Texas. In the first note, Clarke's father learned that it was "true now that we are to go to Arizona and relieve the 3rd Cav…. Some of the forts will be as nice as this one; others will be intolerable. Hughes and I have hopes of going to Hdqrs at Prescott [Arizona] as our two captains are favorites of Grierson's and have the best troops. But then it is no telling. For me I would as soon go to Huachuca which is a delightful post on the Mexican border."[58]

This offhanded mention of favorites was not unusual. Factionalism existed in the Tenth Cavalry and other regiments.[59] Douglas McChristian provided a useful summation pointing out "the Tenth Cavalry, like so many other regiments experienced disharmony among its officers, sometimes to the point of open conflict. Given the factors of isolation, crowded living conditions, inadequate compensation and vicious competition for promotion to often non-existing vacancies, such incidents came as no surprise." So pervasive was this atmosphere that Bigelow's granddaughter "commented that her grandmother" decades after the fact "had an intense dislike for the malicious gossip and back-biting that seemed to be an integral part of life on officers row."[60]

Of this tempest arising from many causes, Powhatan suspiciously added: "Between you, I and the gatepost the reason we move is that the colonel owns too much land here, the quartermaster too much of a ranchman; several trials have shown the lax discipline among the officers which … had done us a great deal of harm in the Regiment."[61]

In his diary, Bigelow chimed in with parallel private opinions that "two special reasons" existed "for the lowness of tone in the regiment, one was the easy, *laisse aller* character of the Colonel; the other the inferiority of the officer personel [*sic*] with which our regiment, in common with other colored regiments, is stocked."[62]

Whatever the reasons for the transfer, Clarke professed his regret at leaving Fort Davis "as I have become very attracted to it and have always had a splendid time here." Nevertheless, the prospect of marching 600 miles "'a caballo' [on horseback] to Arizona" appealed to him. He closed with the promise he would let the family know when the move from Fort Davis was going to take place.

In a follow-up note to his mother, Clarke announced: "it is fixed that orders are out for us to change with the Third Cavalry."[63] He recapped that the regiment had been in the Department of Texas for a decade and the Tenth was in "ill disrepute [*sic*] with Headquarters." Further, Clarke told his mother: "We are going to march on the 1st of April as a Regiment." All troops concentrated at Fort Davis "so that we will become acquainted which is very rare when a Regt is so scattered" as was the rule rather than the exception until later in the century. Since the late 1870s, when approximately 25,000 officers and men garrisoned "the more than 250 small posts" that existed "about the country, mostly in the West," this distribution pattern supposedly meant that "small remote posts contributed to the army's isolation and lack of expertise in large unit operations…."[64]

Breaking that mold, the companies assembled. Clarke asserted it would take them "six weeks to go to Deming [New Mexico] where we will meet the 3rd Cavalry." As he prepared to relocate, Clarke could have reflected on what he had learned during his inaugural year as a second lieutenant bored by garrison duty. He was not living a romantic page out of Sir Walter Scott's tales of knights and ladies, nor was he even a "Leatherstocking" figure from James Fenimore Cooper's fiction. These notions, and stories about rousing fights between North and South from his father's generation, were but fanciful impressions that bore little resemblance to his experiences to date. Would this disappointing reality change once he reached Arizona?

Chapter 4

"Oh, It's Old Arizona"

After nearly two decades of service in Colorado, Kansas, Indian Territory, New Mexico, and Texas, the Tenth U.S. Cavalry faced new challenges in another hostile environment. In the spring of 1885, orders uprooted the regiment, including Clarke, setting wheels in motion for a mass transfer.

From Spanish colonial times, Arizona experienced frequent violence. For successive generations, Spanish, Mexican, and American forces faced a formidable nomadic people who became known and feared as the Apache. So it was, in 1848, after Mexico ceded most of today's Arizona to the United States by the Treaty of Guadalupe Hidalgo, and the follow-on 1853 Gadsden Purchase, the final push to end warfare with the many American Indians in Arizona began. It soon became evident that the U.S. government must dispatch troops and build forts to protect travelers and settlers on what historian Earle Forest dubbed "Arizona's Dark and Bloody Ground."[1] The Tenth U.S. Cavalry was about to join the long list of foes of the Apache. This force, along with white troops and Indian scouts already mobilized, would hound three dozen men, women, and children of the *Bedonkohe* band of the Chiricahua Apache.[2] At the end of the contest, nearly one quarter of the entire U.S. Army trailed them and their leader, *Goyaałé* (aka *Goyakla* translated as "He Who Yawns")—or as he came to be called by Mexican and American pursuers alike—Geronimo.[3]

The terse conclusions of Texas-born Third United States Cavalry Lieutenant Britton Davis reflected the attitude of a goodly number of those who met Geronimo in his heyday. Davis maintained: "This Indian was a thoroughly vicious, intractable, and treacherous man. His only redeeming traits were courage and determination. His word, no matter how earnestly pledged, was worthless. His history … was a series of broken pledges and incitements to outbreaks."[4]

A true depiction or not, it was during the last stage of this age-old conflict, that Clarke and the Tenth Cavalry (over six hundred strong) rode from the Department of Texas to the Department of Arizona following the course of the Southern Pacific Railroad. Clarke's occasional companion at Fort Davis, Forrestine Cooper, left a breezy recollection of the exodus. Among other things, she related that "the families decided to go by rail to avoid the thirty-day trip, camping each night." Somewhat to her chagrin "the 'Triple Alliance' of the Regimental Infants, as Mrs. [Virginia Maxwell] Keyes had nicknamed" Miss Cooper and fresh-faced Lieutenants Jim Hughes and Powhatan Clarke, "was doomed to be dissolved."[5] Before taking their leave, the three youngsters attended "a farewell hop" at Fort Davis. The following morning "the whole regiment, headed by the band" rode forth making "its first camp about ten miles distant, so that evening many of those who waited to make the trip by railroad later drove out to the camp and had dinner there."

At one point along the route, Miss Cooper and some of her fellow train passengers spied the column as it plodded along "coated with alkali dust, while many wore handkerchiefs over noses and mouths. But as the train rushed past, two officers galloped beside the track, waving their campaign hats and whooping like Indians." Showing off, Powhatan Clarke and Lieutenant Leighton Finley kept up their "race as long as they could, and then with a final whoop, gave it up."[6]

Continuing her narrative, Forrestine Cooper reported when the troops "reached El Paso" they discovered "the Rio Grande was so badly swollen that it was unfordable." The only means of continuing was a "bridge over the river … three miles below the New Mexico line and that bridge crossed into Mexico." This forced the column to halt, and remain immobile for a week to carry on negotiations between officials in Mexico and the United States. As the "red tape … was being unwound to permit the crossing of that solitary bridge" the main body waited. Finally, regimental officials concluded arrangements with Mexican authorities so that the Tenth Cavalry could pass south of the international border.

Negotiations completed, the mounted cavalcade and train continued westward, the latter arriving first at Willcox, Arizona, which "was about a hundred fifty miles" distant. There, "typical of the old frontier days," they found that Colonel William R. "Pecos Bill" Shafter, commanding the First Infantry and also Fort Grant, had sent transportation for the women and children.[7]

Soon, all the elements gathered at Bowie Station, Arizona, where the various troops dispersed and scattered to their new posts.[8] Fanning out, the regimental headquarters under Grierson reported to Fort Whipple outside of Prescott. He and key staff officers, not a few of whom to Clarke's disdain were Grierson family members or part of the colonel's inner circle, arrived with the regimental band and Troop B, the former element boasting excellent musicians and an impressive library of musical scores. The other troops of the regiment went to Fort Apache (Troop A), Fort Thomas (Troops C, F, and G), Fort Grant (Troops D, E, H, K. and L), and Fort Verde (Troops I and M).[9] With the regiment's arrival, Arizona Territory's relatively small African American population expanded significantly just as it did when black troops deployed to Montana, Utah, and Wyoming.[10]

Even before many of these men could settle in to their new posts, on May 19, Troops D, E, H, and K (Clarke's troop) received orders for field duty in New Mexico.[11] This deployment coincided with a May 17, 1885, bolting of an estimated fifty Apaches of various ages and of both sexes from the hated San Carlos Reservation, which a character from one of Owen Wister's short stories described as a place with no streets or houses and "there ain't any land and water in the usual meaning of them words…. Mix up a barrel of sand and ashes and thorns, and jam scorpions and rattlesnakes along in, and dump the outfit on stones, and heat the stones red-hot" and you "had the hell on earth—San Carlos."[12]

This powder keg reservation housed both Apache and Yavapai people, neither of whom were particularly friendly to each other.[13] By the Tenth Cavalry's appearance in the territory, Brigadier General George Crook, who had been the commencement speaker at Clarke's graduation, had held command for nearly three years. He had come to Arizona in 1882 (his first posting was between 1871 through 1875). From long years of personal observation, Crook concluded: "*the torrent of invective and abuse* which has universally been indulged in *against the whole Apache race*" was a common trait found "on the frontier from a certain class of vampires who prey on the misfortunes of their fellow men and who live best and easiest in time of Indian troubles." This group, Crook charged, disdained peace because it killed "the goose that laid the golden egg. Greed and avarice on the part of the whites—in other words the almighty dollar—is at the bottom of nine-tenths of all our Indian troubles."[14]

In fact, the economic impact of military posts and operations in Arizona and elsewhere in the West proved a powerful force, one that led to mixed messages when it came to ending Apache violence. Peace was preferred, but government contracts provided a lucrative livelihood.[15]

Although Crook's words indicated a great degree of sympathy, he was a realist when it came to the Apache raids. The experienced general knew after Geronimo and others jumped the reservation his only recourse was to mobilize "from all points forces to intercept them" including elements of the newly arrived Tenth Cavalry. Moreover, he deemed "it prudent to … warn the citizens" of the mass, murderous exodus from San Carlos.[16]

Crook's concern for local residents was well founded. The San Carlos fugitives headed south toward Mexico leaving a swath of destruction as they descended along a route toward refuge south of the border. As Dan Thrapp indicated in his study of the Apache campaigns, this tragic bolting "would cost the lives of ten American officers, nearly one hundred settlers and peaceful Indians, and no one could guess how many Mexicans, and … would be prolonged for two years."[17]

Experienced, battle-hardened fighters Geronimo and his group wreaked such havoc. Among the ranks was the veteran warrior, *Chokonen* Apache Chihuahua (aka *Kla-esch*), who according to historian Dan Thrapp "loved the forbidden tizwin [a fermented alcoholic beverage brewed by the

Apache and other native peoples in the Southwest] and wanted the freedom to beat his women when he chose." As with so many of the leaders of the Chiricahua and other Apache groups and subgroups, Chihuahua was associated by birth or marriage with several notables including his brother Joanie (Ulzanna) as well as such in-laws as Kenasewah and Ka-ya-ten-nae. A participant in raiding and outbreaks of the early 1880s, Chihuahua allied himself with Geronimo although at one juncture he considered killing him.[18]

Another warrior who fled the reservation and boasted battle capabilities was Mimbres Apache Mangas. Despite impressive family ties, this son of the "redoubtable" Mangas Coloradas ("Red Sleeves") and brother-in-law of Cochise, as well as uncle to Cochise's two sons, he did not enjoy the significant following of his larger than life father. Nonetheless, after coming to San Carlos in the wake of the relentless 1883 Sierra Madre Campaign, Mangas had achieved some stature. Using his standing, in the words of Britton Davis, he not only "egged on" Geronimo because of his own motives, but also did so due to the goading of his expert tizwin-making Mexican-born, white-hating wife Huera, who had " 'sufficient intelligence to be troublesome.' "[19] Eventually, according to Davis, "Geronimo thoroughly dissatisfied, took advantage of this situation" of discontent on the reservation, but as the lieutenant further believed, neither Chihuahua nor Mangas "wished or expected the trouble to go so far as the outbreak."[20]

Besides Chihuahua and Mangas, two other significant figures joined the flight. One of them, Naiche (aka Nachez, Natchez, Nachite) was the youngest of Cochise's sons. During the controversial 1861 Bascom Affair at Apache Pass, the lad Naiche and his mother became captives. The military released them soon afterwards. By 1876, after Cochise's death and the death of his eldest brother Taza "in Washington, D.C., Naiche became the last chief the Chiricahuas ever had." Another participant in the 1882 and 1883 raids with Geronimo, he once more fled San Carlos in 1885 bound for the Sierra Madres where he held out until September 1886.[21]

Despite his age, the venerable, "good-sized … fat, and stout" *Chiehenne* (the so-called Warm Springs Apaches) Kas-tziden (aka Nana) also numbered among those with the Geronimo in 1885.[22] Born around 1800, this "Mimbres leader was neither a chief nor a sub-chief" but was considered by some to be "the tactical brains behind" the much vaunted Victorio, a name that resonated long before Geronimo began to make the headlines. Despite Nana's advanced age, rheumatism, and "failing eyesight," Thrapp pointed out that "in 1881 he led one of the legendary Apache raids into southwestern New Mexico …" laying waste wherever he and his as little as fifteen followers descended. He, too, went to the Sierra Madre in 1883, and again in 1885.[23]

Efforts to locate, capture, or engage the San Carlos defectors resulted in Clarke and troopers from Troop K vacating their new quarters at Fort Grant, barely after settling into the garrison. Clarke and his men were to play their part in Crook's multilevel strategy.

As was the general's practice, he relied extensively on Indian scouts, including other Apaches, much as he had done in the first foray into Mexico during 1883. While not the originator of the employment of scouts, Crook wholeheartedly embraced the use of Indians permitted by the 1866 Congressional "Act to increase and fix the Military Peace Establishment of the United States." His propensity to field scouts predated his service in Arizona, and could be traced to recruitment in both Oregon and California.[24] With this background and having reached the conclusion that "regular troops are as helpless as a whale attacked by a school of sword-fish" when it came to defeating the Apache, Crook heavily relied on scouts.[25]

During the early 1870s, Crook had followed his instincts and engaged the Coyetero and White Mountain groups, followed by recruitment of other Apaches as well as such diverse peoples known at the time as Hualpais, Maricopas, Pimas (Akimel O'odham, also spelled Akimel O'otham), Paiutes, Navajos, Yaquis, Yavapais, and Yumas.[26] In the end, Crook came to favor Apaches because he believed "to polish a diamond there is nothing like diamond dust."[27]

Regardless of the affiliation or ethnicity, the scouts would be commanded by army officers and civilians under the designation of "chief of scouts," who among other things could serve as trackers and interpreters. In the former category, Crook displayed a capacity for selecting "as leaders of the scout detachments the types of officers who were not only able to adjust to having the undisciplined Indians under their command but [also] were efficient and physically fit enough to be accepted by the Indians as leaders."[28] Eventually, Clarke joined this select band of officers detailed to command scouts.

If Clarke listened carefully to Crook's commencement address at West Point in June of 1884, he would have gained insight into the general's strategic thinking. The general articulated his theories in some detail under the title *Resume of Operations against Apache Indians, 1882–1886*. In this combination report-manifesto-apologia the "Gray Wolf," as some of the Apache called him, set forth such principles as the necessity "to secure the protection" of local people and property "to prevent if possible, their [Apaches] recrossing the line" back into the United States from Mexico, where they had taken up sanctuary in the security of the rugged Sierra Madres. Crook envisioned troops "stationed along the frontier. To each detachment was assigned five Indian scouts to watch the front and detect the approach of the hostiles. These troops were stationed at every point where it was thought possible for hostiles to pass."

The ambitious concept was to guard "every trail, every waterhole from the Patagonia Mountains to the Rio Grande.... The troops were under the strictest orders, constantly to patrol this line, each detachment having a particular section of the country assigned to its special charge."

For a backup to this primary force Crook established "a second line ... in the rear of the front, both to act as a reserve, and to prevent the passing of any hostiles who might elude the vigilance of the first line." Finally: "behind this again were stationed troops on the railroad who might be sent to any desired point on the whole front, forming thus a third line."[29]

As part of this scheme, on July 7, 1885, Crook informed the assistant adjutant general of the Division of the Pacific of his intention to place details from the Tenth Cavalry "in the rear of the advance line ... to intercept parties should they succeed in sneaking through the first line."[30] This deployment disappointed "every young officer" in the Tenth. Many, if not all, sought action instead of rear echelon postings. As Forrestine Cooper pointed out, this mission caused men who sought combat experience for the possibility of promotion, adventure, and other motives to plea with Crook "to be sent out to field duty," rather than remain in garrison or away from the scene of fighting.[31]

Clarke bristled at being kept out of the fray. So, too, did James Hughes. Like Clarke, Hughes deplored his stay-at-home assignment at Fort

Whipple, regimental headquarters, doing tedious work that he despised. Given that Fort Whipple also served as Crook's headquarters, Hughes's determination to taste combat meant he "practically trod on General Crook heels when that old soldier" was at the garrison. Hughes's "persistent request to be sent out on Indian duty met with refusal that enough were already in the saddle." Undaunted, Hughes cajoled, "'Well, won't you send me out to guard a waterhole ...?'" In reply, Crook quipped: "'There are more second lieutenants now than I have waterholes to guard.'" If Hughes, who had direct access to Crook, failed to persuade the departmental commander to release him from being shackled to a desk, what hope would Clarke have to be ordered to the field?

Again, Forrestine Cooper noted the repeated endeavors to participate in the something more real than West Point summer camp. She indicated that after four years at the Academy followed by a relatively uneventful stay at Fort Davis: "Down at Fort Grant, Lieutenant Powhatan Clarke's troop ... was still inactive and the young officer was fretting at not being in the field. Several times he went to Fort Bowie, only to return with the same information as Crook had stated to Lieutenant Hughes."[32] Much to his chagrin and that of like-minded officers in the regiment, the Tenth was not to take to the front, at least not for the time being.

At least there was some good news in that Clarke had landed at Fort Grant, which some pronounced as "one of the most desirable stations in Arizona," or in army jargon of the era a "gilt edged" (prime) assignment complete with "Lake Constance" on the parade ground. Be that as it may, the months of routine there wore thin for Clarke.[33]

As he marked time in the daily routine of garrison, all was not drudgery. For example, during the summer of 1885, Forrestine related how she and several of the other younger residents, including post surgeon Dr. William Corbusier's rather rambunctious boys, headed to Grant Creek. As the carefree party passed the post trader's store "Lieutenant Clarke popped out the door of the club room, demanding to know what was happening and where we were going." After explanations, "he joined the caravan...." Before long, the boy in Clarke emerged. He had discovered a "rock nearby and investigated. It was covered thickly with small brown frogs. It took only a minute or two for the children to follow his suggestion of having a 'frog race.'"

Losing track of time, much as he evidently did at West Point, Clarke heard the bugle call and cannon announcing *Retreat*, which jarred him back to reality. "Clarke started to his feet and exclaimed, 'Retreat! By jove, I'm officer of the day and I've missed it!'" He started to hurry off when Forrestine asked, where was his saber? Exasperated, he replied he had taken "it off in the club. That's how I forgot about retreat. I would have remembered if I had worn my saber. And I would have thought about retreat if I had seen it,' was my only chance for sympathy or help," Forrestine responded. Powhatan had but one thought about this incident: "'Shafter will court-martial me and have me shot at sunrise, I guess.'"

Powhatan departed. The next morning, Forrestine attempted to learn of his fate. Her family's cook reported that Colonel Shafter in fact placed the lieutenant under arrest and confined him to quarters, or so the servant had been told by one of the soldiers from Troop K.

With her father away, she turned to Clarke's fellow Tenth Cavalry officer, First Lieutenant Levi Hunt, who had known Forrestine since she was a baby. She "had also attended his wedding to Miss Haidie Badger." She related: "He was the smallest officer who had ever been graduated from West Point, and the nickname of 'Dad Hunt' always clung to him."

Because Hunt had assumed the duties of officer of the day, she could ask him "why Lieutenant Clarke was under arrest, He replied: 'Absent from retreat while officer of the day, and he refuses to give a satisfactory explanation to the commanding officer.' Then I told the whole story and offered to go with Lieutenant Hunt and explain it to Colonel Shafter." Hunt ordered her to "'keep out of official matters, young lady.'" Further, Hunt interjected, "'Clarke evidently does not want you dragged into this. Go home. I'll see Colonel Shafter myself.'"

The exchange with Hunt bore fruit. "That afternoon," while sitting on the porch, she spied Powhatan come "whistling down the front line" of officers' row and "turned toward our steps before he saw me there." Delighted to tell her the news, he blurted out: "'Colonel Shafter just released me from arrest....'" Innocently she asked: "'For being absent last night?'" His interest piqued, he quizzed, "'Did you say anything to him?'" Once more pretending ignorance, she retorted: "'Certainly not. I never meddle in official matters. I know better.'"

Believing her story, Powhatan "went on, 'Old Shafter's not so black as he's painted. He just sent for me, and when I got there he gave me a stiff dressing down about neglect of duty, then released me. I thanked him and started out when he called me back, and this is what he said: 'Oh, Mr. Clarke' (he was mimicking Shafter's voice to perfection), 'hereafter when you are officer of the day, I want you to remember that you belong to the army, and not to the navy. So if you didn't see him, how the dickens do you suppose he knew about that frog race yesterday evening?'"[34]

Clarke owed Cooper a debt of gratitude. He would repay her kindness during an afternoon ride. "My horse, Don," recalled Cooper, "was a fractious animal and hard bated … and it seemed impossible to ever thoroughly break him." Not unexpectedly, "Don decided to run away" just as a wagon approached them on the same narrow lane. The harnessed team "bolted toward us" Cooper said, and she "could not stop Don," while the driver "could not stop the team in time. It meant a crash of my horse into the team, or my being dragged into the barbed wire fence."

While Cooper claimed she "was not really frightened. I had not time to be, when I heard Powhatan call out, 'Sit steady! Drop your stirrup!'" As she rode sidesaddle, this meant she only had to free the one foot on the left side allowing Clarke to crowd "up beside Don, and then said, 'Ready, let go!'" At that point, he plucked her from the saddle. Don galloped on without her. Easing her down to the ground he proceeded to lecture her, then dashed off "on a wild chase after Don and finally caught him."[35]

The harrowing outing triggered a response, one that may have been simmering for some time, from Cooper's father. Soon afterward, he instructed her "to 'cut' Lieutenant Clarke, but would give no reason for his command." Apparently, Captain Cooper numbered among "some of the old commanders in the department" who regarded "Clarke as a 'broncho' in barracks…."[36] This group may have seen him as having the raw clay to become a soldier, but he was not a suitable suitor for young ladies.

While she previously never disobeyed her parents, this prohibition seemed unfair. "Rankled," she "refused to do as he asked" unless her father gave his reason for the unwelcome restriction, but he "considered his demand should be sufficient and I became angry and stubborn, so he left the room."

Forrestine assumed "the sudden change of attitude toward the young officer, who had always been privileged to come in and out of our home informally" was a temporary situation. She thought this situation would "'blow over' and everything would be as usual. The Geronimo campaign was getting on the nerves of officers who were kept in the garrison, inactive. The younger officers were bombarding their superior officers and also General Crook with requests to be sent 'out in the field.'" As such, she "understood all this."

What shocked her was her father seeking out "Clarke that afternoon at stables, and stated that the young officer should stop calling at" his family's quarters nor should he "connive at meeting" his daughter secretly elsewhere emphasizing "his attentions to me were obnoxious to my parents. 'Suppose I do come?' Clarke asked coolly." Her father shot back: "'If you will not comply with my demand as a gentleman should, I will kick you out like a cur.'"

Not known for his patience, "luckily" as Forrestine recollected, "the hotheaded young officer kept his temper and merely replied, 'You wear a pretty good-sized boot, captain. I will not invade your home, but I will not make any attempt not to meet Miss Birdie elsewhere in an honorable manner unless she forbids it herself.'" This ended the exchange, particularly because Captain Cooper's Troop H received orders for the field "the latter part of April 1885" and was not to "return to Fort Grant until May 4, 1886."[37] By that time Clarke had left Fort Grant.

After the captain's departure, Clarke strode up to the Cooper family's quarters "one day and announced, 'I'm not officer of the day this time, so come on down to Frog Headquarters with me.' The frogs were ahead of us, covering the huge boulder. It appeared truly a frog convention. Over the rock two immense sycamore trees formed a perfect arch of interlacing boughs. The twisted white roots were bare under the ripples of Grant Creek, and reflections of roots and trees so distinct as to appear four trees growing from a single base."

As they enjoyed the setting, the pair "sat there talking." Clarke reported General Crook at last granted him permission "to get into field duty, and that he would start to Fort Bowie the next morning before daybreak." Following this news, he romantically took out his knife, proposing to carve a monogram of their "initials intertwined" on the "white bark of one of the twin sycamore trees." This gesture provoked "an animated discussion," the couple talking and working "out the letters by drawing various designs in the soft earth until satisfied with the result. When the monogram was completed, he cut the outline of a large heart surrounding the letters" then declared: "'Someday we will come back to our tree.'" In Victorian novel fashion Clarke supposedly urged: "'Promise it.'" Then they bid, "'Au revoir,' instead of 'Good-bye,' and walked back to the garrison."

With no band playing or much fanfare, the next morning Clarke and Troop K pulled out for the border. Riding past the Coopers' quarters, "though it was not quite dawn ... he jumped from his horse to say a farewell word. 'I don't know when I'll get back. Don't forget our tree.'" Forrestine did not, nor the promise, but with Clarke's departure for the field, what might have been a budding romance ended.

When she later attempted to send him a note that "referred to the talk at the sycamore tree," she failed to receive a reply. She mistook "the silence as confirmation of what had been told me as to his attitude," which meant he was not interested in a relationship.[38]

Cooper's note to Clarke never arrived, and little wonder. After receiving orders, he remained in the field for over a year, bouncing from one camp, fort, or site in southern Arizona and Sonora to another sometimes with Troop K and alternately with elements of other forces sent to rein in Geronimo. In fact, his assignment to Troop K proved fortuitous at least in terms of his career. Clarke finally had his chance as a campaigner. This opportunity would change his life.

As he soon discovered, the impact of the Apaches on the locals weighed heavy, and accurate intelligence about the movements of the enemy was nonexistent as he disclosed in a June 2, 1885, letter to his mother written from Alamosa, New Mexico.[39] After passing through Fort Bayard his practical education in guerrilla warfare began. Mounting up and heading after Apaches was only the first part of a knotty equation. He summarized: "the Indian scare was so very bad that we traveled five days without seeing a soul passing from two to four ranches every day but they were all deserted and some of them showed from the way they were left that the inmates had not stopped eat[ting]." Clarke added the recurring challenge that it was "utterly impossible to obtain the least information about the Indians. Yesterday when we made the first inhabited place the information we received would have astonished a lower gossip. They said the whole Mescalero and San Carlos agencies were out and even the scouts were deserting; also that twenty-five soldiers had been killed...." Then, as now, obtaining viable intelligence from local sources was a Gordian knot.

Furthermore, Clarke concluded: "It is no wonder cavalry can not catch these chaps as they have all the beef they need and know every nook in the mountains." Clarke, however, relieved his mother's anguish, assuring her: "Do not have any fears of my getting hurt as I fear I will not have a chance to get a shot at an Indian all summer." This prophecy proved accurate for the time being.

A few weeks later, Clarke sent his second letter from the field. This June 20 message followed along with an entry in his small pocket journal revealing glimpses into his transformation from the parade ground pretender to fighting man.

First, his June 20 letter contained a description of a classic Apache bolt from the reservation followed by a frustrating army response to interdict them.[40] The novice campaigner described the challenges faced by the troops sent against an adept foe and included his low opinion of the local citizenry as well as the Western press. His experience dashed any notions of a rousing dime novel chase or classic standup Napoleonic and Civil War engagements studied at West Point.

The quarry managed to pass on the American side the border making for Mexico, while Clarke and the patrol headed north in the opposite direction. Exasperated, Clarke threw up his hands relating: "It is nearly impossible to catch them as they raid in such small parties over such a large area so that their trail is nearly imperceptible. They have plenty of horses, all the provisions they need and they know the country thoroughly."

Disdaining the locals, he quipped: "Troops have to rely on information from the most cowardly lying population that infested the globe. You cannot imagine how the romance of the Frontier is rasped out of one on a first scout. I do not know what our first settlers were but for the good of my ancestry I hope they were not like these."

He followed with an almost comic, but no doubt annoying account of what troops in the field faced from the civilians they were to protect. Clarke plied his mother with a story of "two cowboys armed with proverbial six shooters and corn juice fresh from a barroom [who] galloped into camp with news that the Indians were in [a] cañon and making toward town." Unchagrined, the battalion commander "paid no attention to them until five Mexicans and the most reliable citizen came up on a dead run with information that they were attacking the town or rather a ranch below the town firing from both sides of the cañon. The schoolmaster had seen an Indian fall." With that the senior officer "had one troop saddle up and go down on a gallop for six miles but not a sign of an Indian did we see."

The entire event proved to be a case of mistaken identity. The Mexican thought "the two cowboys were Indians and ran them through the ranch howling like a hurt dog 'los Indios'" while the cowpunchers believed he was an Indian and erroneously sounded the false alarm. Clarke confided he sought relief from this phony war to be sent to Mexico where he could get into the thick of things. He informed his mother that if he engaged the enemy it would have to be done "from behind trees and rocks and on foot by a line of skirmishers each man looking out for himself as much as possible but as the Indians are … not as good shots as the troopers in a fight they usually get licked but rarely the living or dead are seen as they carry them off so that the troops cannot tell what … they have accomplished…." Clarke's parting words foreshadowed his actual first combat not many months later.

By July Clarke was off again. This time, he communicated with his father from Fort Bowie. On July 8 he indicated being diverted, at least for the moment, by less onerous tasks than during June.[41] Indeed, he expressed the delight of a young bachelor born and bred in a trio of interesting asides describing flirting with young women, indulging in horse racing, and watching a baseball game. To heighten these 4th of July festivities, Clarke enjoyed the company of "officers and ladies" from the Tenth Cavalry who came down from Fort Thomas along with “some very pleasant ladies from the neighboring ranch.”

Additionally, as did George Custer’s Seventh Cavalry at Fort Leavenworth nearly two decades earlier, Bowie’s celebration included a “slow mule race which … was very amusing.”[42] The outdoor activities concluded with “athletic sports” usually pitting enlisted men of one unit against another. The officers and their ladies capped off the day with “a delightful hop.”

Clarke’s pleasant pastimes gave way to martial matters. To his “great pleasure and happy disappointment” at 10 PM on July 5 the post commander sent for him and handed over a telegram from Crook with orders for field service. The general had relented. Consequently, the next day Clarke “rode to Willcox 27 miles with the thermometer at 104 Far. in the shade, found a fair hotel and good stable and yesterday made thirty miles.” After reporting he “was given command of 50 Mojave (Mohave) scouts.” An energized Clarke was to “leave for the border and scout along the frontier to prevent the return of any of Geronimo’s band who may not be corralled by the troops in Mexico.” At last he had a field command. His “only hope now is that we may have a chance to get something going for ourselves.”

After sharing his glee at an opportunity to see the elephant, Clarke added observations about his life as a frontier officer, which contained some insights that must have been music to his father the former Confederate. While a fair number of Southerners now held commissions after the end of Reconstruction, their presence was not as prevalent as in the antebellum U.S. Army.

Clarke noted: “I have met many officers of several Regiments but … I am all the more satisfied with our own officers and do not think we are hurt by having many ‘Rebs’ as they … called all of the ‘subs’ but one being a southern man and I only hope that some of these conceited 4th Cavalry lot may come to our post some day that we may show them how little ‘nigger’ officers know about politeness. The 6” [*sic*: ordinal 6th] Cav and the 1st Infantry have as nice a lot of gentlemen as I have ever seen the 3” and 4” [*sic*: 3rd and 4th] Cav have several screws loose and I will be glad to get into the field.”

Here Clarke displayed unit pride, having developed an affinity for his regiment. His respect for most fellow Tenth Cavalry officers had emerged. Additionally, his views about the enlisted men under his charge appeared to be leading toward a defensive posture if not an outright acceptance of the troops he commanded. With the passage of time, Clarke eventually displayed respect for his troopers, just as after reflection and more experience, he gained a different perspective about some of his brothers in arms from the Fourth Cavalry.

Evidence of this latter change in thinking appeared in a July 18 letter from Bisbee Cañon. Clarke now had been detailed to command of an Apache scout detachment, an assignment indicative of the trust by his superiors to take charge of one of Crook's much vaunted trackers.[43] Clarke told of how he with "Troop 'H' 4" Cav (Captain [John William] Martin), a company of Apache Tonto scouts under Lieutenant [William] Shipp 10" Cavalry and my own company of Mohave and Apache Yuma" left Fort Bowie. "After two days march," he continued, "I separated from the rest and with twenty scouts, twenty pack mules and five packers. I reached Mud Springs which is a range running off from the Chiricuahua mountains. And which is about twenty miles north of the border. I spent a very pleasant day with Lieut. [Micha] Jenkins of the 4 and leaving five of my scouts and mules started the next morning across the valley…."

Even though he set out early "it was fearfully hot" and many of his dismounted "scouts had some pretty rough feet from being blistered by the hot ground through their moccasins. While looking for the ranch with my glasses I undertook to give my horse a prod with my spur for not standing. He had been looking very tired and I was not a little surprised to have him bolt about five feet and take across the prairie at his best run which is not very slow."

Clarke, who prided himself on skills as a horseman, recounted that he just "had taken his bridle off to let him graze and had been riding him with the halter so that it was utterly impossible to stop so I tried the West Point expedient of catching him by the nose and stopping his wind…." To do this, Clarke caught his mount with one hand and pinched him to squeeze out his breath. Dismounted at this point, he paid the price as the perturbed horse took off and "ran all the way back to Mud Springs with a packer after him and I had to make five miles á la scout, on foot following a long legged Mohave who would look back now and then with the utmost satisfaction at me as

I was wet from head to foot and blowing like a porpoise from trying to keep up with him as I believe he put in his best licks."

This incident demonstrated that despite Clarke's lackluster academic record at West Point, he paid attention to some of his lessons such as equestrian training. It also displayed a developing admiration for the native peoples along with the streak of pride he first exhibited in Texas on the grueling outing with Quanah Parker that he as a white officer was not to be bested by an Indian.[44] Clarke must have appreciated being remounted after his footsore return to the column where his "horse was brought in that night." He carried on his saga, which among other things referenced the ubiquitous pack mules so favored by General Crook.[45]

When one of these prize burden-bearing animals slipped away, Clarke had to retrieve the prodigal and bring it back, making him have to wait until the next morning to start to Captain Charles Hatfield's camp. At camp that night, Clarke witnessed how the scouts in his detachment "caught about a dozen jackrabbits with sticks…." They formed "a sort of semicircle each man at an interval of about five yards and when the 'cityin rabbit', as the darkeys call them, jumps up they all whoop and get them rattled at the same time following him at a dead run and the circle closing on him." Clarke's reference to "darkeys" would not shock his Louisiana-reared mother, and reflected his own Southern upbringing, which remained strong even after he had served with black troops for some time.

In contrast, the quick verbal sketch Clarke drew of the scouts' campaign outfit would have been foreign to his mother. They wore "a head band of cloth around the head to mark them as scouts and very gaudy and shirt, buckskin mocasins [*sic*] up [to] their knees and with their long thick jet black hair may make a very good appearance."[46]

He remained on duty with the scouts in Guadalupe Cañon. Clarke confided that, while not ideal, this locale kept him away from the sameness of Fort Grant or from some other out of the way spot guarding the border with the only enemy being boredom. As he indicated: "I would be lying in a garrison doing nothing at all by myself in one of those border camps with no one to talk to and nothing to see as is the case with some of them. I have enjoyed my trip so far very much and do not see why I shall not continue to do so."

Gaining practical insight into the reality of operations and local mores as well as frontiersmen's foibles, Clarke made the most of his unfamiliar, stimulating adventure. In the process, the gangly inexperienced former cadet began his metamorphosis as a field soldier. As evidence of the change, he imparted a telling detail: "I am afraid you would not recognize last summer's dude as he now appears in iron shod shoes, blue canvas overalls, a cotton shirt and yard wide sombrero with a crown eight-inches high not leaving out the unnecessary six shooter and cartridge belt which I use on rabbit, rattlesnake etc. by way of practice."

By August 8, 1885, Clarke still lingered at Guadalupe Cañon where he described aspects of daily life and his hunger for reading material.[47] After a few references to the movements of troops in Mexico, Clarke again sought support to secure temporary duty at the French cavalry school in Saumur. Periodically the military sent an individual or small groups abroad to observe or receive training with foreign military. Nevertheless, this was not typical, especially for a yet untried second lieutenant.

Regardless, Clarke wanted his mother to do his bidding and "see what chances my application for Saumur will stand and as soon as you can or else I fear someone else will get in ahead of me as for the necessary trips to Washington I will be glad enough to foot the bills I owe. One will have to see Secretary [of War Thomas F.] Bayard and I think if he would ask for permission or approve it, it would be granted by the French war department."

Returning from his hopes for a temporary dispatch to the good life in France, Clarke recounted that: "The Tenth Cavalry troops from Grant are in the Whetstone Mountains west of Huachuca. Several days ago I rode over to Cloverdale where [James A.] Cole of my class is stationed and had a very pleasant afternoon with him and his captain starting at Sunset for Lang's Ranch across a flat valley about two miles wide." With nightfall, Clarke relayed it "became so dark and the ground was so thick with [prairie] dog holes that I had to walk nearly all the way even leading my horse and accompanied by 'Pete' my faithful Indian striker. He is a splendidly built Indian about 18 years old nearly six feet and one of the best walkers.... He is always smiling and calls me Nantan Bejaja or the boy captain on account of my flowing beard and heavy cavalry moustache."

Although proud of his title and facial adornment, the latter would not shield him from the monsoons that drenched him and his fellow Tenth Cavalry officer William Shipp, neither of whom had a tent. Forced to "live under a piece of canvas which unfortunately is now leaking" Clarke could "barely find a dry place to write. In dry weather and light rains we are very comfortable as we have rustic bunks raised off the ground and plenty of grass and blankets." Despite inconvenience, he found the food "good and altogether life passes pleasantly enough" although he "would not like to be here forever" especially given the fact that Troop K was in the field "but no one imagined they would be called out when [I] volunteered for this job." Now he regretted doing so because he wanted to see action with Lebo and his men.

On August 14, 1885, Clarke sent off a brief note from Guadalupe Cañon to his mother in response to one of her communiques.[48] He expressed his want of books, including ones in French perhaps in hopes of a positive response to his bid for the coveted assignment to Saumur. He further recorded the weather had improved and he was well except for a sprained ankle that was "still unserviceable … but is getting all right." Lack of a tent remained a problem, but seemed of little consequence as he pronounced himself "most comfortably fixed" except for having scant reading material as he had indicated in the previous letter. He asked his mother for some catalogues with Spanish and French titles for sale so he could order from them. Clarke ended with a disappointing "No news from Geronimo…."

Late August brought new scenery as made clear in a letter dated on the twenty-fifth. His brief field assignment included his temporarily being "put in command of 'G' Troop 6" [*sic*: 6th] Cavalry whose Captain is at Separ [New Mexico] on a court of inquiry and the 2d Lieut. [James A.] Cole (a classmate of mine) has been sent … in command of an escort for a pack train with provisions."[49] Given the lack of officers as they were flung far and wide with small operational field units during the Geronimo campaign, this unusual seconding of an officer from a black regiment to a regiment of white cavalrymen represented just one of many necessary expedients.

Even with the opportunity to lead white cavalrymen, he must have been envious of Lieutenant Matthias Day and his White Mountain scouts, who according to a courier that trotted into Clarke's bivouac, "surprised Geronimo's camp 200 miles south of the line and captured eighteen women killing Geronimo's son, the old chief Nana and two other warriors. G—was wounded and got off with a four year old son under his arm though he left his mocasin [*sic*] and aiming cross-sticks. Most of the warriors are still out as they were not in camp at the time including chiefs Mangas and Chihuahua. The men and scouts are nearly all barefooted and had a bad time sleeping in wet blankets for 22 consecutive days" and sustained themselves "on peaches and acorns which [the] latter liked to have killed them though the Indians are very fond of them."

Numerous errors peppered the courier's message.[50] This inaccurate rendition added to an earlier muddled account claiming "the scouts killed Nana" who in fact survived, and lived on to a ripe old age, dying in 1896. Supposedly, "Geronimo's son (Chappo), another man, one woman, and one thirteen-year-old boy" also were casualties. "Subsequent information amended the dead to two women and one boy," but one statistic remained correct in that fifteen women and children had been "captured, among whom were Geronimo's three wives and five children…." Additionally, it proved true that "the scouts saw Geronimo pick up his young son and run from the camp through a gauntlet of firepower." Scouts likewise claimed they wounded Geronimo because "he eventually dropped the boy before escaping. But the evidence was at best equivocal."[51] The salient point was Geronimo once more avoided death or capture.

By September 2, 1885, Clarke had returned to Guadalupe Cañon where he informed his mother of continued pleasure from the books obtained after his requests from the previous month. French authors remained prominent in his bibliography.[52] Once more, the miniature library was a godsend for Clarke who complained of being "back to the monotonous cañon of scenery, cactus and sprained ankles when there is good prospect of my remaining all winter if the water holds out, but I do not think it will. You may see however that I am still happy and like Bigelow, from whom I received a letter several days ago, in no hurry to get back to the solitary chair in the Grant Guard House which requires to be sat in for 24 solid hours. Bigelow is out in the Patagonia Mt. S.W. of Huachuca. The troops down in Mexico do not expect to catch up to the hostiles for four weeks even having to wait for supplies of all kind as they are rather destitute of everything."

Meanwhile, Jim Hughes led a more comfortable existence on garrison duty, but Clarke's comrade made it clear he did "not like his post." Clarke sympathized as well as considered joining his old classmate on a proposed two weeks' leave in San Francisco. That prospect pleased Clarke who "would like [to] see the Pacific Slope and wonderful California before going East again but it will depend on my finances."

The California junket never materialized. Instead of comfortable surroundings in the Bay Area, Clarke's fall 1885 entries in his diminutive pocket notebook bespoke of a very different experience where water and rough forage for the animals were the major concerns.[53] This Spartan reality rang through in Clarke's first entry on October 10, which indicated "Left San Bernardino with Troop 'K' … at 5 p.m. marched … and camped above … Guadalupe at 3 a.m. … good water drying up." The next day the detail broke camp at 1:30 "on south plan trail … good water 4 miles not permanent about 5 miles good water in July very little in October good grass. Blackgrama." He went on to report "Trails at this camp … [were] … very rough into Mexico."

A pair of deer shot on October 12 added to the government ration of hardtack, salt pork, and coffee.[54] The next day afforded Clarke his "first vapor bath" which helped purge him of the grime of the trail. The patrol located excellent water on October 15, along with evidence of "plenty of deer," after making nineteen miles that day. The next two days provided a quick layover before resuming the march on October 17 for twenty miles in the vicinity of Elias Creek. Without seeing signs of the enemy, the patrol turned back to the San Bernardino, on October 20. They failed to find the bodies of two men reported murdered at Cowboy Cañon in Animas Valley, New Mexico, as they headed back to base camp. They did link up with Frank Cook and Troop K of the Fourth Cavalry as well as First Infantry Lieutenant James Petitt who oversaw logistics for the units in that area of operations.

Two of the latter officer's couriers were the ones thought to be dead at Cowboy Cañon. In fact, these soldiers from the Fourth Cavalry had been attacked on October 10. An estimated fourteen Apaches ambushed the pair en route to Fort Bowie. Private Samuel Hickman died. Wounded Private Sylvester Grover survived. Grover held the attackers at bay until they broke off the engagement, permitting him to escape with his life.[55]

Likewise, Clarke noted that Emmet Crawford and Wirt Davis reached Fort Bowie to recruit scouts. In turn, William Shipp temporarily halted there. Scout detachments under Matthias Day and Robert "Rosie" Walsh remained in the field. Meanwhile, Major Tullius Tupper's troop from the Sixth U.S. Cavalry ranged about thirty miles east of Lebo's Troop K. These outfits, along with many others in Mexico, futilely sought Geronimo and the remaining Apaches.

Camp routine continued until October 23 when some "San Simon cowboys came in and told us of their losing 24 horses in the last raid and the killing and wounding of Petitt's couriers…." Lieutenant Cook was on hand but suffering from sciatica, while Tucson Mayor Charles M. Strauss (also in camp) fell prey to dysentery.[56] Clarke cryptically mentioned an ailment, stating on October 26 that his hand was becoming too "lame to work" which by the 27th "got worse: and he "had to come to Guadalupe for treatment." He remained there for several days and heard, perhaps with a little envy, in a letter from William Shipp, that Marion P. Maus (First Infantry), Matthias Day, Mason Maxon, and Leighton Finley (all of the Tenth Cavalry) were to "go to Mexico on [the] next expedition."

Clarke would not join them. On October 13 he requested a supply of stationery from Fort Huachuca. Evidently the order arrived because on November 1 he "passed the day writing letters" as well as on board of survey duties plus writing "detachment notes…." By November 5, he ceased making journal entries, perhaps due to a persistent problem with his hand as he scrawled: "Cant [*sic*] write" and placed ditto marks on the single line for November 6.

Three days later, he killed an antelope plus had supper and breakfast the next morning at a local ranch as he headed up a detachment of scouts making their way north. By November 10, he pulled into the Black Cattle Company. The next day found him at San Simon Cienega where he passed four ranches on a good wagon road. He rolled into Bowie on November 12 where, due to an unspecified illness, he remained for two days. Setting out again on

November 14, he passed Bailey Ranch. Clarke pronounced the road good but a "bad taste in the water." At the Solomonville forage station on the fifteenth he took supper and dinner with the owner. During the sixteenth he followed the Gila River toward Fort Thomas. Along the way Clarke would encounter Majors Van Vliet and Anson Mills along with Lieutenant William Read, all of his regiment.

By November 17 he arrived at San Carlos where First Infantry Captain Francis E. Pierce doubled as agent and commander of the local scouts, Robert D. Walsh of the Fourth Cavalry served with his scouts as well, and fellow Tenth Cavalry Lieutenants John B. McDonald and James Watson were on duty.[57] Clarke's mission complete, he turned over nine scouts to Pierce for discharge at the expiration of their enlistments, left his horse, and proceeded in an escort wagon after a day's layover at San Carlos.

Enjoying a visit on November 19 with Mrs. Nannie Viele at Fort Thomas while her husband Charles was in the field, he turned back to San Carlos in a light buggy. The next two days he moved on through Cedar Spring and reached his home base of Fort Grant. After months in the wild, he reported everything was "in splendid condition."

Many of his fellow officers were absent in Mexico by this time. The few who remained behind served on court martial duty. At Fort Grant, Clarke laid out $140 for one of his abiding passions, a black six-year-old Kentucky thoroughbred. On the twenty-third he set out for a gathering at Fort Thomas with Crawford, Maus, Shipp, and others who all attended a "first class hop that night." Boarding a stage at 6:00 AM on November 24, he reached Willcox after 10:00 AM. Transferring to the train, that afternoon he again changed his mode of transport at Bowie Station, this time to the mail buckboard reaching Fort Bowie at 6:00 PM. He brought with him news that the Apaches cut the telegraph lines between Forts Apache and Thomas.

This was not the only action to cause concern. A November 25 report of "Chiricahua hostiles at [Fort] Apache stealing horses" indicated far-ranging enemy activities on both sides of the border. Nonetheless, Crawford and his scouts made their way to Fort Bowie. Crawford arrived in time for Thanksgiving dinner on the twenty-sixth hosted at newly promoted First Infantry Captain Matthew Markland's quarters.

Even after a good meal and rest, on November 27, Clarke's illness continued. As he remained in garrison that same day some Indian prisoners were "released for the time being in order to let the scouts find out what they know." With a telegram on November 28 that Lieutenant General Philip Sheridan (the second-highest ranking officer in the United States Army after William T. Sherman) would appear on the morrow, gaining intelligence from the prisoners may have taken on a heightened importance.[58]

At 2:30 PM, on November 29, Sheridan and his entourage arrived. On the same date Crawford moved out to the Whetstones intent on intercepting the still at-large foe. First Lieutenant Samson Faison as quartermaster followed on November 30 with the pack train in support.

Clarke's unspecified physical condition precluded him from field service through December 9.[59] The next day, the doctor pronounced Clarke fit for duty. This diagnosis proved premature. Clarke remained at Fort Bowie, lamenting on Christmas Day that he "was sick as they make them." Thus, as the year drew near to a close Clarke still had not experienced combat. As was the case with many of his fellow officers, he never saw an Apache, much less fought one. A bland line about Clarke's Troop K and its commanding officer in the *Arizona Weekly Citizen* for December 26, 1885, summed up the frustrating period of waiting without action: "At Mowry, Capt. Lebo is still in camp with his colored troops."[60]

In due course, the idleness of Troop K ended. By then Clarke would rejoin his troopers, and during the next year would experience his first taste of combat.

Chapter 5

"Oh, the Dragoon Bold!"

With winter setting in, campaigning slowed. At least this was Clarke's fate as he headed back to garrison duty in the new year. He first temporarily resided at Fort Bowie where he experienced "the most cheerless New Year's I have passed for some time." A shipment of publications from his mother and correspondence from her shook him from his lethargy, prompting him to write her on January 2.[1]

Her devoted son heartily thanked his mother for "the pretty edition of Tennyson" she had sent him. He assured her it was "a book he had long been wanting…." Receiving it inspired him to think about his mother's "excellent advice about copying good authors." Clarke went on to reveal he "would give a great deal … to write well with at least a little style having a larger number of words at command…." This statement appears to be his first indication of a desire to publish, something that ultimately occurred.

That prospect would be more appealing than the winter the Apaches faced. First, Lieutenant Samuel W. Fountain of the Eighth U.S. Cavalry operating out of New Mexico had seized "all their ponies, blankets and rations" from a "batch that that has been doing so much damage of late."[2] Clarke speculated they "struck for Mexico to join the main body" under Geronimo, where they would find a "more congenial" climate.

Clarke remarked about his Apache scouts, who hunted Geronimo with him. He described how "it is wonderful to see a scout slide out of his outer coverings in a wink when he thinks a fight is at hand. This is as if they know of blood poisoning being sometimes given by pieces of colored cloth carried into wounds by bullets." Because the cause of sepsis was not widely known at this time, such a supposition indicated Clarke's respect for the savvy of his Apache scouts.

Further, Clarke shared that he had not recovered fully from his hand injury sustained the previous year. He predicted it would be on the mend. It still troubled him, and he experienced swelling and acute rheumatism.

Likewise, Clarke shared that when he eventually returned to his quarters at Fort Grant, he intended "to live a little more systematically so as to study regularly and at the same time to have plenty of time for riding…." Perhaps it actually dawned on him that he should have paid more attention to his studies at the Military Academy. At least, this was the gist of telling his mother he wanted "to run over my West Point course again and then go beyond so as to keep up to the times and not be a dunce when I get out on leave." Was this a real resolution indicating that the carefree cadet of old was finally maturing, or just another ploy to please his mother?

Evidently, a gap of several weeks passed before Clarke again wrote home. He penned a pair of nearly back to back letters on January 23 and 25, 1886, postmarked from Fort Bowie, both of which were to his father.

The first of these referred to an unusual incident.[3] It seemed that an Apache scout shot two couriers from Troop C, Tenth U.S. Cavalry, then escaped, perhaps to disappear into Mexico. Other than the ill-fated Cibecue "mutiny" of 1881, scouts usually proved faithful to their oaths of enlistment.[4]

Another cavalryman from the same troop, in this case a corporal, was shot by one of his comrades. Clarke added that the troop commander, Captain Charles Viele, who had been with the regiment since 1870 and whose wife previously had hosted Powhatan, had "all the casualties to himself" meaning these were the only men from the Tenth at that time who had been wounded.

Clarke related that other commands also sustained losses. Among them was a scout from Civil War veteran Third Cavalry Captain Emmet

Crawford's detachment operating in the Sierra Madres. Crawford stood "over six feet high, with a genuine military face, and a spare but athletic form." The Apaches nicknamed him "Tall Captain." He commanded Indian scouts both in the 1883 Sierra Madres campaign, and once more in the 1885 second drive into Mexico.

Clarke believed Crawford's unit could bring Geronimo to bay. He also continued to back General Crook despite many Arizonans expressing displeasure about the lack of results. Because Crook retained the support of "every one in Washington" his position seemed secure. Clarke felt "the people and their little squibs are wasting their time. They are also after their [territorial] governor."[5] As one example, *The Daily Tombstone Epitaph* fired a racist sarcastic salvo: "There was no truth in the report that Crook, [Arizona territorial governor C. Myer] Zulick and Geronimo intend to go into the circus business, with the minstrel and base ball troupe from the Tenth Cavalry as the leading attraction."[6]

As a further indication of many locals who viewed the army as inept, Clarke mentioned that "some of the bills" had been "proposed for organizing these bold frontiersmen" into a regiment to deal with the Apaches, a concept he questioned. He noted that one piece of legislation being considered called for $50 per month for the citizen soldiers, and the same pay received by U.S. Army officers for the commanders of a proposed volunteer unit, as well as "permission to seize mounts even if they belong to the U.S."

Clarke shared another observation "that the male population" of Arizona Territory consisted about "1/3 deserters from the Army who cannot be caught on account of the aid given them by the people...." Even though desertion regularly ravaged the ranks of Uncle Sam's soldiers in the West, with the notable exception of the black Regulars, Clarke exaggerated the demographics of Arizona's population.[7] Regardless, Clarke more rationally remarked, if the lawmakers managed to pass such legislation, he "would like to bet that the frontier Regt ... will be 2/3 'old soldiers' who would not like to see their old Captains until the statute of limitations is operative for them."

In truth, the ongoing Apache campaign required reinforcements, including five companies of the Eighth U.S. Infantry from San Francisco. After becoming somewhat inured to Arizona's climate, Clarke found it "fun to hear them grumble about the cold, dust, dirt" and their posting away from garrison comforts enjoyed in the Bay Area where the unit had been stationed in the main since transferring after a four-year stint in Arizona during 1878, although elements of the regiment returned to the territory as early as 1881.[8]

In his note of January 25, 1886, Clarke spoke of planning leave with Jim Hughes. His classmate began to reconsider until much later when he and Clarke would be authorized longer leaves based on more time in grade.[9] By waiting, they also could save more money, which was "the chief drawback" for both the second lieutenants with their scant pay of $93.50 a month during the first five years on duty.[10]

As the pair of friends contemplated some rest and relaxation, news arrived of Captain Emmet Crawford's death at the hands of Mexican irregulars. Clarke called this event "a miserable treacherous affair." He reported Crawford "had been out all winter and had just made a march of 521 hours in pursuit of the hostiles, surprised their camp and taken all their stock." This remarkable strike left the enemy "in such a forlorn condition that they wanted to surrender" and Geronimo even had "sent in hostages when a party of Mexicans came up on Crawford's battalion of Indian scouts and fired into his camp." To stop a bloodbath, Clarke said Crawford went out to meet with the Mexicans only to be "shot in the head killing him instantly," a statement that was at odds with most accounts that the captain survived for some time after being shot. In retaliation, Crawford's scouts returned fire. The Mexicans sustained casualties including two of their officers. Crawford's second in command, Lieutenant Marion Maus, managed to halt the deadly exchange.

Clarke eulogized Crawford, contending the fallen captain was "one of the bravest men we have and who has spent years of hardship fighting and pacifying the Apaches by whom he was very well liked." That may have been true, but Civil War veteran, and one-time aide de camp to Crook during the general's first tour in Arizona, William J. Ross, offered an alternate take on Crawford. According to Ross, "Crawford was a weak man and a tool of Crook."[11]

Whether Ross spoke from first-hand information, or had less than cordial feelings for his old commanding officer, is unknown. Regardless,

Clarke still supported Crook at this point and disclosed that he wished Maus had not held his men "in check for they have the greatest contempt for a Mexican and on seeing the captain fall they wanted to shoot the whole party" who attacked them.

Clarke maintained the leaders of the Mexican detachment saw both the captain and the lieutenant, but ignored this fact out of greed and hatred for the Apache, as well as having no love for *norteamericanos*. Since the 1846–48 war with Mexico and the Treaty of Guadalupe Hidalgo, Mexican distrust and antagonism toward gringo "marauders" remained widespread.[12]

Indignantly, Clarke railed, "Our good peaceable gov't will certainly not do anything about it." There probably would be no apology, aggravated by the fact that this was the second such offense because the previous summer Mexicans had shot at an unarmed U.S. Army "officer who tried to prevent a similar mistake and finally put him and his ten scouts in jail claiming they had killed cattle."

"The Indian business would have been settled," Clarke opined, "but for this" tragedy, which meant no one knew where and when the campaign would end. Even though Geronimo sent Apache women to speak with Crook, Clarke doubted they would "agree to all the conditions" being demanded of them in order to accept their surrender.

Following his two letters to his father, on February 14, 1886, Clarke sent his mother a quick note.[13] He digressed, adding that the injury to his hand improved.

Clarke then turned to more romantic matters. He mentioned an unnamed young woman with the initials "V.R." (Louisa Van Rensselaer) whom he had known since 1882, the year of his furlough to visit New York and elsewhere.[14] Clarke acknowledged: "he liked her very much for the last three years." He admitted she may not be aware of his affections. Likewise, he could not say whether she had any stronger feelings for him than she held for "her numerous other friends." She had "always been very kind" to him, but that was no indication of her feelings. In confidence, he asked that this frank revelation remained with his mother and father only, and ended his discussion of romance for the moment.

By March 4, 1886, Clarke reverted to typical garrison routine.[15] The regimen once more consisted of serving as officer of the day every five days and going to drill and tattoo for his detachment of dismounted troops. Of more concern was the probability of court martial details and being appointed to the tedious task as either prosecutor or defense that would "leave more work for my pen, writing red tape than I will enjoy."

Turning to more weighty matters, Crook's chances of taking Geronimo captive were remote. Clarke thought it "very doubtful if the latter will agree to being taken and hung when there is no reason why he cannot dance over these rocks for a year or even longer." Continuing, he feared if Geronimo "is not caught before the month is out Gen C- will be relieved from the Department, if he is I would like to see some of the men who have been against him put in command of it as they will find at their cost how little they know about the matter of which they talk so much."

Many civilians and military alike disagreed with Crook's methods, especially the extensive deployment of Indian scouts. Among other things, they questioned their loyalty. One powerful critic, Lieutenant General Sheridan, "reminded Crook that he had many regular troops at his disposal 'and ought to be able to do a great deal with such a force.'"[16] With his commanding officer's censure and Crook's lack of success, fulfilment of Clarke's prediction that "Gen C- will be relieved" was not long in coming.

Clarke further noted Lieutenant Maus who had "rather put his foot in it as some letters which he gave the Mexican commander, if true, are at utter variance with what he and all of his officers and men say took place, however, I have no doubt but that he will be able to explain it all satisfactory."[17] In fact, Maus subsequently provided a detailed version of the clash that led to Crawford's killing. Mexican authorities did likewise in a much abbreviated form. As Clarke anticipated, the response contained no apology.[18]

All these events muddied the waters as far as resolving the Apache conflict, which continued to be a remote story for Clarke. Feeling caged at Fort Grant, on March 5, 1886, Clarke recounted more news about life at a post away from the action.[19]

As usual, horses remained much on his mind. Being officer of the day, he was "obliged to forgo trying a new horse." Similarly, he boasted that his "black gelding is doing splendidly and is by far the handsomest horse at the post. He is a Kentucky horse only five years old." The ever impoverished lieutenant spent $21, or nearly a quarter of a month's pay, for his latest four-legged acquisition. This expenditure may have made his father think about the many times his son noted being nearly destitute. Clarke reiterated his hopes for posting to the French Cavalry School at Saumur.

At that point, he stopped writing, temporarily being "interrupted by a long nosed captain from Pennsylvania, band practice, stable call and a call from a nice little Irish captain of the 1st foot [First U.S. Infantry] who calls me 'small boy' and smokes my cigars but then I smoke his and persecute him by bad billiard playing so that I expect we are even." Among these fellow members of the garrison Clarke "met some very nice men on the frontier, a great many even old foes of yours in 60–65.... I like the officers on the frontier much better than those one meets in the artillery garrisons though a nicer man than [Lieutenant Millard] Eggleston never wore shoulder straps; there seems to be more good fellowship, and hospitality, it is even rash to say than more dissipation out here."[20]

Civil War veterans ran the gamut, as Clarke indicated in mid-March 1886.[21] He demonstrated a lack of respect for the Tenth Cavalry's regimental commander, Benjamin Grierson, whom the outspoken subordinate cast in an unfavorable light. This was in contrast to the post commander at Fort Grant, Colonel William Shafter.

Shafter had assigned PHC to construct a sluice box to power "water for a turbine wheel with which he expects to saw wood from turning lathes and do all manner of things...." Eggleston and Clarke teamed on the project. They "found that our ditch runs up the hill." Concentrating "after two more days" they "succeeded in getting our transit line and profile and were even so very successful that I begin to feel that my genius for surveying was not fully appreciated at West Point."

Clarke added, he "had a very nice letter from Hughes last night. He does not seem very happy at Whipple and I am in great hopes that the recent changes in Regimental Hdqrs will bring us together even though it brings me under Col Grierson (Col of 10" [*sic*: 10th] Cav) again from whom I have taken a complete disgust after being under Col Shafter of the 1st Infantry...." To Clarke, there was "no comparison between their methods or between the two men." He viewed Grierson as "a political general during the war who took a long raid or ride into Tennessee after it had been rendered fit for such travel by better men, returning much faster with his cavalry than he went on account of a 'superior' force of Confederates who seemed to want his horses and blankets." With little regard for the much touted exploit he described the "raid or ride has been beautifully poetically and politically written up by staff officers, country poets, and stump speechmakers and Bvt Maj. Gen. B. A. Grierson Col of the 10th Horse has a 'reputation' among his sisters, cousins & aunts equal to that [of 'Stonewall'] Jackson."[22]

Instead of taking the path of many former Yankees turned congressmen, Grierson supposedly found a "much more comfortable and very permanent" berth in the army "and as more deserving gentlemen of the old guise objected to 'nigger' regiments in 65, the famous ride easily got himself made Col of the 10th Chasserezd'Affrique [*sic*] or as the vulgar would say 'nigger cavalry.'" The last aspersion revealed that Clarke, like so many other military men and civilians s of his era, held negative racial views often evidenced in strong, and by later standards, offensive language.[23]

Clarke argued: "Shafter is exactly the opposite to Grierson." Purportedly, "he rose on his own merits and was a good hard working and courageous soldier which he is yet and runs his regiment and post himself instead of allowing his regiment and post to be run at Headquarters." This style contrasted with Grierson's laissez faire manner at Fort Davis, which made Clarke angry "though at the time not having the advantage of comparison I could not see things plainly as I do now."

Refuting the conventional wisdom about the inferiority of officers assigned to the units manned by black troops, Clarke countered.[24] He thought: "We have some excellent officers in the Regiment and all the young men graduates" as was the norm in all the combat arms regiments of this era.[25] He went on to assert that "in fact during my time at the Academy some of the best men in the upper classes took this Regiment." Conversely, he lamented: "At the same time we have some of the most worthless men I have ever seen 'old warriors' whom the colonel protects in everything: drunkenness, gambling and the rest."[26]

At least Grierson would not remain in command forever, although Clarke realized to his chagrin the mandatory retirement date would not be reached until 1899! After that time, he looked forward to a "little cleaning out that will give us a line of officers of which we can be as proud as any Regt in the service."

Without citing supporting evidence, he asserted that the Tenth Cavalry officer corps contrasted with the Fourth Cavalry. Supposedly, older men were first lieutenants in Tenth Cavalry while younger men had risen to captains in the Fourth, or so Clarke argued. Clarke attributed "this difference … to the fact that [Ranald] McKenzie [sic] would get rid of the worthless" driftwood in the Fourth Cavalry, which he accomplished "by courts martial and retiring boards while Col G[rieson] cuddles all such specimens around and puts them on his staff."

Here Clarke referred to Colonel Ranald S. MacKenzie, who graduated at the top of his West Point Class of 1862 as an engineer. Like Robert E. Lee, he became a field commander. In the post-Civil War, he commanded a black infantry regiment, then transferred to the Fourth U.S. Cavalry, which between 1870 through 1882 he led in Texas and on occasion into Mexico. In contrast to Clarke's opinion about Grierson's lackluster performance, the critical young subaltern admired MacKenzie for achieving results.

Clarke admired MacKenzie, but not Grierson, indicating: "I know you will not think me vindictive in this for Grierson has never had two words with me and has never molested me but I am so utterly sick of having such a fossil at the head of the Regiment and knowing what we might be with a good soldier that I sometimes boil over which is the cause of all the forgoing steam and bubbles."

Regardless of Clarke's often negative opinion of Civil War veterans like Grierson, he did not view all older officers in the same light. In fact, he made friends with some of them and even borrowed Spanish books from his neighbor so that he could improve his language skills. This ability was useful in the multilingual Southwest, especially if Clarke might head to the border again.

That likelihood seemed remote. After the debacle with Crawford's command, it appeared efforts to end the campaign improved. Based on this possibility, Clarke indicated: "We expect the troops in very shortly as a telegram from Bowie says that five hostile bucks have surrendered unconditionally and the rest are near the camp making preparations to do the same. I hope they all come in on Gen Crook's account for he certainly uses only the methods for fighting such small bands and used them well. The greater the number of Indians the easier it is to catch them in such a country."

Clarke went on to recount a St. Patrick's Day ball sponsored by Company B, First U.S. Infantry, which among other things underscored the class divide between officers and enlisted men. He indicated that men from Ireland (typically 20 percent or more) took the lead for this annual celebration.[27] Clarke depicted the stratified event as follows: "The officers usually have the first two or three dances reserved after watching the others amuse themselves retire and leave their hosts to enjoy themselves where I suppose a good deal of the awkwardness disappears. This is only done on holidays and I think it is a very good custom. I had two delightful dances and enjoyed watching the men very much."

Clarke remarked on how some of these white enlisted men were "excellent dancers and they are even very neatly dressed. It surprises one to see how they can make their plain uniforms look on such occasions. For real fun however," Clarke preferred hops given by the men of the Tenth Cavalry. He said these diversions "beats them all especially the ladies though it would surprise you to see how well the darkies dance."[28] Again, he casually used the term knowing full well it would be accepted by his parents with their traditional antebellum Southern upbringing.

After the St. Patrick's Day festivities, on March 22, 1886, Clarke stated his father's last letter was interesting particularly regarding his optimistic prospects for Saumur.[29] Clarke continued to request his father's assistance to secure the overseas posting, which he feared would be pigeon holed.

As in the past, Clarke did not eschew wire pulling. He urged his father to approach a senator or congressman to obtain an appointment to see Secretary of War William C. Endicott so that he personally could present Powhatan's case and secure " 'waiting orders' … to draw full pay…." Otherwise, he could not afford living expenses in France. He would be willing to pay his round-trip fare, and pointed out that this assignment would in no way gain him "very much in a pecuniary point of view." He wanted to attend as soon as possible so that he would study with men of his own age and "while the studies and exercises of West Point are still fresh in my mind."

Clarke reminded his father that he "was familiar with French and want to perfect myself in it." This assertion and the one about his studies were a bit incredulous given his past poor academic performance in both areas, and his continued lack of application to serious study. One additional reason for his desire to attend now was to "take their course in veterinary surgery which is of so much use to a cavalry officer and so hard to get in this country, in fact everything taught there is practical and of the greatest use to us and cannot be learned as thoroughly at Leavenworth, which is the school for all branches and in which most of the work is repetition of West Point."[30]

While he had no desire to escape being sent to the Cavalry and Infantry School at Fort Leavenworth, his lack of seniority meant it would be a "good while before my turn comes." He argued that a year away from his troop could do him no harm, citing that at times officers were away for as much as four years on staff duty, as instructors at the Military Academy, and other assignments, especially recurring ones that took them away from their regiments. His troop, unlike many others, had all three of its officers. Enjoying a "full complement" he thought his services could be spared.

Casting about for further reason to bolster his cause, Clarke concluded the instruction would be of great value "and I think I am enough of an American not to be capable of examining the French Cavalry system without becoming incapable of seeing the merits of our own." Here Clarke played the patriot.

Clarke conceded that the court-martial of Second Lieutenant Samuel C. Robertson of the First U.S. Cavalry, who had been sent to France during the summer of 1881 and extended his stay there through 1882, "for duplicating his pay accounts after getting back" from field duty, dampened his prospects. He had "heard several officers say that it has made a perfect fool of him by being sent to Saumur and was always talking about the French Cavalry but these are faults of the man and not the place."[31]

Robertson's supposed reputation notwithstanding, Clarke contended: "I think I can stand going there without becoming either gambler or spendthrift or being made too conceited to be satisfied with our service in which I expect to spend my life. As for the temptations I am certain they would not be any greater than they are at a frontier post with nothing to do and nowhere to amuse ourselves except at the sutlers."

Clarke struck a chord in that the idleness he experienced at Fort Grant was not too far afield from General Crook's warning on graduation day in 1884 about young officers slipping into bad habits. Indeed, Clarke confided that he "had been doing so little lately that I am ashamed of myself" but blamed some of these circumstances on the Arizona climate and the unfamiliar 4,500-feet altitude which drained his energy leaving him always feeling "weary and worthless." In this regard, those stationed at Fort Grant differed little from many supposed exiles at the isolated frontier posts where drunkenness, gambling, petty quarrels, and a host of other maladies frequently marred life.[32]

Some of his funk probably stemmed from garrison confinement, while many others remained in the field. He expected the troops would return "very soon but we still are in the dark about the surrender of Geronimo." What was known "is that five of his warriors had given up" but beyond that no concrete intelligence existed.

Bored, Clarke whiled away the hours "playing billiards principally by myself but I am learning the game rapidly." Regrettably the post library was only about half the size of the one at Fort Bowie "so that it is difficult to keep up in periodicals." The quality and quantity of the holdings of these post facilities ran the gamut, sometimes being extraordinary; in other instances poor. In due course, Clarke formed a consortium to address the lack of current reading material. For the moment, at least, it seemed that in his malaise he had not abandoned efforts to keep up with national and international events.

Missing his family plus the lack of female companionship added to his feeling of remoteness. He contended: "I have not seen a very pretty girl for so long that I am more than anxious to take leave" and come home for "Xmas if only for long enough to stay in Balt[imore] a week...." Regardless of all his self-imposed woes, one hope stood out for a better future. On the last page he desperately pleaded: "we must make the Saumur plan work."

Clarke's March 28, 1886, letter from Fort Grant once more reflected his longing to be elsewhere.[33] He disclosed: "Reports are rife with respect to the Indians. Crook has left for the border and it is said Geronimo has surrendered so I suppose we will have no more trouble here for some years which makes me very anxious to get leave for Saumur."

Assuming he had missed out on the finale to rein in the Apaches, Clarke concentrated on brushing up on his French for the sought-after Saumur slot. He noted: "One of our corporals here is an Alsatian and a very well educated gentlemanly fellow with whom" he expected to practice his "French a little."

He decried the cost of French language books. As usual, he was "very short of funds after my last purchase of a horse which used up a month's pay for me but he is a good one." Clarke bragged: "You should see this scout horse of mine, he is a beauty." Regardless of the circumstances, he had no compunction about buying fine horses, forming a major part of his off-duty hours which he spent "principally in riding, practicing on a telegraph instrument, at reviews and wading through" the piles of paperwork that burdened officers in garrison. At least when the troops who were out in the field returned, there would be time for "tennis and hops."

For the moment, Clarke and his horse chased "jack rabbits (large hares) with a greyhound that was given to me. She is a beautiful animal and one could enjoy her running forever without getting tired." Despite his constant complaints about the lack of money, Clarke intended to purchase one or two more hounds as the jackrabbits proved "a little too lively for one dog." Evidently, he envied "two beautiful greyhounds from the 3rd Cavalry pack" that had been left at Fort Grant when that regiment changed stations with the Tenth Cavalry, and were said to be speedy enough "to bring down [pronghorn sheep] antelope ..." but with none of the fleet prey in the vicinity they had to make do with rabbits.

At that same time, Clarke resumed his jottings in the pocket journal, noting he had been stationed at Grant until April 13. Although seventy Chiricahua men, women, and children were to be sent to Florida as prisoners of war, Geronimo would not be among them.[34]

This situation arose because of a string of events that began "at 7:09 a.m. March 23, 1886, [when] Crook, his two aides, John Bourke and Cyrus Roberts, and the latter's precocious twelve year old son, Charles, left Fort Bowie" for a parlay with Geronimo. Two days later they met at Embudos Canyon to discuss peace. After an exchange, Crook concluded that Geronimo and others had to surrender unconditionally or face unrelenting pursuit. By the night of March 27, with peace seemingly at hand, Geronimo and many others supposedly became "drunk as lords." Long before dawn on March 30, 1886, Geronimo, eighteen fellow fighters, and twenty-two women sneaked out of camp and headed to Mexico.[35]

Geronimo's actions undid Crook. Failing to take Geronimo into custody, Crook resigned his command, to be replaced by Nelson Miles. This change of leadership brought an end to Clarke's doldrums at Fort Grant, as he related on April 7, 1886. In a pithy summation to his father the formerly unmotivated lieutenant now became excited at the possibility of field duty once more. He sent his "horses and camp baggage" to Fort Huachuca. Clarke soon followed by rail to catch up with his kit and mounts.

Plans for Saumur were postponed. Clarke headed for his troop at Fort Huachuca under Crook's replacement, Miles. Clarke said it "would be amusing to watch the sequel. Crook used the only methods which can be used to advantage, contrary to the opinion of the citizens; Miles is a demagogue and I think will disband the scout battalions using Indians for trailers only." This expectation about the scouts hit the mark, at least during the early part of Miles's assumption of operations.

At first, an unimpressed Clarke forecast Miles would "kill [more horses] and catch fewer Indians in ten years than Crook can in one." Sympathetic to Crook, Clarke asserted it was not "his fault he did not succeed in bringing in Geronimo. The hostiles were well armed and mounted." As such, if Crook, "had tried to capture Geronimo and put irons on him the rest would certainly not come to camp at all. The proof of the methods employed will be shown" to have been correct, Clarke contended.

Regardless of what had transpired with Crook, Clarke indicated he was "very glad to get out again for I am beginning to get weary…" of the tedium at Fort Grant. He looked forward to "being with Captain Lebo and Bigelow again." Clarke ended somberly for those left behind in garrison. Like many others, "Mrs. Bigelow is disconsolate. She was ready to receive John [her husband] when the news of the surrender came and had made preparations for his return, now she does not know what to do." He closed, "I think we shall have some very hard riding to do during the next few months rather enjoy the prospect as I will see more country and am disgusted with lying around water holes" which had been his lot the previous year.[36]

As Clarke predicted it would fall to Miles, whom he gradually began to appreciate as the campaign unfolded, to end the long years of warfare. Taking his lead from Sheridan's censure of Crook, Miles intended to wield a powerful weapon against the Apaches: massed forces to overwelm the enemy by greater numbers. To this end, he deployed an impressive array of combat units from strategic staging centers that crisscrossed the Southwest.

Miles spread his strike force from Texas through New Mexico, and on to Arizona.[37] He depended on amassing a heavy force as Sheridan had wanted, using his cavalry to trail and close with Geronimo and the remaining hold-outs. In turn, the infantry mainly garrisoned posts and held strategic points to deny the enemy means to carry out the age-old guerrilla war.

In the final thrust, Miles fielded nearly one quarter of the Regular Army's fighting men to capture or kill Geronimo. On April 15, Clarke joined the campaign, as he recorded in his pocket journal. Clarke stated that he "left Grant at 6:00 a.m. Wilcox at 12 met [Marion] Maus's command at Wilcox disgusted reached Benson at 2 and Crittenden at 7 p.m."[38] The next day, he left Crittenden on the way to the Mowry Mine where he met Bigelow around noon.[39] Evidently, PHC took to the field unprepared as he left his expensive officer's greatcoat at Fort Grant. To remedy the oversight, Bigelow supplied Clarke an enlisted man's overcoat. After sundown the temperature could drop sufficiently to warrant the warmer outer garment.

Clarke spent the next several days in the vicinity of the mines around Harshaw and La Moria.[40] Nothing of note took place except a communique on April 20 from Miles requesting "men acquainted with Morse code." This directive stemmed from the general's initiative to establish an extensive heliograph system running from Fort Whipple through much of Arizona and New Mexico as a means of rapid communications. This wireless line of sight system used mirrors flashing messages through a code similar to the one developed for telegraphs. It was just one of the tools Miles selected after assuming command of the Department of Arizona.[41]

Admittedly, Clarke had achieved some proficiency in code. Evidently, he did not volunteer that fact. No doubt, perching on a peak to relay messages held no more appeal than his previous year bounding about from one false alarm to another without ever seeing an Apache warrior.

Word came for Troop K to relocate to the vicinity of Nogales. They broke camp on April 25.[42] Clarke and the command reached their new base, and soon were reinforced by seventy Mexican cavalry volunteers under E.C. Ronstadt, who like his father, served in the national guard raised from local Sonorans.[43] In the process, the joint U.S.-Mexico task force discovered the bodies of two of a trio of recently murdered civilians as well as sustained three more casualities among Ronstadt's command. Clarke stated: "all together 9 men killed. It is supposed that they [the Apaches] are now on the trail between" Agua Zaca and Buena Vista.[44]

By April 27, the pursuers trotted through Nogales and on to Calabasas, continuing on to Peck's Ranch, which they reached at 4:30 after briskly moving out for nine miles.[45] When they arrived. they "found Peck's wife shot through the arm and breast—child hit in the head, dogs killed and house torn up."

In a letter Clarke sent much later to his mother. he provided far more detail.[46] Since April 25, Lebo, Clarke, and the men of Troop K had "marched continuously making about 300 miles." During the course of this grueling ordeal, he witnessed "the saddest sight I ever saw or hope to see at Peck's Ranch." Halting at the ranch of Artisan L. Peck, located about eight miles northwest of Nogales and six miles west of the Santa Cruz River, they discovered the results of a raid made that morning.[47] After sunrise, Geronimo, Naiche, and other Chiricahuas killed Petra Peck and her child, then abducted her younger sister, "a thirteen year old girl" (she actually was ten). Clarke lamented "the poor little thing knew nothing of riding" but her captors took her over trails that wore out seasoned cavalrymen.

That same day, Peck fell into the raiding party's hands, but would be released.[48] Similarly, Clarke hoped that by pushing the raiders "they would drop the girl dead or alive."

The killing spree continued, as did Clarke's unsuccessful pursuit, which he privately revealed in his journal through May 2. In the meantime, John Bigelow's writing was meant for a broader audience. In fact, Bigelow publicly shared some of the story of chasing the Apaches from March 1886 through April 1887, publishing his diary entries in serial form under the title "After Geronimo" for *Outing: An Illustrated Magazine of Recreation.* As this subtitle indicated, this periodical was one of the first magazines in the United States aimed at sports and outdoor enthusiasts.[49]

Bigelow faced no obstacle in finding a publisher for his narrative. His brother Poultney Bigelow edited *Outing*; thus the younger sibling easily enjoyed success in placing his first literary endeavor.

This was more than a mere case of nepotism. John Bigelow's position with Troop K afforded him a front-row seat in the Geronimo campaign, a topic of considerable interest to many Victorian readers. Further, the lieutenant's first-hand impressions and straightforward style engaged his audience. Bigelow's words were combined with sketches provided by a number of artists, becoming the mainstay of the then immensely popular illustrated periodicals such as *Outing*.

In the process, Bigelow's afforded readers many of details about the black troopers. As an example, he portrayed the life of his men, which in garrison consisted "almost wholly of guard duty, inspection and fatigue." He concluded: "It would seem that every pleasant and attractive feature of a soldier's life had been purposely effaced and excluded from that of the American soldier" and there was "nothing left but irksome drudgery on the one hand, and idleness and dissipation on the other…."[50] Despite their onerous existence, the lieutenant asserted a black soldier would withstand "more work without grumbling than a white one…."[51]

An astute observer, Bigelow nonetheless exhibited bias and offered opinions that might be challenged. One of his contentions was that the army suffered from indiscriminate recruiting practices, selecting men not fit for duty. Bigelow believed this drawback could be overcome if officers commanding black troops went to enlist perspective soldiers because they were "better judges of colored people" and did not lump all blacks into a single category as all being "alike."[52]

Admittedly, haphazard approaches to fill the ranks plagued regiments regardless of whether the enlisted men were black or white, but this shortcoming particularly proved the case for those African American men who had been enslaved in the South. Antebellum paranoia and prejudice spawned laws prohibiting, among other things, formal education. Supposedly, among the early black recruits almost all were illiterate, which meant "their officers would have to perform most of the paperwork normally assigned to non-commissioned officers."[53]

On the other hand, John Bigelow's privileged upbringing assured he received a solid education that provided him with a fair share of literary tools. With this background, his prose and the added touch of illustration, which the public had become accustomed to in Civil War periodicals, made good reading for vicarious armchair adventurers safe in their Victorian parlors.

Some of the artists who provided illustrations to accompany John Bigelow's narration had honed their craft during that war; others were newcomers. Frederic Sackrider Remington numbered among this latter group of postwar picture makers. Like Dr. Clarke, Remington's father Seth Pierre had served in that conflict, but he was a staunch, early member of the Republican party, who firmly supported the Union.

On September 27, 1861, while nearly thirty-years-old, Seth had enrolled in the Eleventh New York State Cavalry. By March 13, 1862, he commanded Company B as its captain. During the course of the war he rose to major.[54]

The unit history indicated Pierre, as he was referred to by those close to him, gained a brevet colonelcy, which may have been given to honor his valor when a detachment he commanded cut its way through a surrounding Confederate unit.[55] The elder Remington likewise would be compared to Custer because "he was a fearless soldier, a fine horseman, and a kind and gentlemanly companion, 'with a heart in his breast as big as a pumpkin.'"

Tales of the heroic deeds then were the stuff of the Remington household. They intrigued Fred. Writing while a cadet from Highland Military Academy, a boarding school in Worcester, Massachusetts, young Frederic Remington instructed a boyhood pen-pal and fellow aspiring artist, Scott Turner, with whom he exchanged artwork to: "Send me Indians, cowboys, villains, and toughs. These are what I want." What really thrilled both of them were "soldiers."[56]

While martial themes intrigued Remington, his unwillingness to study and adhere to Highland's "strict military discipline administered by cadet officers" mirrored Clarke's "contrary traits" resulting in "a half-hearted compliance" to the commands he received from peers. He seemed to share another characteristic with Clarke in that "his breeziness, inner happiness" and general demeanor "made him popular" with his fellow cadets. Unlike Clarke, he had one other winning attribute, "his ability to draw caricatures of officers and teachers."[57]

After his first year at Highland, Remington returned as a junior, where he remained at "the bottom rung as a third year cadet." Consequently, "despite Remington's sham of applying himself" he could only "volunteer that 'I am well instructed in Upton's Infantry Tactics.'"[58]

Beyond a basic understanding of infantry drill, Fred had little else to show for his time at Highland. It was easy for his father to conclude "that the military would be no career for his son."[59] One wonders whether Dr. Clarke had entertained similar thoughts.

While Remington's father knew that young Fred would not be heading to West Point, he did see his son enter the Yale School of Fine Arts, which had been founded in 1864. Fred began his studies in 1878, but his father would not live long enough to see what became of his burly football-playing offspring, who at that time tipped the scales at around 180 pounds. At Yale, Fred also engaged in horseback riding and continued his childhood pastime of pen and ink sketching, turning out cartoons for personal amusement and occasional appearances in print. Most significantly, at Yale he had the good fortune to meet Lieutenant John Bigelow's brother Poultney sometime before 1879.[60] Remarkably, Remington's acquaintance with this fellow Eli would prove critical in the not too distant future.

Even before this, the elder Remington's health began to fail while Fred was at Highland. Pierre's condition worsened after his son's admission to Yale. By February 18, 1880, at age forty-six, the formerly robust Union cavalry commander died at the family home in Ogdensburg, New York.

He more or less split his estate between his widow and their only child, who as historian David McCullough wrote, would within two years burn through "a sizeable inheritance" of nearly $10,000 (no mean sum for the time) which was "roughly half of what it had taken his late father a lifetime to accumulate."[61] With Pierre's passing and a considerable grubstake in hand, he left the Ivy League to try and make his mark in the world. At this time, his prospects appeared so meager that his first bid to wed fellow upstate New Yorker Eva Caten was rejected by her father.

Making little headway at a career or marriage in the East, Remington set out on a different course than his family could have envisioned, although one that he had dreamed of as a youth. An early leg of his unforeseen, improbable journey was his "first western venture ... a sheep ranch in central Kansas. When that failed he saw his future in 'hardware or whiskey—or anything else....'"[62]

Known to enjoy a drink and a good cigar, it seemed natural that his next endeavor was to throw in his lot as a silent partner in a Kansas City saloon, a fact he kept quiet when he returned to New York for a second, and this time, successful try for Eva Caten's hand. After bringing his bride to Kansas, she found the situation different from Remington's portrayal. Packing up, she returned to her home in New York. With the exception of selling a few pieces of his art, Remington's outlook for the future looked far from certain or hopeful. Going "all in" as the story ran in a Kansas City *Star* piece published much later alleged, he bought a horse for $50 and "sometime in August 1885" headed to the Southwest.[63]

Boldly, the impoverished groom decided to turn to art, but in this case as a livelihood rather than as a pastime. On this next journey of many to the West, armed with artist's supplies and a small volume with blank pages that became his "Journal of a trip across the continent through Arizona and Sonora Old Mexico," he packed his modest travel gear that would serve him well.

Prior to this foray to the Southwest, Remington was a virtual unknown.[64] His thin credits consisted of one modest fledgling effort depicting Arizona cowboys (even though they really were based on cowpunchers he saw during a prior quick trip to Montana). This hastily produced piece was redrawn from this original and bore another artist's signature, the picture running in the February 25, 1882, edition of *Harper's Weekly*.[65]

Now the stout greenhorn gained a golden opportunity to observe a new world first-hand and portray what he experienced under his own name. He filled his pocket journal with brief, memory-jogging notes such as a passing reference to Carter Johnson, whom he encountered after reaching Arizona.

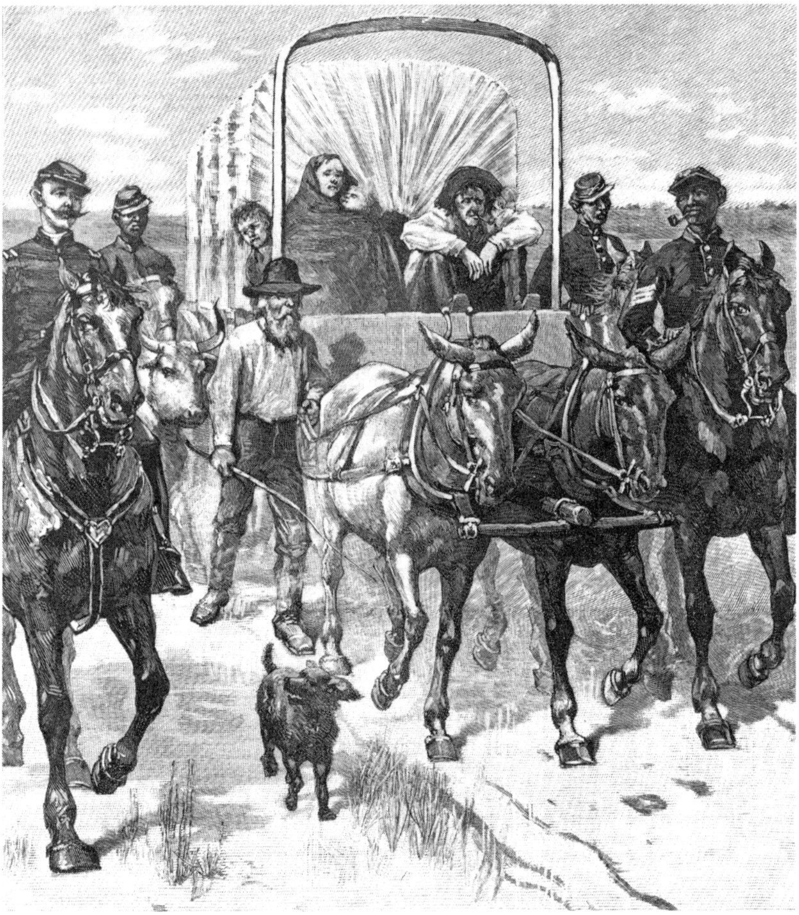

"Ejecting an 'Oklahoma Boomer'—Drawn by T. de Thulstrup from a sketch by Frederic Remington" was the novice artist's first attempt of over one hundred illustrations depicting black soldiers. This image served as the cover for *Harper's Weekly* (March 28, 1885), p. 193 (CR#: 00039) and was taken from a historical topic which he did not personally witness. Consequently, the rendering lacks much of the accuracy of later efforts based on personal observations.

This able Tenth Cavalry officer "instructed" Remington "to go down to Calabasas near the Mexican line" to join Captain Henry Lawton's command.[66] Johnson provided a letter of reference for this purpose, suggesting that the would-be war correspondent plunge in to the life of frontier fighting men.[67]

Rather than link up with Lawton, the wide-eyed New Yorker found other avenues for his introduction to military culture. In the process, he scribbled down a litany of related and unrelated topics in his journal. One of these was the revealing controversy about which army commander had won the hearts and minds of Arizona's citizens. On this matter Remington contended: "The frontier people are well disposed toward Gen. Miles and strongly prejudiced against Crook—mostly on account of his using Chiricahua [*sic*] scouts—which at this view of the proceedings is not exactly a good scheme."[68] In fact, then as now, the wild whiskered Crook in his rumpled canvas hunting suit and the erect Miles with perfectly trimmed mustache and tailored uniform, proved polemic polar opposites.[69]

Here Remington ran counter to John Bourke and others who lauded Crook for his supposedly sage reliance on scouts.[70] Remington opined that Bourke penned his oft-quoted narrative of the Apache campaign "to justify Crook." Remington's private musings demonstrated his formulation of opinions as to the final stages of the prolonged Apache wars. In this regard, he styled himself as "An artist in search of Geronimo" although with a sense of self-deprecating humor, he admitted "in fact it is a matter of congratulations to the artist that he never found Geronimo."[71]

Besides the journal, Remington snapped some amateur fuzzy focused photographs with his lightweight "Detective" as some small cameras of the era were nicknamed. He cleverly combined these reference pictures with sketches of much of what he saw in situ as a formula that eclipsed his haphazard cowboy rendering on scrap paper from several years earlier. The new, more methodical approach combining photography and field drawings worked well.

Possessing an assortment of action-packed images in his portfolio, the budding artist took an eastbound train intent on serving as his own agent to sell his wares. Once home, he presented his illustrations at the New York editorial offices of *Harper's Weekly* where he convinced the prestigious periodical's

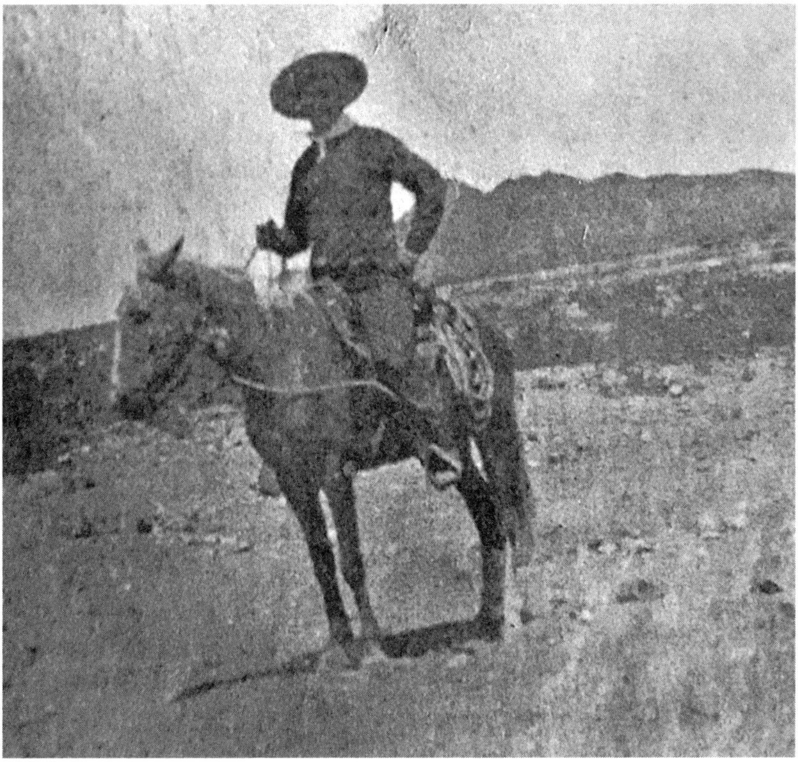

During his trip to Arizona in 1886 Remington's candid snapshots served as "memory aids" for producing accurate, action-packed images that roused his audience and raised him to the highest ranks of the art community. This grainy self-portrait captured him in the guise of one of his long-time heroes—the cowboy. Courtesy Frederic Remington Art Museum, Ogdensburg, New York.

editor, Henry Alden, to run one of the pictures from Arizona. The first published piece ran on January 8, 1886. It bore his signature and ran with the caption "Apache War—Indian Scouts on Geronimo's Trail." That modest opening help launch Remington onto the national stage where he quickly gained notice.

With this success, Remington again triumphed when the editor of the popular *Outing* magazine pored over sample drawings, which as Poultney Bigelow recalled years later in a somewhat embellished narrative, were to his eye "the real thing. No stage heroes these; no carefully pomaded hair and neatly tied cravats; these were the men of the real" West covered "in alkali dust, blinking out from barely opened eyelids under the furious rays of an Arizona sun…." According to Poultney's later recollections that may have been tinged with a bit of poetic license, the impressed editor looked up from the pile of sketches to discover that the creator of these compelling pictures was his Yale schoolmate.[72]

Bigelow's story may have been a bit fanciful, but one thing is true. Remington had brought back a number of views that complemented the running narrative Poultney's younger brother John provided for "After Geronimo." Indeed, a Remington sketch accompanied John Bigelow's tenth installment printed in the December 1886 *Outing* issue, and was among the first of a number of illustrations bought for the magazine at the princely sum of $10 a picture.

Remington probably also was the source for an unsigned brief report in *Harper's Weekly* issue of June 19, 1886. Evidence for his authorship, however, is circumstantial. That the New York-based periodical had multiple correspondents in the Southwest during 1886 was highly unlikely. Further, the heroic officer in the *Harper's* article was misspelled as "Clark," eliminating the final "e." Although not conclusive, all other newspaper accounts except one (The Nogales *Frontier* as reprinted in the Tucson *Arizona Daily Star* for May 13, 1886) spelled the name as "Clarke." Conversely, Remington from his first written reference and every existing later example, consistently misspelled the young lieutenant's surname as "Clark."

While the origin of this snippet of news can be questioned, what is irrefutable, and in fact more significant, was securing the front page of the August 21, 1886, issue of *Harper's*. This illustration once more featured Remington's signature, bringing another major windfall to heighten his visibility.

The foundation for what might be considered to be the work that changed Remington's career path, can be traced to his stream of consciousness pocket notebook's terse, matter-of-fact prose. Remington simply noted he saw a "batch of negro cavalrymen" traveling westward by train whom he pronounced "good style men."[73] By June 10, 1886, the roving reporter-illustrator would have the opportunity to have a closer look at these African American horse soldiers. Writing once more in his journal he summarized: "Got up late after a good night rest at Palace Hotel [Tucson] took camera went to the detachment of 10th Colored Cavalry—took a whole set of photographs." It is interesting to observe that typical of the times, Remington included the term "colored," a similar modifier seldom being applied by him or others to "white" soldiers.

It was at the Palace that Remington met "Lieut Clark … a young slim manly man" who in many ways the artist would come to consider as his military and frontier guide, as well as a kindred spirit. Remington wrote that PHC told the troop's First Sergeant William H. Givens "to do anything for me."[74]

Born in Kentucky, Givens enlisted in 1869 as a private in the Tenth, rose through the ranks to first sergeant, served on the border against Victorio, and demonstrated administrative capabilities that led to his taking examinations for various non-commissioned staff positions.[75] Remington could not have asked for a better introduction to the men of the Tenth. With the first sergeant at his disposal, when the artist asked for "a horse" to be "saddled by the dilletanters of army regulations" Givens saw to it that the request was granted. This allowed Remington to produce an accurate image of the cavalryman's field pack. Then, Remington began to sketch "the housing while surrounded by the enraptured audience of Mexican and nigger soldiers."[76] In his journal he made a note about a possible title for the picture. Would it be "saddle up"? Later, he snapped a few photos around Tucson. Sometime during the course of that day he also interviewed Givens.[77] As Remington recorded in his journal, he stood Givens to a brandy. Over drinks, the seasoned non-commissioned officer told Remington "of a gallant action by Lieut Clark in rescuing Corp Scott who was shot through both legs, under fire—by going to the front and dragging him under cover—a man summoned accompanying him—bullets passed between his arms & legs as he stooped in the heroic act. The Serj. was quite an admirer [of Clarke]. He was one nigger among a million, and a perfect soldier and as near an approach to be a gentleman as I ever saw in a negro."[78]

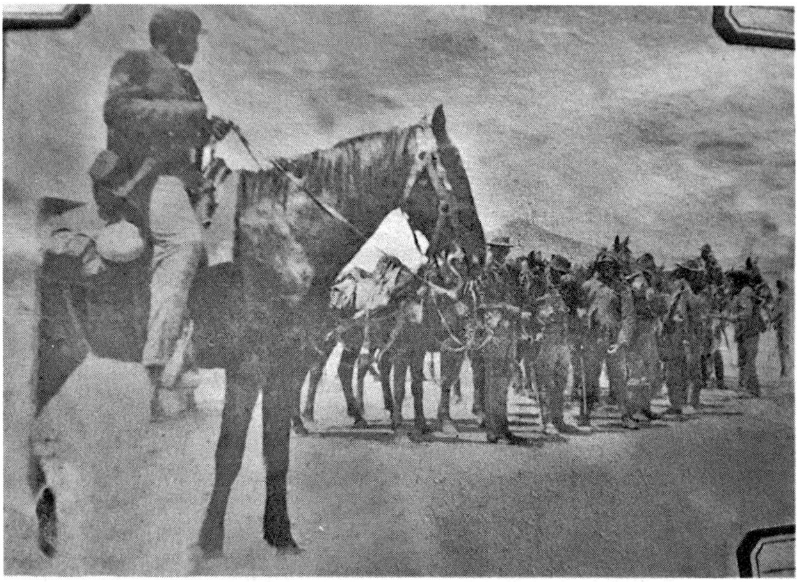

Remington converted this fuzzy image featuring Troop K's First Sergeant William H. Givens into a flowing sketch demonstrating an evolving artistic mastery. Sentinel Peak, also known as A-Mountain, appears in the background as do several buffalo soldiers. Courtesy Frederic Remington Art Museum, Ogdensburg, New York.

The passage indicated that Remington, despite prejudices revealed by the candid language in his diary and renderings accompanying a Bigelow installment (these were more bigoted stereotypes than the later fine art he would produce) began to form a more accurate and sympathetic opinion of black soldiers. In the process, he discovered many things such as the quality of the veteran non-commissioned officers in the Tenth and the pivotal part they played. Further, Remington may have realized he had stumbled on a heretofore virtually unexplored topic—the image of the black soldier in the West.[79] His discussion with Troop K's "top kick" resulted in other benefits, because the war story about Lieutenant Clarke whetted Remington's appetite for more.[80]

What the veteran sergeant had relayed was the gist of an engagement from an April through May 1886 determined mission against the Apache. A detail headed by Captain Lebo gave relentless chase for 200 miles against

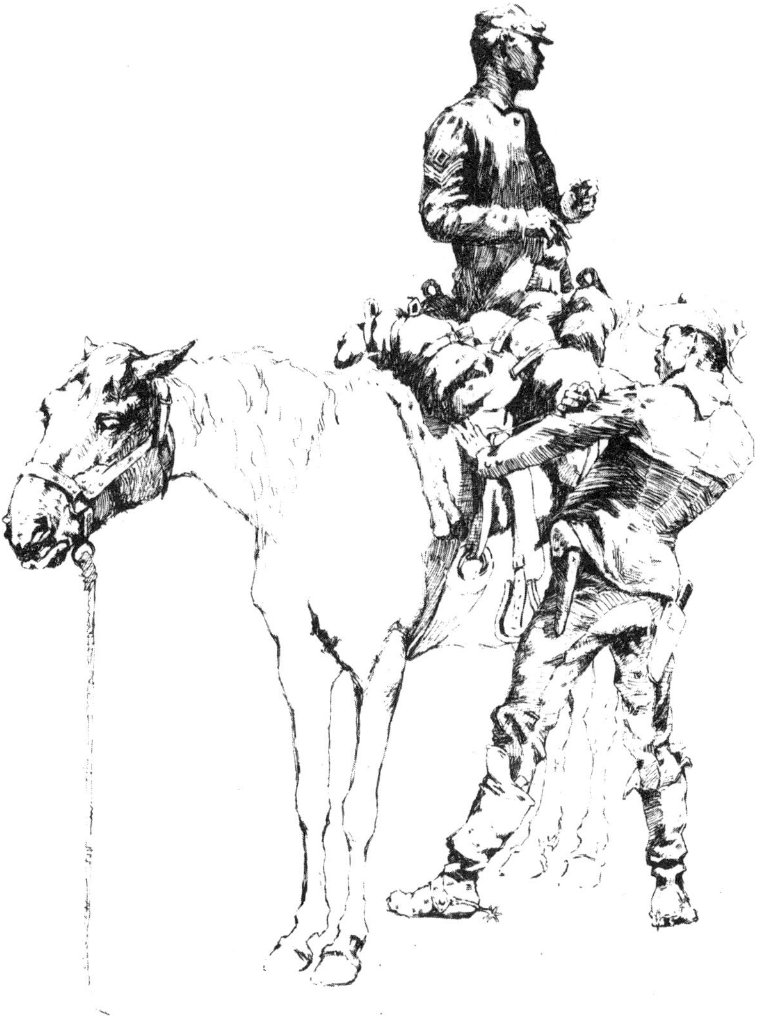

In addition to First Sergeant Givens, Remington's drawing included an African American trooper cinching his heavy laden U.S. cavalry McClellan saddle. The title assigned this work *Tenth Cavalry Officer and Trooper* CR# 00053a Dimensions: 12 3/4 × 8 3/4" Date: ca. 1886 Medium: pen and ink on paper mounted on artist board, is not appropriate given neither of the men were commissioned officers. Courtesy Buffalo Bill Center of the West, Cody, Wyoming; McCracken Research Library; MS 023 Frederic Remington Collection: MS23.78.02.53a.

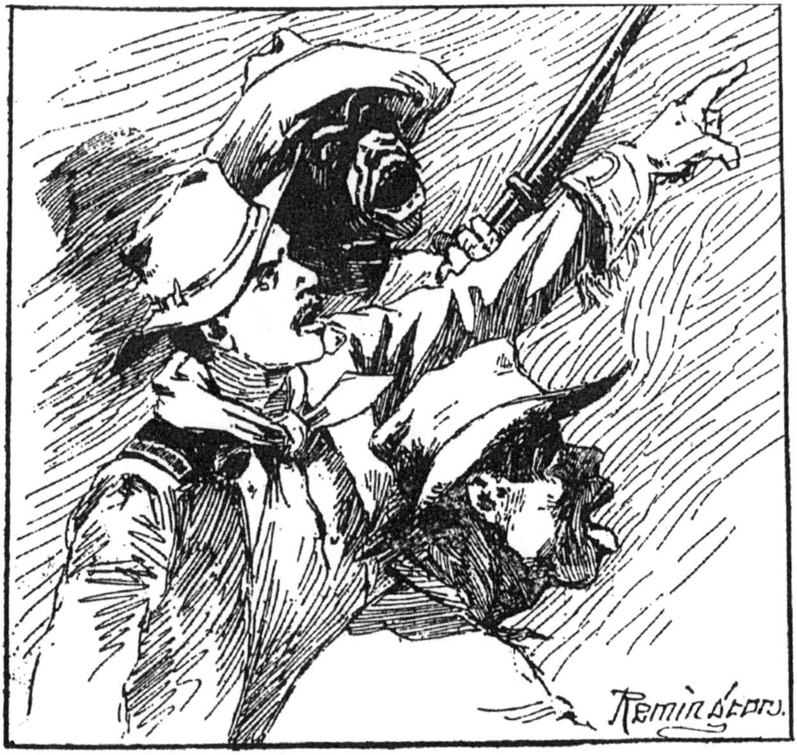

"INDIANS WERE SEEN TO FALL AND BE DRAGGED BACK OUT OF FIRE"

"Indians were seen to fall and be dragged back out of fire" CR# 00107 *Outing* (February 1887), p. 430 represented Clarke's first appearance in Remington's growing repertoire.

a highly mobile opponent passing into a "canyon known today as Cajon de los Negros, named in honor of the black troopers of the Tenth Cavalry."[81] Although in his early forties, Lebo kept up and endured the same hardships as his many younger subordinate officers and enlisted men. His determination finally brought him face to face with the elusive enemy. In an after-action report, departmental commander Nelson Miles lauded the "great bravery" of Lebo's horse soldiers during "this spirited engagement" of May 3 that took place "against an enemy on ground of their own choosing, among rugged cliffs almost impossible."[82]

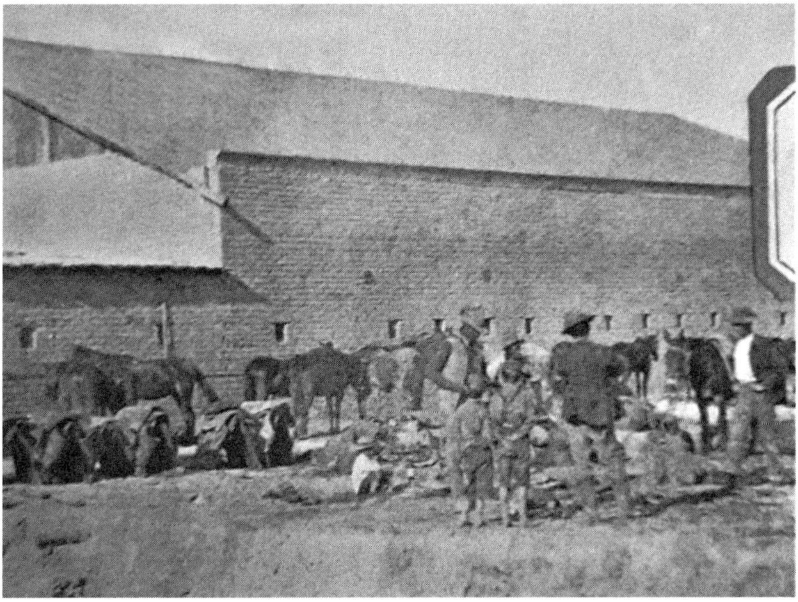

Remington also captured slices of life such as this informal view of men from Troop K, Tenth U.S. Cavalry in Tucson including ubiquitous pack saddles to the left. Remington snapped this picture at the government quartermaster corral in Tucson. Courtesy Frederic Remington Art Museum, Ogdensburg, New York.

According to one running commentary in Tucson's *Arizona Daily Star*, albeit tinged with period language, after Lebo had dismounted his twenty-one men, he sent Kentucky-born Corporal Edward Scott, a veteran of two enlistments, who previously had experienced at least one instance of combat, with several men. They worked their way to the left side of the skirmish line.[83] After doing so, Scott's skirmishers "advanced under the cliff, with the savages looking down on them. No shot was fired. As soon Scott got upon ground high enough to enable him to see the savages he opened fire. The utmost consternation ensued." Replying to the first salvo, the Apaches "opened up on the centre of the troops" managing among other things to strike Scott.

The newspaper account stated the rugged corporal, "after being wounded and while lying on the ground" attempted "to gouge the bullet out

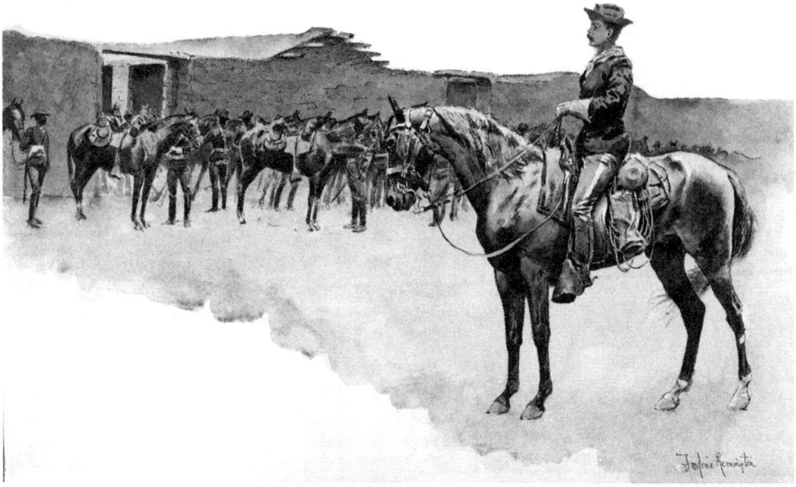

Powhatan Clarke on Horse, CR# 01877 Dimensions: 21 × 28 1/4" Date: ca. 1894 Medium: pen and ink wash with gouache on paper, b/w sheet, would be converted into the opening image for "The Hot Trail," a posthumously published article by Clarke from 1894. Remington based the illustration on his first meeting with "the tall, slim, manly" cavalryman in Tucson, whom he encountered eight years earlier. The government corral appears in the background where the two of them began their friendship in June of 1886. Gift of the Estate of Sally D. Eddy. The Virginia Museum of Fine Arts, Richmond 76.20.2.

of his foot and finger, the Indian who shot him approached near the edge of the bluff and he got his man. The Indian fell over the bluff but some of his companions dragged the body back to the upper plateau and placed it behind some rocks."

Casualties mounted, but "the Indians held their ground and made an attempt to get" the troopers' mounts. These efforts were "frustrated by a covering force and a detail sent to drive the herd to the rear." Each side in the fight supposedly numbered about thirty men. Among them "Three Indians were seen to fall and to be dragged back out of fire, a pretty sure indication that they were killed or mortally wounded."[84]

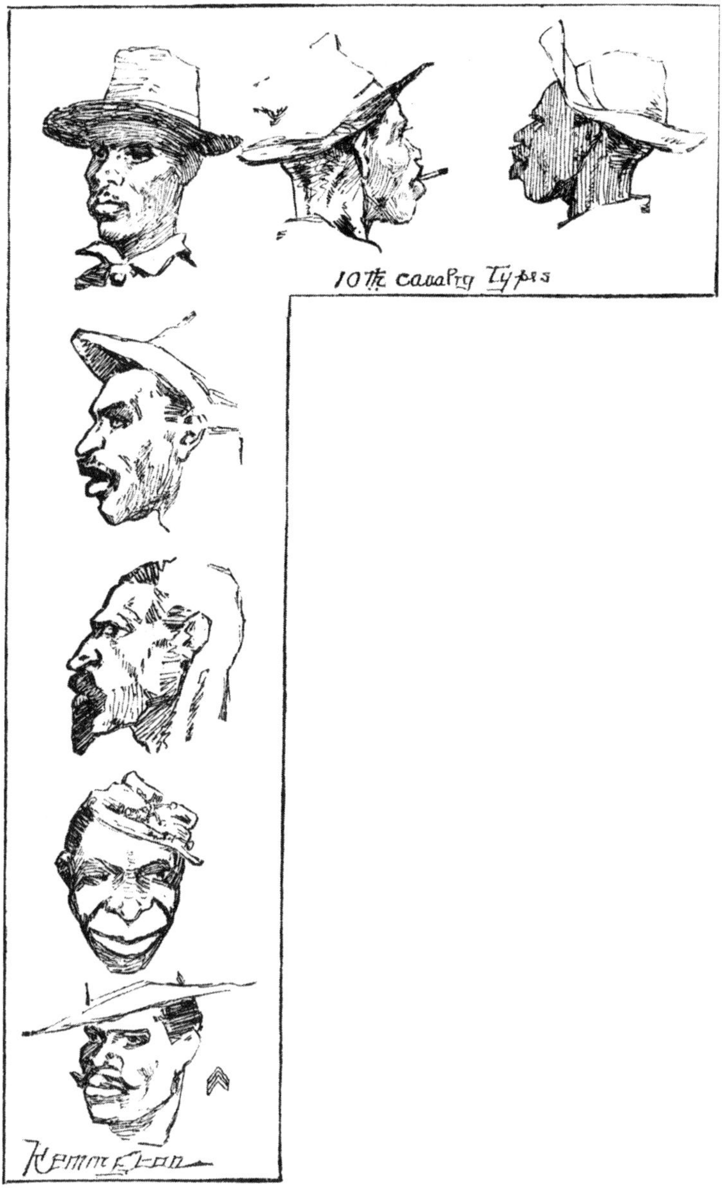

TENTH CAVALRY TYPES.

Remington's "10th Cavalry Types" CR# 00062 *Outing* (December 1886), p. 223, appeared more as caricatures than fine art, bespeaking both of his early, less polished work, and racial attitudes at this stage.

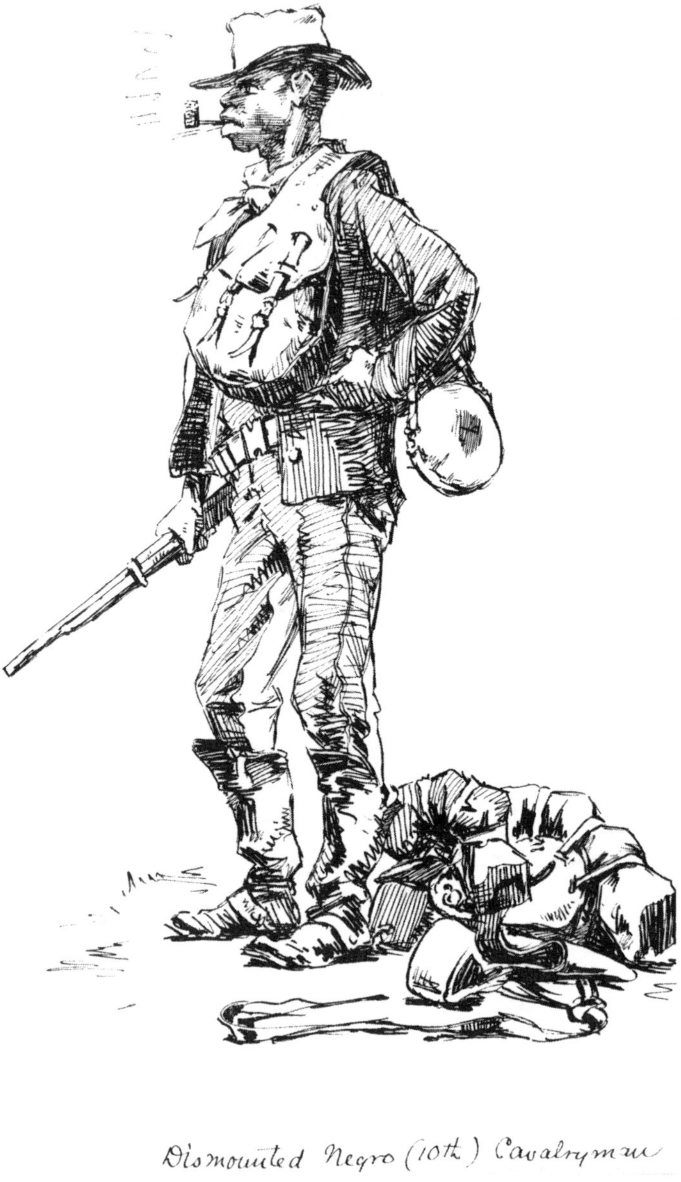

Although still somewhat stereotypical in nature, Remington's "Dismounted Negro, 10th Cavalry" CR# 00060 for *Outing* (December 1886), p. 225 evidenced his growing attention to detail that would set him apart from studio-bound contemporaries.

While the number of Apache dead and wounded was uncertain, what is known was another Troop K corporal from Kentucky, Joseph Follis, was killed.[85] Evidently, he fell during the same volley that brought down Scott, who "lay disabled with a serious wound, exposed to the enemy's fire…." Disregarding his own life, Captain Lebo's second in command, Lieutenant Clarke, rushed to the corporal's "assistance, carrying him to a place of safety."[86] Clarke's own pocket diary entry for May 3 captured this event, which was a textbook deployment based on the U.S. Army's standard tactics whereby the troopers dismounted, sending their mounts to the rear with men designated as horse-holders while the main body fanned out on foot in a skirmish line. In turn, the Apaches responded with their traditional style of guerrilla fighting born of battle experience.[87]

Clarke recorded that the patrol "broke camp at 6 a.m." and an hour later they located a "camp of hostiles" following them along a "rough trail on foot toward Pineto Mts. Found fresh camp on side of Pineto Mts sent McNair [possibly C.C. McNair from the Parajito Last Chance Mine] ahead who discovered Indians on top of a saddle threw out advance guard who opened fire on Indians in this saddle then advanced in skirmish and drove Indians out of saddle." While the Apaches' "main party opened fire … from inaccessible ridge of rocks" the Apaches' "left flank at 300 y[ards]" directed their fire "at the troop's horses" which had been sent to the rear at 500 yards. The Apaches drove back the troopers, in the process "leaving Follis dead and Corporal Scott behind … with several men to defend him while we galloped up horses which had become stampeded."

With no embellishment, Clarke stated: "Brought Corporal down and camped seven miles from the mts at ranch Esperanza on Santa Cruz 12 miles S.W. of Santa Cruz. Found here 7 horses brought in by [Wesley] Lively and [Samuel E.] Potts [privates from Troop K] was sent to Nogales 25 miles to dispatch."[88]

His May 4 journal entry continued: "Arrived there at 3 a.m. meeting 50 Mex Vol en route to Esperanza ranch. Learned at Nogales that [Britton] Davis and [Harry] Benson had left for same place at 1 a.m. no sleep.[89] Left at 8:30 & reached Michililivi [J.P. Millpillas] or Esperanza Ranch at 2 p.m. found detachment B Company 6 Cav. D 10 Cav."

With the encounter fresh in his mind, Clarke added details in a letter to his father about his first time under fire.[90] He repeated the description of the Apaches opening "flank fire from inaccessible rock" that was little more than 200 yards from the cavalry column. Clarke noted that after Corporal Follis fell dead and Corporal Scott received wounds through both legs, he responded, confessing that: "I had some close calls while I was trying to pull the corporal from under fire and I succeeded in getting him behind a bush and you can be sure it was a very new sensation to hear the bullets whiz and strike within six inches of me and not be able to do anything." The lieutenant went on to observe the "men were played out to begin with and from the position we were in, all of us could have been struck…."

A few days later, he recounted this same incident to his mother. Clarke started out casually on May 10 from camp with Troop K about a totally different topic then turned to the recent combat.[91] He modestly started on a note of praise for others, disclosing: "Our troop has been very highly complimented and the captain is the hero of the hour." Previously, the Louisiana-born and reared officer exhibited little respect for blacks in general, but now he challenged: "Do not tell me about the colored troops there is not a troop in the U.S. Army that I would trust my life to as quickly as this K troop of ours."

Clarke described: "The firing was at 200 yards from rocks nearly over our heads. No men could have been more determined and cooler than these same darkies were and as for their officers they like them and will risk themselves for them." Then he praised Scott, whom he indicated would have "to have his leg cut off, the ball that shattered it lodging in the other instep. This man rode seven miles without a groan, remarking to the Captin [*sic*] that he had seen forty men in one fight in a worse fix than he was. Such have I found the colored soldier."[92] Soon, the Arizona territorial press carried this story. Each paper added its own spin based on second-hand information and their own particular editorial perspectives.[93] For instance, one of the earliest accounts appeared in the less than friendly *Daily Tombstone Epitaph* for May 8, 1886, which wryly commented: "And now it appears that instead of Captain Lebo killing a couple of Apaches, with the loss of two or three men," supposedly he did not kill any of the enemy. Instead "the Indians also

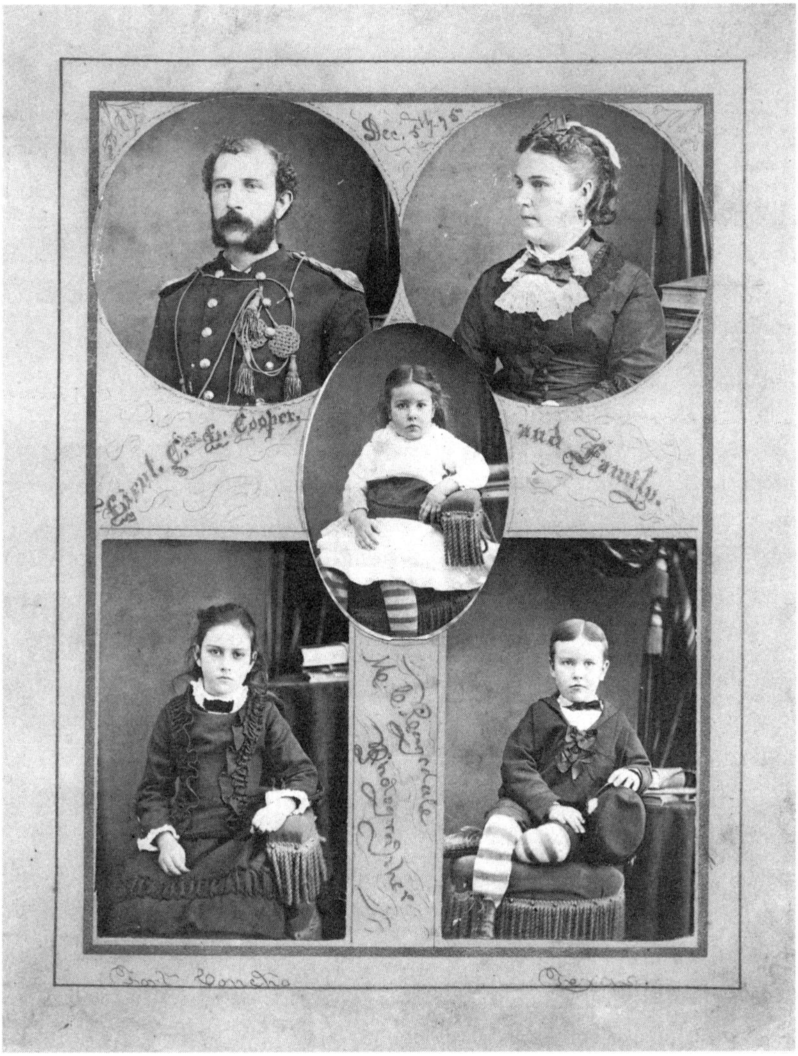

In 1875 Eight-year old Forrestine "Birdie" Cooper (lower left), her parents Charles and Flora, along with her younger brother and sister, appeared in photographs probably taken for the Christmas holidays at Fort Concho, Texas. Nearly a decade later, "Birdie" met Powhatan Clarke at Fort Davis. She soon formed an attachment to the dashing young bachelor. Fort Concho National Historic Landmark.

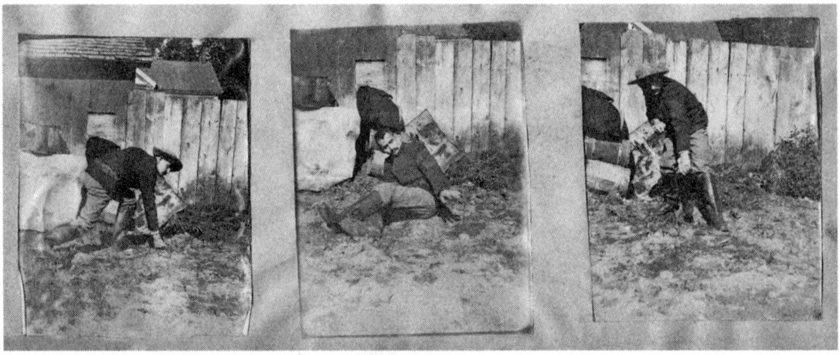

Fort Huachuca's commanding officer detailed a private from the Sixth U.S. Cavalry so the artist could stage the soldier in three poses that he ultimately incorporated into his "Rescue of Corporal Scott." Courtesy Frederic Remington Art Museum, Ogdensburg, New York.

ran off eighteen of the twenty-eight horses in his troop." The article concluded with racially motivated sarcasm: "The Apaches from the time negro troops were first sent against them, have called them 'buffalo soldiers' and seem to have the utmost contempt for them."[94]

Regardless of the reporter's disparaging remarks, Remington formed different views. After his conversation with First Sergeant Givens, he made a special trip to meet Scott at the Fort Huachuca hospital where the corporal had his leg amputated. Interestingly, one of several puzzling elements transpired right after Remington arrived at the post on June 15. The fort's commander, who also was Fourth U.S. Cavalry Colonel William Royall, "turned out a [white] trooper" for Remington to photograph "in various attitudes" and then the artist made "a quick water color" incorporating the three basic stances together into the composition that evolved into the August 21 *Harper's* front cover.[95]

Afterwards, Remington set out to the post hospital where he recorded "an attendant led me over to one [a bed] where a fine tall negro soldier lay. His face had a palor [*sic*] orspreading [*sic*] it the result of the lost limb. I greeted him pleasantly and told him of my desire to sketch his face...."[96]

Comparing an after-surgery photograph of Scott with Remington's depiction of the corporal during the rescue, a far more detailed and faithful image emerges. In every respect this rendering went beyond the artist's

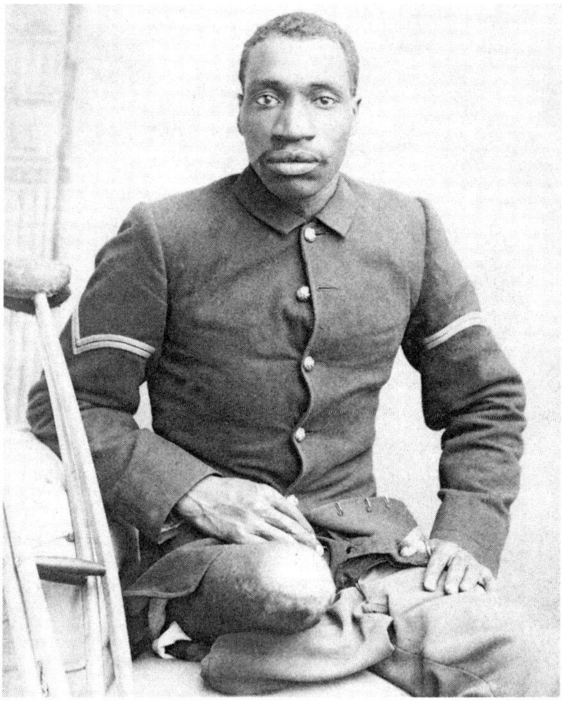

Despite considerable suffering, Corporal Edward Scott survived the journey to the Fort Huachuca Hospital where an army surgeon amputated his leg. Remington went to some lengths to depict both Scott and Clarke in an accurate manner for the cover of *Harper's*. Armed Forces Institute of Pathology, Washington, D.C.

earlier caricatures for Bigelow's *Outing* series. Did Remington add the sketch made from life to the water color he mentioned producing earlier that same day? Furthermore, why did Remington include another enlisted man in the illustration, another detail he evidently had in mind even before his exchange with Scott?

An uncredited article, "Our Soldiers in the Southwest" in *Harper's* for August 21 may shed some light on this additional example of the many unknown aspects of the cover image.[97] That column lauded: "The brave conduct of Lieutenant Clark[e], of the tenth (colored) cavalry, in rescuing, under fire, the wounded Corporal Scott, was such conduct as makes military history interesting." It acknowledged "Corporal Scott's telling of the

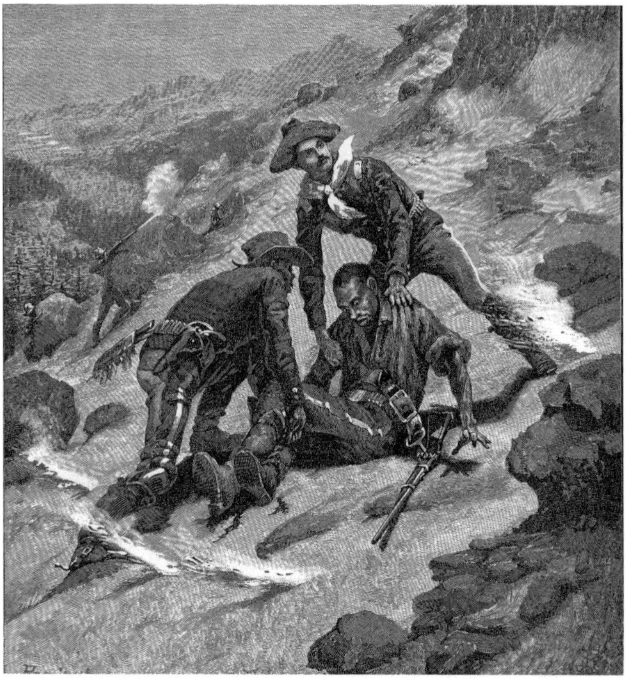

"Soldiering in the Southwest—The Rescue of Corporal Scott" CN: 00049 for *Harper's Weekly* (August 21, 1886), frontispiece, p. 529, along with pictures for periodicals such as *Outing, Youth's Companion*, and the *Century* helped launch Remington as an illustrator and ushered him into the world of fine art. From these modest beginnings, by 1888 some 177 of his pictures were published, making his gamble to take up pen and brush a pathway to fame and fortune.

story, while he lay in the hospital." The interview Remington conducted, had it not been for his reporter instincts, "might never have been heard outside General Miles' camp."

Besides Scott's testimony, the narrative claimed one of Lieutenant Clarke's troopers "who saw him expose himself to the fire of the enemy, in an open space to rescue the wounded man" supposedly expressed "his admiration in the most vigorous language of the camp vocabulary…." Whether the dialect was contrived or real, *Harper's* contended that this unnamed witness indicated: "De Injuns jes fairly ploughed up the ground wid bullets, when he runan' never tuk no notice of what was qwine on no more's if de man's jes fell down in a fiel' anywhar. He'd've fairly dusted 'way from dar to save his own hide whole if he wa'n't a—fightin' man—fighti' man, I tell you an'titjes do 'im good to see a—Injun. An' he don't forget a man in his 'stress.'"

This commentary, as seemingly was the case for the June 19, 1886, *Harper's Weekly*, must have drawn heavily on verbiage provided by Remington. Both stories misspelled Clarke's name, dropping the final "e" as Remington consistently did. Then, too, early Remington biographer Harold McCracken reprinted a much longer piece, which he asserted was an unpublished Remington manuscript, and which contained many exact passages from the August 21 edition of *Harper's*.[98]

Just as Remington's hand in all this reporting cannot be proven with certainty, another anomaly exists related to the *Harper's* cover image—the inclusion of a black soldier aiding Clarke in carrying Corporal Scott to safety. Nowhere is there a mention of who this unknown trooper was save Remington's illustration. Written evidence of another rescuer remains unfound, except one reference to an exchange attributed to Clarke from a May 13 Tucson newspaper account that Remington may well have read. According to the unnamed reporter, during the firefight the lieutenant purportedly admitted: "I was scared to death, but the man [Scott] called to me and I couldn't leave him to be shot to death." Galvanized into action, allegedly Clarke than shouted to a nearby trooper who was "ducking bullets" ordering the unnamed soldier: "Here, help me get this man [Scott] under cover; what the devil are you dodging for—you who was born in the army."[99] Unfortunately, in this instance Remington's unpublished take on Southwestern military operations rightly concluded: "The dusky hero who aided the Lieutenant's noble effort will go down to posterity in allegory, as it were, for I presume that he, like Attila and numerous other men of war, had no time to hunt up stray historians."[100]

All these details were of little consequence to Clarke because he had no time to dwell on his growing public image. As indicated in a May 20, 1886, letter, a series of events kept him "in the saddle nearly every day."[101] Thinking he would attend a hop on May 15, he had traveled six miles from camp, but met a courier riding to Fort Huachuca with news of Captain Charles A.P. Hatfield's firefight that took place earlier that same day ten miles southeast of Santa Cruz, Sonora.[102]

The gist of this May 15 encounter was Hatfield's patrol managed to surprise an Apache camp. Geronimo and Naiche were among the surprised enemy. The Apaches escaped and set up an ambush against their attackers. During the exchange, Hatfield lost two troopers killed and two wounded. In turn, his command captured a half dozen horses and other livestock plus gear as well as supposedly wounded several Apaches but no firm numbers were given.[103] Clarke reached Hatfield after this seesaw clash at 10:00 PM, having ridden twenty miles to link up with the recently engaged troops from the Fourth U.S. Cavalry. Arriving with reinforcements, Clarke found Hatfield reluctant to go after the band he had just fought. The captain would permit the junior officer from the Tenth "to go after the party that ambushed his 40 men with my 26, which he was willing to do with the support of some Mexican volunteers." Hatfield refused to loan Clarke a packer, but would provide three of his pack mules saying he "had orders to go out only in case of absolute necessity."

Clarke's horses had been "very much played out" from their ride to link up with Hatfield so he "would not do any such idiotic thing as to accept the Captain's offer…." Displaying a growing sense of discretion, Clarke suggested Hatfield should "take what men he could" from his Troop D of the Fourth along with the just over two dozen troopers from the Tenth "and push the Indians at least to get their stock." Hatfield demurred. By the next day, when Captain Lebo arrived with more men from the Tenth (Troops D under Bigelow, the remainder of K under Clarke, and Troop L) it was too late to close with the fleeing raiders. Clarke also underscored that only thirty of his men had mounts, so his effective strength was cut by more than half with the remaining dismounted troopers staying back at Hatfield's base camp.

While Clarke hoped to get "fresh horses before long," he took what troopers who were not afoot on a scout from the Mowry Mine where they had camped once again. They covered "a very rough trail down the Patagonia Mts. getting into Crittenden at midnight" after eight hours on the move.

By May 19, Lieutenant Carter Johnson relayed an order from General Miles that Clarke should pay his men with funds delivered for that purpose,

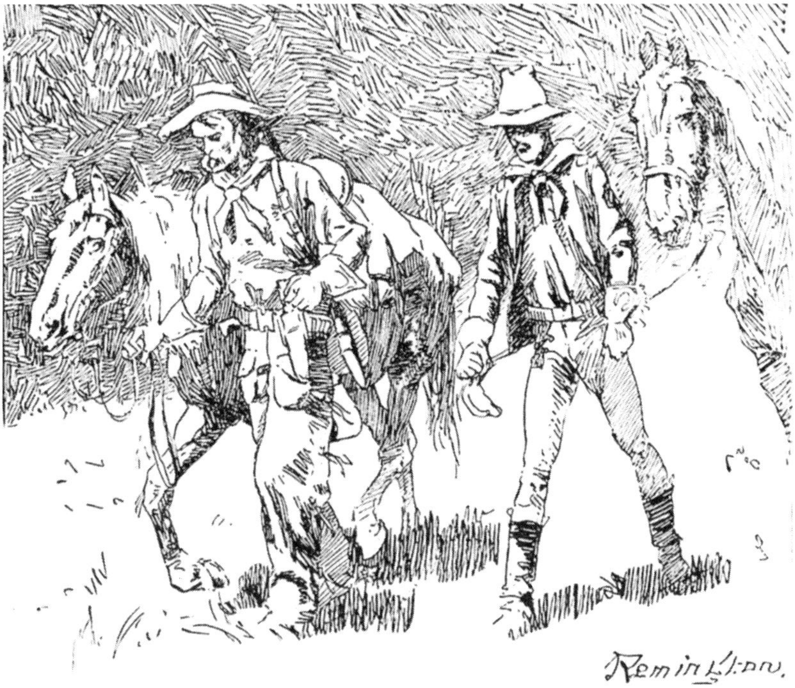

Clarke with his distinctive custom gauntlets bearing a horseshoe motif, later would be seen in Remington's "The government guide looking for tracks" Alternate: "All the Men Were Now Marching on Foot" CR# 00106 *Outing* (February 1887), p. 433.

then head back to Calabasas. "Sick of night marches though the air and scenery by moonlight cannot be surpassed," Clarke nonetheless realized that unrelenting pressure from "all directions" was the key to beating the Apache. The enemy ran low on ammunition "and their stock and themselves have been forced to make terrible efforts to escape the troops."

This tactical situation seemed productive. Clarke, however, feared the enemy would "soon scatter into such small bands that they will escape us and obliterate all trails." He realized "this country is really fearful for marching." Adding to the difficulties, even as he wrote, the temperature reached 107 degrees Fahrenheit in the shade. Conversely, just a few days later, on the trail while halting for the night along the Santa Cruz River, his "two thin saddle blankets" proved insufficient. He "nearly froze not being able to sleep a wink." Such was the lot of operating in the merciless Arizona-Sonora Desert.

Clarke's next letter home captured frustrations experienced by generations of Spanish, Mexican, and American soldiers campaigning against the Apache. From Pantano Station of the Southern Pacific Railroad, on May 21, Clarke rapidly updated his father having just completed another letter the previous day.[104]

Back at Calabasas, General Miles, who took personal control of operations, began telegraphing Clarke "at about 9 p.m. and we kept the wires both between Nogales and Calabasas open until 1 a.m. when he [Miles] decided to order me down four miles between the latter place to investigate a report of Indians." Here was one demonstration of Miles's use of telegraphy and heliography (the terms sometimes being used interchangeably) as a means to coordinate field operations, a factor that ultimately assisted in taking Geronimo.

During the course of responding to Miles's orders, Clarke reflected his general lack of respect for the local Spanish-speaking populace. He shrugged: "As the report came from a Mexican I felt sure there was nothing in it…." With that negative attitude, Clarke rather presumptuously replied to Miles the intelligence was baseless, and informed the general "that Lebo had gone west having me cover the valley of the Santa Cruz and I feared the Apache would give me the slip in case I should go south…."

Unconvinced by his subordinate's analysis, Miles "persisted so I was obliged to break camp at two o'clock in the morning, the four miles turned out to be 19 and we marched until 3 p.m. the next day with the exception of two hours halt to feed and rest." Acknowledging his father's Civil War experience, Clarke admitted: "This march was trying on the men and horses as it made the third successive night march, you know how night marches tell on a Cavalry command."

Vindicated in his response to the general, Clarke emphasized: "The report turned out to be a lie." He followed this by a reiteration of his opinion of the Spanish-speaking residents along the border, bluntly stating: "I do not think these unfortunate Mexicans can tell the truth—when they want to."

Back from this unproductive patrol, Clarke's command "had no sooner unsaddled at Calabasas than Miles telegraphed that the Indians were reported at Tubac, the very place I feared they would cross and to prevent which Lebo had left me at Calabasas." Given that both men and mounts were exhausted from the prior excursion, which Clarke sought to avoid, he and his contingent had to take "one night's rest" before redeploying the next day when the unit "moved north and at Tubac found that at least thirteen Indians had passed there the day before."

After that, they "had a very hard trail to follow as the hostiles passed through horse country and the only track we could depend on was that of a large shod horse with three shoes." Clarke explained it "was arduous work tracking those iron circles over the hard white soil covered with thousands of cow and bare foot pony tracks."

At sundown, having "made forty miles," the tired troopers "camped at a ranch that had been sacked the night before." Clarke observed: "From the worn condition of the horses abandoned by the hostiles" at that site he "felt sanguine until after making a few miles I was told by some Americans that the Indians had captured fresh horses and by marching night and day they had crossed the railroad and were in the Sierra Catalina." Disappointed but not discouraged, the detail pressed on for "nearly forty miles more through a barren country in order to reach this place for water and forage. The day after Lebo joined me with 'D' and 'L' Troops under [William] Davis and [John] Bigelow and on the morning following we reached the foothills of the Rincon Mts when another Mexican … sent us spinning east to find out when we had gone two miles that a man had been killed 15 miles behind us."

Responding to the new information, "Back we came" Clarke wrote, "and at 1 p.m. our trailer … came back at a run having just missed going up to converse with ten Apaches a mile and a half ahead of us. When we reached the spot we found the Indians had taken to the rocks and up the steep sides of the Rincon leaving a trail that the old Nick could not follow." Fortunately, a repeat of the clash in the Pinetos where Corporals Follis and Scott became casualties was not repeated. After that, the combined units pressed on with the trailer "reaching the ranch." Because their guide "had just passed the Mexicans" he thought nothing of the men he saw "lounging around the house dressed like Mexicans. He was on the point of riding down" to speak to them.

His keen sense of observation saved him from what could have been a fatal error. Clarke indicated when the tracker "saw a man dressed in underclothes with his Apache head dress run out of the house, by this time he was 300 yards from the house and in plain sight." He immediately drew his revolver from its "leather holster hoping to get a shot … but our Apache saw this move and jumped for their horses." Alone and with his horse "nearly played out" the tracker "turned back for the command and wasted no time. It was a pretty narrow escape on both sides as the tracker 'was a dead shot'" but so were the Apaches who "usually gets his game when he gets first sights."

Four days passed "spent in the Rincon Mtns. [east of Tucson] They beat anything I have seen yet for trails," Clarke contended. He added "it is walk and lead from sunrise to sunset." Returning on May 31, he postulated the "Indians are now about 200 miles from there going south—so that we hope to get a rest. It is not so hard on us, but the last month has nearly finished our poor horses." This was a common complaint for cavalry operating in such rough country where the Apache had the advantage of stealing horses any time they needed to replace played-out mounts.

With a breathing spell, Clarke, Bigelow, and Dr. Charles C. Barrows provided the officer with "some company which is very much appreciated."[105] He noted the "Doctor and I took a flying [quick railroad] trip to the City of Benson which we enjoyed very much. It seemed like civilization to get into a Pul[l]man car again." He found Benson to be "like most of the stations. On this road a Station house a few shanties, the universal Western bar room in a desert valley between high rocky ranges of mountains." In addition to a bit of rest and relaxation, the respite in Benson hopefully would be followed by the acquisition of much needed fresh horses. Clarke thought "it about time most of our troops being unable to mount more than thirty of the seventy five men."

This all too frequent situation severely handicapped operational effectiveness and prolonged campaigning. That matter weighed on Clarke who confessed he was "to form the least idea as the time that this business will last but unless the government is more energetic it will be years, and many a poor ranchman will pay with his life for the lack of energy with which this thing is run." Although not entirely satisfied with the conduct of the campaign, he admitted: "no general can bring these Indians to terms in such a country as this with the means he has at his disposal." While "many things both interesting and amusing" occurred on campaign, "but on the whole it is very discouraging."

Uninspired by his present circumstances, his thoughts returned to Saumur, but renewed efforts for attending the French Cavalry School would have to wait while the Apache conflict remained unresolved. Before then, Clarke had to refund an overpayment of $172 (nearly two months' pay) from almost two years before, that some astute accountant in Washington discovered. This reimbursement consumed his savings for leave.

Tongue in cheek, he bantered "so that I feel very patriotic" giving money to the government. He had enough remaining funds to cover his "ration of bacon and flour being about $6.00 per month." Conversely he "did not have enough pack mules to carry our officer's mess outfit nor enough men to detail a cook but hope to be better supplied next time."

As May turned to June the campaign continued. With the end still not in sight, on June 9 Clarke reported the killing of a civilian, Henry Baston, plus an attack on a wagon near Arivaca. That night, an estimated twenty-five Chiricahuas raided the town itself for horses.[106] Eleven days later, characteristic of Miles's grass roots style and dependence on the telegraph and heliograph, he sent three communiques from Nogales in rapid succession to Clarke, who was at Calabasas.[107] The first one instructed the lieutenant to "investigate the report of beef being killed by 30 Indians today four miles from Gowns ranch the number corresponds to those in front of Lawton & if true they may attempt to cross railroad tonight between Calabasas and this place [Nogales]."

The next directive indicated First U.S. Infantry Captain William Tisdall, presumably from a stationary outpost with his detachment of foot soldiers, had reported that a party on "Devil's Canon struck quite a large trail going north."[108] Miles telegraphed Clarke: "It is not positive that they have moved north of Tucson road after getting rest move up the Tucson road and see if you horses enough to trail them north if they do I want a command close on them. They may attempt to move … tonight and cross the railroad between Calabasas and Nogales or below Nogales." The general further urged: "you could place your command near them or if you get information that they have passed between you and Lebo you could move back quickly tomorrow & pursue them."

Miles stated he provided Clarke with all available intelligence and spelled out "the main object now is to get some one of command where they can strike them effectively don't go far beyond telegraph communication [possibly meaning both telegraph and heliograph] unless you are satisfied they are going direct for their camp. In case you get any positive information at Towns ranch tonight send me word by messenger at Cosmopolitan Hotel by daylight if that pass over the mountains by Calabasas and Oro Blanco occupied if not send seven dismounted men to occupy it." Later that same day, Miles telegraphed a follow-up which read: "Your command should be ready but not move unless they come in your vicinity. Keep men well out to the south and ask all citizens to give you timely information where troops can find main trail and get your command north of them." In these exchanges, Miles, as did Crook before him, demonstrated a high degree of personal involvement and commitment to maintaining constant lines of communication by every means at his disposal.

By July Clarke reached the Arizona Ranch in Mexico twenty-five miles southwest of Nogales. From there he corresponded with his mother, writing that she probably noticed his change of mood affected what he wrote.[109] For one thing, he "had hopes after posting my mounted scouts at Oro Blanco and taking up my own quarters with Lebo at Calabasas" where "I would have a little rest though to tell you the truth I got weary of the rest during the few days I was idle."[110] Clarke preferred action, so being encamped with nothing to do rankled him. Nonetheless, on the 4th of July he looked forward to having some "ice cream and on the 5th" intended to go "to Nogales five miles below to a great ball [formal dance]." Neither of these routine-breaking experiences came to pass because instead he took "a rattling of twenty miles in the beautiful moonlight on the day Hatfield was ambushed."

Having just arrived from Calabasas on July 3, the next morning Clarke's command mounted up for the field again. Perturbed, Clarke "did not believe the report that was causing the move. I was missing the ball, I had lost my gold watch the night before worth twice its value to me." He also missed one of his favorite treats—ice cream, which was to be served at the ball. Before moving out, Clarke's study of Spanish paid dividends permitting him to post "reward notices in English and Spanish everywhere but had no time to make a search so that I left a hard earned twenty dol gold piece with Lebo for the lucky and honest finder."

On the night of the fourth "after a tail sore hot trip over a mountain trail of twenty-two miles" they reached "an out of the way mining camp in Mexico called Promontorio, a great smuggling camp" where *gambucinos*, miners who worked abandoned sites or those that were too poor to attract major capital for operations, eked out a meager existence.[111] Located approximately seven miles west from ciudad Alamos, this out of the way spot allowed Clarke's command to obtain coffee and "a cup of wheat for the poor ponies" but there was "no grass." The surroundings were not inviting as Clarke depicted the "heavy black clouds" that "made the dark narrow dismal cañon look anything but inviting. The sides of the mountain were pierced in every direction by black mouthed shafts which in some cases held the family of the Mexican miner."

At least there was coffee, and Clarke could buy "a bottle of mescal" which probably was not the most refined libation. After that, he did "not come out again during the whole time" in the camp taking to his bottle for solace. Locals also partook of this raw liquor which Clarke supposed "like many others he digs and blasts for a day after the scarce silver only to get a bottle of the precious mescal." He marveled at the "life these people lead never leaving the miserable settlements and running the risk of losing their lives by Apaches while going to and from their leads." Backbreaking work to extract the precious metals required "the ore from these isolated camps … to be packed for miles over the rough trails to the smelters on picturesque trains of (burros) asses which in Mexico are far uglier than in any other place I have seen."Clarke and his men "gladly left Promontorio and after another hot ride over sierras through rocky cañons where one keeps his hand on his loaded carbine and his eyes in every direction," the situation improved. They came upon a "beautiful valley where for two or three miles" they "passed little fields of barley interspersed with poplar groves and bright colored gardens; to make the change more delightful the hot-clear sky with the painful glare became overcast changing the oppressive heat to a most pleasant temperature."

Such ranchos reminded Clarke "of the old plantations as they nestle down in fertile valleys protected by high steep ranges of mountains. One may march for miles over the hot barren mesas not seeing a living thing and suddenly have spread before him the green fields of barley and tobacco, the hill sides covered with cattle and horses and the large hacienda surrounded by the rougher dwellings of the peons."

At the ranch's headquarters, owner William Barnett "could not have been more welcoming." Halting and unsaddling, the weary patrol "soon stretched out under the poplars beside the stream. Their famished horses recovered "with relish" as they received their fill of "green alfalfa hay." Clarke being the only officer, "took dinner at the house," while his men ate in camp. "After bacon and heavy dough" what "a relief to get beef, cabbage, potatoes, milk and 'lentelles'" (beans) he sighed.

In the morning Barnett had a "fat yearling" killed and butchered and he took fifty pounds of bacon as trade. While fresh beef was abundant on the ranch, bacon was "a great delicacy with the duty being so high as to make it 'contraband.'" Their benefactor also "would take nothing for the two sacks of potatoes, onions, and cabbage sent to the troop."

In passing, Clarke mentioned that Robert N. ("Bob" aka "Little Giant") Leatherwood "an old 'rebel' of [Stephen D.] Ramseur's N.C. brigade" served as his "chief of scouts." He described the man as "a spry little tar heel" who was "a pleasant 'compadre.'"[112] After this satisfying layover, Clarke, Leatherwood, and the patrol left "for Agua Larca a station on the Guaymas R.R." Within two days Clarke hoped to reach his basecamp at Calabasas. Empty-handed, he returned north having "heard nothing from Geronimo whom the troops are following southward. Heaven knows I hope they catch him for I long to see Baltimore again."

He thought "there are four or five Indians in this part of the country yet who either from wounds or lack of arms are afraid to leave the mountains but it is like the needle and haystack to find them and I think I shall leave them for the present." Clarke also shared a report "that an Indian gave himself up at Fort Apache saying that he had lost his gun and horse in our fight in the Pineto Mts. and was cut off by us since which time he has not lead [*sic*] a pleasant life of it. If true this shows that they did not have a picnic with us on May 3rd."

Clarke returned to the Peck's Ranch episode of April 27, 1886. He noted Mexicans managed to recapture the kidnapped little girl, Trinidad Verdin (AKA Berdine) who said: "there are forty bucks with Geronimo, more than we thought by ten." He inserted the former captive recounted how "an old squaw who was shot at the time of the recapture" had taken charge of the girl.[113] Trinidad escaped death, although she emerged "fearfully scratched up from lack of clothes and hard riding but is splendid health." She let it be known that "the Indians treated her very well and had plenty to eat in fact, lived well." Moreover, Clarke asserted a "Mexican with the hostiles" pursued them "to spare Peck's life" but it seemed more likely that it was Geronimo for some unknown quirk who let Peck live.[114] Because, according to young Trinidad, Geronimo could "barely ride being wounded in the back" this act of unusual mercy was even more puzzling.

Ten days after his earlier message to his mother, Clarke set down to write his father from Calabasas.[115] Still lacking horses, Clarke's dismounted, disgruntled troopers had been "posted for the defense of scattered ranches." Irritatingly, Leatherwood's comrades the "Tucson Rangers (3 months men)" had horses. These frontiersmen "encamped 28 miles from here." Paperwork now kept him busy replying to his superiors, as well as filling out the reports and forms required for commissary, quartermaster, and other aggravating administrative matters.

At least he had made his way to Nogales on the train during July 13 to break up the routine. He remained "two nights and a day in the quiet little town whose main street is divided by the international line of the great Republics."

Having struck up an acquaintance with the local collector of customs, he "managed to bring over the few cigars that are necessary for a 2nd lieutenant and various other little contraband that are needed for my personal use. The cigars then are most excellent and in the American saloons in Mexico one can get very good ale, stout and wines which is an attraction even though one be not a taker." This was in contrast to the rotgut sold "in the miserable little places on the frontier even in the post traders."

With "a motley invoice of purchases" in hand, he left Nogales with not only the cigars, but also "a sea turtle, a compass, and a canteen also a pair of spurs" which were possibly vaquero style. The sea turtle came from Guayas. He described it as "a beauty weighing at least 75 lbs and furnishing our mess for two days besides giving soup for dinner to the whole troop, his steaks were delicious very similar [to] chicken or still more like frog legs in taste as he only costs $2.00 and 'two bits' for express." At least they ate well for the time being and with lettuce "and four kinds of vegetables" their fare "should have satisfied any epicure."

He now had been assigned a soldier-clerk to assist with the paperwork, "under a net in the sweltering to keep away from the flies." At 5 PM, Bigelow, Barrows, and Clarke concluded their official day and rode "up to the station" with Lebo "to meet the Northern train, get our mail and then spend a quiet and very enjoyable evening playing 'hearts,' billiards or pool." They also bought beer, but he insisted they were "all temperate" and managed "to have a delightful time all to ourselves the citizens being represented by the R.R. agent and the heir of the Calabasas hotel."

He pronounced this establishment as very comfortable, and was surprised to "find such a tastefully furnished house as this hotel in this wilderness." Not everything was perfect, however, as an incident arose to spoil the mood.

A Mexican came into town claiming the stallion Clarke bought in Fort Grant and for which he paid nearly $200, exhibited the man's brand or one very similar to it at least. Clarke admitted: "When I bought" the horse "I did not have the brand vetted" so there was some question as to ownership. Clarke said the man claimed "to have lost the horse in 83 and that he was fifteen (?) though I know the horse is only four years old. The fellow has not this brand recorded and that will prevent his getting him by law but it does look as if he has a case against me and as these men can get their fellows to swear to anything" the prospect looked bleak. The outcome of this claim and counterclaim is unknown, but as August rolled around, most assuredly Clarke could speak of the constant beastly heat. Once more, he let his father know that he went to Nogales along with Dr. Barrows and Captain Lebo.[116] In turn, Lieutenant Bigelow continued, "busily writing for further enlightenment" of his *Outing* readers. Clarke additionally wrestled with "one of these native fevers … requiring all of my attention and it came near burning me into incandescence." To make matters worse, the "glaring soil with the thermometer at 103 in the shade" left him "a little weak" but he hoped his health would improve now that Troop K had relocated its "camp up on the high sandy hills that are always dry." Likely, Clarke suffered from malaria, the source of which was unknown at the time. Even so, removal away from standing water sources that were breeding grounds for mosquitos had become common practice by this time.

More happily, Clarke noted an enlisted man in the troop had found the lost watch. At first Baltimore, Maryland, native William Turner, who had enlisted in the Tenth in 1881, and who served as Clarke's striker, declined the $20 reward offered by his lieutenant, refusing to accept what amounted to pay for nearly a month and a half.[117] He eventually accepted $10. This incident may well have added to Clarke's growing positive attitude to his black soldiers, a fact that was bolstered by Clarke's suggestion that if his father required any leatherwork, one of the Tenth Cavalry's former saddlers had left service and returned to his home in Maryland. He could offer his services to Powhatan's family.

Clarke further expressed admiration for Dr. Barrows, a graduate of the University of Virginia, who was one of a growing number of Southerners filling "the vacancies left by the 'old heroes'" who were Union veterans retiring from the army. One of those veterans, Captain Lebo, seemingly became more incapacitated from his bouts with the bottle, which Clarke partially blamed on pressures from General Miles. In fact, the lieutenant was pleased that the departmental commander had relocated to Willcox.

He remained skeptical about Miles, as he did the Mexicans. He styled them "vain ignorant" people, and expressed an opinion that he would not be upset "if some European nation should step in" to take charge of the country once more as they did under Maximillian.

Clarke added that he deplored the treatment of the Yaquis whom the Mexican government had persecuted, enslaved, and on occasion attempted to exterminate.[118] Here again, as with his newfound perspective on the black troopers, Clarke's experiences in the Southwest broadened his understanding and in some instances resulted in respect for others whom he previously would have considered his inferiors.

By September, Clarke settled in at Calabasas. Once again, he had access to a typewriter, an invention gaining more widespread use by both civilians and military alike. On the twelfth and again on the thirteenth he sat down at the keys of this writing machine to provide a long review of his current activities.[119]

He opened with an acknowledgement that: "There is nothing like having a correspondent around …" referring to the publicity he had received from the work of the New York artist who recently had befriended him. Clarke acknowledged: "I owe my friend Mr. Remington a great debt if only for being the cause of so many letters from home."

Furthermore, Clarke indicated news from family and friends provided him with additional strength, which he would need in the future when facing "much more severe tests than our little fight in the 'Pinitos.'" He confessed: "to tell the truth your devoted son was very much scared and more and more so than he would like to acknowledge outside of his immediate family."

On a more mundane topic, he told of practicing on the typewriter and hoped to buy one someday as well as wishing he had one all the time "to write up … records of boards of surveys, garrison courts-martial" and for other official "pleasant little duties that fall to the lot of ye second lieutenant in post."

Changing course once more, Clarke expressed joy that "at last … this miserable chase after Geronimo" had ended after intense final pressure had been exerted, and a subsequent meeting by the Apache leader with Captain Henry

Lawton in the Sierra Madres. The war-weary holdouts finally agreed to parley with Nelson Miles on September 3, 1886, in Skeleton Canyon.[120] At this juncture Clarke partially reversed his estimation of George Crook's replacement, calling for everyone to "be grateful to gen Miles for removing the rest of the tribe from Arizona as I have not the least doubt that by so doing the Apache question has been settled … which is a godsend both for the army and the unfortunate people who have to live in this wretched country." Although bloodshed continued for some years thereafter, it greatly subsided but not before Clarke and others would engage in mop up field operations.[121]

As Clarke foretold, campaigning did end. Likewise, so did his prediction that after eighteen months trailing Geronimo, he would return to a garrison. He told his mother he was ready "to get us into a post" and even more anxious "to get leave and see all you again for this life certainly developes [*sic*] ones attachment for home." He recounted how Lebo and Bigelow had been feted by some of the locals, on September 12, before they departed with the troop to Fort Grant the morning of the thirteenth. Clarke did not envy them "the long hot march," which for the time being he would avoid because he remained behind until "the paymaster pays off my Sepoys" as he dubbed the Apache Indian scouts he had commanded since enlisting them in late June.[122] He thought this would take place the following day. Although he acknowledged "a few very pleasant moments" he was ready to make his way back to Fort Huachuca and then press on to Fort Grant.

Even as this letter made its way to his mother, Miles summarized the campaign praising Lebo for "his usual energy, good judgement and gallantry," while also recognizing Corporal Scott, "a brave soldier" who wounded "lay disabled under a sharp fire" but who because of "Lieut Powhatan H. Clarke, 10th Cavalry, a gallant young officer" despite "the risk of his own life, carried … to a place of safety." Miles added: "A youth rescuing a veteran under severe fire indicates the days of chivalry have not passed."[123] Clarke must have been pleased to gain Miles's notice. Perhaps this acknowledgement contributed to a slight increase in respect for his commanding general.

Clarke's campaigning halted for the time being as he had indicated. Characteristic of the end of the field service, as winter approached, Clarke was on his way to the monotony of Fort Grant. It was from there, on October 6, he complained to his father that Colonel Grierson was "letting things slide in his usual way which is enough to make anyone who had any esprit de corps feel disgusted."[124] While far more comfortably situated, Clarke found life "too soft" in contrast to the rigors of field service.

He had hoped to add more, but was called away "to witness the issue of clothing" caustically appending "they have such a high regard" of us "that they require a troop commander to have his clothing rolls witnessed by another officer…." By the time he finished this task, first call for retreat sounded. He only had a brief window to report that he heard from Major General Oliver O. Howard.[125] Although he appreciated Howard's promise to support Clarke's application for a detail to France, prospects seemed slim, as did his desire to take leave and visit his family.

In spite of previous protestations of boredom, Clarke's November 29 letter to his mother indicated he had not written when he had intended because his "many duties" kept him "running around too much."[126] Among other things, he now served as post adjutant, a common assignment for junior lieutenants, which meant he took charge of guard mount at 9 AM, followed by morning reports, oversight of the commissary supplies that included all groceries, rations, toothpicks, and scores of other commodities sold or issued at the garrison. He especially disliked this responsibility claiming there was "too much money to look out for and I always dream I have left the safe open." At least Clarke saw one advantage. He could use such experience in civilian life if he had to resign from the service.

No escape from these matters was in the offing. His efforts to break away for two months on leave came back disapproved. Once Bigelow returned from his leave, Clarke hoped he would be able to secure time to visit the family.

By this time Grierson had been transferred to Santa Fe, taking, as was standard practice for a regimental commander, the band and headquarters with him. The colonel also "promised to have Jim Hughes' troop ordered" to Fort Grant as well as stated he would "try to have the Regt sent to New Mexico."

The first possibility pleased Clarke. As for Grierson's second initiative, Clarke doubted the transfer of the Tenth Cavalry would occur, which suited him as he was "content where I am." That did not mean he enjoyed everything at Fort Grant. For instance, besides being post adjutant, Clarke also functioned as ordnance officer. Because there were no targets for marksmanship practice "to keep in repair at this season" he faced a fairly light routine.[127] The one exception was the fact that the ordnance warehouse was "full of obsolete and unserviceable trash," which required condemnation procedures before he could dispose of the outdated surplus. If he failed to be precise, he personally would have to reimburse any shortfalls.

By December, Clarke fired off several letters as the end of an extremely eventful year drew near. He reiterated to his father that his duties kept him fully occupied, so much so that he had been negligent in his correspondence.[128] Powhatan acknowledged he was "rather selfish about his amusements which I rarely give up" as evidenced by his days at West Point. Nonetheless, his only pastime of late had been "an hour of pistol practice which I am very fond of but never before had sufficient ammunition to make it worthwhile to study systematically." In his capacity as ordnance officer, he had access to "a quantity of obsolete powder and ball ammunition and having a very complete loading machine" he now could blaze away as much as he wished. His goal was to become "a good shot before the winter ends." He had "a quixotic idea" that this diversion was "a good thing" professing "an officer [ought] to know how to use his arms…." In short, he received "a great deal of pleasure from his 'Colt 45.'"

Besides this outlet, which arguably offered a better escape than drinking to excess and other unsavory pastimes, Clarke had reached a new appreciation for his role as post adjutant. This detail was "one of the more important positions" bringing both considerable responsibilities and a degree of power to the lieutenant holding the post because: "All communications with the Commanding Officer came by way of the Post Adjutant, for rarely did the Post Commander directly address officers under his command."[129] As a mark of growing professionalism and maturity, he allowed that being appointed as post adjutant afforded him the opportunity to learn "a great deal about the administration of garrison affairs" as well as gave him "a finger in the pie."

Although he appreciated that feeling, he honestly concluded: "I doubt not that I will tire of red ink as I have tired of other things of the same kind…."[130] For an action oriented cavalryman, Clarke's self-analysis rang true. Once more the irresponsible boy cadet was shaping into a conscientious officer.

He then told an amusing episode about spending three hours "changing the combination" to his safe in the commissary department "after brilliantly sending the old combination on a slip of paper to my tailor in an old trouser pocket." Anyone in the computer age who had forgotten their password can appreciate the frustration and humor of this situation. Clarke wrapped up with word that John Bigelow might be returning to his duties with Troop K toward the end of the forthcoming January. If so, Clarke had renewed hopes of the often-spoken-of leave in the spring.

Although that was months in the future, Jim Hughes, while not having relocated to Fort Grant as Colonel Grierson had suggested, at least now served at nearby Fort Thomas. This meant the two classmates should be able to visit each other. Clarke still looked forward to Hughes's possible transfer to Fort Grant for many reasons including the fact that he found it "lonesome" to be "the only bachelor lieutenant at the post, in fact the only 2d lieut." among but "five officers all told."

Clarke wrote again on December 14, in response to his father's most recent message. He picked up the thread of his narrative.[131] He let it be known he was tiring of garrison duties once more and longed for home leave. As always, he wanted to see action. Perhaps the Utes or Sioux would oblige in the spring. Such a prospect "would be so 'awfully jolly'" and according to Bigelow an outbreak on the Great Plains or elsewhere would bring all the troops together in an uncommon assemblage and provide an opportunity to add to the "'record' for our … regiment." Perhaps even some of the old war horses from the Civil War would "jump at the Retired list" to avoid more campaigning thereby opening some advancements for younger, junior officers.

On the other hand, if campaigning had concluded, he could look forward to taking leave "to pass a few weeks pleasantly" as well as allow him to have his "teeth overhauled" something he would not entrust to "these stone masons out here…." Nonetheless, Clarke found the local surgeons in army blue the "most pleasant and common sensed fellows for companions." As Clarke's medical records indicated, he had ample opportunity to meet "some splendid young fellows in our medical corps and being of a delicate constitution I have a good chance to become acquainted with them…." One of them, Peter Egan, was "a rough diamond but there is no paste about him, he is the one who was the surgeon at Fort Bowie last winter."[132] He equally enjoyed his "very nice comd'g officer at present. Captain [William Boyle] Kennedy who in the war was of the 'California Column' which you let capture Arizona and New Mexico," as he playfully teased his Confederate veteran father.[133]

Clarke dreaded the day that Major Anson Mills arrived to supersede Kennedy. He contended that Mills, whom he knew from his days at Fort Davis, Texas, was "detested in the regiment" supposedly having "had rows with nearly everyone here." He prophesized as soon as Mills arrived there would be trouble. Probably some of it would be serious especially for "some of the reckless ones…." Clarke accused Mills of double standards, being "one of these gentlemen who excuses himself from living up to his rigid ideas of discipline but requires most stringent compliance for his neighbors." There were many such men in the army according to Clarke, who indicated these petty tyrants were even more distasteful when a subordinate was trapped under such a commander in a small garrison.[134] Because Mills and Grierson vied for control of the regiment, thereby creating splinter groups, interestingly Clarke did not side with the colonel's nemesis.

With Clarke serving as post adjutant, he feared his frequent official contacts with the major could result in "a very disagreeable round of duty" and he "would not be surprised" finding himself "on the major's black list." This would mean walking a tight rope not wishing to alienate his friends on one hand because of this "crank" but conversely, he knew he had to "keep pretty level" in order not to cross his capricious superior. Clarke not being one to follow rules during his cadet days, was learning to play garrison politics.

Another sign of Clarke's more serious approach to his profession was acknowledging that he had failed to keep up his ongoing military studies to augment his four years at West Point. He started to remedy the "long months of mental idleness" by purchasing some military law books, which he proposed "to commence and climb through the ponderous volumes."

He also read some historical studies, such as one treating the 1600s. Clarke offered, he was glad to be "a soldier in the 19th century." His return to books coincided with the interest "in military education" of Merritt Barber, the adjutant general of the Department of Arizona. This officer from headquarters spent "much labor" as well as not a little sarcasm in promoting his priorities and policies and resulting in grief for Clarke and Kennedy. In Clarke's estimation, Barber was chief among the annoying bureaucrats, another vestige of the Civil War whom Clarke viewed as superfluous.[135] Clarke, no lover of administrative details, exaggerated: "the staff of our army which by the way is larger than the army itself" was manned by "some of the most idiotic, insignificant offshoots imaginable." In contrast, Clarke preferred his fellow cavalry officers such as James Hughes and William Harvey Smith, who recently paid Clarke a visit. Clarke portrayed this young Tenth Cavalry lieutenant as "one of the nicest youngsters and was in the class of 83."[136]

By mid-December, Clarke had heard from both his father and mother.[137] In the latter case, he enthusiastically ensured "how happy both" letters made him feel. He followed with the announcement that General Miles had called for the departmental headquarters to shift to Los Angeles, California, which did not affect his being bombarded by Barber from afar. He insubordinately boasted: "the poor idiot does not know what a callow sub[altern] he is wasting his time on."

Returning to his days at the Military Academy, Clarke had been "in much hotter water for four years at West Point." He poignantly dismissed the expectation of having everyone "know a whole lot of idiotic stuff about red tape."

The acting post commander, Captain Kennedy, growled and swore, and spent "much time walking up and down behind the lattice of his front porch [placed there for shade and privacy] fulminating compositions that he does not any more dare send Hdqrs than I do." At least he could take comfort in that fact that he was not the only one in uniform suffering difficulties if the rumor were true that Nelson Miles was "in hot water over his Indians." He expressed regret that "some people should be so envious of his success," but bluntly followed with "though between you and me, I cannot admire Gen. Miles as a man, though he has always been most gracious to me."

Clarke thought Miles "seemed too politic and cold," but he conceded the general "was a great man for a young officer to serve with as he will give anyone a chance." With this in mind, Clarke hoped his "prejudices may be overcome some day for he is a successful soldier and they say a very brave man."

Right after Christmas, Clarke completed what probably was his last letter home for 1886.[138] He did not look forward to the forthcoming year, as well as called attention to being impoverished due to his "own idiotic extravagance." This meant he struggled to keep up his "bank account."

His spirits sank even lower when he learned John Bigelow's leave had been extended again, this time for an additional month. Once more, Clarke's desire to visit his own home was dashed. He swore he would "leave as soon as" Bigelow "set foot on Arizona soil." When that happened, he intended to make his way to family in Baltimore and nearby Washington, D.C. where he would try to see the secretary of war. Clarke thought this was the only option that might succeed in gaining his detail to Saumur. As before, Clarke pled his case. He protested that it was "next to impossible to improve my mind out here on account of my very restless and eratic [*sic*] disposition."

Whether his mother accepted this statement or took it as a sign of her son's making an excuse for not applying himself to martial studies out of his typical laziness remains unknown. Maybe Clarke realized her possible skepticism. He added more fuel to his argument that a European war might be in the offing, and sought his mother's assistance, as he had in the past. Clarke wanted her aid to go "abroad in case of a foreign war, for I could then learn that which I could never learn here." In this he mirrored the widespread emphasis of his times on preparing for a more traditional clash with an enemy along the lines of the Civil War or Franco-Prussian War, and failed to realize, as most of his contemporaries overlooked, the value of experience gained from participating in guerrilla warfare. Clarke looked for advancement. He maintained that an overseas assignment would place him in the forefront "in case anything should break out over there which as a patriot I should say 'God forbid' but then I fear I am more of a 2d lieutenant than a patriot."

Indeed, his jingoist bent caused him to declare: "this country needs a war, why of course it does!" In England, Rudyard Kipling championed such sentiments. So would Frederic Remington, Theodore Roosevelt, and others in the United States.

After his somewhat unconvincing argument for sailing to France, he circled back to the holidays. He disclosed that he enjoyed "a very splendid dinner at Captain Lebo's and had a great deal of fun thereafter." Still, he complained that this was not what he had envisioned several months ago when he believed he would be back in Baltimore where the brisk air and possibly snow would make it feel like the traditional holidays. Of Arizona he wrote: "The weather is not much like Xmas just now as it is too warm to play tennis with a coat on and the days are perfectly monotonously clear blue skies, bright sunshine and spring temperatures." Rather than leave the impression that this was paradise, however, Clarke charged the air was "as insipid as the country, dry and never leaving the fragrance that you have in a spring at home."

Now he had to plow into the piles of paperwork that he faced without a clerk for the first time in some months. He had returns to complete that accounted for the personnel present or elsewhere. Further, he took his turn as judge advocate for a garrison court martial against a man who had "slept through 'Reveille'" but he looked at this as "idiocy to try a man when his captain could settle the difficulty."

That matter dispensed with, Clarke proceeded to the commissary for a monthly inventory of the stores, a task that consumed his afternoon, leaving his "head fuzzy with salt-pork, coffee, teas, flour, needles, pins, clothe brushes, and soap." He joked, if his mother found a good position in a grocery store for him, she should drop him "a line and I will resign this position." As "'post powder monkey'" which is to say the local ordnance officer, he claimed to have developed expertise "in expending any ammunition" that may be "ahead" or in other words, outdated.

Clearly Clarke sought a change of pace, but for the moment he could look back on an eventful year. He had endured his trial by combat, performing bravely but by his own admission experiencing fear. In the process, he gained a new respect for his black troopers. His use of racial slurs or disparaging remarks about his troops diminished as he evidently came to look upon them as fellow fighting men.

His deeds also brought him recognition from superiors and from a larger public who learned of his exploits through newspaper accounts, most dramatically through a front-page illustration from novice artist, author, and admirer, Frederic Remington. Clarke's chance meeting with the son of a Union cavalryman led to a friendship that benefitted both men as they began to make their marks in two very different, but sometimes intersecting worlds. As B. Byron Price pointed out in his biographical essay on Remington: "Clarke, a crack cavalry officer, superb rider" and recipient of the Medal of Honor, "became a regular informant and regular sounding board for the artist on military matters and the fine points of army horses and horsemanship."[139] In many respects, Clarke emerged as Remington's military muse, an alter ego, or at least perhaps what the artist longed to be, and with no small dose of hero worship for the dashing Louisiana-born horse soldier.

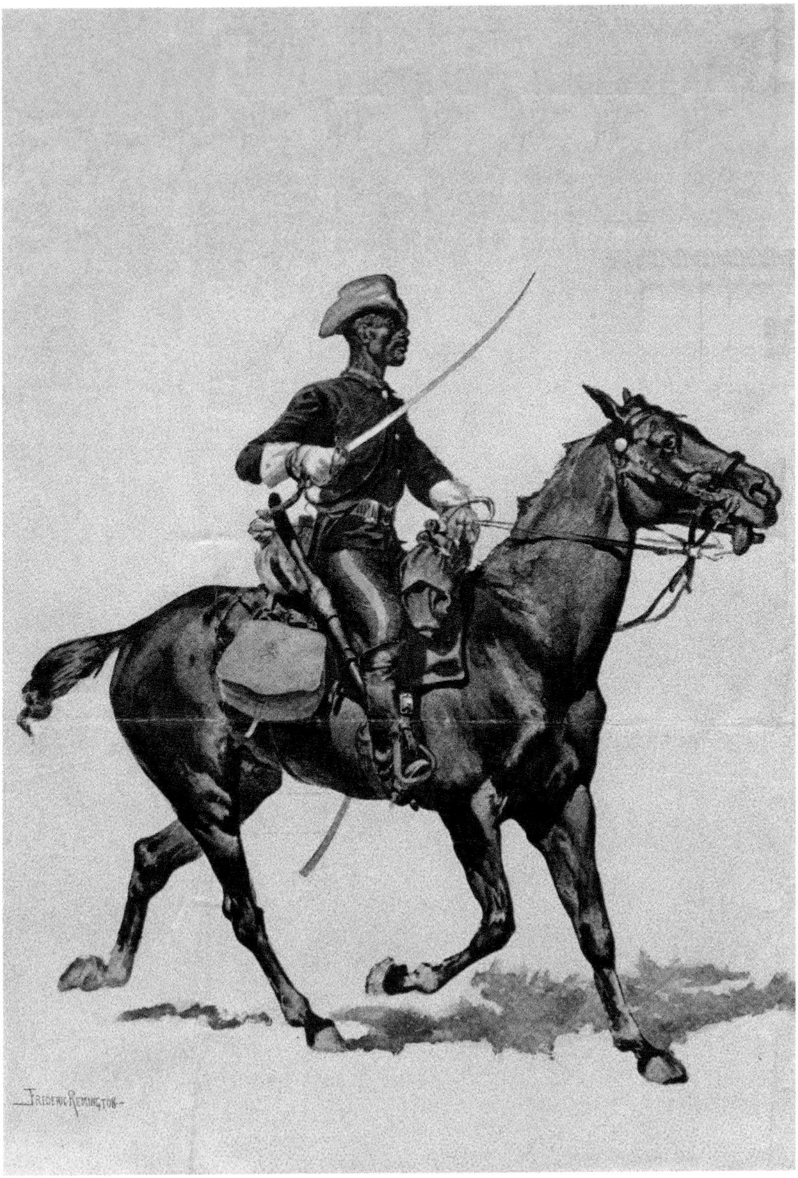

A U.S. Cavalryman also became a color lithograph. It is likely that the subject was one observed by Remington while Clarke's house guest at Fort Grant, Arizona, during 1888. Missouri History Museum, St. Louis.

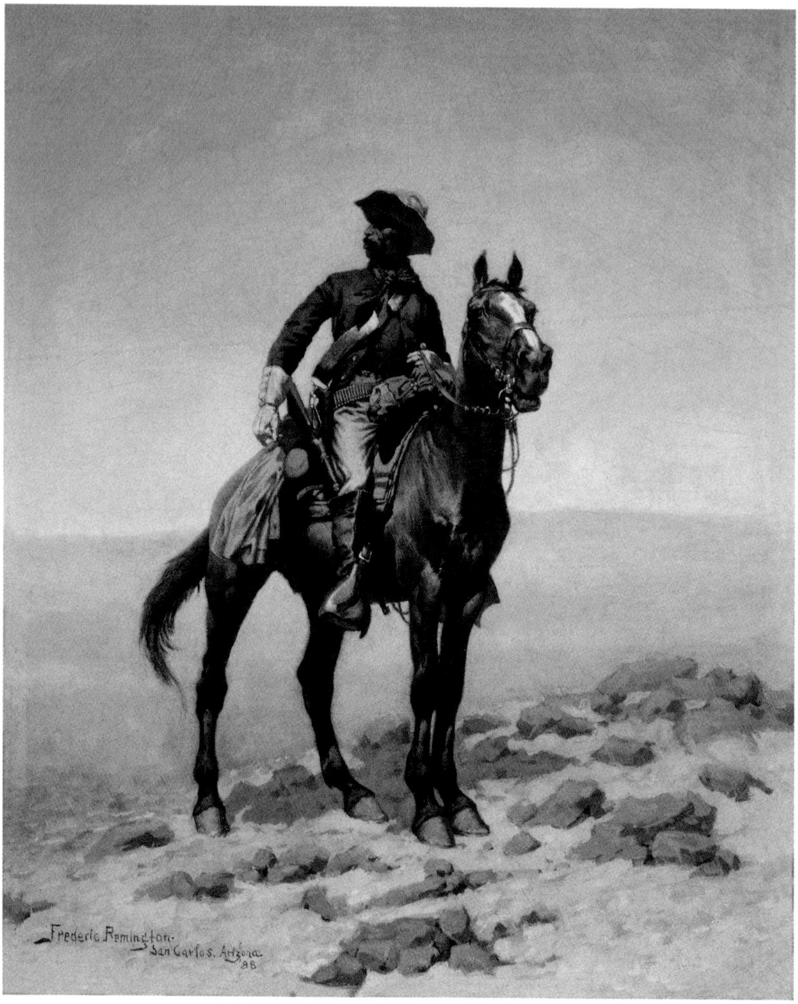

The Alert CR# 00197 Dimensions: 22 × 19-1/2" Date: 1888 Medium: oil on canvas. Inscription: "Frederic Remington/San Carlos Arizona/—88." was another work by Remington that resulted from his experiences at Fort Grant and San Carlos, which among other things emerged as the iconic "Scout with the Buffalo Soldiers." Private collection.

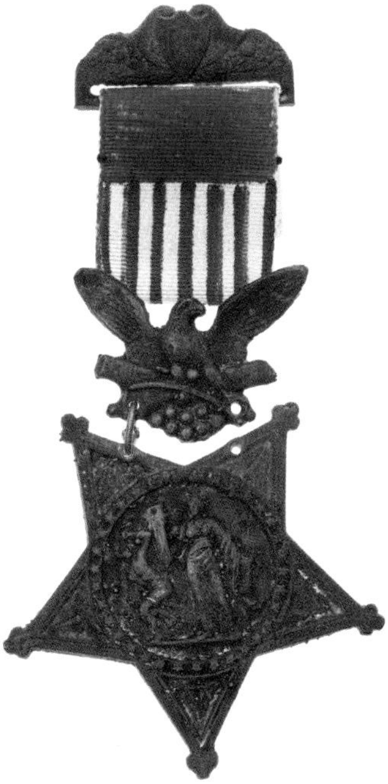

Powhatan Clarke earned this Medal of Honor for the rescue of Corporal Edward Scott in 1886. Missouri Historical Society, St. Louis.

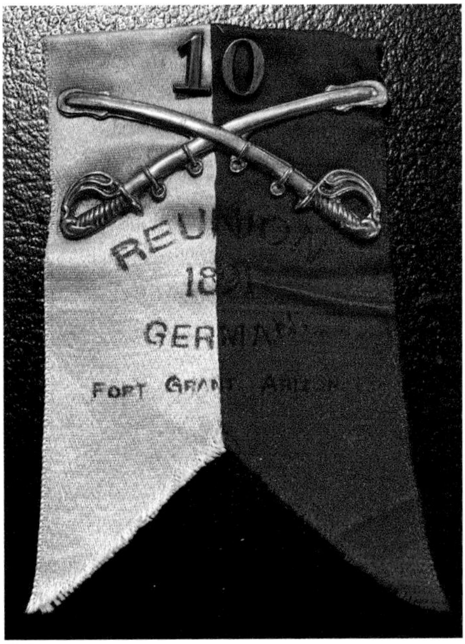

While in Arizona Clarke alternated between physically demanding field operations and comfortable garrison life where dance parties known as "hops" and "Germans" were among the pastimes he and fellow officers enjoyed. A special ribbon commemorated one of these *soirees*. Jack Blades Collection.

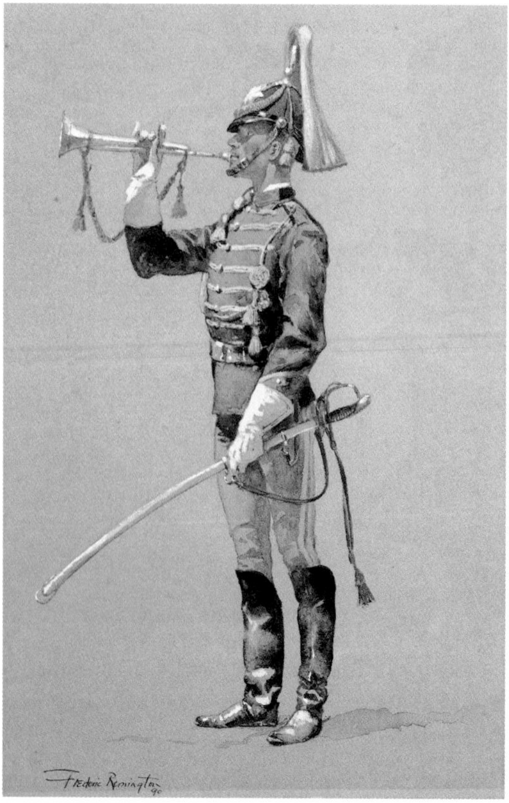

According to historian Thomas D. Phillips, the prolific Remington produced at least 270 images of the frontier army with some fifty or more of these capturing black soldiers. He may have used black soldiers as the basis for depictions of white troops such as his *Campfire Sketch* (1888 CR#004411) from his "Scout with the Buffalo Soldiers" as the basis for his *A Cavalrymen's Breakfast on the Plains* c. 1892 given the placement and poses of the five soldiers in the scene around the campfire. Likewise, his *Taps* (Cavalry Bugler in Full Uniform) CR# 01191 Dimensions" 17 11/16 × 9 13/16" Date: 1890 Medium: Watercolor on paper, may have started as a black trumpeter. While staying as Clarke's guest at Fort Grant in 1888, Remington started an oil of a black sergeant which he produced in his host's backyard, used one of sons of the garrison's doctor as a model on horseback as well as the physician's "striker" in the same capacity, and completed a painting of Clarke's striker. Given these circumstances and internal details of the uniform depicted, the artist possibly converted a black trumpeter into a white one for this painting. Courtesy Frederic Remington Art Museum, Ogdensburg, New York.

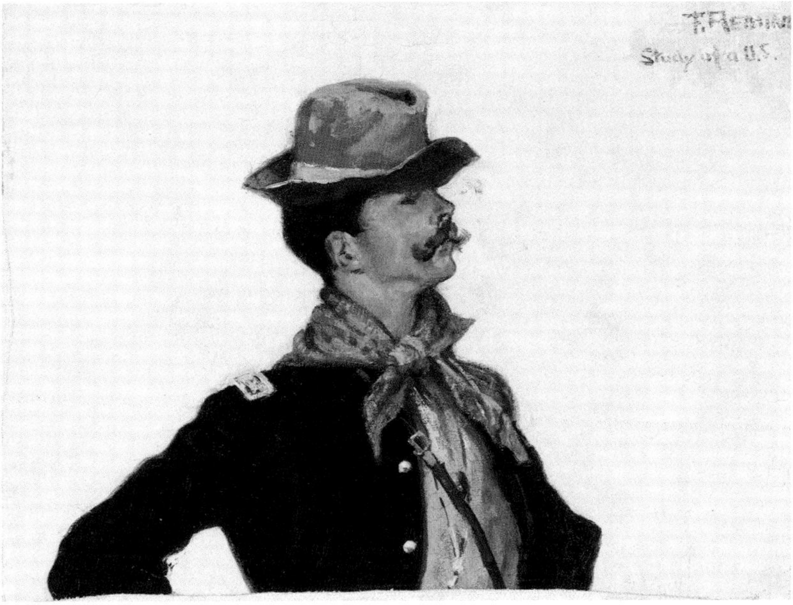

In a September 1, 1890, letter Remington wrote: "Your portrait 'by ME' has the place of honor in our large entrance hall." Here he referred to *Lieutenant Powhatan H. Clarke, Tenth Cavalry* Alternate: *Lt. Powhatan H. Clarke* CR# 01033 Dimensions: 10 1/4 × 13" Date: ca. 1890 Medium: oil on canvas. Courtesy Frederic Remington Art Museum, Ogdensburg, New York. Regrettably fire consumed much of the full-length view of Clarke as Remington envisioned him.

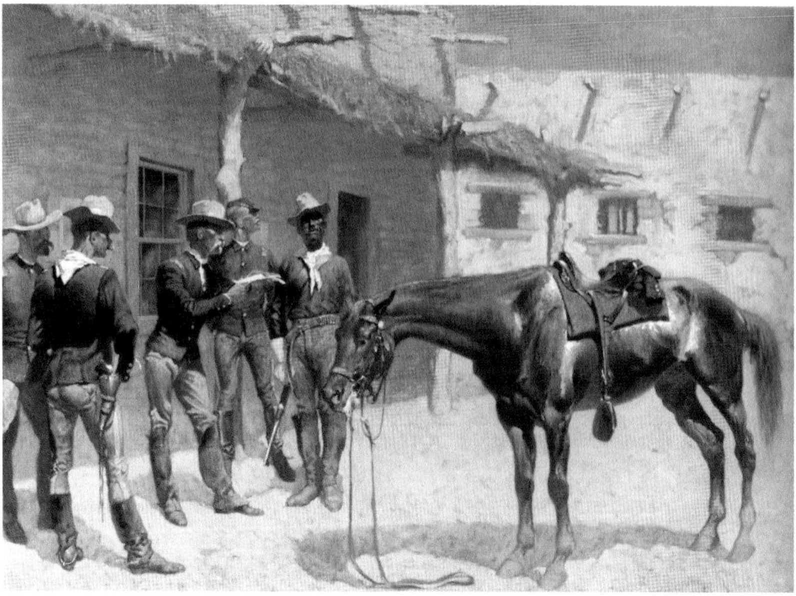

In the1890 *Arrival of the Courier* Alternate Title: *Arrival of a Courier—Arizona Territory* CR# 01139 Dimensions: 36 × 48" Date: 1890 Medium: oil on canvas, Remington included Clarke with his civilian style holster rig and signature handlebar mustache in evidence. The image appeared as a wood engraving in *Century Magazine* (March 1891), p. 646. The R.W. Norton Art Gallery, Shreveport, Louisiana.

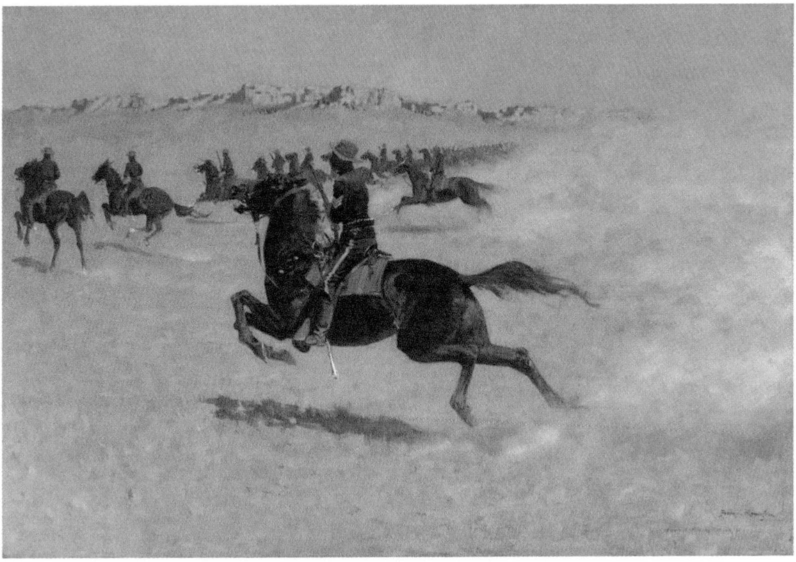

The Pursuit CR# 02137 Dimensions: 27 1/4 × 40" Date: ca. 1896 Medium: oil on canvas. Virginia Museum of Fine Arts, Richmond. Gift of the Estate of Sally D. Eddy. Remington used this image in *Harper's Monthly* (April 1898), p. 733.

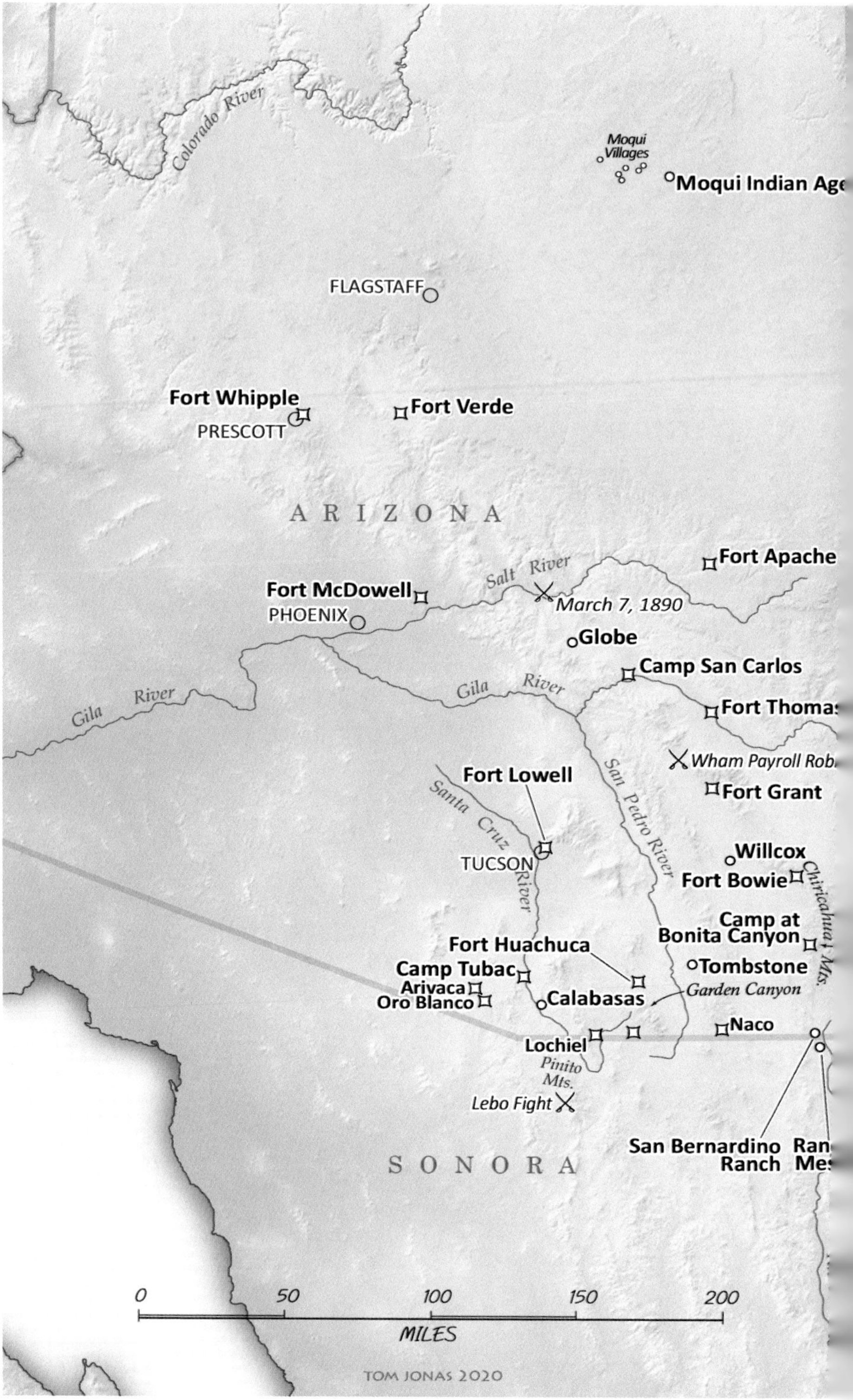

Colorado River
Moqui Villages
Moqui Indian Age
FLAGSTAFF
Fort Whipple
PRESCOTT
Fort Verde
A R I Z O N A
Fort Apache
Salt River
Fort McDowell
PHOENIX
March 7, 1890
Globe
Camp San Carlos
Gila River
Gila River
Fort Thomas
Wham Payroll Rob
Fort Grant
Fort Lowell
Santa Cruz River
San Pedro River
TUCSON
Willcox
Fort Bowie
Chiricahua Mts.
Camp at Bonita Canyon
Fort Huachuca
Tombstone
Camp Tubac
Arivaca
Oro Blanco
Calabasas
Garden Canyon
Naco
Lochiel
Pinito Mts.
Lebo Fight
San Bernardino Ranch
Ran Mes
S O N O R A
0
50
100
150
200
MILES
TOM JONAS 2020

BUFFALO SOLDIERS ON THE BORDER

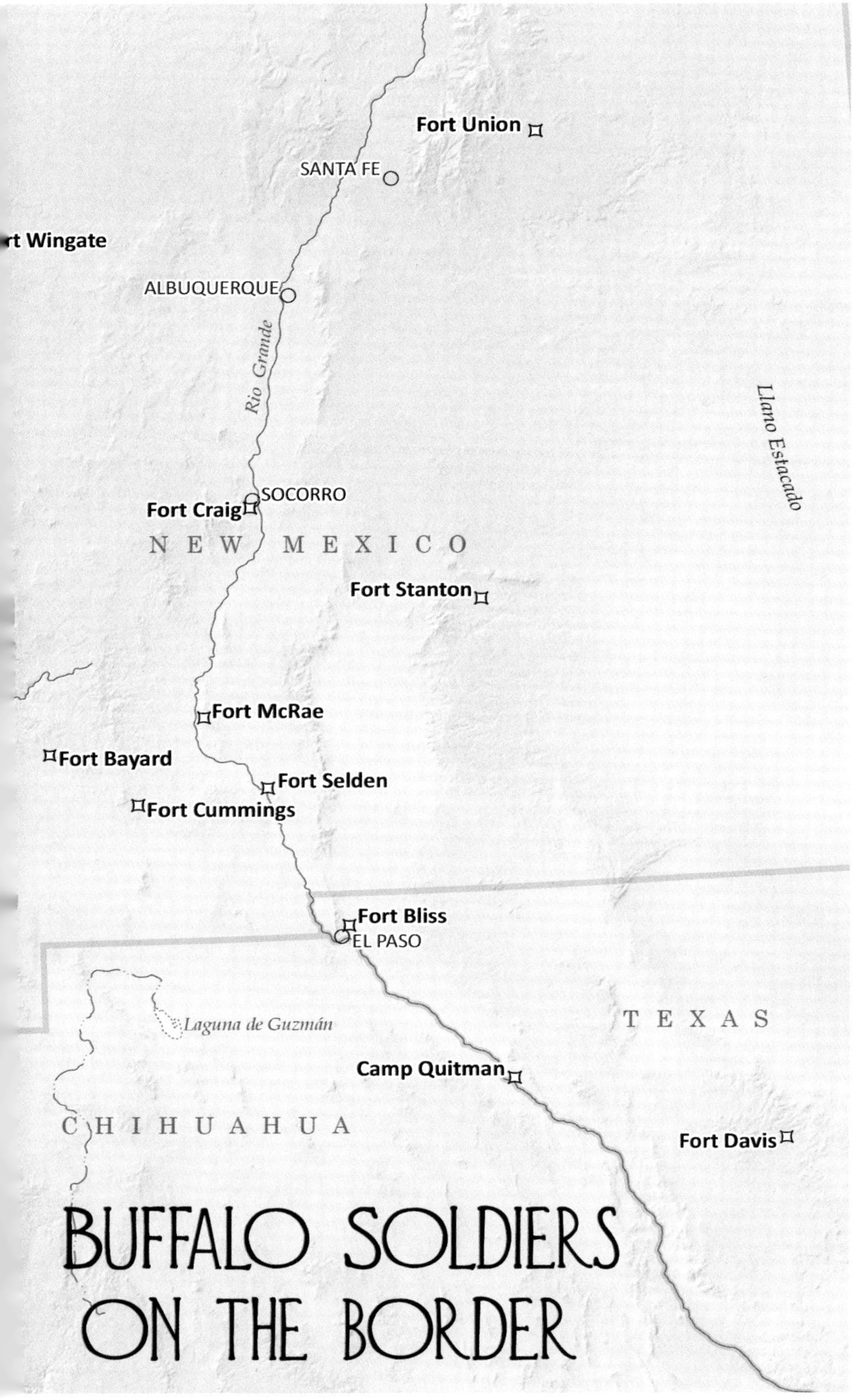

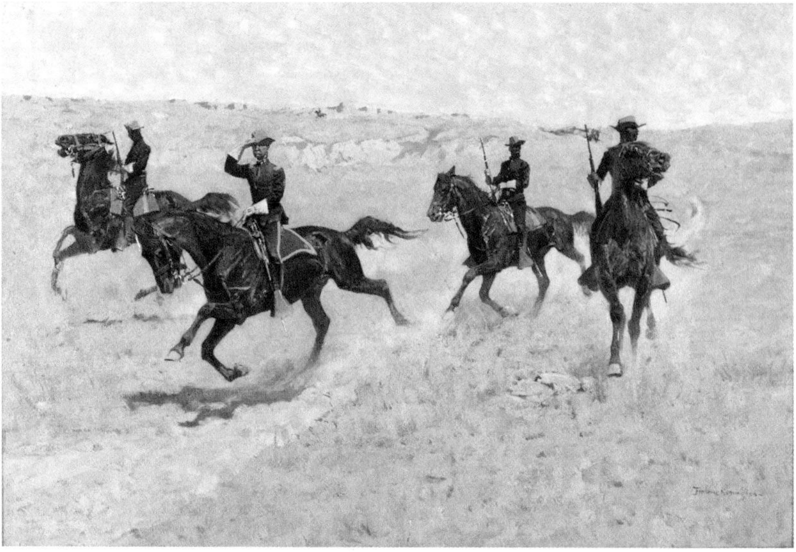

The Advance: General Nelson A. Miles and the Ninth Cavalry on Scout Patrol Dimensions: 27-1/4 × 40-1/8" Date: ca. 1898 Medium: oil on canvas. Despite the title, the officer is not Miles. In fact, the central figure is John Morrison Hamilton, a cavalry officer as indicated by the light blue trousers with yellow leg stripes. Hamilton, like Clarke, had served as Remington's host when the artist stayed with him at Fort Robinson, Nebraska. Years later, on July 1, 1898, Lieutenant Colonel Hamilton was killed at the Battle of San Juan Hill. Image Courtesy of the Desert Caballeros Western Museum, Wickenburg, Arizona. Museum Purchase. Photo © Terrence Moore.

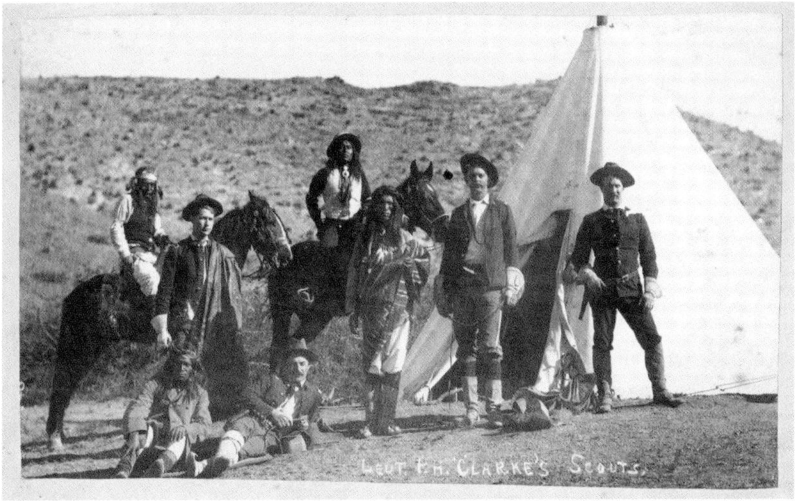

When three of his fellow second lieutenants from the Tenth U.S. Cavalry visited Clarke at Fort Bowie, he assembled them on a hillside next to an army-issue Sibley tent along with three of his unidentified Indian scouts. They are from **left to right**: Melvin W. Rowell; William E. Shipp (on ground); Powhatan H. Clarke; and William H. Smith. Courtesy Buffalo Bill Center of the West, Cody, Wyoming; McCracken Research Library; MS 410 Thomas P. Cuffe Collection, P.410.017.

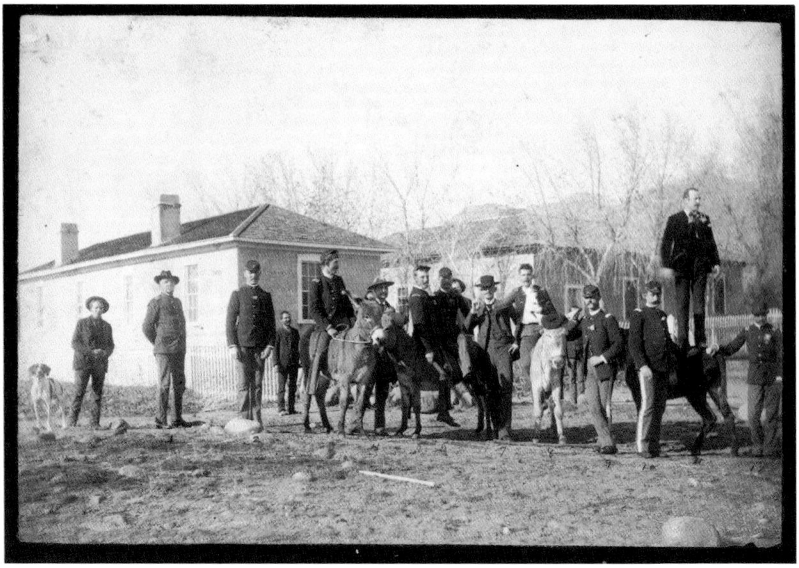

Enjoying the holidays at Fort Grant, brother officers, local civilians, burros, and "Don" Kennedy, a short-haired Pointer, mug for the camera. They are **from left to right**: 1-Captain Joseph Kelley (Tenth U.S. Cavalry); 2-Second Lieutenant Francis J. Koester; 3-Second Lieutenant James Hughes (Tenth U.S. Cavalry); 4-(?) Hershburg from St. Louis; 5-Second Lieutenant William Shipp (Tenth U.S. Cavalry); 6-Second Lieutenant Alexander Dade (Thirteenth U.S. Infantry); 7-Second Lieutenant Robert Paxton (Tenth U.S. Cavalry); 8-Second Lieutenant Powhatan Clarke (Tenth U.S. Cavalry); 9-Second Lieutenant John Little (Twenty-fourth U.S. Infantry); 10-Second Lieutenant Charles E. Tayman, (Twenty-fourth U.S. Infantry); 11-Post Trader Store Clerk Mr. Sheen; 12-First Lieutenant Robert Read (Tenth U.S. Cavalry). Special Collections, University of Arizona Library, Tucson.

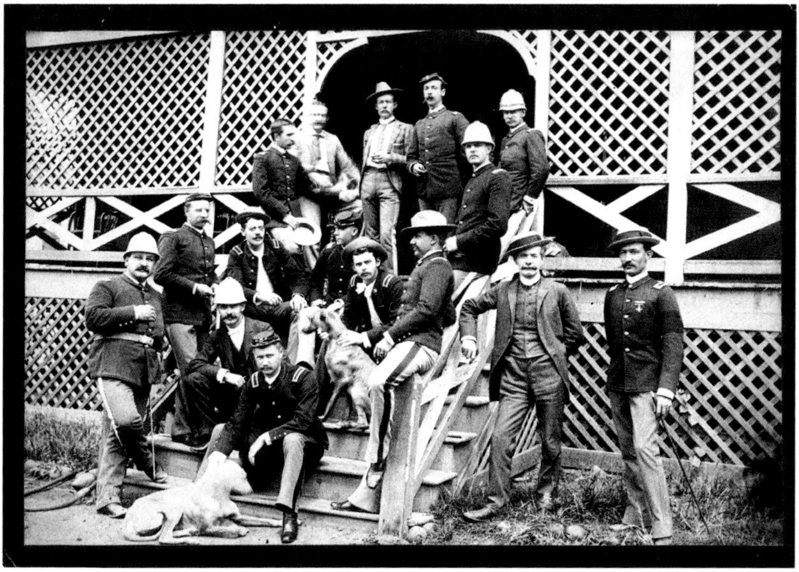

On August 23, 1888, at Fort Grant, Second Lieutenant John Bacon McDonald's marriage to Kate Murphy brought together many of the garrison residents. They are **front row from left to right**: standing in his summer helmet—First Lieutenant William H.W. James (Twenty-fourth U.S. Infantry); Dr. Richard Washington Johnson; Second Lieutenant Alexander L. Dade (Thirteenth U.S. Infantry); seated on hand rail—Second Lieutenant Letcher Hardeman (Fourth U.S. Cavalry); elbow on hand rail—Post Trader John H. Norton; with walking stick—First Lieutenant Robert D. Read, Jr. (Tenth U.S. Cavalry). **second row left to right**: standing-Second Lieutenant Carter P. Johnson (Tenth U.S. Cavalry); Second Lieutenant James B. Hughes (Tenth U.S. Cavalry); Second Lieutenant Withtrop S. Wood (Tenth U.S. Cavalry); Second Lieutenant Powhatan Clarke. **back row left to right**: First Lieutenant John B. McDonald; Post Trader Store Clerk Sheen; First Lieutenant James W. Watson (Tenth U.S. Cavalry); First Lieutenant Leighton Finley (Tenth U.S. Cavalry); Second Lieutenant Henry C. Keene, Jr. (Tenth U.S. Cavalry); and First Lieutenant Levi P. Hunt (Tenth U.S. Cavalry and the bride's brother-in-law). Special Collections, University of Arizona Library, Tucson.

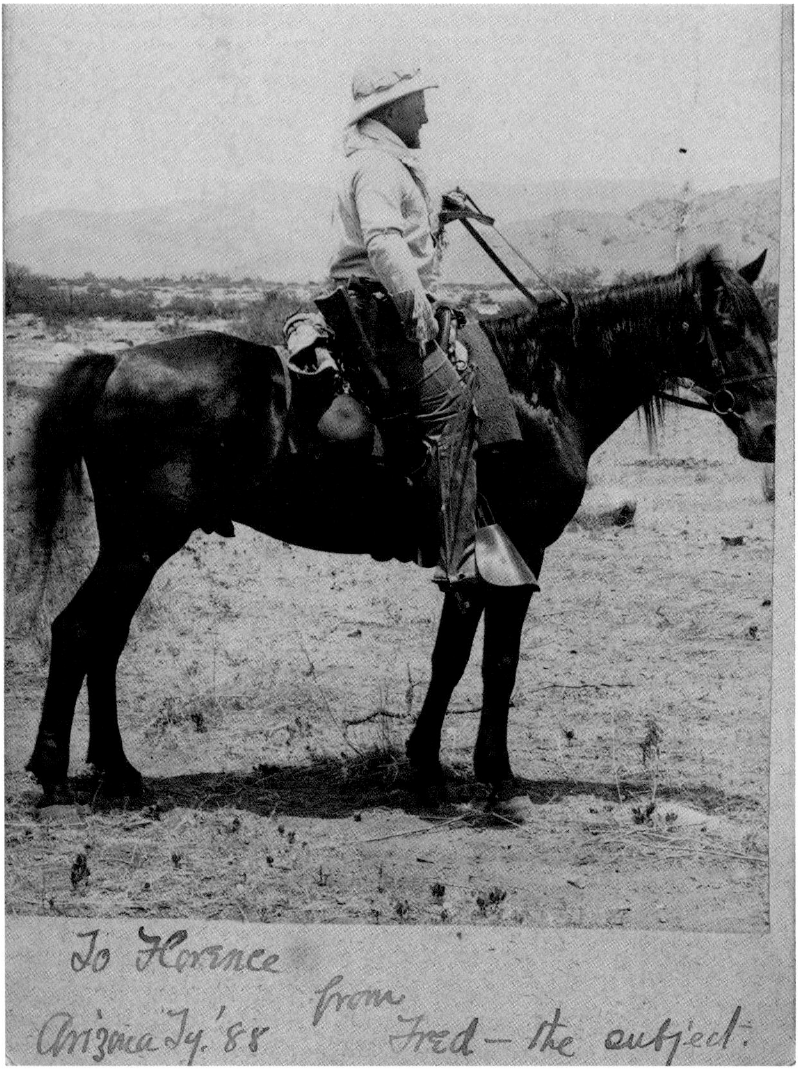

In 1888, during his second trip to Arizona, Remington rode a borrowed U.S. cavalry mount with fully loaded government-issue McClellan saddle. He appeared more like a game hunter on African safari than the want-to-be cowboy persona he adopted for his earlier foray in the territory during 1886. FRAM 1918.76.71.2 Courtesy Frederic Remington Art Museum, Ogdensburg, New York.

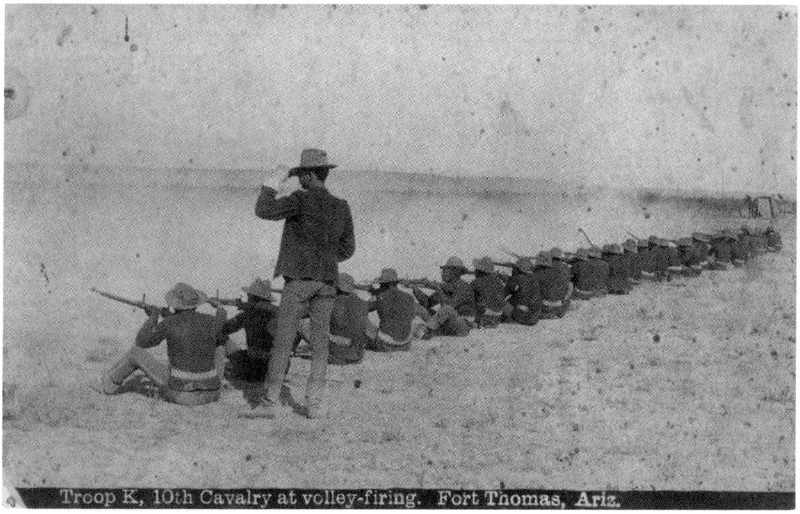

Remington turned at least four photographs, including this one of Fort Thomas's firing range with Clarke at the far left, into a montage published in *Harper's Weekly*. Note the pin holes on the left which are seen in some of his illustrations. Evidently the artist tacked the originals up to copy them while at his easel. Author's Collection.

Chapter 6

"Regular Army Oh!"

As 1887 opened, years of conflict drew to a close in Arizona. Geronimo and scores of other Apaches languished in far-away Florida as prisoners of war. After Remington returned to his home in the East, he built on his success in the Southwest, producing a string of illustrations that enhanced his reputation even as he settled into domestic life. Conversely, lonely bachelor Clarke remained on the frontier desperate to escape to Baltimore, France, or nearly anywhere to avoid the doldrums of Fort Grant.

Clarke's homeward-bound letters reflected the daily sameness of recurring administrative garrison routine. These mundane matters sharply contrasted with his previous excitement of campaigning. For the next several years Clarke's life generally consisted of repetitive post functions governed by bugle calls, as a contemporary newspaper account explained.[1] The military day commenced when *Reveille* sounded "at or near sunrise," the exact time varying somewhat at different posts, through "Taps or lights out" at the end of the official day.

Additionally, three reliefs drawn from the main body of troops each headed by a corporal "and one sergeant of the guard" served "two hours on one post and four hours off, during the tour of twenty-four hours" as an unvarying routine. An officer of the guard, under the authority of the officer of the day, both functions rotating among the lieutenants of the garrison as Clarke often did, instructed each sentinel. Supposedly: "Guard duty is like the reading of the Koran, requiring strict adherence to the rigid rules and requirements."

Added to these martial evolutions, lieutenants typically "had other obligations," including serving as signal officer, oversight of the commissary, ordnance, quartermaster and range functions, post engineer assignments, and depending on circumstances, serving as the post or regimental adjutant, the former duty having been one Clarke temporarily performed after his arrival to Fort Grant.[2]

Clarke's mid-January 1887 account to his mother illustrated some of the regimen that befell U.S. Army lieutenants of the late Victorian era regardless of where they were stationed.[3] As before, Clarke took up the recurring theme of pencil pushing related to commissary and ordnance matters. Even though Clarke found his daily duties at Fort Grant uninspiring, at least the weather could "not be beat." During the day he left his windows open, the scent of geraniums and lilies wafting on "the open air." Although Arizona contrasted sharply with the bitter cold of West Point winters, the downside was that the fort's location at a higher altitude left Clarke "out of breath during the shortest exercise and there is something in the atmosphere that makes one restless." Then, too, it may be Clarke had developed a new excuse for not applying himself to studies. He blamed the "rare atmosphere" for making it impossible to concentrate!

Nevertheless, Clarke continued half-heartedly to plow through military law texts given that like all junior officers he regularly served at courts martial.[4] Clarke also struggled "again with telegraphy" by which he meant the code used for the heliograph system that was so dear to General Miles. Clarke "had been very successful last April" in mastering the flashes that were equivalent to dots and dashes of the telegraph, but an interruption caused "by being sent to the 'Mowry Mine'" required him to relearn the process.

He then dropped a tantalizing reference to the arrival of a photographer on post who charged ten dollars for a dozen images. Ever pleading poverty, Clarke indicated he had not "gone head over heels in 5 × 8's" limiting himself "to a few very good views of Fort Bowie, a cavalry troop enroute and a

Chinaman's picture," unfortunately only one of which survived: the picture of a mounted patrol on the move.

Clarke explained why he purchased the portrait of the "Chinaman," which seemed an unusual acquisition. It seemed he befriended the subject of the photo, a waiter who served at the officers' mess. This unnamed man shared "most wonderful things of his country generally winding up by showing me how insignificant all other countries are in comparison but then he gives me a silk handkerchief and a box of cigars, $1.00 a hundred for Xmas...." Once more, it appears that Clarke learned another lesson about the polyglot nature of Arizona and developed a world view not gained at the Military Academy.

By the end of January, Clarke repeated his impression about the fine weather which reminded him of May back home in Maryland.[5] In contrast to the pleasant temperature, this and presumably other Sundays hung heavy. After the morning inspection of the troops, "the usual routine" ensued which Clarke related led to "a barren sort of day as we are deprived of our mail." A few sentences about the delightful reprieve letters from family and friends brought followed with circling back to Arizona where "the cold, sleet and snow" his parents were experiencing at that time of year did not exist. Clarke confessed he would "regret someday to leave" adding a poetic picture of the scene from the fort's parade ground that afforded him a view of "the tops of mountains nearly a hundred miles away in Old Mexico, sometimes standing out in the mirage like islands in the sea, at other times assuming fantastic shapes."

Other news contained a rumor about two posts in the northern part of the territory being considered for closure in the wake of Geronimo's removal. If the downsizing proved true, that might mean a potential increase in Fort Grant's complement, a "most welcome" prospect in that Clarke could be joined by more fellow junior officers. While not imminent, "as early as 1873 it had been discussed that certain" Arizona posts should be closed. Economic, military, and political factors forestalled this course of action. With the end of the Apache Wars and the expansion of the railroads, it was no longer necessary to keep small groups of soldiers in forts scattered about the territory.[6] Eventually, closure of a number of installations began in the 1890s and continued into the early twentieth century.[7]

Even with anticipated additional comrades, Clarke, as post commissary officer, still faced spending his time "straightening out the meat bills of the Troops, and arranging a new scheme of issue, also blowing up the contractor for tough beef" sold as rations for the garrison. All of these details occupied his Sunday. In a self-deprecating footnote, he professed to be very satisfied about being so " 'important' in this world; so far, however, I have not been important enough I fear."

Clarke had come to appreciate Miles, who had packed up Department of Arizona headquarters for Los Angeles, a move the lieutenant hoped foreshadowed other forthcoming beneficial changes. Moreover, retirements loomed for some brigadier generals. With their departure, Clarke shared that "heaven only knows we hope (some of us) that old Grierson and his whole outfit may be promoted."[8] Clarke's comments continued to reflect the factionalism and charges of preferentialism in Grierson's Tenth Cavalry.

Indeed, as one Grierson biographer contended, the colonel's "lax and familiar method of command" and his focus on personal ranching interests led to him turning over "much of the day-to-day administration of the regiment and post to a small group of favorites" followed by a power struggle within the unit.[9] Bigelow dramatically summed up this state of affairs as "a contest for supremacy, if not the existence of the regiment, between the good element and the bad and that the two elements are pretty evenly matched."[10]

Clearly Clarke saw himself in the former camp, along with Bigelow, Hughes, and others in the anti-Grierson clique. As such, Clarke expressed contentment with his lot. Further, he did not foresee any renewed hostilities with the Apaches. He ended with a cautionary remark: "we will not be able to determine what sort of military year we are going to have until about April."

For now, Clarke enjoyed the "beautiful winter weather" which permitted him to play "a lively game of tennis" as he shared in a February 3 note to his mother.[11] In response to his mother's suggestion that he pursue a transfer, he admitted that he knew of "cases when as high as $5,000 have been paid for the privilege" of swapping with an officer of equal rank in another unit, an exorbitant amount, which for this and other reasons meant the practice generally fell from favor by the 1880s.[12] Clarke flatly indicated that he would not pursue this path. Evincing a positive attitude, he thought "everything will come out right in the end." In part, his optimism stemmed from acknowledging that Miles "has always been very kind to me, and I shall be grateful to him always for my Saumur scheme."

Clarke continued. Grierson let it be known that John Bigelow had requested a place on Miles's staff, which he did not believe. If true, Captain Lebo would counter this as he wanted Bigelow to return after a considerable absence from "his beloved troop." Both Lebo and Clarke missed Bigelow, whom they found "such a sociable fellow." Plus, Clarke had an additional reason to see Bigelow rejoin Troop K—an increased possibility of gaining his own leave of absence, or reinvigorating his overseas plans.

Once more, Clarke was "getting anxious about that war in Europe," which he "would be sorry to miss." Playing the same old tune, he enjoined his mother to cultivate a few "acquaintances in Washington" to assist with his proposal. Clarke added that with recent Congressional legislation relative to U.S. fishing rights, a "row with Canada" might erupt that could bring war between England and the United States. Despite saber rattling, by February 1888, the Bayard-Chamberlain Treaty settled the issue peacefully.[13]

On the home front, Clarke turned to widespread strikes and labor unrest. Starting in March of 1886, protests against the railroads under the banner of the Knights of Labor rippled across the nation. By that May, Chicago police set upon a peaceful demonstration in the Hay Market. Violence erupted with national concerns about anarchists bent on toppling the government prompting civilians and military alike, Clarke among them, to consider the use of martial force.[14] Clarke indicated "that sooner or later Uncle Sam will have to call on his little army to keep things quiet and I do not think it will be very long before he will."

On the other hand, "Poor Lo" (a Victorian-era play on words of Alexander Pope's poem *An Essay on Man*, 1733–34) although "very quiet this year," deprived "the picture papers" illustrated by his new acquaintance Remington and others of "any subjects in the Far West." All Clarke asked was enough of a lull "to let the War Department keep up its scheme of concentration of troops in a few posts, and that the small posts will be abandoned as they are an abomination and a drawback to discipline, esprit de corps and in fact to everything military. I hope to see the day when all our regiments will be stationed in 'regimental' posts or even posts of two regiments." Clarke jumped ahead of actual practice, bespeaking of his growing comprehension of his military profession.

For generations, small scattered posts edged westward, sometimes in the vanguard of expansion. One- and two-company posts remained the norm until the time when it seemed logical to concentrate numerous smaller installations based on factors such as "an expanded rail system" that permitted movement of "troops quickly to troubled spot." By the mid-1890s the army had achieved this consolidation with its troops now "deployed more or less equally around the country on the basis of regional rather than operational considerations."[15]

Clarke also continued to foresee a war on the Continent, albeit proving premature in his predictions. On March 3, from "distant Arizona," Clarke followed European news through periodicals such as *The Herald* from New York, Chicago's *Inter Ocean*, and even *Punch* from England. all available at the fort's library.[16] He yet worried that the "inevitable war" would start before he could "get off to see it." He fancifully expressed: "I would like to turn soldier of fortune and try my chances with the French, and I am fully convinced that they will win in the struggle though it will be a terrible thing." For the moment, he contended Otto von Bismarck and the Pope temporarily would hold matters in check. Several years later, he would change his tune about the French military prowess.

At this time, personal matters were foremost. Clarke expected the Bigelows, which delighted him as he was beginning to think Troop K's first lieutenant was a myth. At least he enjoyed a brief visit with James Hughes, prompting him to relate how much happier he would be if he and his West Point classmate could serve together. Indeed, pondering as if he were a senior officer of long service, if "a few more of our youngsters could be together," military life would be ideal. Clarke continued that the Tenth Cavalry had "the nicest 2d lieutenants I have met anywhere." Displaying pride in the profession of arms "and particularly pride in his regiment" were key traits for an officer, but alas Clarke lamented: "Our men are made laborers and officers prefer to excel on paper rather than the field," which was enough "to knock the Esprit-de Corps" out of anyone who took his role in uniform seriously.

He finished: "I frequently get letters from my artist friend Mr. Remington," a portent of things to come. Unfortunately, none of the correspondence from this period has survived.[17]

Ten days later, Clarke conveyed more welcome news.[18] Approval for two months' leave arrived! With both Lebo and Bigelow away, he could not dash off immediately because as a sign of Clarke's somewhat increased sense of responsibility and professionalism, he concluded this "would throw my troop on someone else's hands in addition to the dropping of staff duties which I am performing." Additionally, he expressed some concern about "a light war cloud over the Indian reserve" but concluded it "would not amount to much." If it did, however, he "could not think of leaving and I feel I would like to ride with 'K' troop over the mesas again even though in as unsatisfactory pursuit as we had last year."

Despite the mopping up efforts of the previous year, violent death remained a very real possibility. The murder of fresh-from-West Point Second Lieutenant Stewart Mott (Class of 1886) offered a case in point. Like Clarke and Hughes, Mott graduated near the bottom of his class. He entered the Tenth U.S. Cavalry, reporting to the regiment in October 1886. Clarke portrayed Mott as "full of life and hope; devoted to his calling and anxious to make a name among his companions."

Without experience, Mott assumed an assignment at San Carlos Reservation assisting the acting agent in distributing farm lands on the Upper Gila. Clarke indicated Mott "was doing splendidly and was liked by the tribe…."[19] Unfortunately, one of the so-called Tonto Apaches became "very insolent and threatening," prompting Mott to incarcerate the man in the guardhouse. Two of the jailed man's sons went to the camp and "sneaked up to the tent" with Mott inside. "Without a word of warning" they opened fire mortally, wounding the unsuspecting lieutenant. Clarke mourned Mott, who died the next day and was buried at Fort Thomas. Clarke recounted that he knew Cadet Mott for many years and the stricken shavetail had been one of his friends at the Military Academy. He thought Mott was "one of the finest men I have known to leave West Point."

Clarke accepted Mott's death with difficulty. It was surreal to him. He indicated: "it is not the first or second situation of just such as assassination and I doubt if ever his murderers will be punished." In his annual report Miles added: "Thus an intelligent young officer gave up his life while in the performance of duty, endeavoring to benefit and guide wild Indians to peaceful pursuits."[20]

Then, as Clarke predicted, several months passed before he could set out on leave. After much cajoling, he finally secured time away, mainly based on medical reasons. Clarke successfully argued that none of the local army physicians possessed the requisite skills to perform the necessary surgery related to his urethra, a condition that in part may have been due to a sexually transmitted disease contracted during his cadet days.[21]

With leave obtained, toward the end of May, Clarke reached New York where he consulted a physician who recommended an internal urethrectomy to correct a urethral stricture.[22] This pricey procedure ran upwards of $500, not a mean sum based on Clarke's pay as a lieutenant. Regardless of the cost, which the military would not bear because Clarke insisted on engaging a private physician rather than army doctor, he underwent surgery.

By early June, Clarke remained in hospital in New York. He hoped to head home soon.[23] Clarke urged his father to help him prolong his stay in the East. He candidly admitted: "I dread going back to Arizona in my present condition." The desperate son asked his father to entreat the secretary of war, making the case that after a recent operation the lieutenant, who still could not get out of bed, would be unfit for duty for a considerable time.[24] Indeed, Clarke remained incapacitated for weeks, which precluded an immediate visit to his family in Baltimore.[25]

While recuperating, he received an invitation from Remington to "come up to New York and visit me for a day or so at least – I want to see you before you go back. Does this reach you as the Irishman said? – write Yours Frederic R." Always looking for an opportunity, Remington's post script indicated that the artist wanted Clarke to take his personal camera back from New York, presumably to snap pictures of interesting subject matter that he could convert into marketable artwork.[26] Remington had come to rely on this "memory aid" to facilitate his rapid renderings as the prolific artist produced more and more illustrations. Clarke evidently would not take up Remington on his hospitality, but their periodic correspondence increased with the passage of time.

In fact, their communications revived after Clarke's sick leave (which extended from April 19, 1887, through October 21 of that year, lasting months rather than weeks as commonly would be the case today).[27] With his recovery complete, and visits with family and friends remaining as pleasant memories, Clarke headed to Arizona via St. Louis.[28] As before, while there, Aunt Mary spoiled him.

He no doubt reluctantly ended his respite, traveling through El Paso where he briefly linked up with friends from the Sixteenth U.S. Infantry as he rode the rails to Fort Grant. To pass the time, he read *Ben Hur*. The novel engrossed him so much that he completed it before reaching Willcox. There he transferred to an army ambulance, in reality a light multi-purpose conveyance not unlike the type of stagecoach referred to as a "mud wagon."

As the now familiar countryside rolled by, Clarke "picked out the old landmarks" prompting him to recall "the old Geronimo days." Back at Fort Grant, he discovered Lebo was ill, yet the captain refused to take sick leave until one of his subordinates was on hand to relieve him. Clarke proclaimed his commander was "the pluckiest man I have ever seen."

With welcomes complete, Clarke immediately fell into his military life starting out the first morning in garrison as officer of the day, followed by serving as the recorder for a board of survey, and on the target practice. Clarke reported he was "back in the traces now and feel like going to work with a will." Of course, he would have liked "to have stayed East all winter," adding "I like the service even more than ever and cannot be more impressed with my good fortune in having such a good berth."

A few days after Clarke wrote his father, he jotted brief lines to his mother.[29] He revealed little of consequence except sporting a "black and blue" shoulder from his time at the firing range with the Springfield so-called "Trapdoor" issue .45 caliber carbine that kicked like an army mule. Clarke said Captain Lebo had encouraged him to qualify so it was "worth the pain and trouble" to please the old man who finally received permission to take sick leave.

Clarke shared that he had two visitors, both officers from the Tenth U.S. Infantry, who were on their way to San Carlos, which he described at one point as "the dreariest place of exile on this continent, and where no officer or man should be allowed to remain longer than six months. White, hot, arid, treeless, restless, desolate, swept for hours each day by clouds of parking dust," or the fine powdered, ever present Arizona soil that covered and remained over everyone and everything.[30] Little wonder that the pair of infantry officers made the "air blue" with complaints about having no housing at their new post, which was located one hundred miles from the railroad, making life difficult for the one who had a wife while the other, who was engaged, had no place for his bride. The plight of these officers was typical. At least Clarke fared better, living in his comfortable bachelor accommodations at Fort Grant. He then promised to "write a respectable letter as soon as I have time."

This he did at the end of October. By that time Clarke had ridden into the nearby Graham Mountains.[31] Just an hour before setting out for this destination, his trunks arrived having been shipped back from his leave. Previously, he made do with limited personal belongings for over a week. Even so, he spruced up his quarters with curtains and a grizzly bear skin, although he expected his lamps and pictures would arrive with the next replacement troops from Jefferson Barracks in St. Louis.[32]

Taking up the subject of target practice once more, with some effort he managed to earn his annual qualification at the range. Passing this hurdle, Clarke happily recalled "the hard rides I have made with old 'K' troop and it is refreshing to hear the troopers African but musical laugh so glad even they to get out of the tedious garrison with its guard duty so tiresome and guard house so threatening, and above all the perpetual, unmilitary work our men have so much to do, poor fellows I felt sorry for them." Displaying empathy for his soldiers, he expressed his anger "when I see the 'fatigue detail' forming every blessed day, to dig and build as men of no other army have to do and which our rich Republic could so easily do for them." While Clarke's protestation about manual labor being unique to the United States Army did not ring true, the use of enlisted men for construction of buildings at forts and other similar work details rankled many soldiers who had not signed on to perform construction. Indeed, one of the major reasons cited for desertions, a persisting problem for the post-Civil War U.S. Army, stemmed from " 'the excess of manual labor.' "[33]

Clarke's expression of genuine sympathy for his troopers demonstrated respect gained from years of service with his men. In this, he mirrored an anonymous officer who similarly expressed appreciation for black troops in a letter in the *Army and Navy Journa.*[34] The unidentified writer acknowledged: "I think the world of the men of my company. When I look at them I do not see black faces, I see only something beyond. For the comfort and pleasant life of the officer on the frontier they are far ahead of white troops. They are more like a lot of devoted servants and retainers. Faithful and trustworthy in every respect, and brave and gallant."

Clarke possibly read this mixed message statement, which while it praised black troops, simultaneously betrayed a degree of condescension. Regardless, it was apparent Clarke had linked his star to the Tenth and its enlisted personnel as implied in the remainder of his October 31 letter to his mother. He evidenced enthusiasm as he regaled her with a tale about "a bright moonlight ride along the foothills, then turned into the mountains for a hard climb coming down we went off the trail." When they could go no farther, they camped.

Clarke's men, along with Carter Johnson's contingent, linked up for a proposed maneuver in which they were to attempt interception of twenty troopers from the Fourth U.S. Cavalry under Captain Theodore Wint, a former enlisted man like Carter Johnson, who obtained a commission. Wint's force was to make its way from Fort Apache to Fort Huachuca without being interdicted by opponents from Forts Grant and Thomas.

The patrols from the Tenth were to catch Wint as part of war games Miles inaugurated that year with troops of cavalry alternating "as 'raiders' and 'pursuers.'"[35] The exercise, Clarke remarked, caused little anxiety as unlike real campaigning there was no fear of ambush. Clarke admitted he would not be pleased to be given "the slip as I fear we will as the men will not be on the alert to such an extent that they would obtain in an Apache chase."

Whatever the outing's shortcomings, Clarke remarked how pleasant his surroundings were. After eating "a delightful dinner of bacon and beans with 'ten pounds to the foot' of soldier's biscuit" he inspected the pickets, played some cards, and then turned in for the night, which in contrast to the "warm and balmy days" were "very cold and even in my blankets and heavy canvas suit … the cold succeeds in creeping in to me."

Clarke was in his element. He closed: "I am not ready to leave the cavalry yet by a good deal, one feels so strong, and hearty." After scanning for sign of Wint with his field glasses, he scribbled a few more lines to end his note in time to send it off with a courier.

This mock foray had the added benefit of bringing Clarke to Fort Thomas to obtain supplies. As he informed his father, the stopover allowed a quick visit with Hughes and two other brother officers.[36] Much to his chagrin Hughes and he "did not get through a tenth of what we had to say." Clarke's reunion came to an end because he had to return to the cat and mouse game against Wint. Clarke left the comforts of the fort for a camp in the "cold dusty air" of the Gila Valley, which he contended was "a most vile region—the days are hot and the nights bitterly cold near the river so that I did not catch much sleep and the next day. I started for Bear Springs where I camped and drank gypsum water and slept in the alkali dust."[37]

The inconvenience did not last long. With the chase concluded, Clarke put away his pipe, tobacco, and other elements of his kit and returned to garrison for "a good warm bath" and sleep "on a good spring bed with slats" rather than the hard, frozen ground.

He found more than creature comforts awaiting him at Fort Grant. On November 12, he revealed the recent receipt of a check as a small payment for "putting my signature in *Harper's Weekly*."[38] He had his new friend from New York to thank for this windfall. Clarke admitted: "I do owe a great deal to Remington." He asked his mother to send Remington a business card from an army ordnance officer of some note, whom Clarke recently met "and also to thank him for the portrait" the subject of which remains unknown.

He went on to mention the ancient Indian ruins he erroneously ascribed to the Aztecs situated in a valley with its "brilliant green cutting sharply, against the reddish 'mesas'" and thought of "the waves that have passed over this half desert country even during the few centuries we have known it." The landscape conjured up images of the "Spaniard … steel clad dons with their long lance and well mounted arquebusers [*sic*] glittering in their inlaid armor … poor chaps it was a long way off to Castile and Leon." Clarke whimsically speculated, "what a meeting it would be if one of those old cavalcades were to be recalled to life in some narrow gorge face to face with my dark Ethiopians. I fear even my Catholicity [Catholic faith which he had in common with the Spanish] would not save us unless our carbines could be brought into quick action against their cuirasses."

In equally colorful prose, Clarke described the vaquero at the "full gallop in their 'rodeo' with his long rope swinging gracefully over the tall peaked hat and the light sparkling gaily on the inlaid bit & huge jingling spurs." One can only wonder what Remington might have created from such vibrant verbal descriptions.

Still in a mood to share his thoughts, the next day Clarke sent another letter to his mother.[39] He delighted in a recent visit to Fort Thomas, spending a few days with Jim Hughes and attending "a most delightful hop, full dress, we danced until midnight and then had a jolly supper at Mrs. Keyes," whose children, as often was the case for officers in the West, were away at boarding school.[40]

The two newest second lieutenants posted to Fort Thomas, Herman Hall and Robert Paxton, both 1887 graduates of the U.S. Military Academy, were on hand prompting Clarke to appraise them as "very nice men and we are fortunate in getting them." Clarke postulated that after the pair from "old West Point" underwent "a few years hard work out here" they would become "very fast friends of us."

While newcomers entered the picture, the old veteran Lebo was about to exit temporarily for health reasons. His departure left Clarke in command of Troop K. Bigelow still had not returned to Arizona. Clarke admitted: "I do not know whether I am anxious to do it or not as there is a good deal of responsibility and I am lazy."

Following up on such uncharacteristic honesty, Clarke indicated how as a commander "the weight of a duty which places the happiness of 60 men in his hands, the watching of the non-commissioned officers, and the handling of the black sheep (very black in this case) requires patience and perseverance, two qualities which I barely possess in the least." In a few words, Clarke bluntly acknowledged many of his weaknesses, revealing a continued race consciousness, albeit one that had been softened from earlier more prejudicial views.

Clarke still cherished the carefree existence of a bachelor subaltern that allowed him to try out his "young hounds." To the action-oriented Clarke there was "no pleasure like that experienced when a fleet long eared jack rabbit springs from almost under one's horse's feet. It is beautiful to see him as he skims and bounds over the level prairie with two good greyhounds, their noses well forward and long ears close to their necks, neck and neck just a few feet behind him."

Such equestrian exertion took its toll, as Clarke remarked. His black horse "was lame from running, a nail in his foot." In the same sentence, Clarke noted his striker "poor Turner is still in hospital." This juxtaposition of mount and man servant may have been indicative of Clarke's equating both horse and horse soldier.

While inconvenienced for the moment, Clarke nonetheless could idle about a great deal, the typical state of affairs for frontier officers especially in peace time. Remington perceived this indolent quiet phase when he decided to draw on the relative quiet to employ Clarke as a source for more illustrations. After opening with advice that Clarke should be sure to "'qualify' [at the target range] – a soldier who cannot shoot in these days is worse than a 'cut' minister at a camp meeting"—he unabashedly gave Clarke an assignment.[41] He urged: "Say old top when you write me write sort of descriptive like – all that you see and do down there while it is stale matter to you [it] is of great interest to the undersigned – tell me what you do and what U.S. soldiers do these days – write any observations you may make or hear relative to Indians or Mexicans – who knows but you might inspire me to make an illustration for which I would get $75."

Anticipating a negative reply from his unpaid silent partner, Remington addressed what Clarke would gain from his efforts. The clever New Yorker allowed you "would not get anything out of that – I hear you say but then proceed with argument I have a clincher – you are a soldier and a soldier has nothing in the world to do in time of peace except make himself and others … happy."

To strengthen his hand, Remington played on their comradery. He asked: "do you remember that big straw mexican [*sic*] sombrero I wore when you last saw me – well that hangs here in my room – I often laugh when I think what an odd figure I must cut down there – I suppose you always remember me as a kind of quasi tramp and always will until your esthetic sense is appaled [*sic*] by view of my really beatic [*sic*] proportions clothed in the vestments allound [*sic*] to be proper in God's country."

If Remington's poor spelling did not offend Clarke, who suffered from the same malady, probably what followed did not rankle him either. Rarely concerned with his language, Remington blurted out in terms not uncommon for his time and class: "I know I can never disassociate you from 'niggers' and 'greasers' and a uniform gaudy but neat. But then I revert to my philosophy which says 'trust not to appearances' and do not doubt but my young indian [*sic*] chasing friend would grace the uniform of a Kings body guard." With that Remington rambled on a bit before placing the jumbled letter into its envelope.

Remington's next letter requested Clarke's Arizona address.[42] After that, he inquired: "How long before you will East again – I so much wanted to give you my 'Detective' [a relatively small camera] to take back with you – didn't know but you would like to try amateur photography and I might avail." In other words, the canny artist had hoped for a source of fresh images as models for new publishable artwork.

That plan thwarted, Remington desired another basis for his illustrations—objects. He collected items while in the West, continuing to amass more during his productive career indicative of his abiding concern for authenticity. He informed Clarke that he wanted the lieutenant to obtain "a buckskin Indian shirt without sleeves – big neck & short skirt – if you got to Tucson look up one at that dealer in Indian curios store – If you find me such a one send it on I will pay you by return mail."

With the order placed, Remington turned to politics and a few other topics in his usual stream of consciousness manner. As a Republican, Remington worried that his party might not nominate James G. Blaine as their presidential candidate, who had lost the election of 1884 to the Democratic party's standard bearer, Grover Cleveland.[43] If the Democrats nominated the incumbent, a disgruntled Remington remarked: "I am for Mrs. Cleveland for President – Grover is no good – he wouldn't fight and if the govt. got into war – the first batch of detail would overwhelm the clerk President."

Remington assumed Southern Democrat Clarke "would quarrel on politics." He ventured that this son of a Confederate officer might join forces with Allen Christian Redwood, a fellow illustrator for New York-based periodicals with a special emphasis on capturing the life of his fellow "Johnny Rebs." Remington expected Redwood to return soon from Arizona on the train where he had been busy gathering material for his own art. Remington indicated Redwood, a Civil War veteran of Company C, 55th Virginian Infantry, was "a refreshing individual – perfectly odd – no nerves – very little of a crank and possessed of the logical mental quality on every thing except politics – in which he was ruined while young" presumably as a determined Confederate enlisted man who survived wounds at Chancellorsville and Gettysburg.[44] Remington implied that Clarke might have met Redwood while the artist was in the West expanding topics for his portfolio.

Jumping to another subject, the ethnocentric Remington related a conversation he recently had with "a young English squid" who had made "claims on the heritage of some hundreds of years of anglosaxon [*sic*] deeds and virtues" as if "I was not entitled to as much credit as he was." This was too much for race-conscious Remington. He lashed out: "there aint [*sic*] a drop of anything but English blood in my veins—pure Saxon at that—no Norman—bred on the soil and Every Remington that a herildric [*sic*] fiend can trace was a British soldier—and the only blot on an English record is that the ancestor of all American Remingtons deserted from the British army and settled on a farm in Vermont when that state was all woods.—since then I have had a direct paternal ancestor in every campaign that Uncle Sam ever undertook except the Mexican War...." Of course, the pontificating New Yorker neglected to mention that the warrior line ended with him. He never wore a uniform save as a drummer boy-mascot for his father's Grand Army post, and during his days in military school before entering Yale.

Digressing further, Remington mentioned that John Bigelow's older brother, who had provided the novice artist access to *Outing* Magazine, had "quit the literary venture—gone to Europe with his rich wife—thereby proving a well known axiom that a young fellow no matter how brainey [*sic*] with lots of money is a wart on the face of the Earth." The elder Bigelow's sabbatical from journalism did not last long. Throughout most of his long life, he remained active in the literary world. Indeed, Bigelow and Remington stayed in contact and even took a jaunt to Europe together in the early 1890s.

Bigelow's temporary hiatus did not dampen Remington's career climb. As an example, he recently met with Elizabeth Bacon Custer. She still wore her widow's black garb more than a decade after her husband's fall at Little Bighorn. Remington found her to be bright. He was illustrating her *Tenting on the Plains* that Charles Webster and Sons would publish that year.

Even as Remington conversed with this imposing matron in her New York apartment, he realized that the bachelor Clarke sought younger female companionship, correctly noting: "you I observe has a gallant appreciation for a pretty girl – I expect some of these dimpled beauties will give you a tierce thrust some day—and then—well we will see whether I get an invitation or not – but every young chap I know usually costs me $10." Remington laconically and somewhat prophetically concluded that he expected to see Clarke wed: "Before I have the pleasure of attending" his comrade's funeral, but once more correctly predicted the two of them would " 'brace a racket' before we wear angel plumage." He encouraged Clarke to stay in the army so they could share some more adventures, adding as a postscript with dogged determination: "Don't forget the indian [*sic*] shirt – you can get me some indian [*sic*] stuff easily I recon and d—me I know you will do it."

Clarke carried out his mission. Around the same time he packed off Remington's requested shirt, he mentioned the pending holidays to his father.[45] During early December, he rejoiced that "Perfection is always punctual and her letters cheer me up.?" Not only was this unnamed female correspondent in the picture, but "also a pretty sweet little friend of mine in St. Louis" was writing him. This was Agnes Foy, whom he had met while passing through the city on his stay with Aunt Mary. Remington hit the mark when he pointed out Clarke's roving eye began to turn toward matrimony.

For the foreseeable future, however, Clarke remained an occupant of bachelor officer's quarters, sharing a house with a fellow Tenth Cavalry officer, Alabaman Second Lieutenant John Bacon MacDonald, another veteran of the Geronimo campaign, who had commanded Indian scouts. MacDonald stood fifty-second out of fifty-three in his West Point Class of 1881. With these and other similarities, the pair of "immortals" bonded and busied themselves with repair and repainting of their joint domicile. Their refurbished "new sitting room" combined Clarke's rugs, curtains, and other touches with pieces of MacDonald's furniture. Pooling their resources, rather than separate accommodations, would "not only be comfortable but will have attained some luxury." In this way, Clarke proffered "we can make our guests more comfortable than if they had to call on us separately."

Clarke described their "cottage" as consisting "of a latticed veranda, five very fair rooms and a warm well lighted bathroom, and outhouse for each of our 'strikers'" indicative of the racial and class divides of the era between officers and enlisted personnel. Clarke also allowed that there was a "back-yard with a large house which I use for my dogs."

He added not having "much success with my dogs but a great deal of sport. The older greyhound is too fleet for the puppies" but "the wise jackrabbits" managed to dodge him and escape in ravines.

Besides this pastime, as always Clarke delighted in a recent visit from Jim Hughes. He looked forward to the prospect of "nearly all the Tenth Cavalry bachelors" gathering at Fort Grant "for a Xmas hop and dinner. I have not seen many of them for nearly a year and we have not been together since the march from Texas," typical of regiments being dispersed at frontier forts rather than serving together, during the more than a quarter of century after the Civil War's end.

At least Clarke saw his promotion inching up with the prediction that First Lieutenant Charles Ward, West Point Class of 1871, would "be dismissed—that will put me 8 on the list of seconds." Because promotion usually occurred within the regiment from second lieutenant through captain, Clarke's somewhat ghoulish glee may have appalled his father, but was not an uncommon reaction. Clarke admitted as much asking: "Charity where art thou? When will I be a captain?"

What followed at year's end were two rather strained letters to his mother. The first evidenced that one of the young ladies to whom he was attracted was Protestant, given the tone of his lengthy discussion about religion to his devout Roman Catholic mother. He indicated awareness of his mother's strict point of view about interfaith relationships and her "feelings toward" this unnamed young woman.[46]

His second piece of correspondence frankly set out that he would send his mother some money toward his younger sister's education, but the funds would not be immediately forthcoming.[47] Just as Clarke indicated in his December 2 letter to his father about his typical halfhearted efforts to apply himself to studying military volumes, he continued his usual lack of wise money management. "Through my own carelessness and extravagance," Clarke conceded he was "about $300 in debt." The upcoming Christmas dinner MacDonald and he were to "give to the bachelors of the Regiment" as "a re-union of our men ..." would compound the shortfall. Despite claiming he had cut "myself down to bare necessity," he was bent on feting "these old schoolmates and fellow soldiers of our Regiment."

Likewise, he betrayed his claim of strict cash consciousness. He spent "$26 for subscriptions to standard magazines." The fort's budget for the library had been reduced. In response. Clarke formed a club with several fellow officers to ensure they had up to date publications. He probably thought his mother would understand this extravagance more than she did the holiday dinner and hop outlays.

Another expense was payment to his striker Turner, who had "been so faithful to me for three years." Clarke felt a responsibility to continue Turner's stipend despite the fact that the trooper had been in hospital for some time. Even a few dollars meant a good deal to a soldier whose base pay started at $13 a month. Clarke dutifully provided part of the amount in cash during this period of illness and used the balance to purchase fresh milk for the bedridden man, a delicacy for a soldier in that era. Compounding the matter, Clarke engaged another soldier servant during Turner's absence.

Clarke juxtaposed his humane efforts with noting that he outlaid $3 each month for his greyhounds. Perhaps hearing his mother's voice in his head, he quickly added: "this is the only amusement I allow myself besides the magazines." He provided some examples of fiscal responsibility such as the furnishing his quarters, most of which was with money "paid out of the sale of one of my horses." Ever ready to justify what may have appeared as selfishness, he pointed out that perhaps as a result of this improvement of his living environment he spent less time "at the 'sutlers' than any other officer (one married man excepted) at the post." Instead he stayed at home frequently.

Besides selling a horse, he raffled his "shotgun in order to send off a few Xmas presents." Additionally, he wore clothes "made of the roughest soldier's cloth and have not a stick of officer's uniform except that which I bought in '84' and an overcoat that I bought last year which I never wear as I do not see any chance of replacing it but wear the soldier's blue overcoat instead."

He avoided other expenses as well, declaring he "did not live luxuriously—for an army officer is not given a salary without requirements being made on him." This lack of money precluded any thoughts of marriage. Otherwise, he contended: "I should be married now without a doubt." To this he admitted that "at 25 one can not always be happy with a horse, a few greyhounds and one companion who is rarely in the house though he is a very fine man."

After more than a year away from the rigors of the field, Clarke backslid into old habits of relative indolence, spending more money than he should, indulging himself with hounds, horses, and hops. He had managed to score a leave in the process, but some of the reasons for doing so stemmed from medical requirements. During this period, the dreariness of the garrison, in contrast to the excitement of the field, tended not to bring out the best in Clarke, as often proved true for his fellow officers who took to drink and other destructive pastimes that marred the record of many an otherwise "fine man." New challenges over the next few years would bring fresh opportunities for the idle lieutenant, offering possible growth, change, and enhanced reputation.

Chapter 7

"We're Fighting Bulls of the Buffaloes"

Clarke's medical leave ended all too soon. This meant by 1888 he returned to sameness of Arizona garrison life. As Oliver Knight described in *Life and Manners in the Frontier Army*: "If one description could alone fit all frontier posts, it would be of a monotonous routine relieved only slightly by the color of periodic ceremony. All posts follow common customs and procedures, but there were all ways 'ground rules'; that is, customs peculiar to a given post."[1]

For Clarke, during these periods of inactivity, mail from home offered continued enjoyment including fairly frequent word from Remington. The first of these notes from New York, written on January 3, 1888, acknowledged receipt of a buckskin shirt the lieutenant mailed for the artist's growing collection of studio props.[2] Remington promised reimbursement for the new acquisition "as soon as I go down to the bank where I do business.... The thing is a little new but I can fix that by having it smoked."

Remington followed with a Clarke-inspired idea about "running jacks" the pastime of chasing jackrabbits through the desert, a subject the New Yorker had depicted in *Outing* the previous year.[3] After several other tidbits, Remington cut to the chase, noting he intended to set out west again in September for three months. He shared: "I want to do 'US soldiers'—some

Pueblo Indians—some Apaches—and then Mexico—I am not going to fool with any d—illustrating but make finished oil studies for painting. I wish you could get a few days off to go to San Carlos with me. I want to make a 'negro cavalry picture.'" Remington's last remark indicated the characteristic Victorian insertion of a modifier when discussing African Americans soldiers, as opposed to rarely adding the term "white" in conjunction with most other members of Uncle Sam's Army. Regardless, Remington's continued interest in black troops, a recurring subject for his growing body of work since meeting Clarke in Tucson in 1886, from an artistic perspective and what appeared to be a personal interest, drew him to this special group who so differed from him.

Even as Remington gave notice of another western trip, Clarke had stored his campaign kit to engage in less strenuous activities, not the least of which was his desired reunion with many fellow young officers during the holidays. This meant he spent considerable time away from Fort Grant as a guest at Fort Thomas, a distance of around fifty miles as the crow flies.

By early January, he briefly returned to his own post from where he sent a few lines to his mother.[4] Sitting at his "carved desk in old oak" rather than the quartermaster issue "with pigeon holes on top" that once served him, he expressed satisfaction "to my heart's content." Changes were on the horizon. A new colonel was to arrive. This meant Major Mills would relinquish command of Fort Grant. Clarke happily anticipated "quite a sweeping out."[5]

On another optimistic note, Clarke hoped to be a first lieutenant by his next leave. Given that no vacancies existed in that grade within the Tenth U.S. Cavalry, his prospects were slim. In fact, some other second lieutenants in the regiment stood in front of him for promotion including Jim Hughes. Clarke's outlook for more rapid advancement would be increased "if only a little war would come along or a great big Indian racket" erupted. Either possibility seemed unlikely. In a rare good mood Clarke chimed: "I doubt if I will be any happier than I am now … and heaven knows I have no right to complain unless some chap comes along and ranks me out of my house."

Housing aside, Clarke turned to a topic of even more importance to him. He took pride in the assertion that: "'My' troop is in splendid shape." Clarke's emphasis on retaining his command stemmed from John Bigelow's prolonged leave, along with Thomas Lebo's absence due to sickness. Clarke bantered that if his mother saw Bigelow during his eastern excursions to let John know "that my troop is getting on swimmingly" without him. Further, he hoped Captain Lebo would not rush back, but not for selfish reasons. Clarke truly desired his often-ailing commander to report for duty only after he was "thoroughly braced up."

For once Clarke seemed happy to stay at Fort Grant rather than heading to the field. He had "never spent one summer there yet and I want to see what it feels like" he offered. Supposedly "it is quite cool" at the post during the season.

The next month Clarke indicated he missed receiving mail from his mother.[6] In turn, Clarke had forestalled answering correspondence as he partied with friends, new acquaintances, and dashed back and forth between Forts Grant and Thomas. On one of these jaunts, he and a newly posted recent graduate of West Point to Arizona, Virginia-born Second Lieutenant Robert Glasgow Paxton, decided to take "a rattling gallop regardless of prairie dog holes" to see Jim Hughes and cheer up their comrade who was "in a most sad state of mind on account of the dullness of his post [Fort Thomas]."

The two subalterns may have been motivated by more than sympathy for a downhearted comrade. They had heard a rumor about a "Honolulu belle" who recently stopped at Henry C. Hooker's Ranch, the home of the newly married Forrestine Cooper Hooker's father-in-law. The curious cavalrymen set out to meet the young visitor from across the Pacific. They would be disappointed in their quest as the young lady in question was indisposed. Frustrated, they left without an audience, riding back to Fort Thomas. The following day they breakfasted, played tennis with Hughes and finally paid their respects as Clarke indicated to "the Maori, unfortunately she was from Illinois and though a very pretty girl she has that insufferable Illinois voice, moreover she is a trifle passive, and a blond, and has been spoiled by Naval officers of all nations."

Clarke and Paxton made the best of their situation. They spent five hours on the tennis courts, afterwards enjoying "a charming dinner at Col [Fredrick] Van Vliet's" followed by spending the evening listening to Mrs. Van Vliet at her piano. The next day, they turned back to Fort Grant making for "battalion drill … a trifle weary" but not so much as to prevent Clarke from planning a repeat outing to Fort Thomas at the end of the week. He looked forward to a hop and the opportunity to don dress uniforms and dance until the next morning.

Not everything Clarke did that winter involved pleasantries at the post. He divulged in a late February letter to his father that although Geronimo and many others had been removed from Arizona, all was far from quiet in the territory. Clarke wrote from the nearly abandoned community of Tres Alamos in Cochise County: "I left Grant day before yesterday rather unexpectedly on account of Indian rumor, made forty-five miles over the worst country I have ever seen to the hot springs and found that several Indians had been there and had shot at a man cutting his shirt with the ball."[7]

The fortunate civilian survived this close call from what Clarke considered a hunting party. After his patrol scouted for twenty miles along the San Pedro River and conducted more tracking, Clarke halted the command after concluding seventy-six miles of unsuccessful trailing over two days.

By February 27, he resumed the march from Hooker's Hot Springs.[8] As Clarke suspected "the alarm was due to a small hunting party of Apaches" who had slipped back to the San Carlos Reservation. Both Clarke's Tenth Cavalry troopers and another detail from the Fourth Cavalry dispatched from Fort Huachuca under First Lieutenant James Russell Richards (who was back in Arizona after forming part of the guard escorting Apache prisoners of war to San Augustine, Florida) had little to do but play whist until two o'clock in the morning. The officers also passed time by sharing "some most delicious claret" with Tres Alamos resident Thomas Dunbar.[9]

After a diverting evening, they parted. Clarke set out for home through the Winchester Mountains where they rode thirty-five miles then camped for the night. Just as he and his troopers halted, a courier caught up with them carrying a dispatch from General Nelson Miles to Major Anson Mills, and another from the major to Clarke instructing the lieutenant to return to the Hot Springs with a report of his scout. Clarke pronounced the requirement "rot" but complied. Striking camp at daybreak, his patrol reversed its course for twelve hours "after marching 25 miles over such rough ground that I had to lead about ten miles." They dismounted to link up with First Lieutenant Levi Pettibone Hunt of the Tenth U.S. Cavalry per orders delivered the prior day.

Hunt decided to await further instructions. He gave Clarke's weary detachment a rest. The joint command could not find "any trail to follow."

Never reluctant to call on his father to lobby on his behalf, the always financially strapped Clarke based on a combination of low pay, high local costs, and his recurring inability to adhere to a budget, requested the doctor to "use your eloquence against" a bill proposed by a member of the House of Representatives from Indiana, George Washington Steele. This Civil War veteran introduced H.R. 1347 "to increase the efficiency of the army."[10] Clarke expressed disapproval relative to several aspects of the legislation. At the head of his list, he strongly objected to a pay ceiling of $1,500 a year for six years "instead of 1,500 the first" year and thereafter $1,650 per annum. Next, he decried the plan to abolish "the grade of 1st lieutenant making us all lieutenants but the worse feature is that it makes promotion lineal in each arm [of the service] instead of Regimental so that the senior lieutenant of a Regiment would go to the next vacant captaincy in the cavalry" as would an artilleryman or infantryman to the next open captain's slot in that branch. Clarke contended this scheme would "knock the Esprit de Corps out of the whole service and be the ruination of these colored regiments. It would knock my promotion as our prospects in the Tenth are splendid and moreover I am so thoroughly satisfied where I am that I would hate to go to another Regiment."

Clarke stressed that the regimental organization served as the bedrock "for discipline and esprit de corps ... and we cannot afford to transfer our officers around as they do in the Navy." He argued: "A man takes some time to learn to know his men and his companions and it does not do to change methods with men any oftener than absolutely necessary."

Clarke's loyalty to the Tenth Cavalry seemed well intentioned. Interestingly, his arguments smacked of an uncharacteristic defense of the status quo, which he often fought at West Point and elsewhere. His aversion to change and what may well have been a paternalistic view of his troopers appeared to cloud his judgment. He failed to realize that breaking from the long-standing policy of advancement from second lieutenant through captain that customarily took place within the same regiment one joined at the beginning of a military career, tended to stagnate promotion.

Although the proposed legislation worried Clarke, his friend Remington concentrated on an entirely different matter. Politics weighed on the artist's mind. With the election of 1888 looming, a rambunctious Remington berated the incumbent, Democrat Grover Cleveland. His message to Clarke included a demeaning cartoon of the chief executive from Remington's new neighbor and fellow artist E.W. Kemble.[11] Cleveland's stand for free trade versus his Republican opponent, Benjamin Harrison, who championed high tariffs, formed a cornerstone of the campaign. Remington sided with the Republicans telling Clarke: "Why Harrison hes [*sic*] all right" but retorted "Grovers [*sic*] a chump."

Nonplused about the contest for the Executive Mansion, Clarke remained focused on his small corner of the world in Arizona. As Clarke informed his father, he continued to relish visits from Hughes, Finley, and other young companions.[12]

Conversely, Clarke's distaste for Major Mills heightened. He charged, "Mills went off the handle the other day and gave me some very unnecessary and annoying orders." Displaying his anti-authoritarian bent, he related how the major informed him not to use a "horse to superintend fatigue parties and not even ride a horse to breakfast!" The second admonition went contrary to regulations. Clarke realized that even if he pressed the issue, he "would be out in arrest ad interim, which would give my Troop to another officer and in my losing command of it." Clarke reached a conclusion that he should accept the major's lecture in order to remain with his men.

Once more, Clarke exhibited better judgment and patience than during his school days, as well as a certain affinity for his troopers, whom he did not want to entrust to a stranger. After the dressing down, Mills added insult in Clarke's opinion "by complimenting in a most sickening manner" his subordinate's "abilities on the field all of which he knows nothing about."

Mills may have viewed Clarke as a reputable combat commander while rightly detecting the lieutenant's imperfect demeanor when it came to garrison duties. As Clarke admitted, he had a difficult time keeping his "temper but in the end it is best. The worst punishment he could inflict would be to put a first lieutenant in command of me." Clarke valued the independence he had gained, taking pleasure and pride in leading troops.

Desirous of retaining this coveted position of authority, Clarke vowed: "Hence I shall mark down his objectionable orders, his remarks to and about my first sergeant" Givens with whom Clarke had developed a rapport as evidenced by the laudatory remarks this non-commissioned officer shared with Remington in 1886 concerning Corporal Scott's rescue. Clarke had labored alongside his men "getting up boulders and moving rock in order to push the work" by example. When Mills " 'jumped' " Clarke "about being on horseback" the lieutenant reacted. Lashing out he suggested: "I am not likely to be so energetic again."

Still smarting the next day, when the Tenth Cavalry's regimental Chaplain Francis H. Weaver queried why Clarke wore spurs in the club room, the lieutenant caustically answered with "rather forcible language" that he "had to wear them so that I might not forget I was a cavalryman as I had been almost turned into a dough-boy (Infantry)." Mills, who had been an infantry officer early in his career, took umbrage to the remark. Clarke said Mills "was powerful chilly when I next met him."

Tensions on a small, insular post weighed mercurial Clarke down, as did the "rainy, misty, cold" front that contributed to his "melancholy mood after a bright warm week" that just passed. Regardless of the change in weather, Clarke had no choice but to continue with his company's ongoing employment "on 'fatigue' digging and beasting [*sic*], hauling and ploughing and I began to feel that I am a 'section boss.' " At least target practice would commence during the next month, affording a respite. The range also gave Clarke an opportunity to set an example for the soldiers as he intended "in making good shots." How he longed "to get in the field once more."

Fulfillment of that desire neared, as news, which must have lifted his flagging spirits, arrived from an ebullient Frederic Remington.[13] Following up on invitations from Clarke and fellow Tenth U.S. Cavalry officer John D. McDonald, whom Remington evidently met on his 1886 excursion, the artist was "trying to convince these d—publishers that they should send me out on a summer raid in your direction and if so be it why I shall descend on you 'horse foot and dragoons.'"[14] Remington candidly admitted, referring to the lack of creature comforts that would be faced and his growing girth: "I have reason to know that a man is liable to prespire [*sic*] under his arms in Arizona during the summer but a man can sweat and still enjoy himself just how I can ever ride a horse again is raising the duce [*sic*] with my grand tactics but I have read that a troop horse is often burdened with more than 220 lbs so there is still hope that I will not have to do the 'dough-boy' act."

The animated New York studio-bound artist assured: "I should be willing to give ten years off from my life for a trip into Arizona this Spring." Remington promised Clarke in common Victorian era language: "All I want is one good crack at your nigger cavalrymen and d—your eyes I'll make you all famous! Do you know I think there is the biggest kind of an artist pudding lurking in the vacinity [*sic*] of Ft. Grant." Here he pressed for assurance that he would be welcome and have a free roof over his head closing with: "Well write—be gracious. I have made up my mind that you are a corospondent [*sic*] worthy of any ones [*sic*] steel…." This last line revealed Remington's admiration for Clarke, which would be displayed many times in the future both in writing and imagery.

Striking a few days later, Remington fired another round toward Clarke.[15] He confided to his would-be host: " 'The die is cast,['] 'I'll plunge I'll cross,' or in a more prosy diction I will go on and explain that I have beguiled a certain distinguished publisher [*The Century Magazine*] into sending me on an atistic [*sic*] and litterary [*sic*] tour through the Indian Territory and into Arizona."

Uncertain of his exact date of arrival, he indicated the trip would commence in early June or failing that in early July, beastly hot months in either case. His plan was "to do the 'Black Buffaloes' This information you will please keep private as I do not want to be anticipated." Once more, Remington reinforced his persistent inkling that the black soldier presented an opportunity to further his career, but for the first time he referred to them as "Buffaloes," which incidentally was the atypical plural form used in what is considered the regimental song, the opening stanza of which ran: "We're Fighting Bulls of the Buffaloes."[16] Although there is a similarity here, that fact does not provide a concrete clue as to where Remington learned of this term. Because of this off-handed mention, he evidently presumed Clarke would take his meaning. The answer to this line of questioning is uncertain just as the origin and definition of "buffalo soldiers" remain varied and inconclusive.[17]

Regardless of where Remington came by the name, he anxiously sought another opportunity to portray black troopers for his expanding portfolio. The cost conscious and excited Remington ended his April 11 letter with pleas for help, as well as a free place to stay and to dine in keeping with his far more fiscally conservative attitude than during his spendthrift bachelorhood. He leaned on Clarke: "Now tell me candidly—can I have men to 'pose' for me at your post and how can I get bed and board there. I have no desire to impose myself on your good nature on this a purely business venture of mine—of course you can lend me a helping hand and make my road smoothe [*sic*]—that I know you will do." He also required one further detail to set his plans in motion—would Clarke "be there at the above date-at Grant."

It seems Remington received a reply from Clarke in a now lost letter, but one from May 4 written to Dr. Clarke, fills in the gap.[18] Penned from Soza's Ranch, the news Clarke conveyed made it appear problematic that the lieutenant would be on hand to welcome Remington.[19] The reason was not unexpected. Mills, who Clarke contended had "been 'laying for me' for some time," relieved the lieutenant from his desirable troop command. The major did so "in the midst of target practice" dispatching his subordinate on a scout at the far edge of the vast Fort Grant military reservation. Clarke complained he "was very discouraged by this for I had worked hard to get a good target record for my troop and I have had command of it for so much time since I came out in 84."

In fact, Clarke as Troop K's second lieutenant frequently oversaw the unit with First Lieutenant Bigelow's long absences and Lebo often being indisposed or away for considerable periods. Consequently, Clarke's removal as company commander may have been a vendetta.

This particularly stung Clarke. He "took pride in my troop." Fellow lieutenant and friend John McDonald disclosed to Clarke that because he "had not been a tool in Mills' hands," this led to his exile. Clarke acknowledged he could do nothing about this without an iron clad case against "such a sharper as Mills" whom he accused of being "too good a liar" to be undone by a junior officer, an accusation he dare not make outside the strict confidences of his father.

Clarke indicated that his health remained an issue. The strenuous mounted service proved difficult. Nonetheless, the post surgeon, whom he painted as "a weak sister," would do nothing to assist. Besides, he would rather be away from Fort Grant even if it meant suffering physically. He speculated about "how Lebo would swear" once he learned of the situation.

Clarke not only vented to his father, but also launched another diatribe in a partial surviving piece of correspondence from his temporary outpost duty. In this undated note, Clarke again lamented the fate of his comrade Jim Hughes who now served under Captain William "Whispering Bill" Davis. Davis replaced outgoing Captain Robert Geno Smither, a Civil War veteran with more military experience than Davis.[20] In an unsympathetic portrayal, Clarke described Davis as "a loud mouthed, empty headed bore, one of the hardest drinkers in the regiment" and a relic of the Civil War. Clarke viewed most such veterans of the 1860s as holding him back from advancement because he immediately referred to not straining his "head over promotion." It was "too much of a lottery" which in reality was not the case given the lineal promotion by seniority within a cavalry regiment.

A note from Remington indicated Clarke also disclosed his plight to his friend in New York. To this Remington responded: "Your letter at hand—so you are banished as it were—well I hope you are like Cataline [*sic*; a first century BC Roman senator who conspired to overthrow the aristocratic Roman government] in spirit—but go slow my boy—there are a heap of people who need murdering in this world but the job of 'taking hence' of such of those who are unworthy is not for our hands."[21] After offering cautionary words, Remington tipped his own hand. He hoped "the powers may relent before I visit your summer home" that would be "well worth 3000 miles."

Ultimately, Clarke could host Remington in part because Mills left for Fort Wingate, New Mexico, to serve on a court martial. With the major's departure, Captain Alexander Keyes took charge at Fort Grant, soon recalling Clarke from his banishment.[22]

With that reprieve, Clarke's maladies disappeared. His health returned. The way stood unbarred for Remington to travel west and have another go at Clarke and his troopers.

Clarke could show the artist hospitality and accompany him into the field. In the process, he ultimately earned a continued place in Remington's inner circle.

As with his earlier Arizona outing, Remington kept a journal in which he recorded details of the trip including his arrival "at Wilcox [*sic*] in night—next morning found 6 mile ambulance down from Grant awaiting me—was pleasant arrive for post—met Clark [*sic*] on horse surrounded by greyhounds—greeting very pleasant." Remington then "accompanied the Lieutenant on horse out to Keyes & Davis troop of cavalry—watched with great interest the packing of mules—the saddling and mounting of horse.... I accompanied Keyes troop on the march; remarked many peculiarities of the soldier type—to the little inventions of necessity—as it were." Remington delighted at his surroundings, except for Captain William Davis who he thought lacked "the qualities of gentleman to an astonishing degree." As for "all the other officers" he marked them as "thoroughly splendid fellows."

Remington expressed a similar admiration for the troopers being "greatly gratified to be able to say that I like the Negro soldiers [*sic*] character as a soldier in almost every particular—Clark [*sic*] told me many piculiaritis [*sic*] which I hope to remember." He had kind words for the army wives and children he met that day whom he saw as "heroic ... to stand petty annoyances with such grace" or as frontier army wife Martha Summerhayes so eloquently phrased it, those family members who came West endured *glaenzendes Elend*: "glittering misery."[23]

Along the way, Remington chanced upon some officers changing station from Fort Sill, Indian Territory, with their men from the Twenty-fourth U.S. Infantry, another segregated regiment manned by black enlisted personnel commanded by whites. These officers invited him to join their party. He accepted, loaded his camera with film "after dark and went down to the camp and slept there with them under the stars" as there was "no uses for tents and shelters in the country as there is no dew."[24]

The next morning, with only coffee for breakfast, Remington remained with the infantry column, snapping off a dozen pictures before taking his leave of the foot soldiers. From there, he set out for Fort Grant.[25] Ensconced in Clarke's quarters the obliging lieutenant had one of the sergeants from Troop K in his back yard available for the artist to "start a study" but even in the relative comfort of the garrison Remington indicated it was "very hot work."[26]

This was not the only time Remington worked at Fort Grant rather than in the field. For instance, at that post the artist prevailed upon Tenth U.S. Cavalry Private Henry Jackson, a part-time soldier-striker to the garrison's military surgeon William Corbusier, to serve as model for the now well-known illustration of a lone trooper descending a steep slope with his mount checked by tightened reins. Similarly, one of Dr. Corbusier's sons, Claude, galloped up and the down the parade ground performing other mounted displays for the artist so he could use these equestrian feats as models for future work. Indeed, as Claude's mother, Fanny Dunbar Corbusier, recollected, Remington "made many of his watercolors in the shade of our quarters, and Claude rode Fan" his horse through various paces while Remington "took snap shots. He frequently sat on our gallery at sunset to absorb the surprising colors of earth and sky at that hour."[27]

Taking a break with a bugle sounding "some very inspiring call" the artist joined Clarke for a ride up a nearby canyon. The young cavalryman impressed his guest with "some military trick riding." Then they "climbed up a very steep cliff" to observe "a view of sun-set on the mesa." Awestruck, Remington found the experience "simply one of those phenomena of color beyond the province of art to portray. – The yellow sand of the mesa – far higher than gold and framing [the] black mass of our side of the mountains behind which the sun had set for our foreground—the purple of the far mountains and the whole prism in the sky" ended the outing on a spectacular note. Turning back, the two riders holed up at Clarke's quarters sitting "up until all hours" while Lieutenant Carter Johnson regaled them with "some amazing stories about experiences with the Cheyennes" and their horses.[28]

With stories of the Plains Indians filling their imaginations, the time had come for the scouting outfit to gather. The rotund reporter-artist would be equipped with a loaned big army horse he claimed was a "dandy" and an issue McClellan cavalry saddle fully loaded for an excursion from Fort Grant to Fort Thomas and San Carlos Reservation then back.[29] The original detail consisted of Remington, Clarke, Sergeant Brown, an "amazing tall man," and two packers, who led four mules. The small band left the garrison striking "off up Sulphur Spring Valley and then into the Taylor Canon Pass of the Sierra Bonitas."

In a quick one-page summary written to his wife Eva on June 17, 1888, Fred added details. Clarke, a sergeant, four cavalrymen, and two packers were making ready for a two-week adventure bound for the San Carlos Reservation. With a "nice big horse from K troop an orderly" and other trappings, Remington was ready to go. He admitted "enjoying myself beyond all question or anticipation. I am getting material such as will make your eyes open." Remington reiterated the use of his camera to capture details as when his hosts at Fort Grant "turned out a troop with pack mules" so he could photograph them a half dozen times watering the livestock.[30]

With this positive beginning, the party was in the saddle. Not far from Fort Grant, the rugged terrain required everyone to dismount and lead "horses up – up as steep as a pair of stairs." Remington confessed he "was almost dead from fatigue." Still, they pressed through the rugged countryside. At "one place we hesitated" he said, "but went down & Clark[e]'s horse slid on its rear elevation all the way."[31]

In another quick musing, Remington displayed racism tempered by his genuine admiration for the black troopers. He remarked: "These nigs are the best d[amned] soldiers in the world." He noted the only reply ever heard from them was " 'Yes sir' … and that comes like a period to one of Clark[e]'s sentences."[32] At this point Remington pulled out his camera once more to snap some photos of the camp before moving out for Fort Thomas.

They trail continued to prove difficult. Nevertheless, Remington hauled out the camera to record the scenery in this "waste of sand" inhabited by "lizards, jack rabbits … rattlesnakes" and other creatures living among the mesquite, cactus, and chaparral. As they plodded along on the long ride which was "slow & hot" a "fine dust" sifted "over everything." Clarke's greyhounds were "badly plaid [*sic*]." Unused to such strenuous efforts the relatively sedimentary Easterner groaned his "rear elevation" had become "very sore," which meant when they "finally got to Fort Thomas" they were grateful, especially for their "very fine reception" that included some strong spirit liquid refreshments.[33]

Rejuvenated from their overnight stay, they woke "and pulled out in the morning" reaching San Carlos. There, much to Remington's chagrin, the Apaches prohibited him from making sketches of them, perhaps out of suspicion or superstition. In turn, the white troops stationed there would not have objected, yet they were not worthy subjects. Remington thought them "rough careless chaps—hard featured—with very little of the suggestiveness of the smart soldier…."[34] This sharp contrast between white soldiers and black soldiers, as enumerated by class and race conscious Remington, was a telling one. Perhaps, as evidenced by relative high desertion rate among personnel in white-only regiments, many of these enlisted men saw their enlistments as a job of work or an interim step to other civilian pursuits. Conversely, their black counterparts consistently posted low desertion rates and substantial numbers of men who reenlisted, making the military a profession.[35]

Remington may not have realized this distinction, but did appreciate waking early to experience the stunning coming of morning light in Arizona. He "saw the sun rise and day break—yellow green blue … lots of high color near the East." As he did so, he noticed "the soldiers stand about the campfires and watch the breakfast with longing eyes." They faced another "25 miles over dusty" trails that day. Along the way, they chanced upon "a company of doughboys lying about with their shoes & stockings off resting until the sun got lower." While the foot soldiers rested Clarke's men "went into the water to drink … it was very picturesque leaning down to fill a canteen from [the] saddle" as Remington noted.[36]

Having completed the trip, the detachment made its way into Camp San Carlos adjacent to the Indian agency headquarters where several officers greeted them. One of them, Captain Charles Viele, invited Remington "to his 'large hotel' as he called his tent of a frame work" which because of the intense summer heat many had pitched "to make it possible … to live through these days here and that's about all." Viele, whom Remington perceived as "a very humorous chap," jested " 'it cooks the immortal soul out of a fellow.'" Evidently, one of Viele's solutions to cope was the admission he "ran out of excuses long ago to take a drink—he takes one now for fun."[37]

As had become habit since the trip when he first met Clarke, Remington grabbed his favorite *aide-mémoire*, a camera, and took pictures that he could use later in his studio as the basis for his art thereby allowing details and accuracy. Accompanied by Captain Viele, they "went down to the agency after breakfast" and photographed ration issue "to my hearts [*sic*] content." The next morning, the patrol, accompanied by Lieutenant Watson, an orderly, and another pack mule, struck out from San Carlos. As before, Remington appreciated that he never heard one of the "hard worked men those cavalrymen" ever complain. The most he ever observed was when questioning an old sergeant "How do you like this kind of life man" the response was a "surly look" but this was the result "of overwork … hunger [,] heat" and other factors, but not a lack of discipline.[38]

Another overnight camp in the "very cold" mountains followed with a surprise visit of a rattlesnake to Remington's bedding which fortunately he discovered before turning in to his blankets. He passed a relatively sleepless night, rolling out early the next day to watch the troopers, who he considered "a funny lot … full of merriment" playing card games such as Monte and Draw. Ever looking for details, he observed they used a Mexican-made deck and many of them used their boot tops to "carry everything," a point he subtly illustrated in one of his sketches. They also had picked up an expression he ascribed to Indians—"'Maybe so.'"[39]

Circling back to San Carlos, after they halted, Viele tagged along with them when they left the following morning. That day, "the heat was awful and the dust rose in clouds." Marching fast they went into "a comatose state" suffering in silence. Reaching Fort Thomas, Remington and probably Clarke, gratefully bathed away the "mass of mud" that encrusted his hair and beard. Clean at last, he welcomed the brief, less arduous final ride to Fort Grant where, thinner and with skin peeling off his face, he "was elected an honorary member of the cavalry."[40] Now Remington proudly claimed he had the mettle of "the class of men who constitute the negro soldiers of to day," ones that greatly differed "from the old troops of the war," possibly referring here to the tens of thousands of African American who volunteered as United States Colored Troops during the Civil War.[41]

Remington bid Clarke and his compadres *adios*.[42] From Arizona he traveled by train to Texas and Oklahoma. There he gathered more references before taking his amassed collection of photographs, art work, journal accounts, and vivid memories to his New York studio.

With Remington literally back at the drawing board, Clarke returned to the daily garrison regimen. One bright flash during the dull routine came on August 23. Clarke's comrade and quarters mate, John McDonald, married Kate Murphy, the sister-in-law of two fellow Tenth Cavalry officers, Alexander L. Dade and Levi Hunt, demonstrating the tight-knit Tenth U.S. Cavalry's officer corps. The wedding took place in the post chapel, a building that was a new hall the ladies of the post draped "with flags, curtains and evergreens and covered the floor with rugs, so that it had a very festive look and especially so when the officers in their uniforms and the ladies in their handsome gowns had assembled."[43]

After the ceremony, a reception and supper capped the nuptials. The next day the newlyweds were off to Auburn, Alabama, where McDonald had been detailed to college duty in his home state.

A bit tardy, Remington dropped a note to Clarke asking: "When is Mac [McDonald] sacrificed [*sic*]?"[44] An oblivious Remington missed the date of McDonald's wedding.

Regardless, he assured Clarke that he was hard at work on the "10 Nubian Horse" (one of Remington's euphemisms for the Tenth Cavalry and a term not foreign to Clarke) project not the least of which were efforts "to make some illustrations for it before which the world will stand in a grim and terrible awe."

In the meantime, Remington considered entering "a small study of 10th Trooper in the N.A. this Fall" meaning he was preparing a piece for the fall exhibition of the prestigious National Academy of Design. Possibly Remington based this oil painting in progress on the models provided at Fort Grant, including the session in Clarke's backyard. Remington asked when Powhatan Clarke and Carter Johnson were coming East, implying he would reciprocate their hospitality.

At that point travels east of the Mississippi were out of the question. Clarke had to be content with correspondence, such as writing his mother on October 18, 1888. His paternalistic yet humane view of the soldiers appeared front and center.[45] As usual, he also referred to being low on funds, but in this instance not entirely because of his personal spending. That shortfall would be corrected on payday when he would be "able to collect a little amount from some of my nubians [*sic*]." While he insisted that he made "it a rule never to lend them any money but frequently one can not refuse the poor fellows" because he thought when the men came into a town it was "only right to let them have enough to get some fun out of life for their lives are most dreary in the posts and they are like a lot of overgrown children." As an aside, he admitted that "some of the officers are in the same boat."

Perhaps Clarke had lent money to his troops on a recent ride to Fort Lowell, which brought them in proximity of Tucson, one of the communities that could offer an assortment of diversions not available at Fort Grant. There was another advantage to the brief excursion to southern Arizona as part of maneuvers to catch a unit portraying "raiders." Clarke could take a break from garrison routine and briefly relax in Tucson. The outing was not without consequences.

For one thing, Lieutenant Colonel Edward Pennington Pearson, the new commander at Fort Grant, placed Clarke and his troopers under one of the other recently arrived officers from the Twenty-fourth U.S. Infantry. Clarke balked, privately insisting in his letter that this officer, whom he did not name, was "a sad specimen" who was "a man without a spark of soldier in him." Along the route from Fort Grant to Fort Lowell, this new thorn in Clarke's side remained mounted up a steep hill where the cavalrymen toiled "along on foot to save their horses." Adding to the poor impression, the infantry officer had the "impudence" to inform Clarke "he made a mistake not to go in the cavalry and that he was as active" in the field as the Tenth had been.

With ruffled feathers about his branch and regiment Clarke came "near breaking" the neck of this outsider "by taking him over a rough piece of cañon" where the infantryman's horse fell, causing the rider to clutch the pommel of his saddle for dear life. The horse turned around requiring Clarke "to get on it and force it over" the steep incline. In the process, the accident put a dozen of the troop's best horses "in a fearful flight."

Clarke intended to report the incident to General Miles because as he asserted "my troop is everything to me and I am going to run it or have trouble and would be a sorry stick if I did not." After ten months at the helm with both other officers absent from Troop K, Clarke would brook no interference.

In his private correspondence, he faulted Pearson for putting such "a 'thing' in my command." Even though Clarke expressed frustration, at least he initially viewed Fort Grant's new commander as "a good just man" but one that did "not know human nature."

In spite of complaints, the few days' ride southward had its moments. Clarke wished his mother could have seen her son and his troop "as we rode through the Hot Springs of [the] Cañon." He asked her to "imagine coming from the dusty plains over arid cactus covered mountains to suddenly descend to the bed of a beautiful sparkling stream" where one could enjoy "seeing the horses thrust their heads into the crystal water and how happily their great lustrous eyes look."

Clarke related how difficult it was for someone who had not experienced the pleasure of leaving "the scorching barren hills to ride for miles under the shade of the tall trees that barely reach the summit of the high perpendicular walls." Struck with his surroundings that were so different from those of his youth, Clarke described: "The scenery is really grand, almost sublime, at times the narrow trail carries one beneath massive overhanging walls while one is sprayed from the hundred dripping springs that issue drop by drop from invisible fissures in the granite; on either side from the long line of springs lay long curtains of maidens hair fern interspersed with bunches of brilliant wild flowers."

Above them, the troop passed by "high caverns … succeeded by strangely carved pillars. I have never seen the cañon look more beautiful though in the winter moonlight—with its strange shadows and silvered tones it does instill one with awe," Clarke enthused.

Inspired, Clarke shared he was "going to try to get the General [Miles] to let me take a ride to the Grand Cañon of the Colorado … though it is several hundred miles from us…." Clarke never made that trip. His descriptions of the majestic formations were moving.

In addition to Clarke's prose about the ride to Fort Lowell, he shared some thoughts about the two days he spent in Tucson after reaching that fort. In nearby Tucson, he recounted about having "a pleasant time meeting a great many old acquaintances." Among the locals Clarke mentioned "some very pleasant Jews there who are always extremely hospitable."[46] He followed with a remark once made by a major "that Tucson was composed of the elite & the Israelite." To Clarke this old "chestnut" rang true. Interestingly, he found "the latter more pleasant than the elite," an interesting perspective for a Roman Catholic.

Besides socializing, Clarke listened to "a very good Mexican orchestra from Guaymas and that was a treat." Unfortunately, music made him homesick, depressing him after he heard it.

Perhaps that longing for family induced him to seek a position at West Point as an instructor in the French department, an utterly misleading statement given Clarke's mediocre performance in what should have been one of his stronger subjects at the Military Academy. The drawback was that this assignment would take him away from his "Regiment for four years" as well as would necessitate leaving behind his trusted striker, Turner, plus his faithful greyhounds. Did he consider all of them as pets?

A week later, Clarke's family remained much on his mind. He conveyed happy birthday wishes to his mother.[47] Clarke mischievously commented little did his mother know when he was a babe in arms "what a great soldier you were preserving for your country." In an additional playful moment, he wondered what she would have done if she realized that her new born someday would wear "the detested yankee [*sic*] uniform commanding a troop of 'Ethiopians,'" once again one of many names he freely bandied about in letters to his parents and no doubt others as typical of the era and his upbringing.

Turning to Lebo's return from a lengthy absence, Clarke said the captain was "in splendid trim" and "seemed well satisfied" with his junior lieutenant's "management of the troop." With the arrival of the company commander, Clarke also might break away for a hunting trip. At least he could sleep later without his striker, Private Turner, waking him so early each day to report for his command duties.

On the same day Clarke completed his mother's birthday salutations, Remington penned a few lines, not the least of which was a mention of "the photo of yourself. I can't say that it flatters."[48] Evidently it was good enough to keep. He used it as the basis for later illustrations. For the moment, portraits of the gangly cavalier had to wait because the artist was "rushed to death" preparing two manuscripts, a few dozen pictures for *Century Magazine*, four chromolithographs, a page for *Harper's*, and "an oil painting to make before the end of next month and that wont [*sic*] give me much time to 'monkey.'"

Before he completed this marathon, Remington at least had "sent an oil of a "10th Cav. Trooper to the Fall Ex. Academy" which indicated he followed through on completing and submitting his painting to the National Academy for the fall exhibition, another milestone in his advancing status in the art world.[49] He had not completed as intended "a water color with my compliments" of Clarke, "but don't know when I will get at it—before the years end though."

Again, he indicated, Carter Johnson, who was going on leave "must come and see me when he is here or I will enclose a formal note which you will hand him. These soldiers are hell for documents conveying authority." He promised to write often, reiterating he wanted to know when Clarke anticipated his own leave.

Good to his word, on October 31, 1888, Remington expressed delight at Clarke's "discription [*sic*] of the cook fires at night" which the lieutenant had included in a response to Remington. He then referred to "some ideas for a new U.S.A. uniform" sending a few quick sketches for the lieutenant's comments.

No doubt, Remington's proposed military outfits intrigued Clarke more than his next appearance for court martial duties at the beginning of November.[50] Just over a week later, he had completed this undesirable assignment to find himself in a less typical position: forming part of a detail dispatched from Fort Grant to meet an incoming train with some significant passengers from California.[51]

Clarke, along with Captain Joseph Morgan Kelley and a detachment of troopers from the Tenth traveled to Willcox, "that most villanous [*sic*] frontier town" in Clarke's opinion.[52] They had been "sent there to escort six [actually five] pardoned Apaches for fear the people and civil authorities would seize them."

Clarke admitted he would not have blamed the locals if they lynched the released military prisoners as they were the ones who had "fired on Captain Pierce of the 1st Infantry and wounded the chief of scouts [Al Sieber] then taking to the hills they killed a few citizens and were finally driven in by [Carter] Johnson & [Jim] Hughes." Indeed, the men were none other than the Apache Kid and four other scouts court-martialed and convicted the previous year of mutiny and desertion.[53]

The main subject of this outburst was a young Aravaipa Apache who bore many names including the one evidently given him at birth—Ski-be-nan-ted.[54] White men knew him as the Apache Kid, "a protégé of Al Sieber" who first enlisted as an Indian scout in 1882.[55]

A half decade later, the Kid wore the chevrons of a first sergeant charged among other things with preserving "order on the reservation."[56] Supposedly, in this capacity, during June 1887, he and some of his fellow scouts killed "the former Indian policeman known as Rip." Complicating matters, the Kid and his detail had been drinking, a common accompaniment to violence at San Carlos. Further, Rip reputedly had killed the Kid's father, marking the incident as a traditional example of kinship revenge.[57]

After Rip's death, one contemporary source indicated the Kid thought Captain F. E. Pierce, the reservation's acting Indian agent, and the chief of scouts Albert Sieber "would give him credit for what he did." Instead, orders for disarming the Kid and his group awaited them at the agency. Shortly firing erupted. Sieber was wounded.[58] The Kid fled, and the former first sergeant became a fugitive.

Although the Kid and his associates would be captured, tried and sentenced to imprisonment for life, General Miles called for a reduction to ten-year terms for each man. The officer who served as defense during the court-martial continued the appeal process. He eventually secured their releases from the military prison on Alcatraz.[59] Clarke decried their being set free as a "shameful …display of stupid philanthropy," an opinion shared by some Arizona papers.[60]

The predicted mob did not appear. That was not to say the escort detail found their stay in town a calm one. While Clarke and Kelley "were quietly reading" one night "two or three pistol shots" disturbed the two officers. There had been "such a commotion in the street, the town being filled with drunken cowboys of the Chiricahua Cattle Company" the outbreak came as little surprise.

Despite taking the disturbance casually, Clarke "feared some of our men might get into a scrape." He left his tent to order the men "all back to camp though I did not relish going into such a mob…; on reaching the long crowded bar room I found that no one had been hurt."

Relieved, he might have smiled when he witnessed some of the patrons "pointing to the bullet holes in [the] pannelling [*sic*], it was a picture worthy of Remington." Indeed, as he looked around and revealed what he observed, Remington would have reveled in the scene Clarke described:

> the "boys" were in full war paint, six shooters, tall Mexican hats, long rowelled [*sic*] silver spurs, and the inevitable "shaps" [chaps] or leather overalls with fantastic fringe—a faro game at one end and some "girls," daises [*sic*] of the prairies, with blossoms and an alkali complexion, some of my men who seemed a little excited and such a pandemonium, "One of your fellers liked to killed a man lieutenant [.] he must have burst his coat" said one festive cow boy.

Clarke turned to his troopers. He asked who the shooter was, and received the not unexpected reply: " 'don't know nothing about it sir we's just come in' a most brazen lie," the young officer concluded. At that "a jubilant vaquero grabbed" Clarke by his arm and urged: " 'We have you this time lieutenant you have got to take a drink.' "

Before Clarke could react, everyone rushed for the exits, leaving the lieutenant alone in the saloon. "Expecting the shooting to commence," he realized the drover who had been fired at by one of the black soldiers "was coming back for blood." With that thought and knowing he was "entirely too prominent in my uniform," discretion became the better part of valor. In a split second, Clarke dashed for the closest door, which received his "most quickly, electrified, retreating self, boots, spurs, six shooter and all." Thinking he had reached an exit, much to his chagrin, Clarke discovered he was "in a little closet piled up on about forty men and the door was barely closed when the shooting commenced."

Where all the bullets went after this "revenger" emptied his revolver was a mystery, but no one was hit. After the firing stopped, everyone tumbled out of their cramped shelter unscathed. Clarke immediately hurried to Kelley in camp requesting four men with whom he could go back to town and round up the remaining troopers. Leading this detail armed with revolvers and carbines, Clarke made the rounds of the saloons, He eventually arrived at the one where the firing had taken place.

Clarke's detachment spied the man from Bitter Creek with "his compadres … taking a drink and as I feared they might bull doze my men I told them to get their pieces ready and if any one hurt one of them I wanted them to fill him full of lead." Fortunately, none of the civilians made a play as they "did not seem inclined to pick a quarrel with carbines."

The tense situation ended without violence. This may not have been the case according to a story a southern Arizona quartermaster agent, C.M. Renaud, related to Clarke.[61] According to this local source, if the troopers "had not a white officer with them they would never have gotten out." Renaud also believed: "there would have some very dead cow boys 'tambien.'"

Clarke reported the incident had not been an accident, given that he "found out that some of the cow boys had been spoiling for a fight saying that they were going to kill a 'nigger' that night and at the bar room one of them had jumped up swearing a soldier had hit him," which the lieutenant dismissed as untrue. The accuser pulled "his pistol on the soldier trying to shoot him but the gun missed fired and the soldier instead of running 'like a nigger' coolly pulled out his government Colt and opened up on the cow boy who fled."

The lanky lieutenant noted the cow puncher was a Texan, who must have headed to another water hole to fortify himself with more liquid courage. His feelings hurt and being run off "by a 'coon' … he got back on his horse and caused the stampede" in the saloon where the drama first unfolded. Clarke assured his father: "not a civil officer in town even attempted to arrest this man nor any of his friends." Because locals in Arizona often viewed the military with disdain and vice versa, the lack of response by law enforcement came as no surprise.[62] That tension seemed heightened because of the added racial element involved.[63]

No blood was spilled. The detail soon broke camp without further clashes to make their way to San Carlos with the five Apaches. Upon their return from Willcox, an unexpected, unusual reception awaited them because "after crossing the Gila at San Carlos, the Tenth Cavalry Band met them at the river and serenaded them into camp which caused a great deal of ill-feeling among the people at San Carlos."[64]

If Remington ever heard of this incident is not known, but in a December 27, 1888, letter, he did make note of an obscure tale about a black corporal shooting a sergeant at Fort Grant.[65] He next mentioned an illustration captioned, *Bringing in a Deserter*, which appeared in *Harper's Weekly* for December 8, 1888, expressing his pleasure that Clarke liked the picture. Remington joked to the lieutenant: "Was there a military error in it presume so."

In another reference to Remington's ever-expanding list of published drawings, he shared that he had sent Carter Johnson "a lot of papers" probably meaning he forwarded several copies of the December 22, 1888, issue of *Harper's Weekly* that carried a rendering of Clarke's fellow Tenth Cavalry officer. The shrewd artist added: "I sent a paper to Gen. Miles. Was that a good scheme?" In just a few scant years, the formerly obscure, scrambling-to-make a-living New Yorker had progressed from association with junior officers to elevating his standing to include high ranking military men such as Miles.

Remington had not forgotten the lower echelons as he referred to several efforts depicting enlisted men such as his "10th Cavalryman" which he sold at the National Academy of Design exhibition. His major news, however, was a painting for the Water Color Society based on a study he produced in Clarke's backyard at Fort Grant. Eventually, the final version possibly morphed into *Taps*, which showed a white cavalryman rather than a buffalo soldier.[66]

This was not the only time Remington converted an image based on black troopers. In its final form, however, Remington depicted whites most probably because the practical painter realized this substitution made better

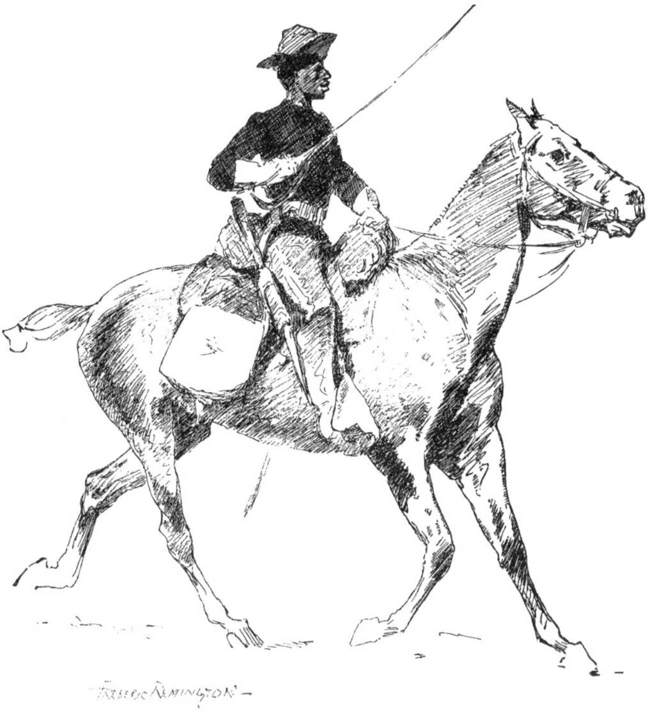

* No. 314. A U. S. Cavalryman—Frederic Remington.

SOUTH GALLERY.

NO.	SUBJECT.	OWNER OR PRICE.	ARTIST.
293	Cabbage-field,	$20.00	Chas. C. Curran.
294	"That All!"	25.00	Wm. J. Hays.
295	The Author of "The County Fair,"	Mrs. Charles Barnard,	Wm. Wallace Scott.
296	Bed-time,	30.00	M. L. Stone.
297	Ivory Miniature,		Mary C. Pursell.

18

Remington included *A U.S. Cavalryman* in his exhibition for The American Water Color Society, New York, 1891, as this line engraving indicated from the accompanying catalog. He assigned the same title to a rendering of a white horse soldier in 1888, which may have started as a depiction of "buffalo soldier" that he converted for artistic reasons and to enhance the ability to sell the original. Author's Collection.

financial sense when it came to a prospective buyer. Moreover, he probably thought art critics might find this adjustment more acceptable.

Being swamped with projects, Remington apologized to Clarke about his promise "to do some work for you [Clarke's portrait?] this year but I have got a mass of stuff to wade through which I can not see the end of and I am afraid I wont [*sic*] get around but be of good heart—Ill [*sic*] get there some time if death dont [*sic*] intervene." While the lieutenant had to wait for his gift, the artist at least urged Clarke to write "Garrison Life in the South West." He encouraged Clarke to "write way up—racy—real—unconventional—and Ill [*sic*] see what I can do with it."

At approximately the same time Clarke heard from Remington, he sent what seems to have been his final letter of 1888 to his father. Clarke's alternating downcast and hopeful tone stemmed from a projected visit with family and friends the next year.[67] That being impossible for the present, he spent some of the holidays at a reception the Vieles held for him and a few other young bachelor officers. After that, they took to their horses and "had fine chases" followed by "an exquisite dinner, which lasted until 4 a.m." At noon the next day, they ran a burro race with Clarke and the chaplain in the lead. They followed up with having a photograph taken and making calls before settling in "spinning yarns and talking about our various experiences since the last meeting. Altogether we had a very gay time of it."[68]

James Hughes also managed to pass through Fort Grant on his way to Fort Apache and San Carlos. Clarke and his classmate were joined by a third officer. Hughes had "a great deal of fun out of [William] Shipp," who formed part of the trio, badgering his comrade who evidently had become engaged while in Louisiana earlier in the year.

Once all had departed, Clarke confessed: "I am about as lonesome as old Graham Mountains." That feeling disappeared as 1889 brought many new experiences. Clarke shared one example of a break from the mundane in a January 9 letter from his new staiton at Fort Thomas.[69]

At nearby San Carlos, a disgruntled Apache, whom Clarke called Childmana, reportedly had "21 men ready to take to the field," which would have meant a campaign to keep the troops "busy for quite a little while." Clarke declared: "if he goes to killing you may count on about 80 to 100 settlers going to the happy hunting ground" but fortunately Clarke hoped ongoing negotiations would preclude another outbreak of violence. None the less, he cautioned his father not to share "anything about Indian news … for such things are generally kept quiet to avoid the brilliant Washington people from getting excited." He added that it was not wise to publicize "such small matters until negotiation fails."

Clarke mitigated his characteristic disdain for authorities in Washington with a desire not to cause undue excitement in case the situation ended in a peaceful solution. In fact, the Apache Chil-chu-a-na, as he was referred to by the Globe *Arizona Silver Belt*, had "transgressed disciplinary regulations" which landed him in the Fort Grant guardhouse. The resourceful prisoner managed to take "French leave of his custodians. At last accounts be was ambushing around in the hills in the vicinity of his wickiup on the Rio San Carlos, on the reservation."[70]

Despite Chil-chu-a-na's brief breakout, the reign of terror Clarke predicted did not come to pass. The situation stabilized so that there was little to do but daily drill and ten hours sleep a night for Clarke to consider requesting a brief leave to visit Jim Hughes, who by that time had transferred to Fort Apache.

Toward the end of the month, Clarke remained at Fort Thomas where in late January he indicated being "more contented with life as I find it."[71] Soberly, he went on to say "that an army officer has no business marrying at least not in our army." In fact, it was at least for the enlisted men a bachelor army for the most part, almost as if the attitude were "if the army wanted you to have a wife they would have issued you one." For officers it was slightly different, but here again the adage in the later Victorian military was lieutenants never marry, captains and major may, lieutenant colonels can, while colonels and generals must. Of course, in the concrete, the situation varied widely.

Without prospects of a bride, he likewise despaired of ever being posted to an eastern station. He especially believed this would be his fate because of John M. Schofield.[72] In 1888, after Philip H. Sheridan's death, Major General Schofield, who had served as superintendent of West Point during part of Clarke's cadet days, assumed command of the U.S. Army. Clarke viewed Schofield as "all artillery and hates colored troops." Clarke based the first part of his statement on Schofield's original commission as an artillery officer, but also to the young lieutenant, the general represented a certain mindset of those who served in that branch tucked away in comfortable coastal fortifications near major cities where spit and polish and paperwork ruled.

Clarke charged nepotism because the commanding general's son Richmond McAllister Schofield obtained a direct commission from civilian life in February 1889 as a cavalry officer. He decried his view that Schofield's son, who he referred to as "this man boy," had managed to secure a commission in "a choice regiment" while Andrew Greg Curtain Quay, son of Pennsylvania Senator Matthew Quay, landed a posh assignment at Fort Myer, Virginia, adjacent to Washington, D.C., in a staff position.[73] Clarke complained that Quay was but "6 months from the Academy, and as you remember that when I tried to go to Saumur it was urged that I had not been with my Regiment 3 years!"

Adding to his disdain, Clarke noted one of his fellow Tenth U.S. Cavalry, who had only joined in 1885, had "been in New York for nearly one year and a half." A discouraged Clarke declared: "at times it is enough to make a socialist of one if it were not for the many pieces of good luck I have had...." While he stood against "favoritism in a Republican Army," he admitted, "this is the only country in which I would not stand heart and soul for a throne. It's a heavy gilt edged affair, but it can't weight people down."

In the midst of the protestations about the good fortune of others, Clarke revisited his old dream of being sent off to Saumur. Acknowledging the improbability of an assignment to France, Clarke indicated that he was "always glad to get back to my work, the horses and bugles." Of course, he would not mind a little excitement, sharing: "If we could only have a good first class Indian chase with hard marches and bad water and picturesque climbs among the mountains just to stir ones blood up I would not 'kick.'"

In reality, Clarke amused himself with snipe shooting, which he found more of a sport than going after quail. What he really wanted was to kill his first "deer antelope." Such outings provided a bit of diversion and supplemented the issue beef and pork available on post.

He turned to another matter, telling his mother he was about to make his way to Fort Grant to pick up the rest of belongings. He admitted this would do little to make his new quarters more attractive. He hated "to give up his pretty cottage" at his former post, which had been his home for two and a half years.

Clarke's assignment to Fort Thomas came about as part of a regimental reorganization that took place after Grierson's elevation to command the Department of Arizona, ending the colonel's over two-decade tenure with the Tenth U.S. Cavalry.[74] This change meant that long-absent John Bigelow would return to Troop K, as Clarke mentioned in a January 25 note to his father.[75] Most probably, both Grierson's relocation to his headquarters in Santa Fe, New Mexico, and Bigelow's rejoining of the troop came as welcome news to the lieutenant particularly because Captain Lebo remained at Fort Grant leaving Clarke the sole officer from Troop K at Fort Thomas.

He believed it would be important for all three officers to be re-united because as one of his initiatives to reshape the army, General Schofield had "directed that all troops in each division be massed every summer in a large practice camp." If the plan came to be, troops from Arizona were to rendezvous at Santa Barbara, California, a prospect that pleased Clarke. The coastal resort would be most welcome, but Clarke rightly postulated the related expenses of such exercises would be denied by Washington.

Clarke prepared for this possible deployment by "drilling away like a Tartar." Such efforts frustrated him because, like some of his fellow officers, he complained about the quality of recruits sent to Tenth Cavalry. Clarke expressed his exasperation with a threat that he "would like to knock the heads off some of the recruiting officers … for some of the specimens of 'nigger' they send us, it is shameful. They could get better men if they would try." Clarke claimed recruiters simply did not care. His solution to this problem was to have "all recruiting for Colored Regiments … done by officers of such" a suggestion that he shared with not a few other commanders of black troops.[76]

In spite of challenges, Clarke punned he "would have 'K' in better shape than ever before, as I have no 'Mills' to grind and the Captain gives me full swing." At least relocation to Fort Thomas had ended Lieutenant Clarke's duels with Major Mills.

Still, he sought greener pastures. Clarke wondered if his old alma mater, Maryland Agricultural College, might not be in need of a "competent instructor of cavalry." To this end, he asked his father if he knew a faculty member there whom he might contact. While this would not be as prestigious or potentially as career enhancing as Saumur, being detailed as an officer at various land grant and other institutions to oversee the training of cadets was a common practice, as evidenced by John McDonald's assignment following his wedding.

Clarke's next letter to his mother made mention of Bigelow, who by now had fallen from favor with Troop K's second lieutenant.[77] He judged: "I do not think there is a beam of righteousness in the entire family." One wonders what Clarke's friend Remington would have thought about this pronouncement against an early patron?

Similarly, Clarke continued to show little respect for "Old Grierson," who despite leaving the regiment had "ordered that the Thomas and Grant garrisons would relieve the troop at San Carlos every two months, that is a troop would be two months at Thomas, two months at San Carlos & 6 months at Grant." Clarke expressed no concern about the scheme per se, were it not for the many married officers. Additionally, Mills would not have to move from Fort Grant where he would remain permanently so as not to be inconvenienced by periodic relocations, while Lebo was to remain at Thomas in command of the post. Once again, this would require Clarke to take charge of Troop K most of the time.

Grierson's plan following past practice also placed all his "pets" at Fort Apache "to make their life easy" for the favored few. Clarke also lashed out: "It would never enter the old pensioner's head to make the 4th Cavalry [which also was stationed in the department] do any of the dirty work."

As he previously indicated, leaving Fort Grant made Clarke sorry he had to abandon his comfortable "little house." At least he had escaped Lieutenant Colonel Pearson whom he denounced "as great a fool as Mills was a rascal." Clarke wished he could be under Van Vliet or his favorite—Shafter.

In fact, at Fort Thomas, he had occasion to spend time with William Shafter. As an example, he related that the pervious Sunday he dined with the colonel and his wife along with their daughter Mary and her husband William H. McKittrick, who had a ranch near Willcox.[78]

After "a swell dinner" at Hooker's Ranch they all went outside for a walk. Clarke's greyhounds provided a bit of entertainment when they chased "an immense hare," which they herded "within two feet of the ladies."

The next day, Clarke attended a hop on post. On Tuesday, Mrs. J.H. Norton, the wife of the post trader, included him at her musicale, which proved a treat as she "plays to perfection" he gushed. Likewise, the McKittricks, who possessed fine voices according to Clarke, "surpassed themselves." He admitted originally being "quite loth to return to [Fort] Thomas" but that opinion had disappeared as he did "not find it so bad after all," concluding that when he put his "quarters in shape I will be quite content." What was more, he briefly joined Dr. R.W. Johnson on the march to San Carlos, along the way shooting nearly a dozen snipe for supper.

Although Clarke seemed to have a great deal of free time, routine duties remained. For instance, as he closed his message home, he related it was his turn to serve as officer of the day.

Nearly a week later, Clarke dashed off another quick reply to his mother.[79] He put aside criticism of General Schofield, or at least in so far as he might be able, to obtain a favor from the army's commander. He suggested if his mother met the general, she should pass on her son's "compliments and tell him I think he has a good head [and] he has made some excellent moves." Given Schofield's lofty position relative to Clarke's low standing in the military hierarchy, at best he might have taken this as idle flattery; at worse he could have seen this as a pretentious comment from a very junior subordinate.

Once again, Clarke remained single-minded. He must succeed in securing permission from Schofield or the secretary of war to approve a year at the holy of holies—Saumur.[80]

With Miles as divisional commander, perhaps he hoped his prospects would improve. As before, he blamed some of the lack of success of his scheme to go to France on First U.S. Cavalry First Lieutenant Samuel C.

Robertson's making "an ass of himself." He revealed that he might have to ask his father to approach Schofield, who he now portrayed as "a thorough gentlemen" unlike some of the previous commanding generals of the army, although Clarke conceded some had been "good soldiers" even if they were Yankees who had bested the South.

Clarke expressed an abiding interest in his profession. He wanted "to see something of foreign armies and the military systems of France & Germany." The much-desired trip to Europe would improve his military education and language skills, or so he maintained. Perhaps he could even return to fencing, boxing, and rowing, all athletic pursuits he claimed he had to abandon after leaving West Point.

Despite his pleas, a year in France never materialized.[81] No reasons were given, but a litany of objections could have been made by his superiors. At least Clarke seemed safe from prying superiors at Fort Grant for the moment. In the spring, he enjoyed a good ten-day visit from Jim Hughes, who secured leave from Fort Apache allowing the two immortals to spend time together.[82]

Also, at that time, Remington reentered the picture, which should have bolstered Clarke's spirits even further. In his March 14, 1889, note, the frequently traveling artist shared that he recently returned "home from the city of Mexico where I have been doing the army. They are immensely picturesque and I have some good subjects."[83]

The extent of Clarke's interest in the Mexican military compared to his fascination with the French and German armies is unknown. Assuredly, Remington's other news caught the lieutenant's attention. Remington shared: "Our article comes out the 1st of April." At last, this meant the long anticipated "A Scout with the Buffalo Soldiers," would be published in *The Century Illustrated Monthly Magazine* for April 1889.

Remington added that if Clarke obtained leave, he should visit. The ever ready to enjoy himself Remington confirmed: "We will have a great little time here—I am full of work but a 'loafer' dont [*sic*] bother me." Also "Missie," the nickname used by those who knew Remington's wife Eva well, also chimed in telling her husband to invite "Mr. Clark [*sic*] to come on East and see us."

Early the next month, Remington followed up with acknowledgments of a photo Clarke had forwarded, one of a rabbit that he proposed to use "presently for an illustration."[84] He assumed that by the time his April 2 correspondence had reached Clarke, the lieutenant should have received the article in *The Century*. The author-artist candidly and somewhat immodestly remarked that it "reads well and has nothing else to recommend it."

Additionally, he commiserated about a medical problem with Clarke's eyes, but hoped "they may bring you East" which actually proved the case later in the year.[85] If so, he mightily looked forward to a reunion reflecting "it would not be a high carnival for you but then little things make life."

Clarke seemed optimistic that a medical leave would be forthcoming, as Remington indicated when he dashed off a few lines on April 15, 1889.[86] "Dear Old Boy: I m [*sic*] glad you are coming East," he said. Although he had much work he promised "that we meet this trip.—You have got to eat my porridge this time or bust a flue."

Before Clarke received the expected permission to travel for medical treatment in the East, as he had expected, an unforeseen incident briefly sent Clarke back into the field. The story began as routine duty for a joint Twenty-fourth Infantry and Tenth Cavalry detail dispatched to escort $28,000 in army payroll being distributed by Major Joseph Wham at Forts Grant and Thomas.

As the detail headed northward, they neared a narrow part of the road in the vicinity of Cedar Springs, where the soldiers spied a boulder in the middle of the path ahead impeding their passage. Some men went to remove the obstruction. As they did so, a single shot shattered the silence, followed by some fifteen or twenty other rounds. A gang had sprung an ambush.[87]

Caught without cover, the troops made a brave stand. After a sharp, short firefight, lasting about thirty minutes, eight of the eleven soldiers had been hit, including Sergeant Benjamin Brown, who had sustained two wounds, one of which was a dangerous shot in the abdomen. Corporal Isaiah Mays, also of the Twenty-fourth, was one of only three in the command who remained unscathed. He decided to crawl away from the assault. As soon as he thought it safe, Mays ran for nearly two miles to Cottonwood Ranch where he sought help for the surrounded patrol.

Eventually, Company K of the Twenty-fourth arrived in escort wagons, but they responded too late. The payroll was in the hands of the thieves, none of whom had been struck by return fire from the troops. In turn, eight of the dozen defenders became casualties "while bravely doing their duty under a murderous cross-fire," as Major Wham later reported.[88]

As soon as the battered escort made its way back to Fort Grant, an investigation and pursuit of the perpetrators commenced. Both civilian law enforcement and military patrols responded, including a contingent led by Clarke.

While Clarke's element of the manhunt rode, he received a message from Lebo with the "description of some of the robbers as given me." The captain continued: "I have notified C.O. of post & civil authorities." Aware of local sympathy for the culprits, Lebo cautioned: "Don't place too much confidence in the guide you have.... Think that if any men in this vicinity are concerned he would not act in good faith & mislead you in the trails."[89]

Lebo kept Clarke abreast with an update about a reward of "$500 for each man" involved in the robbery, and the fact that civilian law enforcement officers were at Fort Grant as was the departmental inspector general and Major Wham also conferring and coordinating the investigation. Lebo added a postscript. Another military contingent from the Fourth U.S. Cavalry would join the dragnet on May 15.[90]

Clarke's persistence resulted in the apprehension of one of the first suspects. Learning of this, Lebo ordered: "Keep your prisoner at Camp Goodwin tonight & bring him in tomorrow morning unless you receive other orders [from] me."[91] Having succeeded in this mission, Clarke returned to garrison. Soon afterward, he boarded a train to embark for his approved medical leave in the east.[92]

Even after departing Arizona, Clarke followed the court proceedings, which began in June. By that time, he was in St. Luke's Hospital where he had undergone a urethra surgical procedure in 1887. From here he wrote his mother: "That Wham Robbery Trial was a farce even for Arizona." He denounced the preliminary hearing as "ridiculous. Boodle and private interest, antipathy to the 'nigger' & government and hate of the staunch Marshall who had brought in the suspects and a litany of political machinations."[93]

Clarke also let his mother know he expected to be released in a few days and would join the family first in Baltimore and later at their summer home in Canada.[94] Recuperating through September, Clarke managed a visit to West Point. He may have spent time with the Remingtons as well.[95]

Now that medical matters had been addressed, along with a much-desired respite among family and friends, Clarke all too soon entrained for Arizona. This meant ending his journey at Willcox and returning to the routine of Fort Thomas, broken at the beginning of November by sitting on a court martial with several fellow officers at Fort Grant.[96]

With business as usual, letter writing returned as a means to retain contact with loved ones across the Mississippi. One of the lifelines came from Clarke's father, who remarked that the Remington picture "is very striking & certainly a fine work of art, but I agree with your mother that it does not look the picture of a gentleman. Yet there is a growing fascination about it."[97] It is unclear whether Clarke's father was speaking of the *Harper's Weekly* images of the lieutenant as they appeared in "A Scout with the Buffalo Soldiers" or another picture, perhaps the portrait Remington had "intended to do you up in water color with my compliments," but had not delivered until Clarke's visit during his medical leave.[98]

This was followed by Remington's next letter in which he requested Clarke's opinion, as was typical of many of the artist's notes to the lieutenant.[99] After listing four new works that had gained note in some instances, he queried: "What did you think of My Mexican Army in Harper's Magazine," referring to a November 1889 article published under that title, penned by Thomas Janvier, and illustrated by Remington. To this Missie added a post-script: "You ought to leave the army, get married & come & live next to us if you want perfect enjoyment."

Eva Remington also wanted to know if Clarke still paced "the floor with" his hands in his "pockets and talk war." This was a rhetorical question. She wrote: "I know you do and still I love you." Assuredly, the April 1889 issue of *The Century Magazine* not only did much to reinforce the comradeship between Clarke and Remington, but also the fact that Eva expressed a fondness for the quirky, gangly cavalryman cemented this bond even further.

Although the Remingtons included Clarke into their realm, the lieutenant's core remained family as intimated in a lengthy letter sent to his father near the end of December. Next week, he would be off to Fort Grant and hoped "not to get as drunk as I was last year. I have really been very good since my return and begin to think I have about sewn [*sic*] my … wild oats. We are going to have a splendid time all the same."[100]

He added: "Miles & Grierson have both sanctioned officially our re-union at Xmas, the latter sent a very nice circular to the Post Commanders telling them to give us all aid—that it is considered good for the 'Espirit de Corps'. This meeting will be more dignified and not a spree for we have determined to make a Regiment of the Tenth Cavalry."

Again, he sang his old tune that harkened back to the cadet drinking song "Benny Havens, Oh!" One stanza ran: "in the army there's sobriety, promotion's mighty slow."[101] On one hand, sobriety was not always the norm in the oft hard-drinking army. Clarke pointed to this fact in his letter about attempting moderation during the holidays, but assuredly climbing the military ladder, which at that time from second lieutenants through captains could only take place within regiments, was "appallingly slow unless speeded up by deaths of friends and comrades."[102] As such, Clarke once more expressed: "I am really frightened about the infernal attempts Schofield is making for 'lineal promotion.'"

Clarke questioned whether his father knew someone "of influence you can talk to—it will spoil the happiness of my military life." He challenged: "We should stick to Regimental promotion and then there will be some chance of our having esprit de corps and good efficient regiments. When I am to be promoted to first lieutenant I do not want to be sent to some Regiment that I do not know and where I will have to begin afresh to make new ties and a new record and then none of us who wish to have the friends whom we have tried for long years under such crucial tests as those through which Arizona has put us all." Content with the traditional system of regimental promotion, he laid the proposed new scheme at the feet of "a few growlers who get their promotion, it is sickening this eternal sacrifice of interests of the service to a lot of grumbling stay away and political soldiers."

Clarke was not above some of his own nest feathering. With France disappearing as a dim possibility, he intended to ask his Aunt Mary, who planned a trip aboard, to speak to German general of cavalry Maximillian von Versen "to get me to Berlin.... I am all the more anxious for a detail to Europe."[103]

He noted: "the catarrh does not seem to get better but is even getting my throat" and was taking treatment. Regardless of continuing physical issues, Clarke's life was far better than it had been. Nearby friends in Arizona, such as Jim Hughes and other brother officers, as well as some delightful civilian companions helped improve his off-duty lot. Thanks to Remington, he gained some popular national exposure, in the process enjoying a warm friendship with the artist and his wife. Clarke even managed a trip east, where he could reunite with many of those by whom he well regarded besides enjoying some different scenery in Canada and elsewhere.

All in all, he was fortunate, even though he bemoaned that the lack of advancement, the dream of a posting abroad, and his bachelorhood were not necessarily ideal. In this final category, a possible lady to end his single state had escaped him as his one-time fellow Fort Davis and late Fort Grant neighbor related in her memoirs.

The day before Christmas of 1889, Mrs. Forrestine Cooper Hooker, now the mother of a little girl who was almost three years old and a boy of a year and a half, was visiting her father-in-law's ranch.[104] Four young officers of the Tenth Cavalry who had known her as a teenager (Charles Grierson, James Watson, Alexander Dade, and Powhatan Clarke) learned she was at the Henry Hooker Ranch, ten miles from the garrison.

Learning of her presence, they "rode over with invitations for Mrs. Henry Hooker, Mrs. Ida Stewart (my sister-in-law), and myself, to attend the dance and stay overnight as the guests." It so happened that Powhatan elected to serve as Forrestine's "escort that night, and between dances we tried to puzzle out what had happened" to a note she had sent him while he was in the field, "which he had never received, and his note that had never reached me, asking me to write. The statement as to his reason for applying for field duty had been with out any foundation, and he said that he was sure 'I under stood, and would wait for him to come back.'"

She added: "It was a frank talk on both sides, and we understood each other perfectly. The next morning I went back to the ranch, and then to Los Angeles. He returned to his station at Fort Thomas, and we never saw one another again, but I heard from him by letters at intervals."

The gist of the conversation had to do with a message she thought Dr. Peter Egan would deliver to Clarke. Inadvertently, the note had been thrust into a pigeon hole of a local rancher's desk, never to be handed off to the doctor until discovered years later. Philosophically, Forrestine commented: "So the story ended. But I have never forgotten, and I know that he [Clarke], too, always remembered the old sycamore tree up Grant Creek, and the monogram he had carved the day I promised to 'come back to our tree.'" That chance of fate, she said "changed the course of both our lives, as well as influencing others." While the pair never saw each other again, both going their separate ways, romance, adventure, a bit of notoriety, and even a posting to Europe, although not as originally conceived, awaited the goat of West Point's Class of 1884.

Chapter 8

"We Went to Arizona for to Fight the Indians There"

Ironically, while Clarke returned to the "wilds" of Arizona to spend the 1889–1890 holidays in comfort, the usually well-situated Easterner Remington was roughing it. As indicated in a January 9, 1890, letter about his "Ten days before Xmas," the artist and "another man who was also insane and I started to make a dash for the North Pole—we got as far as Matawa Canada, and then concluded to hunt the 'festive moose' as you would say."[1]

Indicative of Remington's growing success and fame, he offhandedly remarked that General Nelson Miles "sent me a nice little note—wanted all my work." Since the end of the Geronimo campaign, Miles began his steady ascent up the U.S. Army command ladder. In fact, by 1888, the death of the U.S. Army's commanding General Philip Sheridan resulted in a series of promotions and reshuffling of the army's upper echelons. Among others, Miles moved up a notch from heading the Department of Arizona as a brigadier general to the next tier as Division of the Pacific commander, which soon brought him his second star as a major general. As Robert Utley summarized in *The Commanders*: "Both in Arizona and in San Francisco he [Miles] kept himself in the public spotlight and cultivated influential friends" as he sought his second star and looked beyond to even loftier goals.[2] Remington's association with this rising power proved a boon to both the artist and the general, and possibly assisted Clarke's future advancement.

Remington had advanced considerably since his days as a hand-to-mouth illustrator. Nevertheless, he still looked to the bottom line. Remington "gasped" at Miles, who asked for free samples of articles. He considered making the general "pay for it—but the Kings [*sic*] request is a demand so I … got the plunder to gather [*sic*] sent it to him with note all about how happy I was," and asked why "the general thought so much of the art."

Providing the general these publications worked to Remington's benefit. Possibly Remington's interactions with Miles aided Clarke as well. After the packet arrived from Remington, Miles "replied by a very graceful letter missive which is now pasted in my scrap book but seriously it was good of the Gen. to like my stuff and I was duly honored etc. he asked me to come out next summer.… I recen [*sic*] you & I could get a pack train if we wanted it."

While building a relationship with one of the army's top leaders, Remington remained busy in his studio "at work on that big cavalry picture … got smoke and blood a foot thick on it—think it will get there." In addition to this major canvas, he wrote Clarke on January 30, 1890, that he began "slicking" up the lieutenant's portrait for an exposition "of the Society of Am. Artists" to be held in the spring of 1890.[3] Remington shared: "it was a rather good bit of painting," humorously adding: "You remember it.—something like this." Here Remington included a caricature.

Unfortunately, only a portion of the painting survived. A black and white full-length published version, however, appeared in *Harper's Weekly* for March 22, 1889. It was one of two images individually depicting Clarke along with a rendering of his fellow Tenth Cavalry officer, Second Lieutenant Carter Johnson.

Remington then indicated he would take Clarke's advice and subscribe to *The Cavalry Journal*, but not immediately because he had "joined every d– association in America in the last 6 months but that I have bought a house have got to buy another horse—two wagons—everything I am hopelessly bankrupt—but if I can have six months I will get my second wind and then I'll join the C.A. [Cavalry Association] & run for Congress; or scuttle a ship."

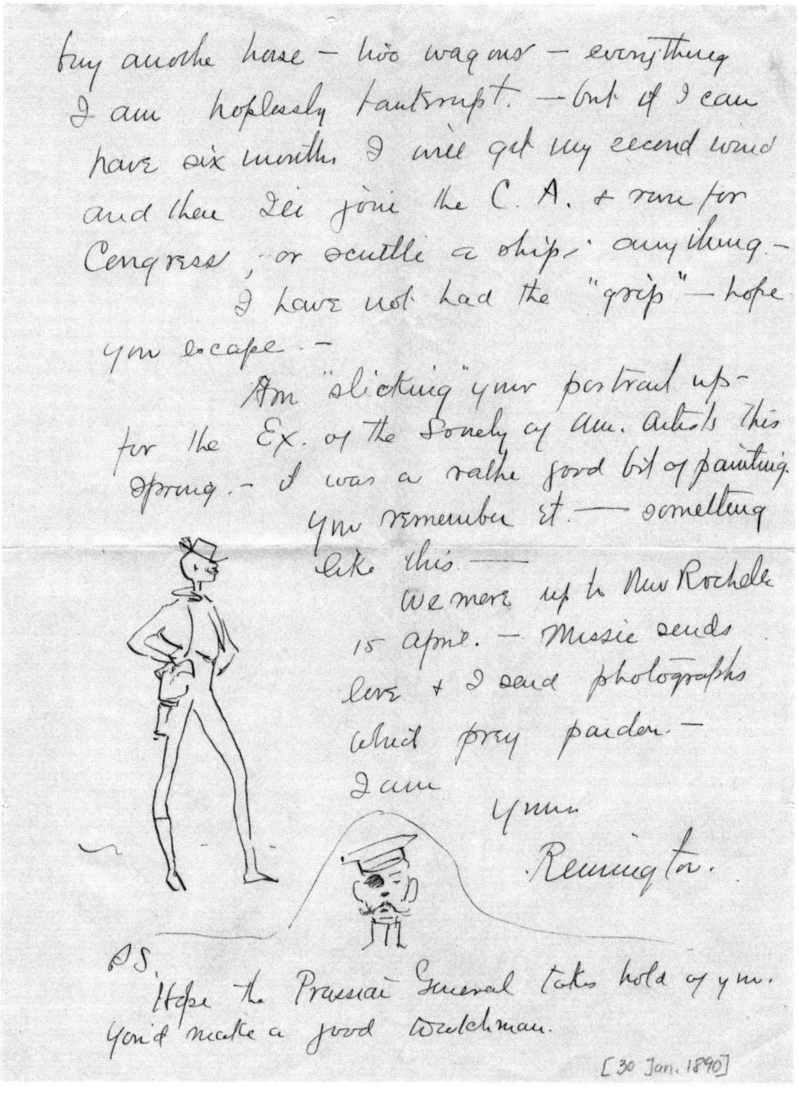
buy another horse — two wagons — everything
I am hopelessly bankrupt. — but if I can
have six months I will get my second wind
and then I'll join the C. A. & run for
Congress, or scuttle a ship; anything. —
I have not had the "grip" — hope
you escape. —
Am "slicking" your portrait up —
for the Ex. of the Society of Am. Artists this
Spring. — It was a rather good bit of painting.
You remember it. — something
like this. —
We move up to New Rochelle
15 April. — Missie sends
love & I send photographs
which pray pardon. —
I am
Yours
Remington.
PS.
Hope the Prussian General takes hold of you.
You'd make a good watchman.
[30 Jan. 1890]

Pleased with his latest painting, Remington told Clarke in a January 30, 1890, letter: "Am 'slicking' your portrait up for the Ex. Of the Society of Am. Artists [American Art Galleries] this Spring.—it was a rather good bit of painting. You remember it.—some like this—" Missouri History Museum, St. Louis.

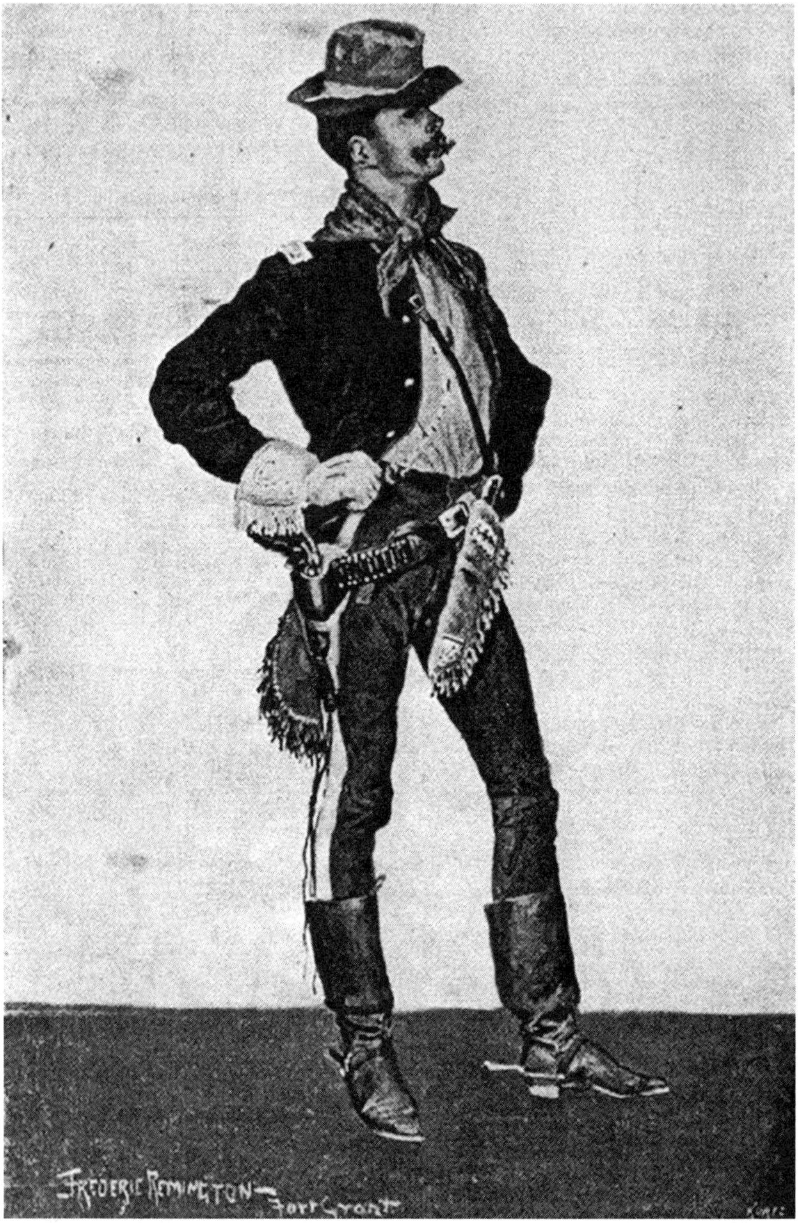

Remington transformed a disheveled, gangly Powhatan H. Clarke into a noble knight errant with dashing cavalryman's handlebar moustache for *Harper's Weekly* (March 22, 1890), p. 216.

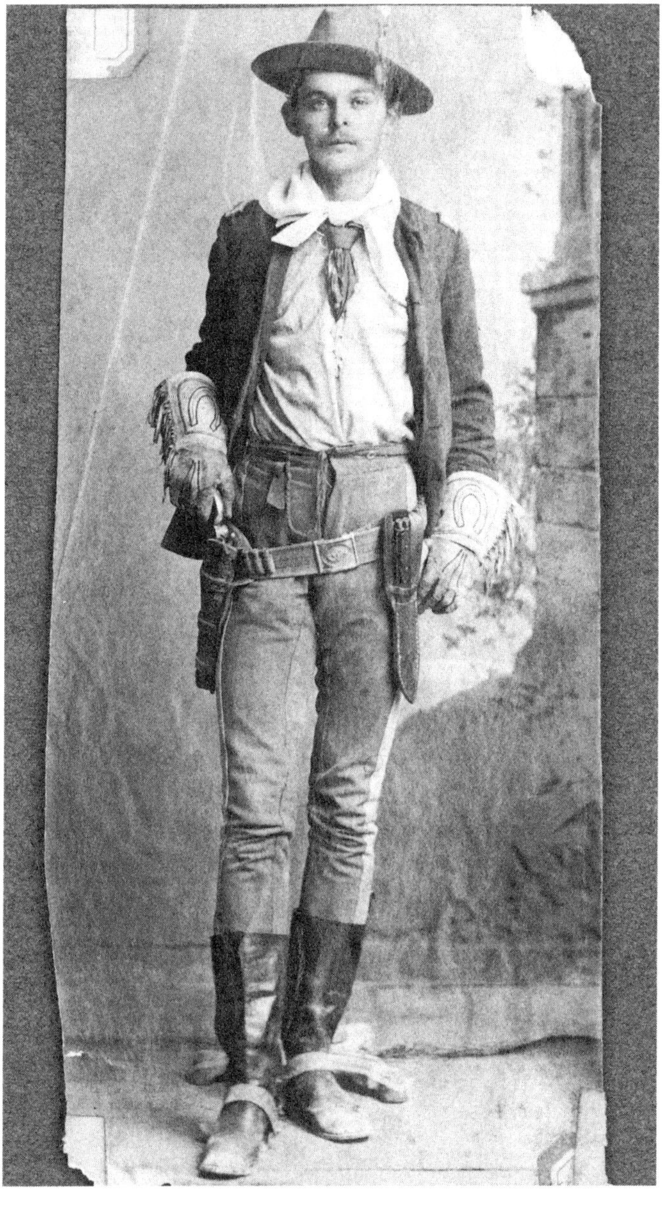

Tucson photographer Henry Buehman's portrait of an awkward Clarke with a wispy moustache portrayed a man far from the *beau ideal* of a frontier horse soldier. Courtesy Frederic Remington Art Museum, Ogdensburg, New York.

Besides cash-flow, Remington concluded that the content of *The Cavalry Journal* might be of limited use. After all, "soldiers by profession" dealt with the future. Remington remonstrated, he did not "care a d– what you cavalry-man are going to do—its [*sic*] what you have done" that interested him.

Thereafter, Remington boasted: "My big 'cavalry fight' is going to be a 'corker'—I tell you boy I've got 'em to fighting—blood by the bucket full—smoke enough for Chicago in '70." Then he gently prodded Clarke for the lieutenant's "views on the reorganization of the army—'socilistic [*sic*] & general equality racket' etc." Further, Remington cautioned: "you would be better off in a new deal—this scheme of [your's] the man who has the best vital organization and who takes the most care of himself eventually getting to be General of the Army is tough." He added a postscript: "Hope the Pussian [*sic*] General takes hold of you. You'd make a good watchman," referring to Clarke's latest plot to reach Europe.

Having failed in his attempts at a posting to French cavalry school, the capricious Clarke set his sights on another European assignment—Germany. While Clarke possessed no German language capabilities that fact did not dissuade him.

Once more, Clarke sought family connections to promote his most recent venture. He persuaded his mother to intercede with her sister, Mary Boyce, to "touch up" General Max von Versen who had been made "commander of the Cavalry of the Guard" in Germany.[4] Clarke reckoned the general's "influence must be great." Given von Versen's lofty position, it seemed improbable that a lowly, unknown American lieutenant could catch the German general's eye.

The fact that the general had married a distant relation of Mark Twain, Alice Bryan Clemens, one of twelve children of a prominent St. Louis businessman and banker James Clemens, Jr. and his wife, made the impossible, possible.[5] Mary Boyce's social standing in St. Louis meant she was connected by blood, marriage, or social ties to all the upper crust there. In fact, it was the first factor that came to play. Alice von Versen and she traced their lineage to a common ancestor. That happenstance provided Clarke a conduit to the German nobleman-general through his wife.

One of the supposed assets Clarke could bring to an overseas assignment was his marksmanship. He was "putting in about 2,000 rounds of revolver ammunition a month and getting so that tin cans can be hit at a gallop at twenty yards." While dismounted, he was "also doing good work at a hundred yards." He believed these capabilities would impress either the French or the Germans. It did not matter to which country he went. He simply did not want "to spend my days in a two-company post" any longer.

Yet Clarke told his mother that his posting to Arizona really was "quite decent at times when I am home here with my Africans and my dogs."[6] Nonetheless, neither possible relocation of his Troop K to a better military installation someday, nor a potential transfer to Troop L at Fort Bayard, New Mexico, which he portrayed as "a gay post near Silver City," satisfied his wanderlust.[7]

Heading to New Mexico ran contrary to Clarke's Troop K loyalty with whom he had served for a half-dozen-years. Clarke admitted to being "such a slave to my own comfort that I do not like to leave Turner" his valued striker, and "my cozy quarters" that he had settled into at Fort Thomas. Going to Fort Bayard meant starting over and hauling only his books with him. "Moreover I hear there will be some scouting after Apaches in the vicinity in March," a prediction that proved accurate. If so, he did "not want to miss that—in it alone is there any chance for reputation, but for that matter even if I go to 'L' I would come back for the scouting."

Torn, Clarke stated if "offered the command of the troop I could not refuse it." That would mean "the labor required, the skill, tact, punishment that have to be employed with these mobs which have been thoroughly ruined by inefficient drunken officers" who previously held the command. He believed it would take years to undo the damage requiring "the tough element" in the ranks to be "entirely eradicated" for the sake of bringing the troop up to his standards.

Rumors of an opportunity for scouting were one thing. A determined Clarke felt Europe held a greater promise.

Falling back to the past discourses, he once more implored his father to champion the cause. This time he required Dr. Powhatan Clarke to travel to Washington to meet the U.S. Army's adjutant general, John Cunningham Kelton,

West Point Class of 1851. When the former Confederate officer requested a posting abroad for his son, he maintained the desire for duty in Europe was "no freak."[8] Instead, he contended his son did so out of "intense pride in the service." Afterwards, Dr. Clarke laid out other particulars to strengthen the case, to which the adjutant general responded: " 'You will have good news of him soon!' "

While in Washington, the ever-ambitious Clarke wanted his father to pursue more than a possible sponsor "about foreign details" which he was willing to undertake with his own funds. He likewise stirred old coals. Clarke had the audacity to add that Dr. Clarke "bear in mind whenever he meets a politician who takes any interest … he must impress upon him not to favor the 'lineal promotion' bills." Once more, he groused this policy would set back his promotion to captain by five years "besides breaking up our regiment."[9]

Dr. Clarke seemingly sidestepped this second mission from his son, but did manage to secure some promising news from Kelton about Europe. He noted the adjutant general "told me you will have something by January you can much understand how satisfying it would be if von Versen can initiate supporting you to go to Germany if anything happens I shall see that von Versen soon hears it."[10] Dr. Clarke also mentioned returning a letter from Remington, which indicated that Clarke shared some of his exchanges with the artist of potential interest to his family.

As Clarke dreamed of a European billet, Remington reappeared on the scene. This time he announced: "I have been elected to a life membership of the Cavalry Association," thereby being one of the first to be so honored to attend this recently formed organization (1888) at Fort Leavenworth, Kansas.[11] He accepted "the favor with avidity and the greatest pleasure." Under the circumstances, Remington reversed his previous course, stating tongue in cheek, he would "be glad to 'cough up' the dues, initiation fees, real and personal taxes, insurance gas and water rates and would even be glad to enrich a post trader for a basket if I could do so."

Continuing, "I suppose there must be [*sic*] for a member of the Cav. Ass'tion. I'll be blowed if you can ever make me walk up hill like a dough boy, now that I am a cavalryman." Light-heartedly, the New Yorker teased: "Of course my acceptance of this honor is conditioned on the understanding that I am not to go to war. My business in life, as a painter and illustrator is to give other fellows the credit that is due for gallantry. I desire no honors of this kind myself. In the public judgement of to day I am accorded the benefit of a doubt as to the heroism of my moral nature and I never want to get up very close to an evily [*sic*] disposed person with a gun for fear that the doubt might be dissipated."

Later that same month, Remington offered another interesting morsel.[12] His association with Nelson Miles had advanced to the point that the newly promoted major general, who had been in New York for a week, invited Remington to Governor's Island, the long-time military installation that once served as part of the city's harbor defenses. After many iterations, the post had become a major army administration center and recruit rendezvous. Regrettably, the artist "could not go."

Remington reciprocated Miles's offer with a counter suggestion that the general "ride and dine with me" adding the "he feels very kindly disposed toward me—he liked the article just published in Harpers" referring to the March 22, 1890, piece featuring Lieutenants Clarke and Watson. Remington related that the general "spoke very highly of both of these officers" as well as "inquired about you in many ways and I made remarks calculated to do you good."

Remington lobbied to further Clarke's career. For this same purpose, the savvy New Yorker also advised: "You just be good to Gn. Mils [*sic*] and your day will come—he is disposed to treat you with consideration—bide your time don't ask small favors but wait until he is in shape and then you can bet a favor that you want and that is of importance." If Clarke followed this path, Remington foresaw his friend would get "to that d– French Cav. School or to Washington one of these days if we have to burn New York City."

Remington's good deed for Clarke came with a small price. Fred asked if Powhatan was acquainted with any officers at Fort Wingate, New Mexico. Remington was considering this post as a jumping-off point for another excursion to the Southwest.[13] He also wanted to know: "What are the hotel accomodations [*sic*] there" perhaps really seeking that information, or possibly fishing for a free roof over his head as he had when he stayed with Clarke at Fort Grant a few years earlier.

Turning to Remington's most recent *Harper's Weekly* submission, the story and illustrations recapped a recent break in the relative quiet that had settled over Arizona with Geronimo's incarceration in the East. As the regimental history of the Tenth Cavalry recorded, while "The Indians were … fairly well settled down to farming on their reservations" there were "sporadic outbreaks" that brought the restless Clarke back into action. The lieutenant "with a detachment of picked men and scouts, had a roving commission to run down the hostiles still 'out,' and did excellent work."[14]

Once more, Clarke escaped "the infernal … clerical work such as courts martial & Boards of survey" in garrison for the exhilaration of the field.[15] Tragically this opportunity came because of the death of Frank Herbert at the hands of El-Chees-Choos, Nas-good, In-dees-doo-day, and two other warriors at Black Point (also known as Point of the Rocks) seven miles northwest Fort Thomas.

Prior to Herbert's killing, on March 3 and 4, 1890, Mexican troops had clashed with Apaches including Hale (Miguel) where in the wake of the two-day fight, a watch belonging to Sheriff Glenn Reynolds, who had been killed during the escape of the Apache Kid and his followers, on November 2, 1889, was recovered.[16]

The story of Reynolds's murder went like this: After the Kid's return to Arizona and as he was being escorted back to San Carlos, the army determined that they should not have tried him and his companions by court-martial. Instead, they should be judged in the civil courts.

A new trial held at Globe ended with the Kid, Say-es, Pash- ten -tah (Bach-e-on-al) and Hale (Miguel) being found guilty of the attempted murder of Al Sieber. Convicted of this crime, all these former scouts were sentenced to seven years at the Yuma Territorial Prison. These four and a like number of other Apaches named Hos-cal-te (Tonto Tag Number 60), El-cahn, Has-ten-tu-du-jay, and Bi-the-ja-be-tish-to-ce-an, along with a Mexican convicted of horse rustling, were on their way to the railhead at Casa Grande. They were guarded by Sheriff Glenn Reynolds and W.A. "Hunkydory" Holmes, in a wagon driven by a third civilian, Eugene Middleton. At Kelvin Grade in the Tortilla Mountains the incline became so steep all the prisoners dismounted their moving jail. En route, they overcame their guards, both of whom died in the escape attempt. Making good their attack, they scattered, leaving behind a wounded Middleton and the stunned horse thief.

Some four months later, one of the fugitives, Hale, had been brought to bay. At the time, the Mexican forces under Moscow-born, now Mexican officer, Emilio Kosterlitzky, had no idea about the relationship of their two-day fight with the Apache Kid and his fellow runaways.[17] Not until Kosterlitzky expressed the watch and chain to authorities in the United States, along with a revolver bearing some initials and a money pouch with U.S. currency, did it become clear that these were all items from Sheriff Reynolds' body.[18]

Three days after Kosterlitzsky's fight in Sonora north of the international line, another two Indians were killed and three captured. The survivors, El-Chees-Choos, Nas-good, and In-dees-doo-day, remained at large, trailed by an unusual composite force during the days of a segregated army. The patrol consisted of hand-picked African American veteran soldiers from Troops I, K, and L of the Tenth U.S. Cavalry, a small detail of white enlisted men from Troop L, Fourth U. S. Cavalry, and Indian scouts, all White Mountain Apaches save one Yavapai.[19] Clarke explained why this outfit as selected from several sources. He maintained: "an American troop will have in it only a few splendid riders and a lot of men who are absolutely worthless." This meant that for serious duty, such "as an Indian chase, we take selected men from several troops."[20] Clarke's hard-earned years of experience paid off as this red, white, and black strike force under Lieutenant James Watson, with him as second in command, closed with their enemy three miles north of Roggenstrohs's Ranch near the mouth of Cherry Creek at Salt River.[21]

A succinct recap of this engagement appeared in Tucson's Spanish language newspaper, *El Fronterizo*.[22] In crisp prose, the reporter recounted the "5 renegades who murdered the driver George Herbert last week were hit yesterday, 30 miles north of here, by the troops of Lieutenants Watson and Clarke, a rough fight ensued which resulted in the death of two hostiles and the capture of the remaining three." The clash took place after a chase of "more than three hundred miles through the most rugged country of the territory." The two dead Apaches were buried where they fell. The prisoners went to Globe before being "taken to San Carlos and then handed over to the authorities of Graham county."

On the same day (March 15, 1890), a Tucson English-language paper, the *Arizona Weekly Citizen*, provided its version of the confrontation as well as a report for Washington, D.C. regarding deliberations by the House Committee on Indian Affairs to relocate Geronimo and other Apache prisoners from the East to "be safely confined on Fort Sill reservation."[23]

Addressing the former topic, the reporter added details such as the fact that the command led by Watson and Clarke overtook "the renegades on Salt river, about 30 miles north of Globe in a rugged and almost impenetrable locality. The troops surprised the renegades at 1 o'clock, p.m., on Friday, and after the first exchange of shots the renegades took to the rocks and began a determined fight for their lives." During the course of the action, "The troops and scouts displayed great bravery …, although at a disadvantage" in their positions against a well concealed enemy. Rare praise from locals called this "the best piece of work ever accomplished in the pursuit of Indians in Arizona, and the greatest credit is due to the lieutenants for their splendid work, and those under them especially 'Rowdy' and other scouts, who resolutely stuck to the trail until the fugitives were sighted."

This last-named participant, Yavapai scout Sergeant Rowdy (a Tolkapaya, at that time erroneously referred to as a Yuma Apache) boasted considerable previous service.[24] Rowdy, known to be an "excellent shot," and loyal soldier proved his value on more than one occasion.[25]

The March 15, 1890, edition of Globe's *Arizona Silver Belt* further praised the scout and the young officers. In no uncertain terms, the paper credited "the experience and determination of Lieut Watson and the faithfulness of the scouts. In fact, had it not been for the admirable performance of the trailers, especially Rowdy, capture of the renegades would have been impossible." To express their appreciation, the citizens of Globe held an impromptu celebration in honor of the good work.[26]

Taking a similar approach, Florence's *Arizona Weekly* lauded the "lieutenants for their splendid work, and those under them, especially 'Rowdy' and other scouts, who stuck doggedly to the trail until the fugitives were sighted."[27] In this instance, twenty-eight-year-old Sergeant Rowdy, who had been "described as 'old in war—loved campaigning and fighting and killing … even better than he loved whiskey" received recognition rarely accorded Indian scouts by the frontier press. Because of the major role Rowdy played in leading the detachment to the enemy followed by his valiant participation in the subsequent fight, he became one of eleven American Indians from Arizona to be awarded the Medal of Honor.[28]

In fact, another report from Globe's *Silver Belt* described the intense action as the patrol closed on the renegades. Both Watson and Clarke led from the front, intent on reaching the mouth of a small cave, which colorfully was described as "not as deep as a quart mug." Clarke, the first to appear in front of the enemy hideout, shot one of them "twice though the body. 'Rowdy' the Indian scout shot the Indian, breaking both arms, thus saving the life of 'Tucson's own' Lieut Clarke" who had a bullet hole "through his hat and also one between his legs."[29]

Likewise, Sergeant James T. Daniels of Troop I, Fourth U.S. Cavalry and Sergeant William McBryar of Clarke's Troop K, joined Rowdy in the elite pantheon of Medal of Honor recipients. Daniels would be commended for "Untiring energy and cool gallantry under fire in an engagement with Apache Indians." McBryar would be singled out "for coolness, bravery and marksmanship while his troop was in pursuit of hostile Apache Indians."[30]

In McBryar's case, as Frank N. Schubert underscored in *Black Valor*, the army approved his medal "with almost no delay, making him the first man in the Tenth Cavalry to be so honored." Schubert postulated: "The speed with which this award was made suggests that McBryar did indeed distinguish himself. Frequently, years passed before officers got around to submitting recommendations, and sometimes the soldiers themselves had to start the process."[31]

The long-time colonel of the Tenth Cavalry, Benjamin Grierson, now Department of Arizona commander, recommended the prompt award of brevets and medals usual in cases of distinguished gallantry.[32] Additionally, he echoed others when he stated: "This is one of the most brilliant affairs of its kind that has occurred in recent years and has had a very quieting effect upon, and will no doubt prove a lasting lesson to, the Indians of the San

Carlos Agency. It was, therefore, extremely gratifying to congratulate the commanding officers of San Carlos and Fort Thomas, and especially Lieutenants Watson and Clarke and the troops under their command for the persistent pursuit and complete success."[33] Even Remington took heed of the affray, turning it into "Two Gallant Young Cavalry Men" for *Harper's Weekly*.

After much fanfare, Clarke made his way back to Fort Thomas. Almost as soon as he arrived, notice came of another additional duty. He was made acting signal officer, which required him to remain "in readiness to take charge of divisions or stations during the general practice" that would be held in the near future.[34] Clarke's heroism and recent fame aside, he reverted to business as usual.

Clarke's next letter to his father reflected as much.[35] Another brief diversion from garrison matters sent him "to Black Rock out on an Indian rumor." After a rapid jaunt and because his "scouts found the signs of Indians but the trail was too old and spoiled by wind and loose horses" his patrol quickly turned back to the post.

In garrison once more, Clarke enjoyed periodic visits from three junior subalterns "owing to the band of Apaches over whom they and their troops were acting as guards." As a result of the Apache Kid and other raiders, the government devised a strategy to end the last vestiges of the Apache war, prompting Clarke to remark, "it is strange how our race reasons 'to its own advantage[;]' it is a pitiful sight to see a whole tribe took up and shipped away because it has shown sympathy and given shelter to some of its renegade members."

Clarke found official policy "necessary to bring about the capture of the renegades" distasteful. He contended the forced removal of families and friends of the men being pursued "would not have been very digestible to the sensitive abolitionist. . . ." On the surface, their departure seemed "picturesque enough in the excessively bright light—the long rolling cloud of dust—the heavy lumbering Army wagons filled with men, women and children, the advance guards and long lines of troopers and the debarkation was really well worth seeing." Clarke concluded: "They may say what they choose but the Apache is a fearless and at times handsome man with all his cunning and craft for both of which qualities he well deserves the same praise we give our own." He added that the government's removal of possible accomplices from San Carlos was wrong.

While this forced relocation went into motion, Clarke's father took time to write his son. He acknowledged receipt of a copy of *Harper's Weekly*.[36] The doctor assured: "It is a great pleasure as we advance in life to find comfort and take pride in the conduct and character of our children." To assure that his lieutenant son did not become too self-important after being praised by his father, Dr. Clarke recounted how his wife reacted to "Powie's' photograph, or woodcut" in *Harper's*. Clarke's mother maintained it "did not do him justice. He looks too much a 'bronco breaker' and the white stripe on the right leg of his pants blending with the ground of paper on which it is cast, gives him a 'spider legged' appearance in that limb," she criticized. Despite misgivings, the proud mother read the article to others. She also borrowed from Remington's language about Clarke's ancestry hoping that her son's "Western frontier life will not contaminate that refinement which he inherited from his 'Virginia, and Louisiana French blood.'"

A few days later, Dr. Clarke indicated that a reporter from the Baltimore *Sun* came to their house. The professor asked the reporter if he "had killed anybody. 'No sir, but your son has!'"[37] Then the doctor shared a recent dispatch from Washington indicating that Grierson requested Powhatan's promotion, which in essence was an endorsement, but not necessarily within his ability to set in motion because of the time in grade rule required for advancement. The reporter followed with a request for Dr. Clarke to forward a copy of Remington's *Harper's* story to him. The next day the Baltimore paper published a complete rehash of Remington's article, but made no mention of Grierson's dispatch. Dr. Clarke felt "tempted to let him have extracts from your very interesting letters, but thought it best" not do so.

He asked Powhatan if he sent Aunt Mary a copy of *Harper's*. Powhatan responded: "I believe I did, but I'm not sure. On reflection I did not. Shall I send her one?" Because the lieutenant looked to his Aunt Mary Boyer for aid in his bid for a German posting, providing her this latest story might have aided his case. Clarke intended to visit her during his leave, which he planned to apply for in "late in May or in June."[38]

His energy levels had reached low ebb. He said: "I am generally so tired out from target practice which leaves me in the sun from 7 AM until noon and on horseback from 1:45 till four that I do not feel like writing." Clarke asked to be forgiven if he sounded disrespectful in any way in an earlier letter; "either the heat or the target practice or these odious medicines," which he did not name as to the type and the malady for which they were prescribed, "make me feel like an electric battery all day and I will be glad to get away for a few months." Given that Clarke continued to suffer from a sexually transmitted disease, the many heavy metal "cures" such as mercury pills, employed to combat venereal ailments, typically proved dangerous, painful, and ineffective. Clarke's lament was not unfounded.

As Clarke wrestled with his health issues, his mother informed him she had been in New York visiting a sick relative. This was why she had not written recently.[39] While there, two families independently bought her copies of *Harper's*. She was told "it was time for you to bring suit against Remington for libel methinks perfection perfectly absurd."

Powhatan viewed the article in a different light. Letters kept arriving from his New York admirer. In fact, Clarke sent thanks to Remington, who on April 9 responded: "Your letter at hand—don't mention it old man you chaps deserve that sort of thing and I propose to do it as much as I find occasion for."[40]

Of further interest was Remington's painting of Clarke, which now hung in "the American Art Association Galleries and is admired by thousands—they think you are a d– tough looking cuss but you can stand it—got you between a d– greaser and a bad cow boy and they [sic] suffer by comparison. I have made a hit on the Exhibition I think." In closing, Remington commiserated with his cavalry hero ending: "Sorry you couldn't give the French dough-boy a 'whirl'" because Saumur had been denied.

While military authorities squelched Clarke's bid for France, he assumed at least a planned leave would be in the offing. He begged his mother not to worry "so much about my eyes, a leave and plenty of rest will do them good. The surgeon at Grant told me to apply for six months leave."[41] The surgeon had provided "a certificate so that I shall not have any trouble getting my leave," he assured. Also, a transfer between John Bigelow of Troop K and Robert Read of Troop G was in progress "so that it will surely be a go, then there will be two officers with the troop."

Eye condition or not, Clarke still spent considerable time on horseback. For instance, he rode from Fort Thomas "to Cedar Springs 24 miles between 3 o'clock and six Monday evening; left Cedar at 5:20 AM yesterday; Thursday took breakfast with the Vieles at 8 o'clock … put on my full dress and appeared as a witness before a court [martial]." This official matter concluded, he ate "lunch, left Grant at 2 PM and got to Fort Thomas at 7:30 and got up" the next morning "feeling splendidly after my 62 mile ride of yesterday." Clarke's reemergence early for duty that day surprised his superiors.

With his ability to endure such hard riding evident, he regretted the need to take sick leave. He felt he must do so, however, noting he would "put in my application in a few days." After that, he would follow the paperwork through the chain of command including contact with General Kelton "to let you know when it is acted upon and you can wire me." Evidently, Clarke felt he had sufficient stock with the army's adjutant general to jump over the military hierarchy in this matter. Offhandedly he mentioned a photograph "of the rabbit and dogs" for one of his friends, which incidentally he had supplied to Remington. Eventually, the artist's rendering of the greyhounds chasing a jackrabbit would serve as a distinctive letterhead for Clarke's stationery.

In addition to riding, Clarke remained "very much interested in revolver practice." He hoped that his enthusiasm would inspire Troop K to have "one of the best records in the army."

As for other news, Grierson "made general 'at last'" motivating Clarke to ponder "if our new colonel has any 'snap' and goes for drunkards poor chaps, I will soon be a 1st lieutenant but I may wait years. The list is now Johnson, Hughes, Clarke…. It will be lacking in modesty to tell you that Lieutenant Watson commended me for gallantry" for the action in early March. Ultimately, Clarke would be recognized "for prompt and indefatigable pursuit of a party of renegade Apache murderers, and for conspicuous gallantry in the successful encounter of March 7."[42]

Returning to confidentiality, Clarke admitted that the rescue of Corporal Scott took "what little courage I have," and was not something from within himself. He modestly asserted that his bravery came "from Heaven and my only dread in life is that I may lack it someday. This is for you alone."

Perhaps in part humor and part seriousness, he added: "If Remington knew how little I love the sound of bullets he would not write such articles. How lucky I am I suppose when I tell people so they think I am hiding my self-conceit however it is luck."

Although not confident of continued valor, Clarke seemed self-assured about Germany. One major stumbling block presented itself. Mary Boyle revealed from her contact with General von Versen, that "it costs an officer $4000 a year with any of the [German] guard regiments and $3000 with an ordinary cavalry regiment." Rhetorically, he contemplated: "I would like to know where the average German cavalry officer gets this amount notwithstanding the fact that they are all 'vons'" or in other words members of noble families with private means.

Clarke could not "live at the rate of 3000." This was well over his annual base pay of $1800. This financial stumbling block came as a great disappointment, dashing his goal to "get to Europe both for my education and also for my health."

There was a ray of optimism. One of Clarke's champions "told Von Versen that he would assist me and that he felt sure that I could get the detail if the general was to have me attached to a Prussian cavalry regiment." As another option, he could adopt a frugal lifestyle, as his sometimes impractical and contrary aunt proposed, and "live on half my pay." In the same letter, she reversed her course ridiculing General von Versen and going on to point out that it was impossible to go "to Germany with an idea to economize." Clarke remarked: "Queer world this," but cautioned that his mother should not "repeat this" knowing how it might strike her rather flighty half-sister Mary.

After considering the matter, the economic challenge of a posting abroad could only be overcome by the aid from his aunt or General von Versen. He could not bring himself to ask for the funds. Clarke complained this was "nearly double my pay," a frustrating hurdle that seemed insurmountable.

Falling back to his previous plot, he sought one last time for his mother to return to his original goal of Saumur. He asked his mother if she would contact a cousin in France to aid him "in any way in getting to a French Cavalry Regiment." He felt he could "easily live on my pay" there. Plus, he predicted, perhaps ignoring the lessons of the Franco-Prussian War from two decades earlier, that "after all the French are going to win the next war if there is any" future fighting in Europe. Clarke postulated his mother's contact "ought to know some cavalry colonel who would be willing to have me attached to his regiment."[43]

Escape to Europe was not Clarke's only hobbyhorse. He remained fixated on target practice with a handgun. "I am beginning to think that I could make a man move at 30 paces with a revolver," he bragged. As if he had been reading dime novels and romantic tales of duels all his life, he went on to say: "I have always wanted to be a good snapshot and I am going to keep at it until I am for I would hate to refuse to fight with any decent weapon and I would still ever hate to get hit but I am not getting bloodthirsty."

Although writing in spring, the heat was "coming on again" adding to the discomfort of his ailments. He had "given up the Hot Springs because although the hot water clears out my head," unfortunately it did little "good for the catheter [his urinary track complications] and I find it better since I have quit. I hope I make it right … if I do not, I will not be fit for cavalry long." With proper medical attention and time away from Arizona's "trying climate" he promised "I will do all I can to get cured."

Evidently, Louise Clarke shared the contents of this letter with her husband as Dr. Clarke's next good-natured note disclosed.[44] The doctor stated: "I sympathize deeply with you in your isolated life and the coming heat. I am sure you will get your detail to France next fall. So shoot away at 30 paces and get ready for the Frenchman."

By May, Clarke placed alternating thoughts of France or Germany in abeyance because he received orders to appear at the hearing of the three Indians he had helped capture. Apaches were not the only former persons of interest to be back in court. Clarke noticed that Ed and Lyman Follett had been charged with cattle rustling as were Gilbert Webb and Marcus E Cunningham, "all of them who would be connected Wham robbery."[45]

From Solomonville, Clarke rode three and a half hours on the thirty-mile route to San Carlos. Clarke arrived on May 18, linking up with his striker Turner and twenty-five of his men from Troop K. By May 19, he assumed another assignment gathering a half-dozen of his troopers and six infantrymen as another payroll escort for Major Wham. In this case, the journey to Fort Apache proved uneventful. Having completed this mission, on May 22, Clarke's contingent departed Fort Apache, camping that evening on Ash Creek.[46]

By the twenty-third, they were back at Fort Thomas. Clarke stayed overnight before turning around for San Carlos on Saturday, May 24. Upon his arrival at the agency he ended up "in bed with measles caught in Solomonville." This malady laid him low for two weeks.[47]

By June 20, he was on his feet and off to Fort Thomas to serve on yet another of a countless round of courts-martial, the bane of his existence and that of most of his contemporaries.[48] Courts martial were far from Clarke's favorite duty; thus a breezy description of life in New Rochelle by Eva Remington must have been welcomed.[49] She detailed the house and grounds, carriage ride, and the fact her "Darlin" Fred had added five pounds to his expanding girth.

Eva longed for Clarke's visit during the forthcoming fall. Of most importance were her remarks that: "I am so glad Gen Miles is such a great admirer of yours and I told him all the good things of you I could think of. He is awfully nice and I very much admire him." Here again Clarke's stock grew with a highly placed military man in part due to the favorable impressions he gained from both of the Remingtons.

Several days later, Remington broke away from a fishing trip and labors in his studio long enough to catch Clarke up with the latest.[50] Because Remington contemplated a return to the Southwest in September, he wanted to have as many potential hosts as possible. To this he added, "Don't go to the Grand Canyon without me."

Clarke had written his mother back in 1888 about a desire to visit the Grand Canyon. He must have shared this in a missing letter, of which there seem to be many. Indeed, there are numerous pieces of Clarke's correspondence that no longer exist, but not so with a June 2, 1890, response from father in which the doctor expressed concern for the health of his son.[51] "If you wish or are ever willing to telegraph me," the doctor promised to "go at once to see Gen. Kelton and ask him" how he could have his son sent "away from Thomas" for medical reasons.

Even while it appeared that Clarke, who was in garrison, might be permitted another sick leave, some of his comrades actively stayed in the field chasing the ghostly Kid and others. Concern over these marauders reached the highest echelons. President Benjamin Harrison ordered: "The Secretary of War, with these directions, will take prompt and effective measures to protect settlers, and capture and bring to merited punishment any hostile Indians who have been concerned in the killing of our citizens."[52]

In typical government fashion the action rolled down through channels until reaching Powhatan Clarke. Once again, Clarke was to form another special team of troopers from the Tenth U.S. Cavalry and White Mountain scouts from Fort Apache "to be used along the Mexican border."[53] This meant Clarke would not take sick leave. The prospect of action away from Fort Thomas once more seemed to improve his health. Clarke's desire to depart Fort Thomas for a climate more conducive to his well-being would be overtaken by other matters—the post's abandonment drew near.

By the end of June, Clarke's letter to his father supplied the backstory and a brief description of his latest escapades.[54] He began with a retrospective of how earlier in the month he had marked time at Fort Apache, where he looked forward to being posted someday. Clarke had experienced "a few days at Apache" that seemed like "Paradise after San Carlos" as well as better than Fort Thomas.

For the present, Clarke assumed he would be confined to Fort Thomas where he would face a "dull hot summer … weak physically" as well as emotionally spent. Fate intervened. Assignment to the field resurrected Clarke like Lazarus, beginning with a telegram from Carter Johnson. Interrupting Clarke's dinner on June 20, Johnson's message informed the pensive lieutenant of a recent directive. Johnson was "to select an officer to take command of 15 scouts and did I wish it; well I did under any circumstances." Having accepted the detail, Clarke appreciated that Johnson "gave me the pick of his scouts and from first glance they seem a good lot of men." Enthusiastically, he indicated: "there is something I like about the Apaches. They are far cleaner and more intelligent than the stuff one sees at Castle Garden [meaning European recruits fresh off the boat in New York] but this would be the slightest of compliments." Of course, there were drawbacks, especially in terms of language. At best, a few army officers had a smattering of local languages. Fortunately, Clarke's Spanish was adequate. Because a number of scouts could converse in Spanish, and had some English, officer and men could communicate adequately.

In addition to the scouts, Clarke was to "have five men of my troop including Turner," his indispensable striker, "and as I picked them all and know them I have a nice little outfit. I am never sanguine about Indian chasing." Here he realistically inserted: "I have really no hope of catching the Kid and his seven bucks." He knew this "would be too much luck and a splendid stroke all of which will not prevent my trying."

Being savvy and conscientious about livestock, Clarke began with "easy marches to put my ponies and mules in shape." He described where the patrol had camped the previous evening on Black River. The site allowed him to "see far across the valley of Ash Creek the Gila range, before which lies Thomas."

To provide more protection from the elements, Clarke's fellow Tenth Cavalry officer James Finley "fitted me up a light tent with jointed poles and light iron pins, a jewel in its way." Typically, Clarke declined such shelter, which he considered a luxury during campaigning, "but on such a trip when I may be in the mud at some waterhole … during the rainy season I shall have a tent."

While on detached service, Clarke's troop relocated to Fort Apache with its "attractive location on a plateau surrounded by mountains and covered with pine timber."[55] Dreams of living at this verdant garrison again proved short lived. He soon returned to Fort Thomas, and after that was bound for San Carlos. He then returned to Fort Apache. There he assembled the nucleus of his detachment, fifteen scouts and three men from the Tenth Cavalry's Troop B. After a short visit with Smith and Finley he reversed course for Fort Thomas.[56]

Happily, he would be ordered out from there for the field, as terse journal remarks such as the ones on July 3 noted. He expected Second Lieutenant George Stockle from Fort Apache to "bring down the scouts and soldiers." By the Fourth of July the men had gathered and would be off to Cedar Springs.[57]

As Clarke scouted once more, he explained to his father what had turned his world topsy-turvy. He began: "I came in yesterday and will be here several days owing to telegram ordering me to wait for 15 scouts, men, mules etc. so that my command will have 40 men."[58]

Continuing their southerly march, they passed through Fort Grant. By July 6, the column headed into Willcox where Clarke caught a "Mexican selling whiskey to Indians."[59] The illicit transaction and resulting drunkenness that Clarke indicated was "prevalent amongst Indian scouts" brought an arrest to the seller and stern punishment for two scouts involved in the spree. To demonstrate Clarke's serious view about this infraction, he requested and received permission to put in irons "any Indian scout found drunk, and to deliver him to the commander of nearest military post for confinement and trial."[60]

After that, Clarke and his men rode off to Fort Bowie, where they arrived on July 8. Reaching the now familiar post, Clarke heard from Corporal W.E. Ewell that the detail's second-in-command had not arrived.[61] Not waiting for Stockle, on the following day the patrol headed out, consisting of thirty scouts, Sergeant Spear, Privates Wilson and White of Troop E, Privates Harris and Gray of Troop H, along with Corporal Ewell and Private Turner, Walker, Johnson, and Roper of his old Troop K. Clarke marched the unit twenty miles, encamping in Pinery Cañon where it "rained fearfully."[62]

On July 10, the patrol struck Rucker Cañon (Clarke alternates between Cañon and Canyon when he mentions the Rucker camp) which would be a frequent camp site, remaining there until 1 PM to dry out. They "got tangled up in Rucker and camped a mile from [Lieutenant Alfred M.] Fuller ... and pulled up to the foothills of San Bernardino flat."

The hunting was good. Scouts killed six deer. This allowed the men to have fresh meat and Clarke to spend the evening reading and writing a letter to his classmate Jim Hughes.[63]

On that day, news came from Carter Johnson about the status of one of the scouts. A telegram reflected an interesting concern for the well-being of the scout Katoggies, whose child was ill. The clipped message reported the ailing "child is much better." Also indicative of a concern and awareness of the scouts, the experienced Johnson imparted sound advice not to "let them disarm your scouts. Better communicate wish [to the] department on the subject at once. Indian will refuse to cross border unarmed." After Geronimo's imprisonment in the east the Mexican government directed that only a few Indian scouts, who were to be unarmed, could pass into their nation with U.S. Army patrols. Thus, Clarke had been required to obey this restriction which had been agreed to by officials in Washington.[64]

Another fellow Tenth Cavalry officer, James Watson, brought his comrade up to date. He shared that $112.50 reward was offered for each of the murderers of Sheriff Reynolds. The wanted notice read: "Should be three of them. No reward offered for and also necessary no reward offered for those who recently joined Kids outfit."[65]

The Apache Kid and those associated with him were not the only ones to disrupt peace along the border. Among those sought in the ongoing manhunt was Masia (also spelled as "Ma-say," "Masai," and "Massia"), who supposedly was "the only Chiricahua now known to be at large" and who was portrayed as an equal of "the wildest romances."[66] A former Warm Springs scout who had been in Emmett Crawford's command, Masia's loyal services did not prevent him from being uprooted and transported with Geronimo and others first to Florida then to Alabama.

As the prisoner traveled eastward, one contemporary account claimed: "He escaped from the train in Missouri and made his way back to Arizona where his record has been that of a fiend, killing cattle, stealing horses and shooting a stagecoach driver from a rocky bluff." Further vilifying Masia, he reportedly met an Apache mother "and her fourteen-year-old daughter." He killed the mother, took the horse, "and bore away the daughter. When closely pursued, he killed the horse, took to the rocks and carried the girl to Mexico. After keeping her a year, he returned as far as Bowie pass, pointed out to her the Apache White Mountains, gave her beef and a horse and sent her home. The girl is now demented." Later, Masia purportedly kidnapped another girl.

Cattlemen and the government officials saw Masia as a brigand and murderer. They posted rewards to bring him to justice.[67] Similarly, there was a price on the Kid's head as these two high profile fugitives remained free to strike with impunity.

Headlines reflected the widespread ire against "The Kid, one of the worst of the renegade Indians, and his few followers."[68] Perhaps some publishers exaggerated and sensationalized their reporting to sell papers, or even to influence the government to reconsider closing military posts in Arizona.[69] Regardless of possible motives, the southern Arizona press kept fueling the fire, even as Clarke continued on his mission.

In this regard, on July 12, Johnson sent Clarke a second telegram stating "the last woman taken off by Masia has never returned. It was so reported but not truly. She was kidnapped last November."[70] With Masia added to his roll of fugitives, Clarke's command remained active. That afternoon, they reached San Bernardino Valley where Clarke reminisced "five years have passed since I have been at the old camp "occupied by Captain Joseph H. Dorst's Troop. On July 13, they entered the now familiar Guadalupe Cañon site of Clarke's old deserted camp. Unlike years past, there was no water because of the earthquake of 1887, which changed the course of the stream.[71] The lieutenant sent eight men to reconnoiter the canyon in quest of water.

On July 14, they started in the direction of Cloverdale.[72] Again, there was no grass. Water was depleted by cattle. Because of this situation, Clarke was "afraid to go into the Animas" due a lack of feed for the livestock and he turned towards Guadalupe Cañon.[73] By July 15, Private Gray's horse "played out" in San Bernardino Valley forcing Clarke to leave behind the man, a sergeant, and one scout. This new turn of events caused the frustrated lieutenant to remark: "The devil save the man who has to scout here in the future, dry & dryer."[74]

A break in routine came on July 16, at San Bernardino, when they chanced on "the Slaughters of Tombstone and a 'cow-belle.'"[75] (Clarke's nickname for working ranch women) Having exchanged a few pleasantries with the family of the storied rancher and lawman "Texas" John Slaughter, Clarke and his men rode on in the rain and heat. Another highlight occurred on July 18, when Clarke bought a horse for $45. Clarke seemed delighted after "a two hour squabble over some horse trades between my scouts and cow-boys." Among the *remuda* was "a beauty three years old iron gray about 15 hands" high which he bought for himself. With "Cyclone" and the brown pony, Clarke felt prepared for endurance riding. Likewise, he made "some trades" to replace horses for his scouts.

Clarke's concern for his men showed through when he reported: "Some of my scouts are badly mounted and I have already had to go security for about $400 in ponies for them." This was a sizeable sum, but out of necessity, because locals would not accept army promissory or due bills and he had no choice. Clarke stated he would be "glad when payday comes and I have this risk off my mind" of expending the money from his own funds. He really was not concerned as they were good solid horseflesh, and if need be, he could resell them or trade them.

During another stop at the San Bernardino Ranch, Clarke spent the evening playing cards "with two cow-belles and some aristocratic cow-boys. Well the cow-boy is picturesque even if he does smell bad but ye cowbelle ringeth—no chimes to my ear, and I had to listen" to their singing such as it was.

The overnight at "Old Tex's" (John Slaughter's) ranch headquarters prompted Clarke to suggest Remington could use the cattleman-lawman as a subject with his "squirrel gun, his cur dogs and an old tent that looks as though it had come from the mountains of Tennessee." Just as Clarke had sat down to his journal update, he reiterated having "Harrison of the Second [Cavalry] to dinner." He "bought a chicken" from Slaughter to which the old gentleman added a sack of vegetables from his garden. "Imagine the feast Harrison and I had chicken, venison, beets, carrots, potatoes, onions, and cucumbers with brown sugar for dessert and people call this hardship," and after that, "Harrison being junior I talked him to sleep about my exercises." Beside the meal at Slaughter's San Bernardino Ranch, Clarke added that on the march they "had lots of venison and that keeps everything in a good humor but I have had no barley and scarce grass and I can tell you how that worries the soul of a cavalryman."

The environment continued to appeal to him as well. One night the men "dammed a dry wash down which some muddy rain water was flowing and pitched our packs in a most beautiful spot." He slept from three o'clock in the afternoon until 5 a.m. the next morning. Clarke "woke up looking upon a most beautiful 'echappie' [*sic*; *échappée* French for vista] of green grassy mountains crowned with the crumbling mound of an ancient volcanic battlement of black basalt with bronze like mass, the whole dotted with cedar and oak." He shared an important truth in the desert noting: "How much water adds to a landscape."

At that point, Harrison amused his messmate Clarke "with his collection of scorpions, centipedes, vinegaroonsect [*sic*] which he caught here and I don't envy myself the creepy nightmares that I am to have." Bad dreams or not, it was time to turn into his blankets. His "festive Apache" scouts had at last "ceased chirping leaving the field to some rheumatic old crickets that must have come out with old Tex" Slaughter. As the camp cook "poked his stubborn fire to the doleful tone of plantation minstrelsy" at "ten o'clock blissful drowsiness" conquered Clarke's "fear of bugs."

On July 19, they reached the Chiricahua Cattle Company Ranch. Not long before that, men from this outfit had harassed Clarke's detail in Willcox while they served as an escort for the Apache Kid and the other four prisoners bound for San Carlos.

On the same day, they reached "CCC" Ranch, Florence's *Arizona Weekly Enterprise* mentioned Clarke's patrol. The paper continued to support him and his mission "to capture, if possible, the renegade Apaches now off the reservation. Young, fearless, ambitious, and not afraid of hard service, we believe there is no officer in the army better fitted to perform this difficult task than Lieutenant Clarke."[76]

While Clarke made good press, his new second in command was an unknown. Young George Stockle, a "green" former infantry second lieutenant commissioned from civilian life, had no field experience.[77] When the onetime foot soldier reported to Clarke at Fort Bowie, he arrived so unprepared that he did not even have a proper mount that could keep pace with Clarke's horsemen.[78]

The lack of a suitable mount for Stockle was only one missing necessity. Not all of Clarke's men packed carbines, the basic firearm for cavalrymen of the era. His request for their issuance resulted in being informed that no spares existed "at any post."[79] Even in combat, red tape had to be surmounted. Clarke was informed that he must "forward immediately a special requisition for such ordnance and ordnance stores as you need for your whole detachment and an effort will be made to it obtain them."

During the layover at Fort Bowie to rendezvous with Stockle, Clarke learned of "a fight with broncos [Apache raiders] near [San] Carlos – one killed, four surrendered." Clarke cryptically mentioned "tiswin" (also spelled "tizwin") an intoxicating corn brew, which may have been, as in many cases, at the root of the violence.[80] At least the tired command had the opportunity for a hot meal. Unfortunately, the respite proved all too brief. On July 21 they pulled out in the direction of Riggs Ranch.[81]

On the way, one of the scouts fell ill. Nonetheless, in June 22, they made it to Rucker Cañon. By June 23, they scrambled to the top of the "Chiricahuas over a very hard trail," their difficult climb being rewarded by a "beautiful camp in a glen with icy water" as their campsite. The next day was a different story. A mule strayed, forcing Clarke to retrace his course with a scout nearly all the way back to where they had camped the previous night.[82]

Clarke shared a number of other incidents in a richly detailed correspondence such as a letter to his father July 26 from Rucker Cañon, disclosing that he had not received mail from home "since leaving Bowie."[83] This was of little consequence "as the work keeps me from getting homesick and restless and I have these tough ponies for this work." Regardless of the hardiness of these mounts, the sympathetic equestrian lamented: "I would like to see my horses get a good square feed and two or three days' rest."

The animals and men had been pushing hard. At one point, for three days, they cut "straight across the highest point of the Chiracahuas" prompting him to divulge: "The older I get the rougher the trail gets and such [a] trail was this one over loose blocks of granite and through forest of quaking aspen that tears the packs off the mules."

As disclosed in his private journal, but now shared with his father, on a stormy night one of "the mules strayed away from the herd and I had to return to the very foot of the mountains & sixteen miles with one scout to find him, and such a sweet time driving him back up the trail." With dark setting in, they could go no farther through the impassable canyon. They had no alternative but "to drop in our weary tracks and sleep in the rocks." On the next day, the situation scarcely improved. Declared Clarke: "we got up the mountain through the cañon that no man on horseback ever attempted." Here the trail, such as it was, passed "over fallen timber and over great polished boulders then up along a narrow ledge. Really people in the East have no idea of the places an Indian can get a horse over."

The tired column reached one place that "was so bad that I feared a mule would fall off and he did with my bedding and some dutch ovens." Doubting that his father would accept the story's veracity, he underscored: "You may find it hard to believe, the mule fell rolling and tumbling over one hundred and twenty feet landing in the stream amongst the rocks. I went down to shoot him thinking to find him all broken up but when freed from his pack he got up and shows no sign of his fall except one eye that is all swelled up and [a] rough gash in his head." Clarke proffered: "The immense pack saddle evidently keeps these animals from being torn to pieces on these falls. This place was nearly perpendicular."

After this grueling escapade, Clarke and the scout rejoined the patrol where they "heard that the Kid was in the Mule Pass Mountains trying to steal into Mexico. This sounds very clear but it is my opinion that if the Kid wanted to get to Mexico he would have been there long ago." Despite Clarke's doubt, he gathered his detail "to go over and 'investigate.'" As predicted, they "did not find a sign of the 'broncos' nor a trail in the Chihuahuas and it will be a cold day when Joe Bush [Clarke's self-bestowed nickname] goes into that scenery again."

If Clarke were not on a mission, he "would love to be able to camp a week off in those tall pines with that delicious odor and clean grass that reminds one of Virginia." That was not possible. He had a duty to perform, causing him to "wish I could hit a trail and 'chum' Mr. Kid."

One of the barriers to capture or kill any Apaches arose from the latest of many snags in relations between the United States and Mexico. As Carter Johnson warned, "the agreement between the United States and Mexico for the passage of troops across the border when in pursuit of hostile savages … prohibits the use in such service armed Indian scouts; they can only be used as guides or trailers without arms, and only two scouts for each company or each separate command."[84]

This was despite the fact that the Mexican minister in Washington signed "an agreement with the United States government for the reciprocal crossing of the dividing line by forces of both countries in pursuit of hostile

Apaches."[85] Reversal of this arrangement placed severe limitations on the deployment of scouts, hampering Clarke's effectiveness.

Higher headquarters realized this restriction's impact. Clarke's superiors reacted to the decision by the Mexican government, which distrusted Apaches even if they were scouts.[86] First, the Division of the Pacific commander directed Grierson that "in case Lieut. Clarke should cross the line," he was to "leave all the scouts but two," but to offset this reduction of troop strength, "his force of soldiers should be increased so that he may have from 15 to 25 men besides the scouts." Grierson ordered all "commanding officers of the posts in the southern part of Arizona and New Mexico … to put a force of troops on the trail of the Indian outlaws, whenever they may develop their position, so equipped as to follow them without cessation and so closely that they may be captured or their trail not be lost again." In the event the party dispersed, "or should the trail become scattered or for a distance obliterated," the pursuers were to "continue their search and follow the outlaws wherever they may go, notify the post commanders, and obtain supplies as heretofore directed."

In addition to being hamstrung by international politics, Clarke and his men dealt with a more immediate issue, the fierceness of summer rains. On July 28, the rains poured down so hard that a house in the town, where the patrol had stopped, was "taken away" and two men drowned. To keep out of the rising water, the command sat on their saddles.[87]

The downpour prompted Clarke to complain in his journal on August 1: "too much rain" as well as pondering about the prospects of "cholera morbis." He must have been pleased to start back to Fort Huachuca on August 2, which they reached on the following day.[88] By August 4, Clarke should have felt vindicated when another search party, one maneuvering in Mexico, returned to the post without the Kid or even a sighting. With that failure, all the patrols were called back on August 5, save Clarke's outfit.[89]

For the moment, Clarke's command remained the only one on patrol, mounting up on August 6 for Bisbee. Along the way, the recent rains inhibited movement. An added challenge cropped up when two mules bogged down "in quicksand; we have a hell of a time" extracting them, he recorded. Losing two pack animals paled in comparison to Clarke's August 7 journal entry about picking up the newest member of their party, "the company surgeon"

Dr. Thomas Darlington, Jr. Clarke commiserated because the "poor fellow just lost his young wife."[90]

With the contract doctor added to the rolls, the column left Bisbee on August 8 to encamp in the Sulphur Spring Valley where they experienced "another wash out."[91] On August 9, as they slogged over the usually baked desert to Riggs Ranch, the storms had turned the twenty-five-mile route into mud in which two mules fell. At least the downpours had one positive effect. Clarke marveled how "green and beautiful" the countryside was.

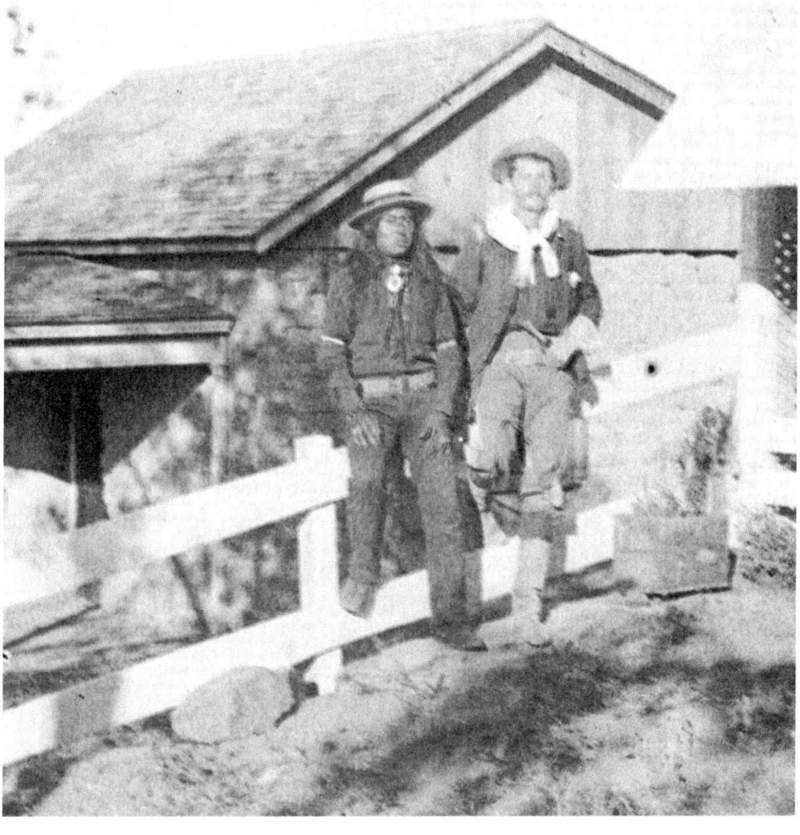

Periodically Clarke resupplied, rested, and paid his Indian scouts at Fort Bowie, where a fellow officer, Second U.S. Cavalry First Lieutenant Alvarado Fuller, photographed him with one of his scouts. Collection of Stephen C. Gregory.

Once at Fort Bowie Clarke and his men enjoyed a break from the field. He even may have received a letter from Remington there, who at that time praised an article Clarke had submitted to the *Journal of the United States Cavalry Association*.[92]

Clarke's fledging effort to publish, in this case on one of his pet subjects—the pistol—indicated he sought to establish himself as a military professional.[93] Apropos to Clarke's personality, his article appeared in the "Discussion and Criticism" section of the *Cavalry Journal*. As such, he felt no compunction about expressing his dissatisfaction with the two types of revolvers issued to the army at that time—the Colt and Schofield, both in .45 caliber. He dogmatically set down the type of handgun that should be issued, how it should be carried, and when it should be used, along with other recommendations as to training and an array of other improvements. Clarke went on to extoll the virtues of "snap shooting," which he had practiced at the range expending thousands of rounds of ammunition.

This early effort seemed to please Remington, who related: "Saw your article on 'pistol'.... Solid as the devil. You take it off as hard and sound as a veteran of 1000 battlefields!" Remington also thought Clarke's "experience with these Apache scouts is great." To this he added: "make notes–observations and when this cruel war is over you write some magazine articles which I will have published & will illustrate. You have rare opportunities to do a good thing which will compensate you for the hard times you are having."

With a bit of black humor, Remington wished Clarke "would get the 'Kid' but please do not let the devil kill you – it would be a rather tough final for a career which might get a better chance to go over the range. However you will get a proper obituary – bet on that. But how little an obituary interests a dead man."

As for the selection of a campaign mount, Remington concurred in a run-on sentence: "You are sensible in riding a pony they are better than a big hoss for that work and it don't [*sic*] cost as much." He further commiserated with "poor Turner – he will have more trouble with his monthly drunk now that his base of retreat is cut off" probably meaning Clarke's striker would have no place to sleep off a drinking bout as he could in garrison. Remington wished Clarke "luck with the 'kid' and when you come

East headquarter here." He then ended with a toast: "here's to the health of the scout—standing up."

After welcome words from Remington, Clarke wrote his father about being paid "yesterday and I collected $315 that they owed me for horses etc. not a kick about one charge and I did not lose $.10."[94] Because his father knew all too well about what a spendthrift his son was, the lieutenant jibed: "Do you not think I am improving in my book-keeping."

One thing his father must have respected, however, was the son's appreciation for horses. Pleased with himself, Clarke let it be known that his men were "splendidly mounted." Regardless of the quality of horses, he admitted the recent riding all "over the country has worn me out." He also must have been proud that his Apaches gave him "about $300 to send to their wives," which as he pointed out, indicated their trust in him. Now he hoped the money would safely reach Carter Johnson, to whom he sent the funds at San Carlos for distribution to family members.

After this respite, on August 18, Clarke returned to the trail. That evening, his scouts were "preparing an Indian dance." This led to a round of drinking, forcing him "to wait for drunken scouts." Another problem with his scouts soon occurred, when along the way, one of them fell by the wayside."[95] Pressing on, by August 19, Clarke's detail camped at Stein's Pass where he had not been "since '85."[96]

This time, they were fortunate to have grain and hay for the livestock and breakfast for themselves. With men and mounts fed, they were "off for the Hachita– no one knows the way nor distance," but the cavalcade pressed onward along the unknown route. They chanced upon a rancher, who informed them that Tenth Cavalry officer Edward Keyes was "on the trail with five scouts" to which Clarke confided in his journal: "I had no idea he had a scout" given that he thought all scouting parties, except his, had been recalled. With Keyes ahead of him, he reasoned it was time for "me to camp at 5 P.M. in a pouring rain under a haystack by a mudhole—weary—weary. I'm in the mind to have a glorious nap in my slicker." Seeking some relief from the weather may have been comforting as perhaps Clarke's supposed Keyes was in hot pursuit presumably on the tail of the Apache Kid and some of his fellow raiders.

As the damp command entered Hachita on August 20, Clarke took shelter and sent a note to his mother.[97] When Clarke received information of another killing by the raiders, he informed his mother about being ready at 5:45 A.M. with "everybody … in saddle, rations drawn and packs but I had to wait half an hour for my head Indian." He admitted that this important piece of the puzzle "had gotten so drunk that he could hardly sit a horse."

Nonetheless, they made a night march in the "pitch dark … and at 3 A.M. I was at Stein's pass station, 32 miles. I was happy enough to get grain and hay and even a bottle of Anheuser beer!" Drinking by scouts was one thing, but rank had its privileges. He shared the brew with young Stockle. The two of them stood "blinking at each other by the light of a stable lantern with a quart cup in one hand and a chunk of bread in the other. We had no dinner and I should smile that bread and beer did not seem a feast."

Dead tired, Clarke fell to sleep by 4 AM, but after an hour of rest, he rose at five "and at six we trotting blithely over the green valley of the Animas." Along the way, Clarke confirmed Keyes rode in advance of him, a fact that some of the papers praised when carrying stories of this new headliner, even as they now barely noticed Clarke and his "colored troops," as a Tombstone newspaper insisted on using as a modifier.[98] With "no map and no one could give me satisfactory directions" Clarke finally made camp. Once there, he regretted that he had skipped breakfast "to go look for a mule that got away from my scouts" plus dealing with "some drunken miners" thereby cutting the letter short.

While often repetitious, Clarke's journal included details not included in his letters. As an example, the August 20 entry revealed the quest for the "horses and mules" drove him to "profanity" forcing "all scouts and I [to] turnout." They soon caught "all but one mule … but 'Gay–yay'" one of the scouts, had brought the wandering beast back a bit later. The recent Apache marauding also panicked the locals. One of the few remaining mine operations, the "Copper Dick," closed down. The miners headed to town "on a bat" looking for liquid courage in one of the saloons.[99]

For the remainder of August, Clarke's contingent ambled from place to place. Some locales were familiar, such as a camp where the lieutenant recalled playing "euchre in a dugout" in 1886. Other times, Clarke wound up in terra incognita, as he did on August 22, 1890, when he scribbled a question mark because he did not "know just where this is except that there is a wind mill and reservoir of the San Simone." When they entered Rucker Cañon, he once more reached recognizable ground, and a launching point for a ride to Fort Bowie. There, a dry berthing and food awaited them. No longer "cold, wet and hungry after a ride in the mist and rain" Clarke saw to resupply of his patrol. Additionally, he obeyed orders, probably reluctantly, to "send four men to [Fort] Apache with 19 extra ponies."

Having regrouped and re-provisioned, it was off to Rucker Cañon, Clarke's preferred hub of operations.[100] After they arrived, he discovered they were short on bacon, a staple of the field diet. On the upside, Clarke expressed delight that he was "getting lots of butter and milk"—luxuries on the march.

Without a sergeant, Clarke pressed one of the men into the role of acting non-commissioned officer to fill the slot. Likewise, his junior second-in-command, freshly assigned Stockle, took on some of the burden of leadership. Clarke trusted him, and split the force. He detailed acting Sergeant James Spear and four men as well as a dozen scouts to Stockle, dispatching the detachment to San Simone. In turn, Clarke took the "rest of the outfit" through the Animas Valley.[101] Along the way, Clarke received news that the "Kid is on foot going westward!"

This intelligence failed to help Stockle or Clarke, as a September 6 letter demonstrated.[102] He mentioned to his mother about going on "another wild goose chase. I would not have left Rucker Canyon on the scanty information I had but the commanding officer at Bowie hinted rather strongly for me to come up this way" toward Willcox.

That suggestion sent him in the wrong direction. As Clarke "expected Mr. Kidd [Apache Kid] had gone the other day over towards Tucson. It's going to be a long trail after the Indian and I do not believe they will get him soon so they put every Apache scout in the field." Among those scouts were Clarke's detachment who provided "lots of fun to see these Apaches watching the railway trains. The 'iron wagon' fascinates them … furnishing them no end of enjoyment and wonder." Paternalistically, he viewed them "as if children" who he had "to look out for … in the matter of their rations and horseshoes and 1000 things but they are far from children when it comes to their craft." On the trail, "from morning till night," they could study "the surface of the earth … as the printed book on which they read the record of every living thing that leaves a track."

Clarke noted that to the casual observer, they appear to be "unconscious in their saddles" but come to life "suddenly when the leader moves to one side and there a group chatter" and their spokesperson reports to him: "'tenant [lieutenant] me like hunt that deer maybe so one hour ago by this place maybe so two hours … a big black tailed deer' and in a few hours after there is venison in camp." Although his mother may think that her son's tale echoed James Fenimore Cooper, he speculated if "the old novelist" could "look down on these Apaches it will ease his mind to find that he was not as great a liar as he thought himself to be."

He added that Remington had sent him a camera. He hoped "to get some interesting pictures to show you by the time I get on leave again. I think I will hold on to this camera as long as I can." Clarke reiterated that he considered establishing their "regular camp at Rucker Canyon. It is a glorious place our shelter tents being spread on a grassy lawn and most shady oak trees are on a plateau as smooth as a tennis court. There is a delicious pool into which I can plunge and the ranch house of Mr. Gray has a large spacious cool room where I can relax and write." Plus, there were other advantages. They had good beef aplenty and to satisfy Clarke's sweet tooth, Mrs. Gray made "delicious chocolate."

This was the sort of detail Remington urged Clarke to capture. In a letter Remington penned at the beginning of September, the New Yorker spotted raw talent and possibilities for his friend.[103] To cultivate this potential, he insisted Clarke had to "make copious notes of your present experiences in the vain [*sic*] in which you write letters to me." If he failed to do so, the lieutenant would be "thrice d–fool." Remington had shown some of Clarke's correspondence to a "half-dozen literary ducks" who told him the officer's writing was "plumb and full of guts – I'm going to let Harper [the publishing house] read it and I will put up a job of some magazine stuff to be written sometime hence."

The enthusiastic mentor further urged the key to writing was that Clarke "must be yourself—untinctured by other people's ideas—you certainly have a well-defined personal view now be true to it." Remington expressed faith in his friend, predicting: "I want to make it clear to you that you might write some charming reading" particularly because he maintained Clarke possessed "the facility of not taking people or life seriously and that's at the heart throb of modern literary men."

Remington confessed he lacked this trait. He called himself a fool for being "too serious." He then assumed Clarke had received the camera from New York. Once more, he advised: "get some good single figures in the foreground – have yourself taken."

In the meantime, Remington was not idle. He spoke of working on "an enormous canvas now, 'The War Path'—a vast mass of rushing ponies and ferocious naked figures. I'm going to take it to London with me next winter." Additionally, he "made a painting for the fall exhibition titled 'The Arrival of a Courier'" and Clarke must have been pleased to learn he appeared in the foreground.[104] Similarly, Remington included Clarke in *Harper's Weekly* montage adapted from some photographs Clarke had furnished from Fort Thomas.[105] Four illustrations depicted target practice. Remington said he would send a copy to see "what you think of it."

He also remonstrated in his last sentence: "Well take care of yourself – Make Notes – Make Notes – Make Notes!" To ensure that his pupil absorbed this lesson, the teacher also included a quick sketch of Clarke speaking to a scout and in a bold Spencerian script again wrote: "Make Notes!" Underneath that he scribbled: "get the color of the eyes."

By this time, it was clear Clarke dabbled in photography at Remington's urging. In fact, he referenced this avocation in his September 9 journal entry. At a stopover in Willcox, Clarke tried "to take photographs with Remington's machine" but failed to produce usable results. To compound his lack of success, he misplaced the camera. He proved unsuccessful in relocating it.[106]

In the former instance, Clarke shared his mishaps with Remington about recent unproductive efforts.[107] Grabbing a piece of stationery from John H. Norton & Co. General Merchandise, a store owned by the former Fort Grant

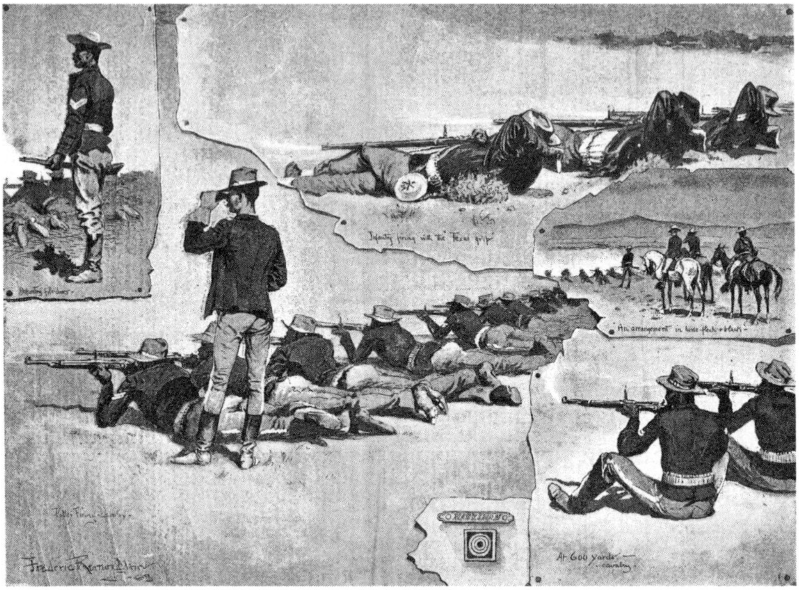

Remington's "Skirmish Line Target Practice in the Regular Army" appeared in *Harper's Weekly*, October 25, 1890, based on photographs provided by Clarke. Note the pinholes in the renderings, which coincided with the ones in the photo Clarke sent the artist. Author's Collection.

post sutler, the frustrated photographer recounted how he "spent the day in a dark room trying to get right diaphragm and speed on shutter." His first attempts came out "splendidly," but he had to keep adjusting to end up with "very distinct images" so he "bought some chemicals intending to keep on" with his picture taking.

He further explained how he lost the camera. For some unknown reason, after boarding a train to Tucson on which a fellow officer spun some creative stories about his pursuit of the Apache Kid, Clarke left the camera on board. He called back to the brakeman to put the equipment "off in Tucson" and received an "'all right'" from the brakeman who promised: "'I'll put her off at Benson, next station.' To cut story short the camera has been traced to Oakland, Cal. and traces lost but little chance of turning up so that I will send you the one I have ordered to replace it and any balance that may be due in

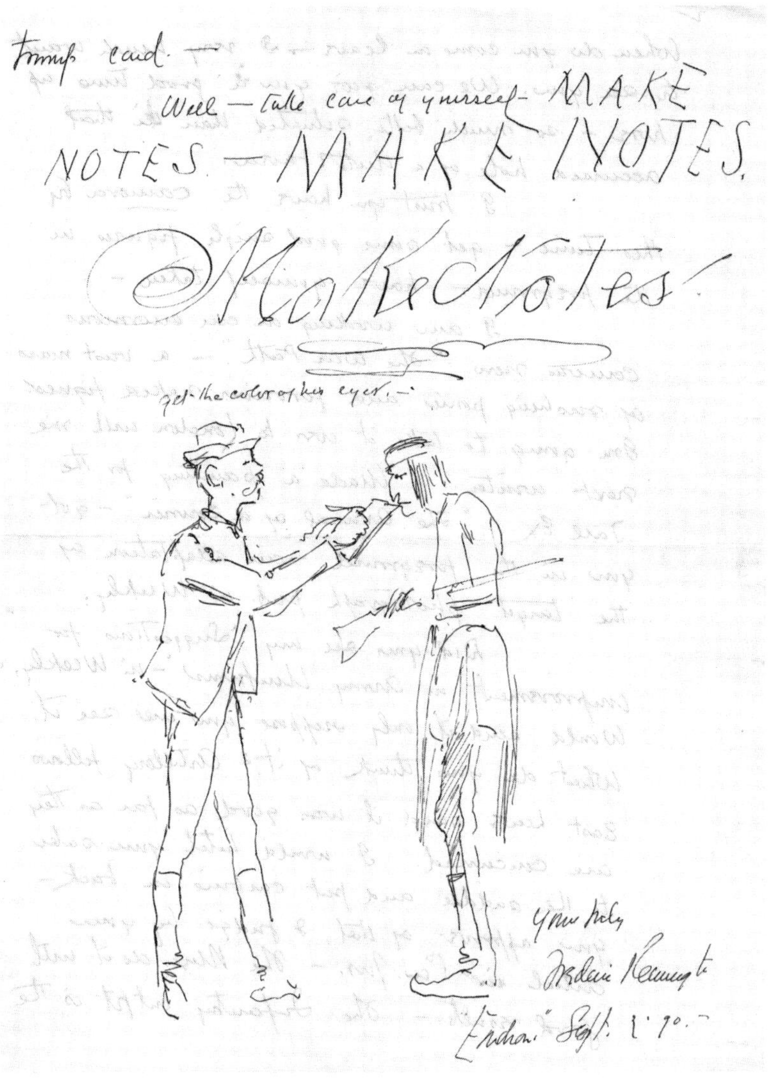

On September 1, 1890, Remington encouraged Clarke to "augment your income and increase your fame by literary effort." Remington added that the lieutenant should "MAKE NOTES—MAKE NOTES—MAKE NOTES!" so that his writing would "have a well defined personal view…." Missouri History Museum, St. Louis.

difference of price business is business." This mishap on the Southern Pacific Railroad prompted the ever cash conscious Clarke to make out a check to Remington for $100, including his estimation of $90 for another camera that he wanted the artist to order on his behalf. With that payment, Clarke was off to Fort Bowie; thence to Rucker Cañon where he promised to "keep a diary that is like cutting nicks in the memory bumps—Guess you are right—life is too short to be taken seriously."[108]

His recent loss of the camera was another matter. He vowed: "wait till I sic my nigger on that brakeman." In anger, Clarke probably gave vent, threatening to send his striker Turner to do his bidding. His ire also may have contributed to his racially charged term, but given the recipient of the letter he probably thought nothing of how Remington would react.

On the same day that Clarke wrote from Willcox, Remington took up his pen.[109] He informed the lieutenant: "photograph the whole lot" meaning "those savage Indians" who served as scouts as well as the "half savage 'Congoes,'" which was another of Remington's euphemisms for the black soldiers. Further, he told Clarke to "send your plates to me and I'll have them developed." He wished he "was going along" with Clarke, but in his absence, they should be able to "get up a great article on the affair" about chasing of the Apache Kid. Longingly, Remington said: "I want just one more whack at Arizona before I die."

Clarke's exploits on the frontier prompted Remington to query if the lieutenant had been "reading any of the stories of Rudyard Kipling about British India. He is a second Bret Harte." Evidently Remington equated Kipling's newly published poem *Tommy* with Clarke and the other American frontiersmen in blue doing their part to conquer the last few Indians at large in the West.

Remington took a different tangent. Ever desirous of expanding his artist props, in almost childlike terms, he pleaded, wanting an "Apache saddle so bad that I cant [*sic*] eat till I get one." Moreover, he said he received a letter from Leighton Finley from Fort Apache. In his note Tenth Cavalry officer Finley strongly disagreed with Remington's suggestions "for a cavalry uniform," which the artist had devised based on his limited experience.

Remington closed, but not before his wife Eva used some white space in the margins to request that Powhatan "have some more pictures taken." She repeated that Fred was "anxious to see Arizona."

Eva's spouse could not resist having the last word. In another marginal note, Fred discussed "a strange incoherent telegram from you to go buy a camera. I am not going to trifle with your soldier nature by disobeying my orders—I shall buy a camera." Not as yet realizing Clarke's loss of one on the train, Remington wondered "what in thunder do you want of two cameras?"

In early October, Remington received Clarke's convoluted tale of the camera.[110] Clarke's "letter and check at hand" and an offer to pay rather than have Remington out of pocket, cleared up the matter. Remington was more concerned whether Clarke had received the camera he just procured in New York for his colleague in Arizona. He let it be known that the camera was "a good one." Remington also advised to "remember that you always over-expose in Arizona."

To alleviate Clarke's guilt, Remington remarked: "So my camera has gone astray. Well its [*sic*] of no consequence. The camera was not just what I wanted." Further, he would not hear of Clarke buying a replacement "camera to give to me—nonsence. [*sic*]" It had been his idea to send it to Clarke. Additionally, he considered "the camera is yours and that settles it and if you ever send it East It will go back by the next train."

These exchanges over picture taking reflected the fact that both men were intent on recording one of the final Indian campaigns, although on a minor scale. Regrettably, none of Clarke's images have surfaced, indicating that perhaps he did not master photography or his labors have been lost. Among these pictures were some taken on October 4, while at Rucker Canyon. Clarke's journal testified he was "photographing" using dry plates per Remington's urging. He followed suit on October 5, when at a local ranch he observed branding and "good roping."

Roundup activities went on for several more days such as in October 6, at the San Bernardino Ranch, possibly on the Mexican side of that significant spread, which stretched across the international boundary. Clarke witnessed more "branding, good roping and riding." All this activity was novel to

Clarke. It seemed worthy of "some photos." After shooting the branding, he tried developing the plates, but they were "fogged."[111]

Perhaps it was more than Clarke's lack of technical proficiency that resulted in his poor results. He noted in his journal on that day he had hooked up with Jim Potter and eventually went "to get a sip of mescal." Undeterred by the previous day's dubious photography session, on October 7, Clarke again tried to capture pictures of the riding. Once more, light-leaks spoiled his efforts.

It was time to take a break for other pursuits. On October 8, he was off to a ranch beyond the southern boundary of the San Bernardino.[112] His destination was Mescal Ranch where he explored a "'vineteria' meet E.F. Foster 'contrabanista' [*sic*] eat and drink mescal and see the operation."[113] In other words, Clarke visited a bootlegger-smuggler at his Sonoran distillery. The operation was not illegal per se, but the product was subject to duty in the United States, which Foster ignored.[114]

After partaking of the potent liquor on October 9, the time came to head north again. The problem was Clarke unwisely took a "mescal toddy with Potter," which led to some more liquid refreshment. The first farewell drink downed, Foster showed up "with a new bottle and he gets laid out." Not to be left out, Turner's effort at cooking dinner were disastrous as he tried "to outdo the 'smuggler'" in matching shots. Turner failed to best his drinking partner. He fell by the wayside, forcing Private Gray "to cook supper." Observing the festivities, Clarke's scouts joined and got "full and go down." The drunkards decided it was time to kill the mescal distillers, not realizing that in their intoxicated state they were about to end the source of their liquor. Grabbing ten of the "'mescalleros'" the Apaches intended to shoot the distillers. Fortunately, this ill-conceived execution did not take place.

The row did not end there. One of the scouts, "Tzezecoe gets mad and finally tries to shoot 'Moseby' for which I put a set of general charges against him and send him to Bowie with Corporal Ewell" (a nickname given him by the U.S. Army after the former U.S. dragoon officer and later prominent Confederate general Richard Ewell), and three scouts as an escort.[115] Clarke realized he had to end the volatile situation. Brawling and drinking, two activities that often went hand in hand, must end.[116]

While Clarke had no compunction about personal consumption of alcohol, that same privilege did not extend to his scouts who continued to wrestle with the negative impact of drink. As evidence of his concern, on October 11 he recorded "Mister Indian drunk all night and gets up rocky some of them fall over themselves. Can't get the outfit that sells them the mescal."[117] It was time for the bleary-eyed revelers to resume their mission, and avoid the fate of Emmett Crawford's command, which set in motion what became a tragic end with a drinking spree by scouts, including the Kid, in a Mexican village.[118]

Perhaps Clarke was a bit hung over himself in that he failed to date his next letter to Remington as well as tended to be more blunt than usual in his opening.[119] He wrote, "My dear compadre: you are wasting your life – I am wasting glass plates." After blurting out these random thoughts, he changed tone: "I wish you could be down here on the day we got in the fracas about eight Magdalena Mexicans branding cattle – it was immense – some of the animals were corkers and more than one rope snapped. I never saw such pretty roping in my life…."

Clarke transitioned to describing a "long lank 'Texican' big rusty spurs, large hat and rusty face" which was the lieutenant's impression of his fellow mescal swilling acquaintance, Jim Potter. Clarke wagered Remington would pay dearly to have an "hour for a pose" with the cowpuncher. If only the artist could see Potter "swing his rope" or "get his pony catching his cow by the neck with its white teeth to get a move on her the devil seem to take such huge delight in chewing fresh rawhide but it's supreme pleasure is when the critter is on the dead jump whip goes the rope – two turns around the pommel … the little bay lays back; the leather in the saddle creeks [*sic*] and the cinches groan, the cow stands on one horn but the cigarettes in the old 'Tajouoas' mouth never quivers."

Potter spun yarns for Clarke and Stockle, both of whom had "been stretching our eyebrows for an hour listening to Jim and another picturesque old devil tell about the Lincoln County war." The pair of gregarious cowboys claimed: "'It all started about a wider 'woman' the lawyer beat the dame out of ten thousand insurance on her husband's life—her friends got in attachment for the lawyer's cattle and in return he raised a fighten party."[120]

With the somewhat dubious history lesson concluded, Potter commenced "playing hell on a scweekay [*sic*] old fiddle."

After enlightening Remington about the Lincoln County War, Clarke recollected his own escapades about the trip to the Vinetoria. They set out in the "clear cool morning everything bright as gold—springy pony—the packer—my old sergeant and our [Private Neil] Roper who you may recall." Making good time, the party logged "eleven miles in an hour over the hills and draws to [a] wild picturesque spot hidden in the hills a few miles from the line [the border with Mexico]."

Once they reached their destination, they spied "little patient burros even trotting in with their immense loads of the mescal plant to the great white piles." Four men took these loads and swung "their bright axes cutting and beating the cooked plant into a pulp—it's splendid stuff to eat rather sweet but nicely flavored." The mash then went into "rawhide vats where fermentation goes on" followed by placing the juices into a "primitive still out of which the clear white liquid is poured into cases then from the case to little brown jug and then Wow!" Clarke damned the swells of the elite New York Fellowcraft Club with their fine *Veuve Clicquot* champagne. This was a man's drink, which Clarke and company took advantage of "by loading their canteens and some bottles then taking a start for horses we loaded ourselves just a little and struck for home while able."

This unmilitary conduct would scandalize the adjutant general "to see my dignified old Sergeant trying to preserve both gravities and two bottles under each arm getting from his horse to our tent while the festive scouts sat on their haunches and encouraged him." Willing on occasion to overlook behavior that may have been contrary to a staunch Victorian's moral code, for the good of troop morale Clarke seemed pleased that: "My Ethiopians are having one hell of a pleasant evening."

While procuring spirits presented no problem, other commodities were not so easily obtained. By October 12, the patrol had exhausted its supply of tobacco and vegetables, which given the season probably were canned. Being without the luxury of smokes rankled those who missed their nicotine, but the lack of vegetables presented a more important matter as it could lead to disease, most notably scurvy. At least there was fresh meat, after an October 17 antelope hunt.[121]

As the end of October drew near, so did Clarke's independence on scouting along the border as he indicated to Remington.[122] He had ridden forty miles up from the U.S.-Mexico line in ten hours to appear at the court martial of the scout who tried to shoot Clarke's corporal at Mescal Ranch. While enduring the proceedings, Clarke kept busy by providing Remington with some of the details, the key one being about the recently assigned replacement for Grierson as Department of Arizona commander. He irreverently noted " 'Gutsy' was here with his aide de camp and son in law" this being one and the same individual.[123] Gutsy was another Civil War veteran, Brigadier General Alexander McDowell McCook, who although routed in the Chattanooga Campaign and relieved of command, managed to retain a commission in the Regular Army after Appomattox, first as a lieutenant colonel and by July 11, 1890 as brigadier general.[124]

Clarke and McCook had at least two things in common. They both graduated from the United States Military Academy, and each had little regard for the other. As Clarke informed Remington, McCook had said: "who is this young man Clark—he seems to be pretty independent and guess we will have to saw his horns or words to that effect...."

"Oh my pride! oh conceit!" cried Clarke. Following this chant, he displayed his bravado to Remington: "I despise from a military point of view and consider very inefficient—the 1st lieutenant" who was slated to assume Clarke's scouting command along the border.[125] Clarke balked that the general's "idea is to give him half of my outfit and have me also dependent on the tenderfoot for orders. The first lieutenant told me this yesterday and I informed him that I would be d—if I would serve under him or any other 1st lieutenant and would apply to be relieved the minute his order came."

Having let fly his frustrations, Clarke admitted: "of course if they wont [*sic*] relieve me I will do my duty but damn these family headquarters," referring to another case of nepotism that had been the norm because, as noted, McCook's aide-de-camp was his son-in-law. With McCook at Fort Apache, where Carter Johnson now served, he wrote requesting that this trusted veteran lieutenant from the Tenth "get the old gentleman to leave me alone or send me back to my troop."

Now that he had exhausted his frustration for the time being, he reverted to what was beginning to be an obsession. He had undertaken some of his experiments with shutters or stops and "developing plates to find out how I was getting on but as soon as I think exposure is ok" the outcome was otherwise. He concluded: "I will let the chemical business alone." At last, Clarke conceded, agreeing to send the plates to a professional as Remington recommended. Finally, if he produced images, would Remington "object to my distributing any of them—except in the case of Lieut. Stockle who has been helping me. I do not care to give any of the prints."

Carbines replaced cameras for another antelope hunt on October 17. Clarke went with Sergeant Spear, Trooper Johnson, plus three scouts—Charlie Shipp, Mechinay, and Goody-pole-nay, but had no luck until nearly sunset when they brought one down at long range. With that Clarke stated: "we put in at dark hungry, thirsty and weary."

It appeared that hunting did not keep the scouts sufficiently occupied. On October 22, the scourge of alcohol reappeared. On that date, scouts May-tay-lay and Pete Closie got drunk and slept in bushes. "The former refused to work before breakfast," so Clarke made the man "haul wood and walk the next day" rather than ride his pony. Both punishments hurt the scout's pride and feet.

After covering forty miles, the next day brought the patrol back into Fort Bowie at 3:30 P.M. Clarke had ample time to clean up in order to join some other officers to play " 'hearts' until midnight." Another diversion presented itself on October 24. Clarke attended a "soldiers' hop" that night. Customarily officers departed early, but in this instance, Clarke seemed to ignore tradition. He had an "Absinthe drunk and raised 'cane.'" The next day he was sick.

Not surprisingly, the self-imposed illness passed quickly. On October 26 Clarke returned to duty seeing to it that his command loaded supplies at Fort Bowie until 4:30 PM, then took off to Willcox and Holbrook followed by a quick stop at Whites Ranch. The rest of the rations arrived on October 27 with Stockle, who also brought along Clarke's precious "photo supplies."[126]

These materials came just in time. On October 29, after another junket to the Mescal Ranch (the scene of their earlier bacchanal) with six of his men, he was back for roundup. Mrs. Slaughter arrived shortly thereafter bearing two pies much to Clarke's delight. Once more, he witnessed roping and riding skills, which would have been an apt subject for picture taking. Clarke, however, failed to mention if he used the camera that day.

According to his journal for October 30 more pressing matters confronted him. Reacting to renewed reports of Indians, his detail went into action.[127] They galloped toward Cottonwood, but found no trail. With that dead end, on November 1, they returned to San Bernardino. For the next two days Clarke had time to "take some photographs and ride with the dames" before all the various Texas buckaroos and Sonoran *vaqueros* departed for their respective spreads.

Election Day on November 4 elicited a comment from Clarke that "both judges democrats and they 'fix' one ticket for a Mexican who swears he will not vote." With the voting concluded, it was off to Guadalupe Cañon on November 5, near the "monument" meaning the marker that delineating the United States-Mexico border. On November 6, they crossed over into northern Sonora's Cajón Bonita, a "lush canyon with a perennial stream just five miles to the south" of Guadalupe Canon.[128] What should have been a bucolic setting turned out to be a "rough trail, hard rain, water high in stream and no game."

At least the lack of game changed when they felled two more antelope. Another positive turn of events came with orders on November 10. They were to go back to Fort Bowie for payment. Happily obeying, the contingent made its way to the post via Whites Ranch where Powhatan Clarke, Assistant Surgeon Charles Willcox, and Second Lieutenant James Hornbrook of the Second U.S. Cavalry met for dinner late on the eleventh. A good meal and sleep followed, allowing for an early start to reach Fort Bowie on November 12.[129]

With a break from the field and enjoying the relative comforts of Fort Bowie, on November 13, Clarke commented about preparations "being made for a 're-union' at Grant. Private theatricals." Jumping to the nineteenth of the month, after receiving pay, Clarke participated in another reunion of sorts with a trio of physicians who happened to be at Fort Bowie that day. Doctors Charles Willcox, Edwin M. Mann, and Charles L.G. Anderson had gathered there giving Clarke an opportunity to visit with all three medicos.

Besides the medical men, Clarke likewise cryptically mentioned a mysterious "Miss 8." She was but one of several women who appear in his private journal at this time, but he consistently remained coy about their names, even in his most private writing. One thing was clear: Clarke seemed ready to settle down and marry. For instance, his journal entry for November 23 contained the single line: "Miss 8 has an understanding." Did this passage refer to matrimony?

Whatever Clarke's meaning, he was not so involved to forgo an impromptu get-together on November 24. Tenth Cavalry comrades William Ewen Shipp, William Harvey Smith, and Melvin W. Rowell, who had ridden "down from Apache 135 miles in 16 hours."[130] They had little time to visit, but managed to be photographed with some of Clarke's scouts.

Their group portrait captured only a brief moment. On November 25, Clarke was off to Fort Grant with scouts and four men with a one-hour stop in Willcox. The layover did not delay Clarke. His detail reached Fort Grant on November 26, arriving in time to witness a "tableau in the evening." This possibly was the "Private theatricals" mentioned earlier in the month, referring to a popular Victorian pastime featuring motionless figures representing a scene from fiction or from history.

On November 27, less static amusements awaited the merrymakers. The day started with a rabbit chase and a polo match, which Clarke's team won. One of his opponents, Smith, ended up with "a wicked cut in the hand and Rowell gets one in the eye." Their injuries did not keep the former rivals from remounting for a champagne ride. Among the equestrian party was "the widow," another unknown woman to whom Clarke paid passing attention.

That night, the officers and their ladies dined at "a splendid dinner" attended by thirty-two people. Clarke remarked how the new commander of the Tenth Cavalry, Colonel John K. Mizner, was more his ideal of a commander. He described the colonel as being "filled with energy and regimental spirit." During the festivities there were "Good toasts! And an exquisite song from McKittrick." Activities ended the next day with refreshments at the Finleys. This left a final day on November 30 to "pay calls and loaf at Grant."[131]

By that time, Clarke should have received Remington's most recent letter.[132] If so, he would have learned that artist's growing fame helped gain an invitation to accompany Major General Nelson Miles "through the North West.—Rode 248 miles in 38½ hours –relays of cavalry horses."[133] This outing gave Remington a chance to see "the 1st Plungers" as he styled the First U.S. Cavalry. He thought them a "nice lot of chaps" but concluded: "Don't [*sic*] think they are a fighting crowd lot of old gentlemen on the upper story—good kids though." He expressed a much higher regard for the "Eight Cavalry" which in his eyes were an "all hunk—good regiment."

This latest trek West also brought him to "Custers' [*sic*] Battle ground" where Remington expressed a view which Mrs. Custer would have applauded: "he would have licked Sitting Bull" if Major Marcus Reno "hadn't been a d—coward."[134]

Having weighed in on the Little Bighorn battle, Remington returned to the repetitive subject of photographs. He told Clarke that he would "take your plates down to-morrow dont [*sic*] know what it will cost" and even then, there was no certainty that any of the photos would be printable. On the other hand, Clarke's correspondence was worthwhile. Remington intended to keep all the lieutenant's "letters—some day am going to have them published—you will edit them or I will or some one will."

Being the more circumspect of the two strong personalities, Remington cautioned: "Keep out of [a] row with old McCook—those old devils are the curse of the army. Old story—youngsters full of enthusiasm—old chaps full of whisky—cant [*sic*] get along-but Death is around and hes [*sic*] got his eye on the fellows of that kind." After this somewhat ghoulish observation, Remington added a rather unflattering, but realistic perspective: "In case of war they would all go on the retired list." Although a civilian, Remington understood all too well the dilemma of the stagnated promotion process.

If Clarke were wise, he would read Remington's closing remarks carefully. In a few telegraphic phrases, the well placed artist revealed: "Gen. Miles spoke very nicely of you and the 10th Cavalry Kids—says you are fightin.—He don't love those old 'coffee coolers' [loafers shirkers, or lazy soldiers who avoided duties]; as he call 'em."[135] In short, Remington recommend that his hard charging compatriot "just keep easy you young bronco and I tell you your day will come." What Clarke needed to do was let influential spokesmen such as Remington do his bidding, rather than plead his own case.

Nonetheless, attaining favor greatly depended on merit. Only a small window remained for Clarke to add to his record. Thus, in December, he brought his command back to Fort Thomas for refitting. Within three days, Clarke and his men were ready for the field once more, this time in a fearful cold snow storm that forced them to camp "in the mud." Braving the elements, Clarke's band traversed familiar ground to Fort Apache where it was "cold as hell snow rain mud and ice" but reward awaited them there for the discomfort. At Fort Apache, Clarke turned his "scouts loose to go to their happy homes."

The Apaches were pleased to be reunited with their families, especially because as Clarke outlined in a December 19 letter to his mother: "Tonight I have bought them a great lot of flour, beef, coffee, tobacco etc. from the commissary out of the savings we made during the last two months on the ration and they are going to have a grand time."[136] He would be celebrating at "a little hop" followed by a get together at the quarters of First Lieutenant Charles Ayers where they "played cards and enjoyed music."

Such pastimes provided only momentary diversion. Clarke longed for a European assignment. By this time, Germany seemed most likely. He felt certain if he maintained strict economy "until April I will then have enough money to go on leave" but all this still depended on "a favorable consideration of my request to Mr. Phelps," the U.S. Ambassador to the Kaiser's court. His hostess, "Mrs. Ayers tells me he was one of the most powerful men in his party." In fact, the former Republican congressman was just that.

If his plans emerged for "leave in the spring [William] Smith will go with me. He is said to be one of the handsomest men in the Army and a charming fellow who usually has about as much money as I have."

Not content to bombard only Remington, Clarke also felt compelled to assail his mother about the latest mania—photography. He seemed more optimistic in his descriptions to her than he did to Remington, asserting his camera was "just beginning to give me some very good pictures and I hope to have quite a selection to show you."

Additionally, Clarke knew his orders had been "mailed from Los Angeles" directing him "to take 20 men and 10 scouts instead of 20 scouts." He summarized that it was the continuing saga—"two men have been killed in the Guadalupe Canyon and the papers are giving it to the 'powers' for withdrawing the scouts so that I do not think there is any doubt that but that I will have as much of this work as I want."

Clarke's comment alluded to the murders of John "Jack" Bridger and N.H. "Bunk" Robinson, and the wounding of August Hickey by attackers who set upon the trio on December 12. The estimated Apache party of three women and two men, one of whom was thought to be Masai, took place fifteen miles north of the international line.[137]

One irate newspaper editor charged: "Hickey came in Saturday night from his mine in the Guadalupe mountains. He brought with him a vest which was covered with blood from the collar to the bottom, the lining of which was completely saturated." Hickey had "found the vest which the Indian had on which Robinson thought he had hit, and which he undoubtedly did severely wound in the neck." While not earthshaking, the next part of the report was the "most startling part of the story" because allegedly "there are at least three men of undoubted veracity who had been with Lieut. Clarke's scouts while he was in that neighborhood, who will swear that it belonged to one of the scouts with whom Hickey had had some previous trouble." Incensed, the paper relayed: "Hickey has the vest at Bisbee and wishes the Prospector to state that Lieut. Clarke can have it by applying for it."[138]

Clarke did not pick up the gauntlet. Instead, he found more satisfying ways to pass the hours at Fort Apache. One of these entailed a Christmas morning ride, which he captured with a surviving grainy snapshot.

While Clarke passed the holidays pleasantly, his journal revealed that this was not a perfect Camelot. A telling line ran: "usual Fort Apache discord" not unlike the garrison tangles he had witnessed at Fort Davis, Texas.[139] Benjamin Grierson's departure from the regiment had not changed the insular nature of his present locale, Fort Apache.[140]

Even so, Clarke left post politics behind for the present. On December 28, he rode out from Fort Apache with "15 men 10 scouts" while Lieutenant Stockle went to Ash Creek. By December 30, Clarke's column appeared at

Fort Thomas, which he remarked was "only an outpost" of Fort Grant by then. There he found his old Troop K.[141]

He then spent New Year's Eve at Fort Grant with Colonel and Mrs. Mizner, whom he thought to be "lovely people" in contrast to his opinion of Benjamin Grierson. On January 1, 1891, after three days on patrol, Stockle was back, so he could join Clarke and the entourage at a "hop that is immense." After enjoying the dance and catching up with other junior officers in his circle, such as one his favorite new youngsters, Alexander Dade, the Finleys hosted a dinner. Clarke completed the day at the home of Major and Mrs. Stevens Norvell where he had "quite a pleasant chat with Miss Dolly" Beck.[142]

Similarly, on January 3, the roving-eyed lieutenant along with Dade spent time in "the company of some ladies" during "the afternoon at McKittricks." Clarke was infatuated, describing Mrs. Mary McKittrick in glowing terms as a "lovely woman divine voice charming hostess in an exquisite gown with a dainty Japanese maid." The two officers remained as overnight house guests, which provided a far more comfortable environment than Clarke faced the next day.[143]

By January 4, he was back on his horse bound for Fort Bowie with "20 men 10 scouts five lead horses." He maintained: "Everything just the same except – the romance with the Y.W. which one of my friends has picked up." Was Y.W. possibly an abbreviation for young widow? If so, he kept details to himself as usual.

The next day, the detachment arrived in time for Clarke to partake of some final holiday cheer, dining with Major and Mrs. McGregor. Another chance to relax came on January 6, 1891, with a "whiskey poker," dinner, and after seeing Dr. Mann off at Bowie Station he hastened to Fort Bowie where he was "back at three and fry oysters until weary and weak." Fresh oysters in Arizona would have been unheard of before the arrival of the Southern Pacific railroad that made such luxuries available, plus Fort Bowie boasted an ice house, which meant chilled wine and other niceties could have accompanied the feast. The good life at Fort Bowie wrapped up on January 7, 1891. At 8 A.M. it was time to embark for camp at Chiricahua Ranch through January 9, followed by a re-ride to the fort.

Another payday rolled around on the twelfth, the same date Clarke and "Hornfrog" (his nickname for Second James Hornbrook of the Second U.S. Cavalry) made preparations for a hunting trip. They loaded "800 cartridges for ducks." After an abbreviated circuit to Separ, New Mexico, that brought them back to White's Ranch, Clarke, Stockle, and others finally went on their hunt for water fowls. Despite packing enough shells for an army, the January 14 safari only succeeded in bringing down a single duck![144]

A greater expenditure of ammunition with far more lethal results had taken place in South Dakota. The national press plastered front pages with articles about the series of events, which began as a desperate, but peaceful religious revival that turned into a ferocious encounter leaving many dead on both sides during what became known as the Ghost Dance. When the gun smoke cleared the media frenzy subsided, but not before declaring the episode as "the last of the Indian wars."[145]

Arizona papers spilled less ink on this battleground to the far north given that the territory still faced its own Indian threat. One account typified this local bent, running a piece about "Lieutenant Stockle with ten Indian scouts and twenty colored men" arriving in Willcox Saturday "en route to Fort Bowie and the southern country recently the scene of Indian hostilities."[146] The article went on to say that the next morning "Lieutenants Clarke and Dade, l0th Cavalry, followed." After suffering barbs in a previous account about the "bloody vest" allegedly from one of his Apache scouts, Clarke was back in the good graces of at least one editor. Once again, he was "that enterprising young officer, Lieut. Clarke" who "in conversation with him didn't seem to be very much put out at the hard things said about him recently in the Tombstone paper."

Clarke took the high road retorting: "he did his whole duty, and the better class of citizens will so say. He said he would, as heretofore, work diligently, and while be perhaps could not rid the country of these roving bands of Indians, he could prevent further murders by them." The trick was "how to prevent" the remaining raiders "from getting arms and ammunition by purchase or otherwise from unscrupulous parties." Further, he correctly realized: "So long as they have ponies and other property to trade, and guns are to be had they will have them."[147]

Clarke's analysis rang true when it came to the Kid and others having the means to continue their marauding. He missed the mark when he promised to halt the slaughter of citizens in Arizona and New Mexico, however. No sooner had he made this promise than news of the "killing of one Chequitte Smith at McGowan's ranch" assumed to be more bloody work of the Apache Kid and four accomplices, including three women, re-energized hot pursuit.[148] Clarke's force took to "the trail at 7 a.m. and a hard one."

According to one of the first newspaper accounts, Smith had been killed at a ranch he co-owned with a brother in the Chiricahua mountains.[149] "The only information regarding the killing," the article stated, was "that Apaches surrounded his cabin at day light and lay in waiting for him to come out."

After murdering Smith, they ransacked the house, taking everything of use then "broke up everything in sight." The story continued: "The spot where the deed was committed is about fifteen miles from Fort Bowie and it is supposed the troops from there were at once notified. The funeral of the murdered man took place yesterday. Further particulars are expected tomorrow."

It was uncertain whether Smith "might be a canard," so the newspaper telegraphed Fort Bowie. The editor received a swift response: "Smith was killed in Morse canyon by Apaches. A courier just arrived reports Lieut Clarke on a hot trail."

Clarke's journal for January 15, 1891, confirmed this. After camping at Rucker Cañon, his patrol moved into the Chiricahuas on "a fearful trail. Men stagger up the hills."[150] Adding to the frustration, after discovering the "camp of the hostiles," which may have been occupied for months or even longer, Clarke's scouts fired "some shots but Masai got away with his squaw who goes in another direction burn his camp and try to trail him on foot but it is no go. Kill some deer and go into camp."[151]

Reversing course once more, on January 21, 1891, the Tombstone *Daily Prospector* turned on Clarke. This time he came under fire for not finding Smith's killers. An initial report pointed out "Lieut. Clark [sic] did not take the trail till Friday last, four day afterwards." Even then, he was near "the five murderers" who "passed close to him on their way down to Sonora where they are now." Rather than close the gap to engage the raiders, Clarke "followed them at a distance of eighteen miles and then returned" so his scouts could "get their pay" at Fort Bowie. Making the most of a damning article, two other territorial papers ran a verbatim reprint of the diatribe.[152]

A barrage of speculation often sprinkled with negativity and doubt followed. One of these appeared in the Tombstone *Daily Prospector* for January 22, 1891. Repeating a Los Angeles paper, the Tombstone edition, at that point, did not contradict what appeared in print about Clarke's "detachment of troops and Indian scouts in pursuit of the band of Apaches who killed Chiquito Smith three days ago at Morse Canyon just north of the Mexican Border. The horses that the Indians were obliged to abandon, have been found on the trail. The trail is fresh, and unless snow interferes, the Indians will be captured."

The narrative likewise reiterated Clarke's analysis that the trail was left by "three Indians in the party, and they are renegades from Mexico, where the trail leads."[153] According to the reporter, the army faced a major obstacle in that military authorities claimed: "the treaty with Mexico should be so amended as to permit United States troops to cross the border. As it now is, they can cross only when in close proximity to hostile Indians and must return immediately on losing the trail."

Blaming international affairs contained some elements of truth partially leavened with excuse, but a single fact remained. Whether there were three or five perpetrators at large, they had avoided the clutches of their stalkers. Clarke was not the only to bear the blame for the ongoing "depredations" as the actions of the Kid and Masai usually were classed in the Arizona Territory. They were seen not as mere brigands, but instead savvy to the ways of the military as former "Scouts" as the Tombstone *Epitaph* made certain to call Smith's killers.[154]

Although Clarke did not always enjoy positive headlines, Eva Remington remained a solid supporter. In early January, she sent some clippings to him so he could "see that you are getting famous, notorious or whatever you wish to term it."[155] She did "not envy you chasing those savages over those mountains and am glad you have not a little wife at the Post in a state of anxiety for you. There is no fun having your better half fighting Indians."

Eva could sympathize to a degree in that her "Fred came home one week ago last Friday and he has come to the conclusion that Winter campaigning is not all together the pleasantest thing in the world." Here she touched on Remington's excursion to South Dakota during the Ghost Dance, a subject he would address when writing a bit later in the month as he promised in a post script appended to Eva's letter. Remington said he could not immediately do so as his editors were pressuring him for copy and images of the recent trip west.

Once Remington had fulfilled those obligations and gained his "second wind," he did write to Clarke. The first order of business was to acknowledge Clarke's "very interesting letters," then he related that he "had a letter from your mother" indicative of the close relationship that had developed since their chance meeting in Tucson's Palace Hotel in 1886.

That must have seemed a lifetime ago for the unknown, financially uncertain Remington, when he entered Arizona. Now secure in professional stature and fiscally solvent, he could afford to spend "a month in the Sioux outbreak" seeking new inspiration, which he would incorporate into his next renderings for *Harper's Weekly*.[156]

Fired with enthusiasm, Remington, whom Clarke rightly had accused in the past of knowing nothing of war, finally "saw soldiers till you cant [*sic*] rest." The Seventh U.S. Cavalry, one of the two main units deployed to the Pine Ridge Agency, South Dakota, was in Remington's staccato verse: "fine outfit—soldiers are all over the room—got the knee action—no funny work and a burning desire to fight—well named—Think their recruits are best—think men like the Regt."

The other cavalry regiment hurried off to Pine Ridge was the Ninth U.S. Cavalry, another unit manned by black troopers.[157] It must have stung Clarke when Remington judged "The 9th is a great Regt. Bette[r] lot of 'nigs' than the 10th—Lots old 10th men in it." The Ninth's field commander, Major Guy Henry, similarly drew the artist's praise as a "gallant fellow." Softening the blow to Clarke's regimental pride, Remington at least allowed the "10th Cav. has best lot [of] line officers I have ever seen."

But of all officers, to Remington the "big G—Miles is the biggest man in America—every soldier ought to be proud of him. He had brains to start

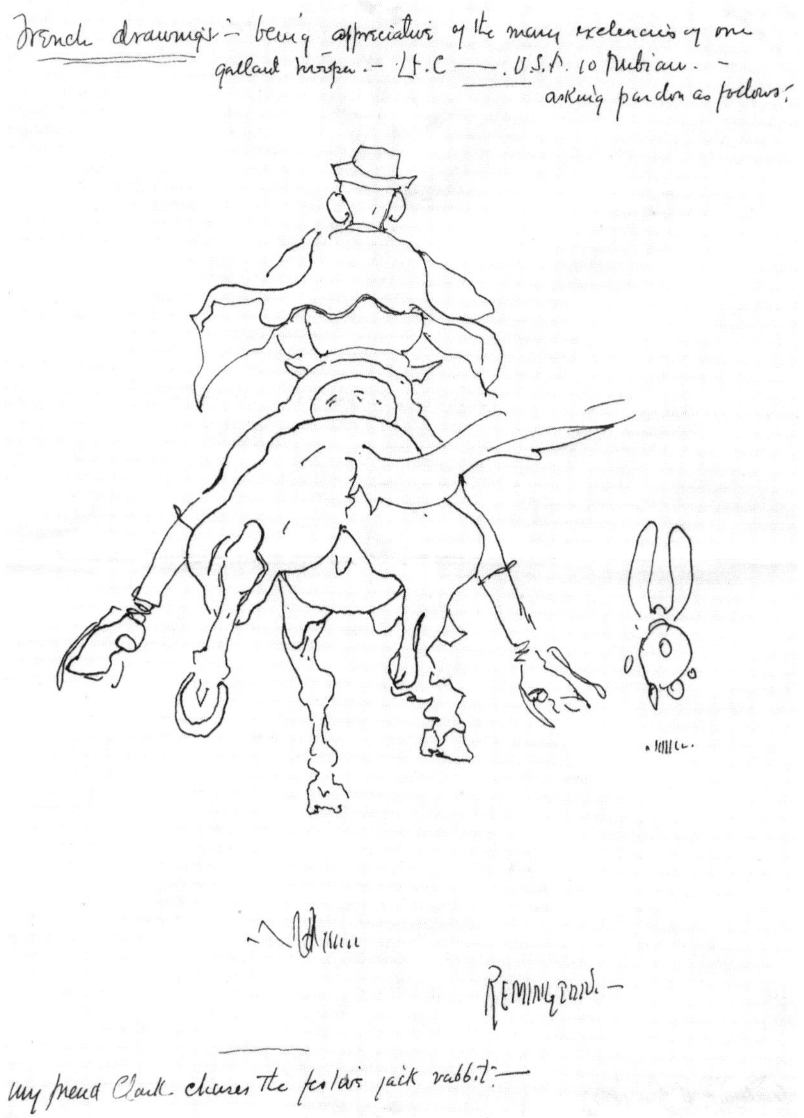

On January 27, 1891, Remington asserted: "… Miles is the biggest man in America—every soldier ought to be proud of him…." The artist added a cartoon of Clarke bounding across the desert in pursuit of jackrabbits. Missouri History Museum, St. Louis.

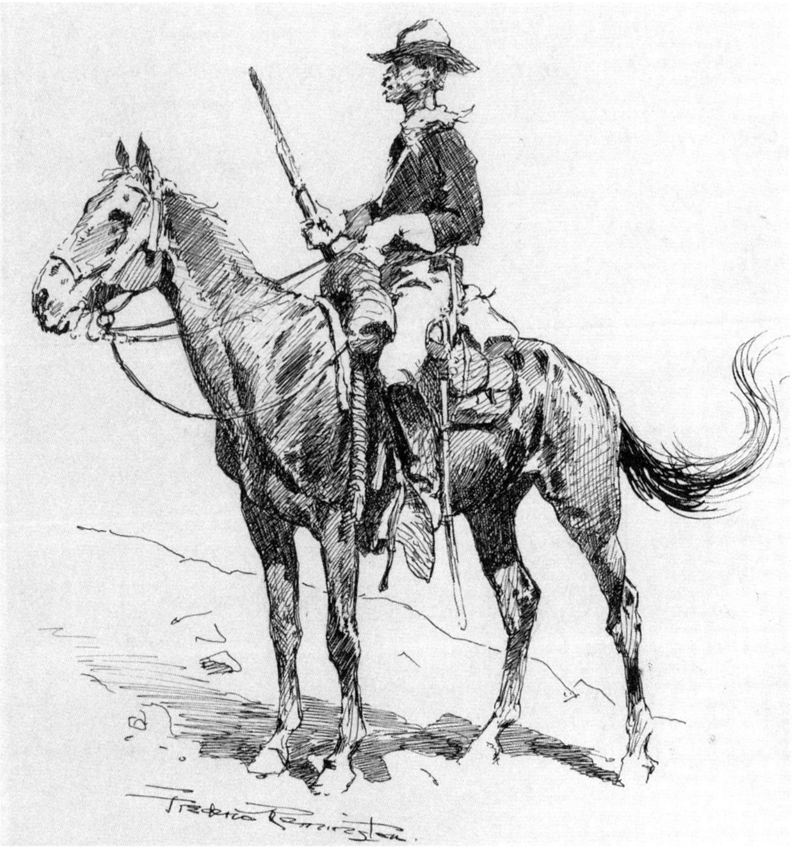

U.S. Cavalryman – Portrait of Charles Ehricke "U.S. Cavalryman" (inscribed) CR# 01380 Dimensions: 10 5/8 × 9" Date: ca. 1892 Medium: pen and ink on paper, indicated Remington's continued interest in black troopers as a subject for his creative endeavors. Courtesy of the Richard F. Brush Art Gallery, St. Lawrence University, Canton, New York, gift of Karl V. Ehricke in memory of his mother, Mary Lawrence Cooke Ehricke.

with and he has cultivated what he had."[158] Whether Clarke agreed or not, he must have realized how important Miles could be in his own ascent up the military ladder.

Meanwhile, Clarke's return from the patrol that narrowly missed closing with Masai, brought unwelcome news. At Fort Bowie, on January 24, 1891,

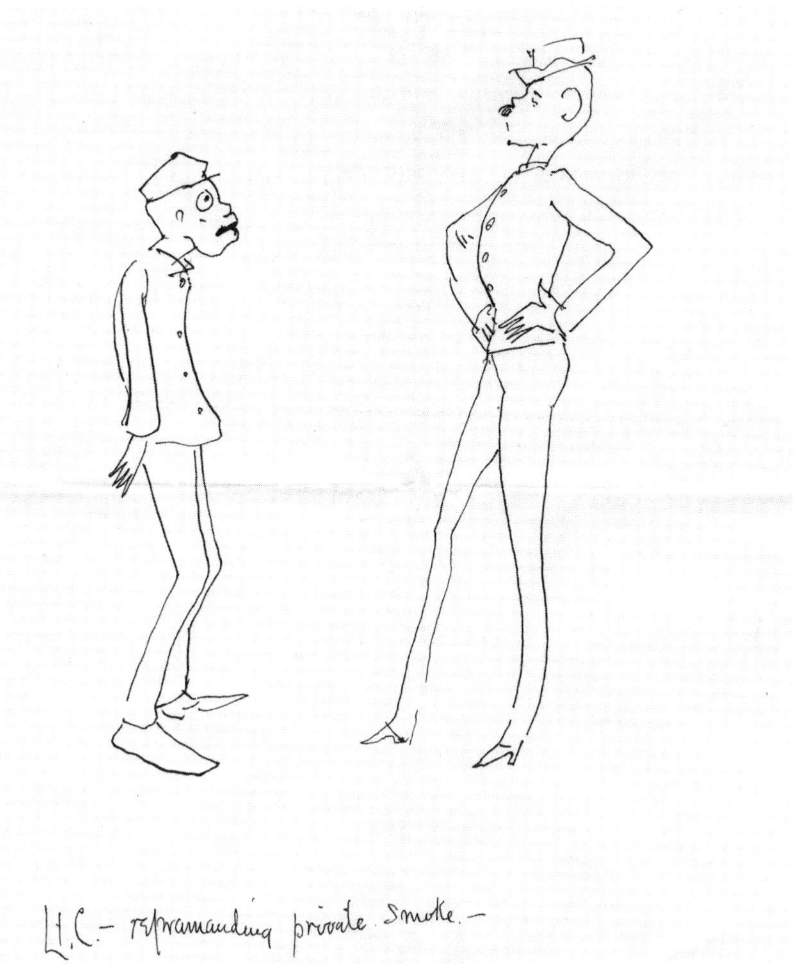

On November 12, 1890, Remington revealed he was keeping all of Clarke's "letters—some day am going to have them published—you will edit them or I will or some one will." Even at this late date, however, his caricature of a black soldier reporting to Clarke demonstrated the artist's continued racist attitude. Missouri History Museum, St. Louis.

he received ill tidings that he had been appointed regimental adjutant. The only positive side to this new assignment was that it came with a $30 monthly pay increase. Accepting his lot, Clarke made preparations to bid "Adios!" He saw Jim Hughes, stopped at the McKittricks, and visited the soon-to-be closed Fort Thomas where he paid respects to his old commander Captain Thomas Lebo and the men of Troop K with whom he had served both in field and garrison for nearly a half -dozen-years. Now it was on to a desk job where he clearly understood it would be "work work—work."[159]

In a way, Brigadier General McCook's threat to saw Clarke's horns had come to pass. Clarke's unsuccessful pursuits of Masai and the Apache Kid ceased—a mission that incidentally no one else ever accomplished. Preventing the violent raiding attributed to these two former scouts, some but not all of which had been of their doing, fell to others.[160]

The curtain closed on Clarke's hard riding adventures as a combat cavalryman. Nonetheless, there were other acts to follow.

Chapter 9

"The Girl I Left Behind"

Clarke's life took a new trajectory in 1891. After nearly a half decade as field cavalryman, he headed to staid garrison existence as regimental adjutant.[1] In a letter to Clarke's father, Colonel Mizner hinted at one possible reason for this posting.[2] The colonel wrote Dr. Clarke: "Although my acquaintance with your son has only extended over a few months I have been most favorably impressed with his natural qualities; so much so in fact, that I have appointed him Regimental Adjutant." In keeping with the former Confederate officer's "natural desire … in securing a full recognition of your son's military services," Mizner prepared "a letter inviting the attention of the War Department to the conspicuous gallantry of Lieut. Clarke." Perhaps Clarke's growing maturity since his lackluster performance at West Point favorably impressed Mizner.

The lieutenant owed a certain degree of gratitude to Mizner. Nearly five years after the rescue of Corporal Scott, for which the lieutenant had been mentioned in reports and even considered for a brevet (a worthless gesture as far as Clarke was concerned), a more prestigious recognition was in the offing. On February 8, 1891, Mizner recommended award of the Medal of Honor based on previous "orders and the records of both the department and division commanders."[3]

Mizner's superiors agreed. On February 12, Department of Arizona commander, Brigadier General McCook, favorably endorsed the colonel's recommendation. Working its way up the chain of command, the major general commanding the army, J. M. Schofield, supported the decoration.

On March 5, 1891, the War Department's chief clerk had a Medal of Honor engraved, bearing the inscription: "The Congress to Lieut. Powhatan H Clarke, 10th cavalry, for conspicuous gallantry in action, in Pinito Mountains, Sonora, May 3, 1886." The official citation added Clarke: "Rushed forward to the rescue of a soldier who was severely wounded and lay, disabled, exposed to enemy fire, and carried him to a place of safety."[4] Clarke would not have to wait for the decoration to be sent via the mail to Arizona. He personally received it on March 12, 1891, in Washington, D.C.

Clarke's star ascended rapidly with help from his father, the Remingtons, and even through his Aunt Mary Boyce. He barely held his position as regimental adjutant for a month, when informed he was to appear before a promotion board to consider his fitness as a first lieutenant. Originally, Clarke was to report to the Presidio of San Francisco for his examination.[5] Orders changed the venue to the national capital.[6] The redirection meant the presiding officer at Clarke's review would be fellow veteran of the Geronimo Campaign, Henry Lawton, now a lieutenant colonel.

There was another reason why the revised location of Clarke's board had consequences. He was in Washington for more than possible advancement. Clarke secured posting to Europe, although not to France.[7] Mary Boyce's familial connections helped pave the way for Clarke's alternate target—Germany.[8]

Adjutant General Kelton shared this news with Doctor Clarke. The general opened: "I suppose you know that our minister to Germany Mr. Phelps has asked to detail Lieut. Clarke to Second Westphalian Hussars to go to the Third Army Corps under General von Versen adjutant to the Emperor and King." In a friendly manner, he wryly added: "I hope he will like the detail. He will receive all the pay and allowances any officer does on detached duty in the country in that respect he will be as well off as adjutant of his regiment."[9]

Clarke, who possessed fair fluency in French and Spanish, but not German, soon was directed "to proceed to Berlin in obedience to the special instructions" that would be enumerated when he reached Washington.

March became a banner month with his receipt of the Medal of Honor and his appearance before the promotion board. Topping it off was a coveted assignment to Europe based on sterling letters of recommendation from the head of the U.S. legation in Berlin and the adjutant general of the German general staff.[10] With this, Clarke had little time to set his affairs in order including applying for a special passport.[11]

Completing last minute arrangements, Clarke boarded the French mail steamer *Champagne* sailing on April 4 from New York direct to Le Havre, France.[12] He arrived safely and so informed his mother.[13] A brief time in Paris was followed by several rounds of sightseeing and social engagements, which included a reception from a French cavalry unit of which a family friend was a member.[14]

In the midst of socializing, Clarke observed that all the towns and villages "were blue with soldiers," and a fort stood "at every step with great guns all tied by little railways. I don't see how the French and Germans can fight on these lines and I will wager that the Belgian neutrality will not last 10 seconds." Clarke predicted a war that would erupt over two decades later. He saw the future all too well. It would have come as no surprise because as he related to his mother: "You cannot imagine how intense the French hate the Germans, it is grown double since 73" in reaction to their defeat in the Franco-Prussian War.

Former Francophile Clarke shifted his esteem to the Germans. Clarke observed with nearly every able-bodied German male having spent a stint in uniform, everyone had a link to the military.[15]

Not long after he reported for service in a German regiment, Clarke wrote: "I have grown to like the young Germans."[16] He complimented them as "goodhearted polished fellows" and "if he had no other engagements I believe I would join one of their regiments in the next war. I do want with all my heart to see them win." He praised his benefactor General von Versen as "my ideal of a soldier."[17] Moreover, Kaiser Wilhelm II impressed him, and he had contact with him several times.

Evidently, via a New York newspaper, the Remingtons learned of Clarke's Medal of Honor and of his detail to Germany.[18] Perhaps in his haste, Clarke neglected to contact them. In this case, however, neither Fred nor Eva begrudged Powhatan for not keeping them abreast of his whereabouts or the many changes in his circumstances. Rather, Remington reiterated his appreciation that Clarke was "a d—good literary man" who should write "some stuff from Arizona and I want you to do all the polishing. It takes a heap of polish to make the thing go now. Mind what I say – write some good stuff – it will do you a heap of good. You play your cards right and you have got the world by the rear elevation."

He beamed at his much-admired comrade's recognition. Remington remarked, he always played a "short horse to win and its [sic] seldom I get

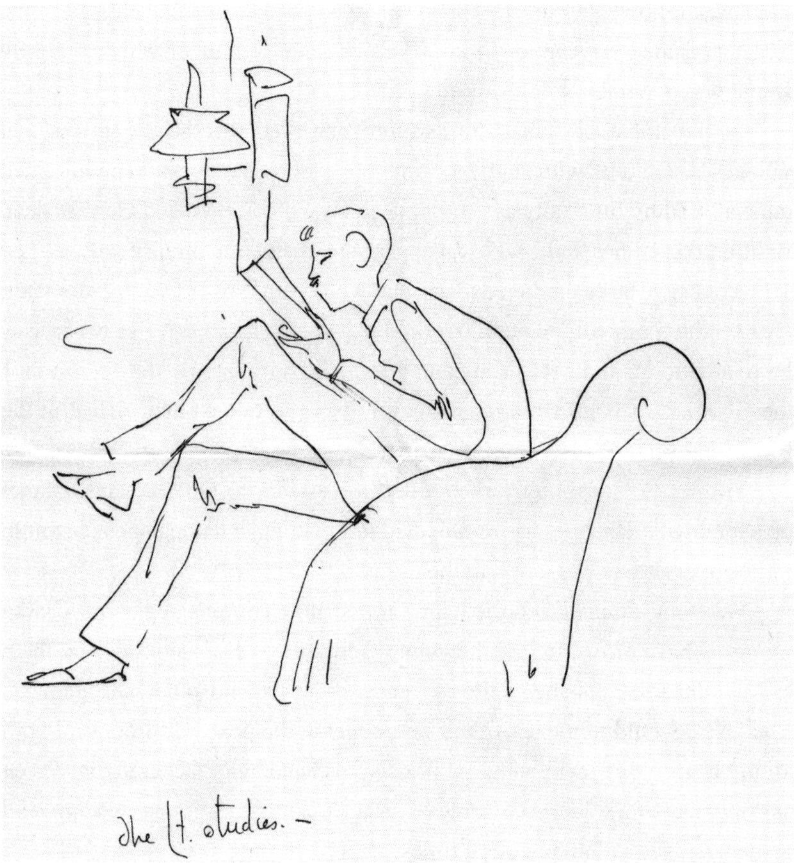

In a note dated October 14, 1891, Remington also lampooned Clarke, who regularly claimed in his correspondence from Germany how diligently he studied. Missouri History Museum, St. Louis.

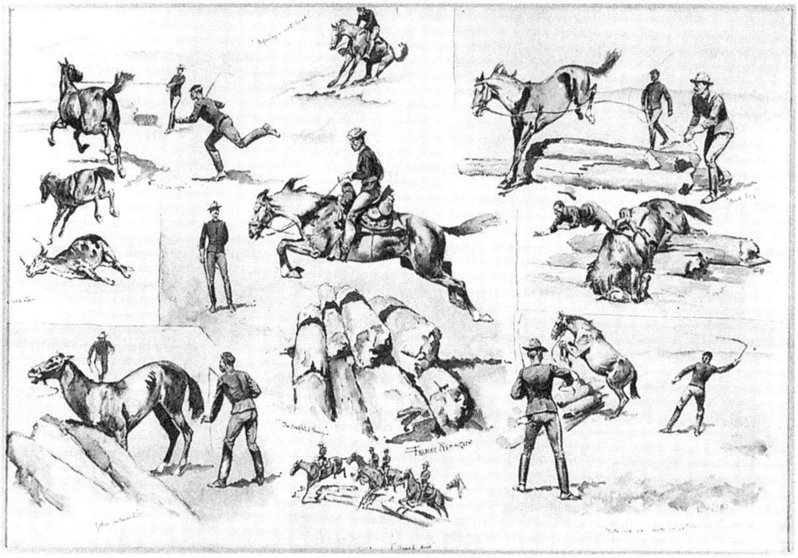

Remington's "Training Horses to Leap Obstacles, Tenth United States Cavalry" Alternate Title: "Nine Episodes at Cavalry School" also depended on photographs furnished by Clarke and a fellow Tenth Cavalry officer for *Harper's Weekly* (September 19, 1891), p. 709. Remington urged Clarke (who at the time served in Germany) to write the narrative, but proved unsuccessful.

them but I got one winner in you." Remington came to rely on Clarke, a real military man, and in the artist's mind a hero, as a window to martial matters. An armchair want-to-be soldier, Fred shared his thoughts and lived vicariously through Powhatan, such as commenting on the potential "blood[y] old war which is so long in coming – you ought to see it and I will start immediately. Wouldn't it be lovely" the bellicose New Yorker proposed, if there were some "real blood letting." In the interim, he suggested Clarke "Spruce up cultivate your intellect write articles and being just from Arizona don't let the German girls get all your substance."[19]

In his next "purely business letter," Fred told Powhatan that Lieutenant William H. Smith of the Tenth, "sent me some horse jumping photos taken by you and himself. I have made a page of horses and call it 'Training cavalry horses to jump obsticles [*sic*]'. We can get no one to write it up and the 'house' instructed me to write immediately and ask if you would not have the goodness to do column and a half for Harpers Weekly at your very earliest convenience."[20]

Remington converted the photos into artwork, diagramming them as rough sketches for Clarke's review and use as a basis for the text. Inexplicably, Clarke ignored the offer to author the piece, eventually requiring Remington to produce the narrative with coaching from Smith.[21]

Perhaps Clarke's unresponsiveness to this collaboration stemmed from long daily military training with the Westphalian hussars, attempts to learn German, and dutifully completing his reports to the War Department along with the detailed fiscal accounting required for him to receive reimbursement from the quartermaster in Washington, D.C. There was one other compelling factor—growing love interest.

In the past, capricious Clarke had dallied with Agnes Foy, a member of a family close to Aunt Mary Boyce. Then, he met Agnes and her friend Elsie Clemens at a posh St. Louis wedding, which he had attended years before while on leave.[22] The "tall distinguished-looking debutante," as the St. Louis *Republic* described Elsie in June 4, 1891, caught his eye.[23] He began to besiege her while stateside and thereafter with a barrage of letters once he reached Europe. Indeed, mounds of correspondence written to her survives in stark contrast to fewer existing letters to others.[24]

Of course, Clarke continued to correspond intermittently with his father, mother, and Remington, for instance, where he observed the French, despite being "out of shape in the military way and yet they want a fight – think of a great nation's fate being in the hands of those willing to thus risk their country's very existence."[25] Clarke could not comprehend how the devastating defeat of the Franco-Prussian War had not provided a powerful lesson. Instead, the French grew "weary of waiting for the war—what a strange epoch in the history of mankind these armies that have never been in battle."[26]

In turn, much of Germany's martial success stemmed from its impressive manufacturing capabilities and natural resources such as coal and iron—the sinews of war. Powhatan witnessed this for himself on a visit to Essen.[27] During his two-day stay there, he was the guest of the chief director for the gigantic Krupp "works." Clarke depicted the complex as "larger than a town with 20,000 cannon and troops" that were "taken by railway that runs all over the place." Clarke was dumbfounded and feeling "small to see these great machines" where the steel was "heated and melted by gas … like so much taffy."

Although this forerunner of the military-industrial complex gave Germany an advantage, Clarke underscored that most junior German officers, unlike a number of their contemporaries in the American military, never had engaged in actual combat.[28]

They did spend considerable time in mock maneuvers. Originally, Clarke pronounced these exercises "quite like real war."[29] He, however, was not blinded by the pomp and relayed: "The drill not withstanding is in small parties at scouting and we have nothing to fear in such matters though they have."[30]

Such observations strengthened Clarke's growing nationalistic self-image as an "American more so than when coming here." He gained higher regard for "how great were the feats of the soldiers of 64, 65." General Wesley Merritt stood at the top of the pyramid of Civil War veterans in Clarke's estimation. He unequivocally pronounced Merritt "the best soldier in our army."[31]

Additionally, Clarke formulated ideas about changes required in the U.S. Army in light of what he observed while abroad. He saw publishing as a means to this end.[32] In this regard, Remington kept promoting other potential collaborations, urging the magazine to accept Clarke's "Hot Trail." While awaiting an answer, Remington was off to New York City "to meet Gen'l Miles on appointment."

Fred passed on a tidbit from another of Clarke's fellow Geronimo campaigners—Carter Johnson. The rough and tumble frontier officer had remarked: "I see Clark[e] is keep[ing] Europe stirred up," which Remington took as a compliment, coaching: "go it old man, just you handle the biggest spoon you can lift."

Embarking on literary pursuits fit with Clarke's plans to return to the Tenth Cavalry upon completing his European detail. Those plans likewise included an end to his bachelorhood and a new bride—Elsie Clemens, who he once told his mother was "a handsome girl and a fine girl but she is proud and has a strong will."[33] Louise Clarke knew the latter trait was what her son needed in a spouse.

Elsie's aunt, who was the wife of General von Versen, played a hand in aiding the young lovers. She also made it possible for Clarke to meet her second cousin, Mark Twain.[34] A delighted Clarke enjoyed not one but two visits with the world-renowned author, sage, and wit.[35]

Clarke's courtship advanced. He also basked in Twain's glory, but his relationship with Remington changed. A rift developed between them evidenced in a surviving letter from Fred to Powhatan. Taking an atypically serious tone, Remington solemnly reminded that regardless of circumstances, "even the crisis which is greater than death does not absolve a man from certain obligations," when it came to friendship.[36] He related that Elsie, whom he knew about at this point, received "the whole bloom in [*sic*] benefit of your correspondence and when the bit is on you, you are a regular case of diahorreha [*sic*] in written words!"

The men patched up differences before he received word of his return to the United States. Also while still serving abroad, Clarke's promotion was conferred.[37] The fledgling first lieutenant spent several months concluding his affairs in Germany including attendance at drills and other assignments, continued preparation of regular reports to the secretary of war, and even did some professional writing for the *Military Service Journal*.[38] Then, Clarke booked passage home at government expense.[39] Finally, he resolutely cast his lot to become a husband and take his bride to his next assignment after reaching home.[40]

With his ticket attached to his luggage, he boarded the *Spree*, landing on May 11, 1892. After he stepped ashore, "newspaper reporters" from the New York *Herald* set upon Clarke, honoring him "with lots of heavy type."[41]

Powhatan Clarke had enjoyed more than a year of good fortune beginning when he received his Medal of Honor and a promotion to first lieutenant through his special assignment from April 1891 to May 1892 with the Twelfth Westphalia Hussar regiment in Düsseldorf, Germany, and culminating with Elsie Clemens's acceptance of his marriage proposal. Upon Clarke's return to the United States, the wedding of Elsie and Powie became the talk

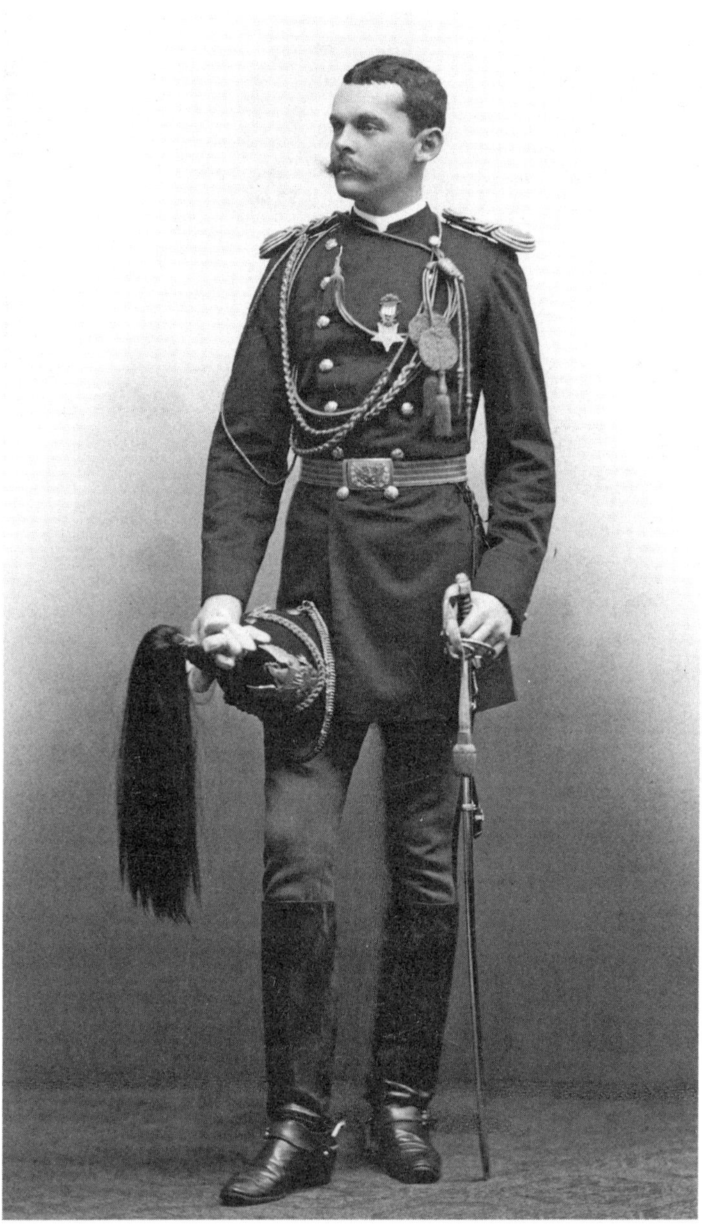

Powhatan Clarke had a series of photographic portraits taken while posted to Düsseldorf in part to win Elsie Clemens's hand. University of Arizona Library, Special Collections, Tucson.

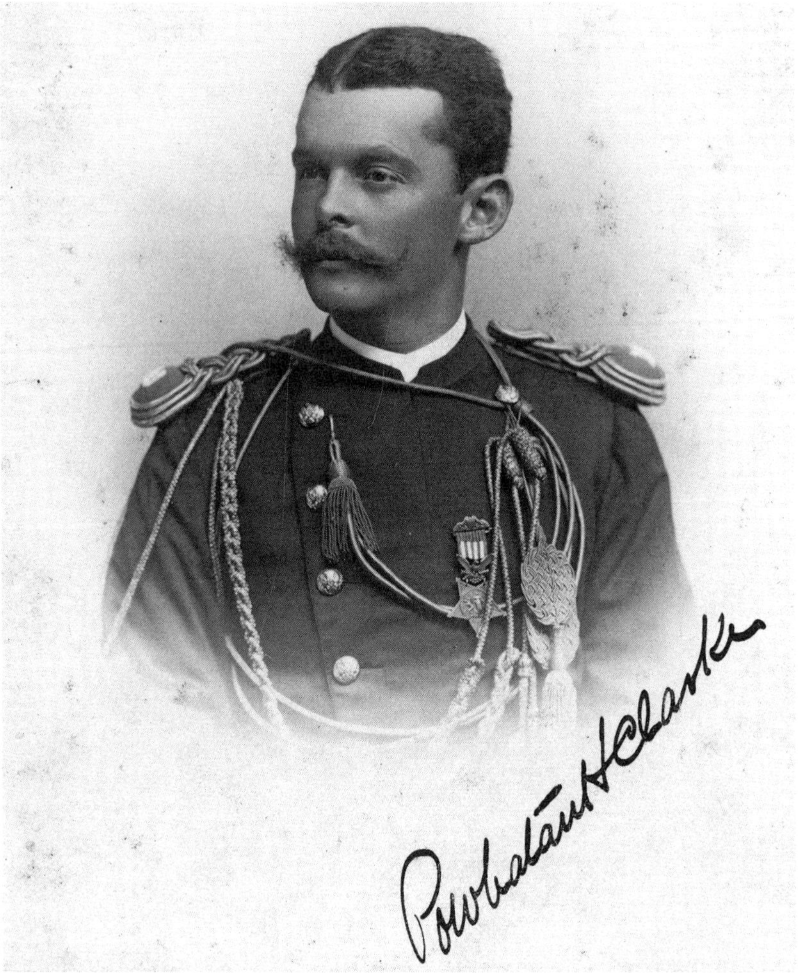

Clarke autographed his bust length portrait that conspicuously displayed his Medal of Honor and *aiguillette* that designated regimental adjutants. Author's Collection.

of St. Louis society and beyond.[42] Indeed, one newspaper in Clarke's home state of Louisiana reported: "the wedding has caused a great deal of comment owing to the fact that the bride, an heiress of one of the wealthiest and oldest St. Louis families, entered a convent two years ago with the avowed purpose of becoming a nun."[43]

At this point, some question remained whether the Clarkes in fact would be sent to Fort Custer, Montana, one of the posts where the regiment had been relocated from Arizona while Clarke was in Europe. Powhatan contacted his superiors about the matter, and found this was to be their destination.[44] After the pomp of their military wedding and their honeymoon in New York and Canada, the couple boarded a train for St. Louis and then on to Chicago. From there they proceeded to St. Paul, Minnesota, where they waited for their connection to Montana on the Northern Pacific Railroad.[45] Leaving in the afternoon, they finally rolled in to Custer, a hamlet that was little more than a train stop on the Yellowstone River slightly upstream from the Little Bighorn River's mouth. Disembarking, the newlyweds took an army ambulance, a generic name for a light multipurpose vehicle, for the thirty-mile overland trip to Fort Custer. They arrived in time for dinner and a serenade by the Tenth Cavalry's band, facts Elsie passed on to her mother in the first of a series of letters that shed light on life for frontier army wives and their families.[46] All the officers and wives turned "to welcome the bride." With the greetings completed, the Clarkes proceeded to the post in an ambulance. At the fort, they became temporary house guests of the First Lieutenant William Harvey Smith, and his wife of less than a year, the former Mary Louise Darst of Ferguson, Missouri.

Anxious to move into their own home, however, Elsie provided an inventory of items she wanted for the kitchen.[47] Her mother might be able to ship these from Jefferson Barracks because a levy of recruits from there was expected to depart for Fort Custer soon. Meanwhile, she and Powhatan had inspected their new quarters to see what must be undertaken to "have it cleaned up."

While they were settling into married life, an official matter surfaced. The military attaché in Berlin transmitted a "'Qualification Report' upon Lieut." made by Lieutenant Colonel von Britzke, "the commander of the Prussian regiment to which he was lately attached for a year."[48] The cover letter indicated this was "a report that Lieut. Clarke & our Army may well be proud of" and indeed it was. The commander of the Westphalian Hussar Regiment No. 11 praised the American as presenting "a fine, military appearance; is a bold and powerful rider; & has a perfect passion for the military service." Adding to the laurels, he judged Clarke as possessing "a clear & sharp understanding; & having a proper military insight, he succeeded in learning our methods & regulations & also in getting a correct idea of the reasons & spirit which control said methods."

It had been a mutual admiration society. Clarke saw much in the German military worth emulation. Ignoring counsel for discretion from both Frederic Remington and William Smith, as well as a former secretary of war Redfield Proctor's suggestions, the headstrong Clarke penned a scathing exposé in the press, a tactic he had conceived while in Europe as a means to achieve his revolutionary makeover of the U.S. military.[49] Clarke boldly signed and included his regimental affiliation at the end of a New York *Herald Tribune*, May 7, 1893, commentary under the headline: "Reforms Needed in the U.S. Army. Systematic and Uniform Training of the Men of Primary Importance. Plain Talk from An Officer. What Should Be Done to Form a Staff Ready for Any Emergency. Red Tape Carried Too Far."[50].

His recurring message revolved around significantly enhanced training on many levels and of many types for officers and men alike. Clarke called for "a more thorough system of practical inspection." General officers, who should conduct such probes, were "so tied down by office work that they" and many "older officers … were physical wrecks from campaigning in and since the war. Some of them may be, but I have not men so feeble that they could not drill their regiments."

According to Clarke, the problem was not physical. He contended the service was "handicapped by men whose highest idea of duty is to do only that which they cannot shirk."

Clarke's letter to the editor in the New York *Herald* ruffled brass in Washington including General Schofield. The army's commander wanted measures taken "with a view to disciplining Lieutenant Clark, and affording an example to others."[51] Major General Wesley Merritt concurred with disciplinary actions, but savvy of the ramifications, indicated that he doubted "the advisability of bringing this officer before a court for this offense. Not that I think the court would not convict him of conduct to the prejudice etc., but because the sentence of the court would not, in my opinion, be productive of as much good in his case as a severe reprimand by the Commanding General of the Army."

In Merritt's estimation, Clarke had a long road ahead of him to reach his potential. "At present," however, the general viewed Clarke as "conceited and vain-glorious, resulting from the attention he attracted for his conduct in an affair with Indians in Arizona, and his detail abroad."

To set Clarke on the right path, Merritt proposed the first action should be "a rebuke from General Schofield." He deduced this "would result in much good to Lieutenant Clarke, while a trial by a general court might be used by the newspapers to make a hero of him, and an opportunity to malign the army."

A few weeks later, given that Clarke had rankled many military men with his charges that "the War Department and its administration, and the character of the Army involving personnel, system of instruction, administration" were subpar, and because "the general tenor involves strictures upon officers high in command and authority," Schofield passed on his verdict to Merritt.

With "discipline and subordination" foremost, Schofield could not abide the army being "made a public debating society, to discuss the official acts or measures of superior authority, and convey censure respecting others in the military service." The means to air concerns, according to the general, was for "intelligent and fair minded officers" to work through channels. Admitting that "honest differences … must arise," these must be "fairly stated for the decision of the Secretary of War or the President, whose final judgment should be accepted with soldierly subordination" and not in newspapers.

Clarke received stern warning that "future publications of a character like that now under consideration, will form a basis of charges against the officer, for trial by Court-Martial." To assure that others in the army understood the serious nature of "the wide circulation of the newspaper article under consideration," a copy of the letter of reprimand went "to all department commanders" and of course Clarke received one and a duplicate was placed in his personnel file.

Clarke avoided dismissal just as at West Point. At this stage of his career, however, he had allies, most notably Remington, who as reported by *Harper's Weekly* insisted " 'the hand of the fat god of rank' is extremely heavy on the army, and effectually squashes the spirit out of the likeliest young officers."

Remington hung his hopes on his favorite, Nelson Miles, whom he correctly foretold would climb to the top. When he did, he would be "in favor of young blood but he is afraid of a cabal on the part of the tubs and waits to keep all his position masked." All Clarke had to do was bide his time.

Likewise, Fred warned that Powhatan should not "antagonize Merritt or any other of the 'Corinthian class' for they will get it in for you. When you want to apparently be forceful be as foxy as you can—or some 'smart fellow' will put twine on you."

If Clarke disregarded this admonition and went down in flames, Remington assured that he would "write you an obituary which will make the blood come right out of the faces of the fellows who jump you." Little did he know that such an action would be necessary sooner than he realized.

Epilogue

"Fiddler's Green"

Clarke may have received Remington's jest about an obituary not long after he and Elsie ended their honeymoon and started married life at Fort Custer, Montana, during the fall of 1892. While the newlyweds had a brief time together, and nearly a year later welcomed their son Powhatan Hughes Clarke into the world, their days together proved all too short. Fort Custer's post surgeon and old comrade from Arizona reported on July 21, 1893, the sad news "that 1st Lieut. Powhatan H. Clarke, 10th U.S. Cavalry, died at this post this date 3 P.M. Cause of death, accidental drowning. In line of duty."[1] A second announcement followed from the Tenth Cavalry's lieutenant colonel who confirmed the sad news of the fatal incident in the waters of the Little Big Horn River in the immediate vicinity of the post, and which added that it was "believed that in diving off the bank Lieutenant Clarke struck his head on a rock which stunned him before his body could be retrieved life was extinct, all efforts to resuscitate him proved unavailing."[2]

With the tragic accident still fresh, Frederic Remington conveyed his shock and that of his wife Eva to Clarke's widow.[3] Leaving the usually gregarious New Yorker nearly speechless, he mused: "It really seems so improbable and we cannot get used to it. We feel deeply for you in your bereavement and mourn the loss of our old friend Clark more than I dare say. We cannot imagine how it came to pass. Missie and I send love."

This fatality resulted from Clarke's efforts to enhance much needed training designed to prepare troops for fording water obstacles on campaign. Thus, he was putting into practice his own admonitions for better and more realistic preparation to improve combat readiness. So it was that "After swimming their horses to and fro across a circular pool in the river not more than 40 yards in its greatest diameter and about six feet in depth the three officers separated, Lieut. Clarke proceeding alone to a pool about the same size only a few rods further up the river." Once he reached the spot, Clarke "dismounted and tied up his horse" then "he almost immediately dived into the pool.... An enlisted man standing near by saw him rise from the dive. It was noticed that his hair was discolored. At the moment, the man thought it mud."

Regrettably, "it was blood, not mud, on the officer's head." Clarke's brother officers and some enlisted men "continued to dive and search for their comrade's body, for it was now felt that the body could only be recovered." This grim task fell to Lieutenant William L. Johnston, "who at the time of the accident was in the post, but to whom the word of danger had come, to rescue the body."[4]

Over the ensuing months, newspapers around the country, including the *Army and Navy Journal* and *Harper's*, which ran "an excellent likeness of the late Lieut. Powhatan H. Clarke, U. S. A.," ran stories and printed obituaries as well as made mention of promotions, which occurred in the wake of the vacancy Clarke left in his beloved regiment.[5] Occasionally, references to Clarke's death remarked about the hornets' nest he had stirred up, such as one which appeared in *Harper's Weekly*. In a piece that Remington could have authored or at the very least agreed with, *Harper's Weekly* lamented the death of this "officer of brains, energy and enthusiasm, and one moreover, who had won the United States medal of honor for special gallantry in action against Apache Indians" and somewhat ingenuously was *sans peur et san reproche* "without flaw and without reproach."[6]

For nearly a quarter of a century thereafter, such positive depictions of Clarke held sway in print, albeit these stories were few in number and released sporadically.[7] As examples, the year following Clarke's death three references appeared about him in the *Army and Navy Journal*. The first two showed up in the April 11 issue having to do with a recent rendering of Clarke's rescue of Corporal Scott. T.H. Lambert presented this "beautiful oil painting of … a gallant and cultured officer," who "drowned it may be remembered, July 21, 1893" to the Tenth Cavalry Officers' Club. Lambert received the members' thanks and a standing invitation to "accept the hospitalities of the club" if he visited Fort Assinniboine, Montana, where his art would be hung. They also gratefully acclaimed "the picture is not only a speaking likeness, but it also recalls in a most vivid manner the incident as impressed upon the minds of all his old comrade officers."[8] Despite this glowing review, Lambert's highly derivative depiction drew heavily on Remington's far more artistic *Harper's* cover. Except for Captain Lebo, none of the officers who gazed on this masterpiece "while downing a drink in Clarke's honor," had been at the firefight. Consequently, none of "his fellow-officers" had the slightest idea if Lambert's brush had captured anything remotely close to reality.

While some eulogized Clarke as "the knight errant" of the buffalo soldiers, Remington provided final lyrics for the unsung ballad of Clarke's life.[9] Uncannily, Clarke's admiring artist friend predicted the untimely end, when he mused: "The little 'cherub who sits up aloft' has his hands full to look after Lieutenant Clarke and keep him from breaking his neck…."[10] Another of Remington's descriptions of Clarke, however, which appeared in the March 22, 1890, edition of *Harper's Weekly*, said it best. Remington claimed Clarke was "adored by his men" and was capable of riding "horses which no one else can." Supposedly, he was "one of those old-time kind of 'ride into battle with his life on his sleeve' soldiers"—not a bad epitaph and one Clarke may have accepted as high honors.

After Clarke's death his widow and infant son remained at Fort Custer until October 1. As Elsie recorded in a rare diary entry years later, their child, who had been born on April 5, was named "Powhatan James Hughes Clarke (after your father and his best friend)." The lad would never know his father, although it is likely he visited the grave with his mother occasionally from their home in St. Louis where Powhatan's remains arrived to be placed in the Clemens family plot at Calvary Cemetery. Living comfortably in the rambling home of her parents, mother and son sometimes traveled such as

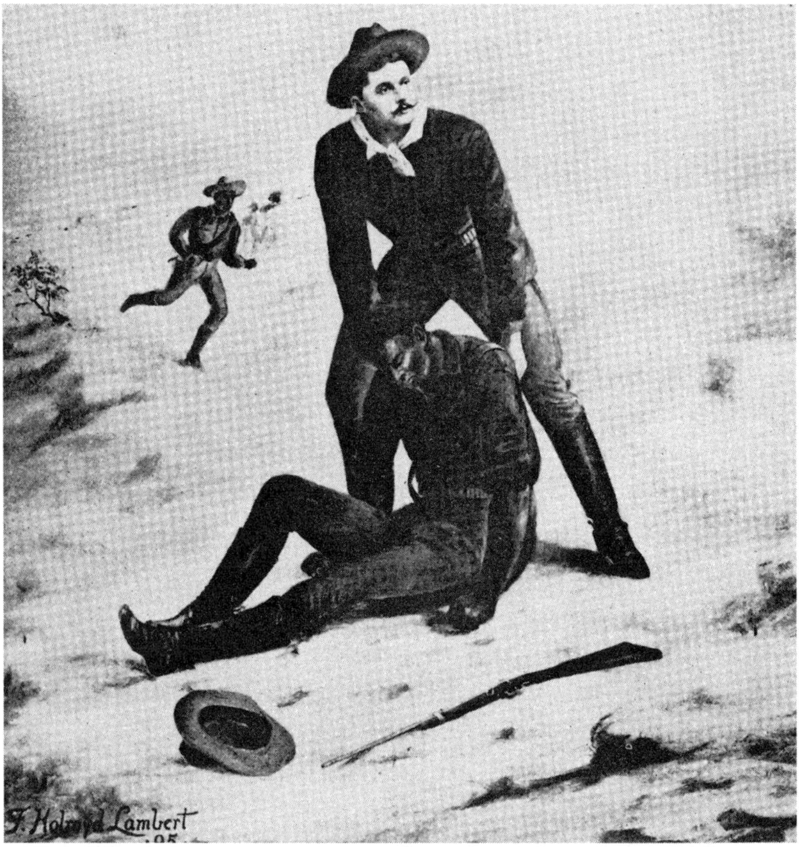

T. Holyrod Lambert's 1895 version of Lieutenant Clarke's saving of Corporal Scott differed from Remington's rendering including a solo act of bravery rather than showing an enlisted man assisting in the rescue.

a trip to Baltimore where the toddler's grandparents watched him "with the greatest interest. When 'dad' [Dr. Clarke] told his stories, you mimicked all his gestures and made all laugh. That same November of 1894 we came back to St. Louis for a brief layover before spending the winter in warmer California climes."[11]

Periodically they spent time in Florida and elsewhere to escape the winter in St. Louis, but for the most part Elsie and "Powie's boy" were homebodies. In the process, Elsie's future dreams for Powhatan James Hughes

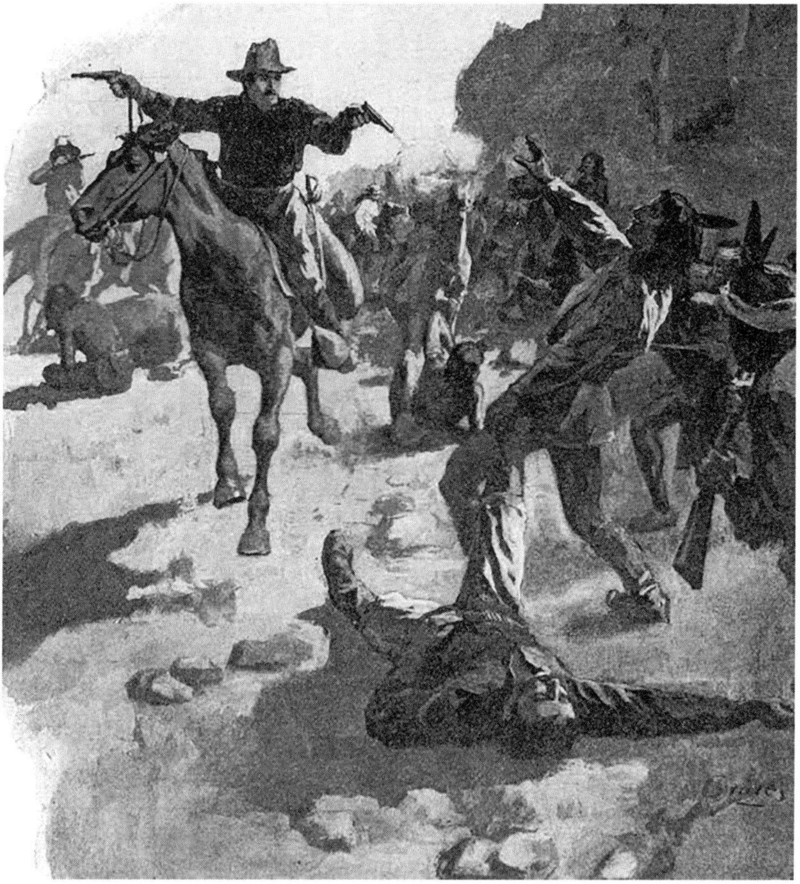

Unlike Frederic Remington, who attempted to capture details based on first-hand accounts, the artist for the two-volume *Deeds of Valor* (1906) concerning Medal of Honor exploits, took great liberties in depicting Powhatan Clarke's heroics during the Geronimo Campaign.

Clarke came true as he was his father's son in many ways. In one particular, however, he greatly differed from the lackluster West Point cadet. The younger Clarke entered Saint Louis University at the age of twelve! By 1916, the barely twenty-three-year old model student had earned his LL.B. (Bachelor of Law) from that institution. Shortly thereafter he would be admitted to the Missouri bar.

After a short time in practice, he put aside the law. On April 16, 1917, Clarke volunteered for the Officers' Reserve of the Signal Corps, Aviation Section, U.S. Army. Passing flight instruction, he received his commission as first lieutenant, the same rank his father held at death, in the Signal Officers' Reserve Corps. By January 1918 he sailed for France, a country his father knew well, and reported to the Twenty-first Aero Squadron.[12]

Not long after he had joined the air service, young Clarke would find his name in print alongside that of his dead father under the byline of Major Edward B. Clark. Combining Apache Wars heroics along with an exploit about a dangerous ditch jump made while posted to Germany to deliver a message from Kaiser Wilhelm, the major cribbed many passages from former newspaper accounts replete with several errors. Regardless, his cobbled together "Germans Sneer at U.S. Soldiers" made it into several papers scattered across the country.[13]

Leading off with a jibe at Germany and "its daily sneer at the American army," he smugly proposed: "The sneer perhaps covers fear." He went on to note that "a boy whose name is Powhatan H. Clarke" had arrived in "Washington to join the Aviation corps of this country." While there, "the elders among the army officers who met him saw in him the virtual reproduction of father," whom the major then resurrected. Summarizing the Arizona rescue, Clarke quickly turned to a longer explanation of the equestrian feat performed in the presence of the Kaiser, now the enemy of the United States. The major ended with his moral that: "Until August, 1914 and perhaps until April, 1917, the story of Clarke's jump frequently was told in the German service. The sneer for American soldier ship officers here say is the sneer of unreason and that the German army knows it."

Now the time came for the young St. Louis attorney turned U.S. Army military pilot to show his soldier legacy. Once in country, he underwent additional flight training. After that, in June 1918, however, instead of seeing combat as a pilot he reported for service with various administrative labor companies, many of which were manned by African American troops. As the war ended in November 1918, Clarke remained with the Air Service when it was redesignated the Army Air Corps. Early the next year he again found himself assigned to administrative duties, the bane of his father's days in uniform. Finally, on September 25, 1919, he boarded a steamer for home where he received his discharge at Camp Dix, New Jersey, on October 25. Supposedly he declined an offer for assignment to military intelligence as a major and instead returned to St. Louis. During a family vacation in June 1920 he and the family visited Gloucester, Massachusetts, where a lung condition meant hospitalization. His health rapidly deteriorated. Less than a year after his return to civilian life, Clarke died on August 30, 1920. He would be buried near his father.[14]

Elsie, alone save for her younger sister, who never married, and who before her death in 1958 donated the Clarke papers to what now is the Missouri History Museum, lived another seven years. Passing at age fifty-six, on August 22, 1927, she would be laid to rest between her knight of the frontier and her knight of the air—the two lieutenants named Powhatan Clarke. Long before that, save for informing Dr. Clarke of alleged efforts "to help erect a memorial of some kind … either at West Point or Leavenworth" and a pair of letters related to publishing Powhatan's "A Hot Trail," albeit posthumously, in *Cosmopolitan* for $75, which he intended to forward to Elsie, Remington seemingly ceased communications with the family of "my friend Clark."[15]

This was in spite of the fact Remington even told Dr. Clarke that the young cavalry officer "was a fellow who appealed to my imagination—he was also a good friend to me and I grew to be very very fond of him." He further confessed that Powhatan had "entered into my life to that extent that I can hardly make it seem that I have got to get along without him"[16] Nonetheless, Fred moved on, seemingly forgetting Powhatan, and striking up acquaintances with other officers and many like-minded civilians who embraced, and in some instances, played a major part in the creation of American Western lore, such as Owen Wister.[17]

That relationship with the rising author of *The Virginian*, however, never reached the levels enjoyed by Clarke and Remington. Nonetheless, Remington with or without such a close connection would emerge as the premier artist of the American West, particularly in portraying the U.S. Army as it began to evolve from a frontier constabulary to an international force. Indeed, Remington eclipsed American rivals, most significantly Rufus Zogbaum and Charles Schreyvogle, who competed with him for a time, but in the end fell into obscurity.[18] Even after Remington's death on December 26, 1909, at age forty-eight, he continued to reign supreme, not only when it came to the U.S. Army of his times, but also arguably as the most significant artist to represent the American West.[19]

As for Corporal Scott, arguably the catalyst for Clarke and Remington being more than passing acquaintances, after over eight years of service the disabling wound in Arizona led to his temporary retirement in the Soldiers Home. Later, he left the Home, married, fathered two children, and resided for a time in Forest Glen, Maryland. Scott ended his days in Washington, D.C., where after his death on July 28, 1913, his widow Sarah eventually applied for a pension.[20]

In turn had it not been for Troop K's the top soldier, William Givens, who first told Remington the tale of the saving of Corporal Scott's life, the chance encounter between Clarke and Remington may have ended on the same day they came into contact with each other. Givens remained with the Tenth U.S. Cavalry, and when it deployed to Cuba in 1898 John Bigelow reported him as "a steadying and encouraging influence upon the men" at San Juan, which contributed to his receiving a commission as an officer to cap his career that ended in retirement in 1901. Givens died in 1907, but not before John Bigelow attempted to secure recognition for the brave veteran's actions in Cuba. Regrettably, Bigelow never succeeded in gaining the recognition he thought Givens deserved.[21]

Bigelow himself inched up the military ladder, along the way authoring many books that followed the first literary efforts for his brother's periodical, and which helped launch Remington's career. Using his influential family, Bigelow enjoyed a second tour of duty at the U.S. Military Academy, reporting there in 1892 as a professor of modern languages. Two years later, in the parlance of the Victorian U.S. Army, another "gilt edged" assignment came Bigelow's way when he reported to the prestigious Massachusetts Institute of Technology as professor of military science. By the next year, he had attained sufficient stature for the acting secretary of the Navy to request him to deliver a series of lectures on land strategy at the Naval War College. The Spanish American War ended all these posh postings. Bigelow joined the Tenth in Cuba and displayed he was more than just a parade ground soldier when at

San Juan Hill he sustained four wounds. A quick trip back with the regiment to the United States ended with being sent to Cuba in 1899 as collector of customs at Sagna la Grande. During this busy time Bigelow released his *Principles of Strategy*, which, like Clarke's piece for the *Herald*, read as an indictment of the state of the U.S. Army at the close of the Victorian era. Far from damaging his career, however, the seniority system that Clarke sometimes spoke of in disparaging terms, brought Bigelow his promotion to major in the Ninth United States Cavalry. A transfer to this brother regiment of the Tenth, meant he commanded black troops at such places as Yosemite National Park (where he also served as acting superintendent of a national park). After spending the summer of 1904 there, he concluded his rich career with retirement on September 15, 1904. Not content to mount a rocking chair, Bigelow taught French at MIT from 1905 through 1910, where he also headed the modern languages department. From there he went on to Rutgers as professor of military science, but left for active duty in the office of the chief of staff of army when the United States entered World War I. He once again put aside his uniform in 1919, meanwhile having been promoted to lieutenant colonel in the process. Thereafter he continued as an author concentrating on geopolitical and military topics. He died on March 1, 1936, just shy of his eighty-second birthday.[22]

Thomas C. Lebo, Troop K's commander when Bigelow and Clarke were his junior officers, eventually became a major in the Sixth U.S. Cavalry just a few days after his former second lieutenant's drowning. He would remain stateside during the Spanish American War, but soon after his September 14, 1899, promotion to lieutenant colonel of the First U.S. Cavalry, he would accompany the regiment to the Philippines. With his elevation to colonel in command of the Fourteenth U.S. Cavalry on February 19, 1902, he would sail for home. The next year, Lebo the seemingly old, confirmed bachelor married Grace Frances Hawkes in Albuquerque, New Mexico. According to the practice of the times, as a Civil War officer, the day before Lebo retired, June 22, 1905, he advanced to the next highest grade, which was brigadier general. Lebo died in Chicago on February 23, 1910, at age sixty-seven.[23]

North Carolinian William Shipp, who attempted to vindicate Clarke in print, also ended his bachelor status after duty with the militia of his native state in1892.[24] During a subsequent detail the next year to Davis School in

Winston, North Carolina, as an instructor of military science, he married Margaret Finley Bisbee. The Shipps enjoyed slightly more time together than the Clarkes. Unfortunately, the year after Shipp rejoined the Tenth Cavalry, in this case a Fort Assinniboine, Montana, he headed to Cuba. In July 1898, displaying gallantry worthy of Clarke, Shipp died fighting in the storied assault on San Juan Hill.[25]

Missourian William Smith, who according to Major General Merritt was "ashamed" of Clarke's attack on the U.S. Army in the press, also would depart Montana in 1898 for Cuba. He, too, fell in action July 1, 1898, at San Juan Santiago.[26]

James B. Hughes, Clarke's closest comrade, classmate, best man at his wedding, and godfather to his son, would display bravery during the Spanish American War. For "gallantry in action against Spanish forces at Santiago, Cuba, July 1, 1898," he eventually received a citation and later a Silver Star when that decoration for valor was adopted.[27] Also, he obtained his captain's bars on July 11, 1899, with the First United States Cavalry. In 1910 he attended the Army School of the Line at Fort Leavenworth, Kansas. On March 3, 1911, Hughes became a major in the First Cavalry. That same year he was appointed as superintendent of the Sequoia and Grant National Park. He likewise served at a number of other postings including Jefferson Barracks, Missouri, on recruiting duty, Forts Custer and Keogh, Montana, Fort Meade, South Dakota, the Philippines with the Fourth United States Cavalry in 1901 and again from 1907 to 1909, along with assignments to Yuma, Arizona, San Diego, and the Presidio of San Francisco, California. Toward the end of his active duty he went on sick leave for an unspecified illness from January 3 to March 9, 1914. Hughes retired on March 7, 1914, "For Disability Not Incident to the Service." Nearly two decades passed before Hughes's death at Walter Reed Hospital on January 21, 1933.[28]

Hughes was one of the last of the Class of 1884 to die. A review of the fate of Clarke's classmates, a number of whom traced their ancestry to leading American families, is revealing. Due to deaths long before most of their classmates, Powhatan Clarke (July 21, 1893) and Ernest Smith Robins (August 18, 1894) ended their military days as first lieutenants. Of the other thirty-five surviving graduates from Clarke's year group, three died or retired early in the twentieth century as majors (among them Hughes), while of the remainder, three became lieutenant colonels, nine colonels, thirteen brigadier generals, and seven reached the grade of major general. These statistics along with comparisons of some of his juniors—most notably John J. Pershing, who would wear the four stars of general of the armies when he commanded the American Expeditionary Force during the First World War (a conflict Clarke anticipated)—raise interesting areas for conjecture.

Two years junior to Clarke, Pershing (West Point Class of 1886) first served in the Sixth U.S. Cavalry. With his promotion to first lieutenant, he joined the Tenth on October 20, 1892. As with many others in the regiment, Pershing mobilized and landed in Cuba, first handling the daunting task of supply as the Tenth's quartermaster officer. Eventually he saw combat as a field commander. In both capacities "Black Jack" Pershing gained notice from superiors.[29] One of them, Theodore Roosevelt, in command of the First Volunteer Cavalry, popularly known as the "Rough Riders," was among those who held Pershing in regard. He proved instrumental in the meteoric rise of the obscure company grade officer to general over the heads of many a senior officer.

Clarke would not enjoy such a fate or gain fame like Pershing; yet his over twelve years in the army starting as a cadet and ending in the Little Big Horn River still merits attention for a number of reasons. Significantly, he reached manhood during a major sea change in national history. The promise of Reconstruction died, Jim Crow emerged as the unofficial law of the land, and the explosion of industrialization gave rise to class conflict between impoverished labor and Gilded Age "robber barons" creating heretofore unknown tensions. The hand of Manifest Destiny had reached from the Atlantic to the Pacific, extinguishing the need for the frontier constabulary of Clarke's experience, eventually to be replaced by a mighty military force in keeping with the United States' emergence as an international power.

Clarke may well have embraced this transformation of the land of which he was so proud. Unquestionably, his ability when catapulted into combat to perform above and beyond the call of duty would have been an asset during the new era.

Receiving recognition for impetuous bravery, Clarke achieved a degree of fame that contributed to his becoming more assertive. Imbued with a sense of self-importance and military prowess, while not possessing the political savvy of John Pershing, or the traits of an original military theorist such as Emory Upton, Clarke nonetheless began to mature as he evolved from a tactical reactor to a strategic thinker. During this metamorphosis he gradually set aside the romantic *bon guerre* views embraced by Remington, Roosevelt, and others to approach an understanding of the cost and scope of modern war.

Clarke's growing insights, which to some degree sagely forecast the outbreak of the First World War, prompted him to take action. True to his long disdain for authority, an ambitious Clarke turned a deaf ear to those who urged temperance. Throwing caution to the winds, he publicly denounced the status quo. The fossilized high command must be swept aside, he publicly argued. The impatient man of action advocated advanced, intensive training under a cadre of competent professional officers, although he had not envisioned the global role his country would come to play.

In the process, the carefree, naïve, boyish "'stainless knight' so brave and pure" began to give way to a more seasoned soldier.[30] Additionally, through prolonged, intense contact with his troops, both African American and American Indian, he developed an appreciation for those he commanded, not as stereotypes, or racial inferiors, but instead as fellow warriors. Additionally, Clarke even achieved a degree of respect for his "gallant foemen" the Apaches, whom he had faced in mortal conflict.

But as Rudyard Kipling observed in his poem "Tommy Atkins": "single men in barricks don't grow into plaster saints." To some degree Clarke could be counted among them. For much of his life Clarke exhibited contradictory traits—some laudable and others less so. While by later standards he might be branded as prejudiced, compared to many others of his era he was far less bigoted, especially when it came to the buffalo soldiers he commanded with pride.

At times, particularly when idle, he could be arrogant, class conscious, impulsive, manipulative, petulant, selfish, spoiled, subject to bouts of melancholy, prone to procrastination, occasionally vacillated, and could be accused of a litany of other faults. In short, he was "such a mixture of all sorts, as only America brings forth."[31] Consequently, his idiosyncratic tale told through his often unfiltered, frank writings, gives pause to anyone attempting to find the rhythm of life.

In the end, Clarke's drowning, ironically, brought about an end Remington thought impossible, silencing his young life scarcely after the playing of its overture. What Clarke could have accomplished had he survived to the Spanish-American War or through World War I, can never be known.

Endnotes

Introduction

1. Oliver Knight, *Life and Manners in the Frontier Army* (Norman: University of Oklahoma Press, 1978), 71.
2. James S. Robbins, *Last in Their Class: Custer, Pickett and the Goats of West Point* (New York: Encounter Books, 2006) explores some of the cadets who graduated at the bottom of their classes at the United States Military Academy.
3. Knight, *Life and Manners in the Frontier Army*, 3–4.
4. Generations of authors have told the story of "the boy general" and his legendary "last stand" such as Robert M. Utley's *Cavalier in Buckskin: George Custer and the Western Military Frontier* (Norman: University of Oklahoma Press, 1988), and T.J. Stiles's *Custer's Trials: A Life on the Frontier of America* (New York: Alfred A. Knopf. 2015), rank high among Custer's many biographies.
5. William A. Dobak and Thomas D. Phillips, *The Black Regulars, 1866–1898* (Norman: University of Oklahoma Press, 2001), 27–8. For more on Custer's racial attitudes consult, Stiles *Custer's Trials*, xvi, 174–5, 213, 228–33,237, 239–40, 249, 251, 277–8, 304, 325, 327, 333, 367–70, 407, 409, 416–17, 431–32, 434. Note, Custer's fellow Union officer took a dissimilar view, for example writing in 1866: "I am anxious to get some colored troops out on the plains and … will send you from four to six regiments of them in addition to the White troops you now have. In the absence of these I think you had better send about two regiments out and trust to recruiting most of them for the regular army afterwards." Ulysses S. Grant, *U.S. Grant Papers: The Papers of Ulysses S. Grant, 1866*, vol. 16 (Carbondale: Southern Illinois University Press, 1988), 93.
6. Dobak and Phillips, *The Black Regulars*, 3–4. During the nineteenth century all but three officers posted to black regiments were white. The exception to this general rule stemmed for appointments of blacks to the military academy starting in 1870 when Mississippian Michael Howard and South Carolinian James Webster Smith led the way making "the long walk from the train landing to the plain" of West Point. In due course, "They were followed in the 1870s and 1880s by twenty others." Of these only a trio "graduated: Henry O. Flipper in 1877, John H.

Alexander in 1887, and Charles Denton Young in 1889. The latter West Pointer rose to the grade of colonel and had the distinction of being the highest-ranking black officer in World War I." John F. Marszalek, Jr., *Court-Martial: A Black Man in America* (New York: Charles Scribner's Sons, 1972), 18–19.

7. Peter Hassrick, *Frederic Remington Paintings, Drawings, and Sculpture in the Amon Carter Museum and The Sid Richardson Foundation Collection* (New York: Harry N. Abrams, Inc., 1973), 16.
8. Hassrick, *Frederic Remington Paintings*,16 and 18.
9. Nelson Appleton Miles of Massachusetts eventually rose from a store clerk to commanding general of the U.S. Army. He began his military career as a first lieutenant in the Union Volunteers, earned the Medal of Honor, and after the war became the colonel of the Fortieth U.S. Infantry, manned by African American Soldiers. During the 1869 reorganization of the U.S. Army he moved to the Fifth U.S. Infantry. On December 15, 1880, he gained his first star as a brigadier general, his second as a major general on April 5, 1890, and in September of 1895 assumed the post of commander in chief of the U.S. Army. He successfully lobbied to become a lieutenant general, which he did on June 6, 1890. Miles, who became a thorn in the sides of the secretary of war and President Theodore Roosevelt, retired on August 3, 1903. He died on May 15, 1925, but not before publishing his memoirs in 1911 titled *Serving the Republic*. Robert M. Utley's "Nelson A. Miles" from the second edition of Paul Andrew Hutton and Durwood Ball, eds., *Soldiers West: Biographies from the Military Frontier* (Norman: University of Oklahoma Press, 2009), 340–57, and Robert M. Utley, *The Commanders: Civil War Generals Who Shaped the American West* (Norman: University of Oklahoma Press, 2018), 90–126, provide brief biographies.
10. See Emory Upton, *A New System of Infantry Tactics, Double and Single Rank Adapted to American Topology and Improved Fire-Arms* (New York: D. Appleton & Co., 1868); *The Armies of Asia and Europe. Embracing Official Reports on the Armies of Japan, China, India, Persia, Italy, Russia, Austria, Germany, France, and England. Accompanied by Letters Descriptive of a Journey from Japan to the Caucasus* (New York: D. Appleton & Co., 1878); and his extremely influential posthumous *Military Policy of the United States Army* (Washington, DC: Government Printing Office, 1904). David J. Fitzpatrick, *Emory Upton: Misunderstood Reformer* (Norman: University of Oklahoma

Press, 2017), provides context and background, as well as added new insights about this influential figure.

11. Nixon O. Rush, *Remington and Owen Wister: The Story of a Friendship, 1893–1909* (Tallahassee: Privately Printed, 1961), 30. Also see: Richard Slotkin, *The Fatal Environment: The Myth of the Frontier in the Age of Industrialization, 1800–1890* (New York: Harper Perennial, 1994), 97.
12. Michael Kimmel, *Manhood in America: A Cultural History* (New York: The Free Press, 1996), 152.
13. Kimmel, *Manhood in America*, 155 and 182.
14. Kimmel, *Manhood in America*, 136. For more on the topic of masculinity obtain Margaretta M. Lovell, "Dashing for America: Frederic Remington, National Myths, and Art Historical Narratives," *The Journal of the Association of Historians of American Art* (Fall 2015): 1–20.
15. See Brian W. Dippie's essay, "'A Very Good Friend to the Army': The Frontier Soldier in the Western Art of Frederic Remington," in R. Eli Paul, ed., *The Frontier Army: Episodes from Dakota and the West* (Pierre: South Dakota Historical Society Press, 2019), 99–118, for a significant perspective on this aspect of Remington's career. Also consult Peter Hassrick, *Catalogue Raisonné* II (Norman: University of Oklahoma Press, 2016), 43–55.
16. Undated notes from a public lecture provided by Thomas Phillips, Ph.D. to the author.
17. *Army and Navy Journal*, May 16, 1891, 643. Hereafter this source will be referred to as *A&NJ.*

Notes to Chapter 1

1. The above synopsis was taken from the following sources: Family Record Births, Box 1, No. A0293, Powhatan H. Clarke Papers, Missouri Historical Society Archives, St. Louis (hereafter referred to as PHC Papers). This same document notes a third son born on December 8, 1824, had been called Powhatan, but evidently, he died young and the name was carried on by the seventh son. "CLARKE. Sons of the Revolution. Virginia" Box 1, Powhatan H. PHC Papers; Francis Heitman, *Historical Register of the Officers of the Continental Army During the War of the Revolution, April, 1775 to December, 1783* (Washington, DC: W.H. Lowdermilk & Co., 1893), and William Thomas Roberts

Saffell, *Records of the Revolutionary War*.... (Baltimore: Charles C. Saffell, 1858); Biographical Notes for the *Cyclopedia of American Biography*, 3. Box 1, PHC Papers.

2. Family Record Marriages, Box 1, PHC Papers.
3. (Baltimore) *Sun*, April 16, 1900.
4. As an aside, one of the enslaved blacks at Ulster Plantation, Polly Mason (1855–1971) who was born on the Boyd estate, provided an oral history interview in 1971. Sound cassette (45 minutes), 10 pages, Location: L:4700.0041, Mss. 4700.004, Louisiana State Library Special Collections.
5. Biographical information Powhatan Henry Clarke's maternal grandfather was taken from the Shreveport *Times* (March 15, 1873), and "Henry Boyce" *Biographical Directory of Federal Judges* (Washington, DC: Federal Judicial Center) www.fjc.gov/history/judges/bouyce-henry.
6. See "Clarke (Dr. Powhatan) Diary," Mss. 893, Louisiana and Lower Mississippi Valley Collection, Special Collections, Hill Memorial Library, Louisiana State University Libraries, Baton Rouge; Powhatan Clarke to General Marcos Wright, May 2, 1888; Powhatan Clarke to Henry Boyce, October 27, 1864, Camden, AK. Box 1; Powhatan Clarke to Henry Boyce, August 3, 1864, Esperanza, LA. Box 1, PHC Papers; and "Powhatan Clarke (19 Sep. 1837-A5 Apr. 1917)," *Students of the University of Virginia, 1825–1872*, www.uvastudents.wordpress.com/ 2012/11/18/powhatan-clarke-19-sep-1837-25-apr-1917 for more information on the Civil War years.
7. Henry Boyce to Col. Powhatan Clarke, January 1, 1873. Box 1, PHC Papers.
8. Mary Goode Lyle Clarke to Powhatan Henry Clarke, February 6, 1873, Box 1, PHC Papers.
9. Powhatan Henry Clarke to Papa (Dr. Powhatan Clarke), August 9, 1873, Box 1, PHC Papers. Hereafter for letters written by Powhatan Henry Clarke, the abbreviation PHC will be employed.
10. PHC to Mother (Louise Clarke), March 29, 1874. Box 1, PHC Papers.
11. PHC to Papa (Dr. Powhatan Clarke), June 4, 1874. Box 1, PHC Papers.
12. PHC to Mama (Louise Clarke), September 17, 1876, Box 1, PHC Papers.
13. PHC to Papa (Powhatan Clarke), December 9, 1876, Box 1, PHC Papers.
14. Award of Merit in Second Arithmetic, January 20, 1877, Box 1, PHC Papers.

15. www.umd.edu/history-andmission/timeline.
16. [Dr.] Powhatan Clarke to Powhatan Henry Clarke, January 10, 1878, Box 1, PHC Papers.
17. [Dr.] Powhatan Clarke to Powhatan Henry Clarke, February 18, 1878, Box 1, PHC Papers.
18. C.S. McCawley to Powhatan Henry Clarke, March 20, 1878, Box 1, PHC Papers
19. C.S. McCawley to Powhatan Henry Clarke, March 25, 1878, Box 1, PHC Papers.
20. 7 U.S.C. § 302.
21. Louise Clarke to Powhatan Henry Clarke to March, 28, 1878, Box 1, PHC Papers.
22. [Dr.] Powhatan Clarke to Powhatan Henry Clarke, May 2, 1878, Box 1, PHC Papers.
23. [Dr.] Powhatan Clarke to Powhatan Henry Clarke, May 26, 1878, Box 1, PHC Papers.
24. PHC to Papa, May 28, 1878, Box 1, PHC Papers.
25. PHC to [Dr.] Powhatan Henry Clarke, May 31, 1878, Box 1, PHC Papers.
26. Louise Clarke to Powhatan Henry Clarke, July 17?, 1878, Box 1, PHC Papers.
27. [Dr.] Powhatan Henry Clarke to Powhatan Henry Clarke, December 9, 1878, Box 1, PHC Papers.
28. To President of the United States from T. F. Bayard, endorsed by Wade Hampton, Richard Coke, M.C. Butler, and B.F. Jonas, April 11, 1879, Box 1, PHC Papers.
29. Each congressional district, U.S. territory, and the District of Columbia was "entitled to have one cadet at the academy. Ten are appointed at large," the last category being at presidential discretion. Hugh T. Reed, *Cadet Life at West Point* (Chicago: Hugh T. Reed, 1896), i.
30. PHC to Mama, May 2, 1879, Box 1, PHC Papers.
31. PHC to Papa, May 27, 1879, Box 1, PHC Papers.
32. R. Graham Frost to Louise Clarke, May 7, 1879, Box 1, PHC Papers.
33. J. Floyd King to Louise Clarke, December 15, 1879, Box 1, PHC Papers. A week earlier the congressman indicated he was working with a fellow Louisiana member of the House to ascertain whether another applicant from the state who had failed the entrance exam would be making a second attempt. J. Floyd King to Louise Clarke, December 8, 1879, Box 1, PHC Papers.

34. E. John Ellis to J. Floyd King, December 15, 1879, Box 1, PHC Papers.
35. E. John Ellis to Louise Clarke, April 12, 1880, Box 1, PHC Papers.
36. J.B. Elam to Louise Clarke, May 3, 1880, Box 1, PHC Papers.
37. Reed, *Cadet Life at West Point*, 21. The appointees in 1880 from Louisiana were:

Cong. District	Name	Age July 1	Residence	Report Date	Remarks
1	Sydney Roman Buchanan	18 yr 1 mos	New Orleans	June 14	Deficient in arithmetic
2	Robert Layton Preston	17 yr 1 mos	Carrollton	June 15	Admitted July 1, 1880
4	Powhatan Henry Clarkes	17 yr 8 mos	Alexandria	June 14	Admitted July 1, 1880
5	George E. Hand				Failed to report

Annual Descriptive List of Cadet Candidates (1880), USMA Library Special Collections, 187, 174–5.
38. Willoughby Walke to (Powhatan Henry) Clarke, June 1, 1880, Box 1, PHC Papers. Walke would graduate with the Class of 1883 in the upper tier obtaining an assignment to the artillery. His successful career in this branch ended in retirement on January 28, 1923, as a brigadier general.
39. Using the "historic standard living value of income or wealth" the sum of $100, in 1880, equated to $2,390 in 2015 US dollars. www.measuringworth.com/uscompare/relaticvevalue.php. This money was to tide him over until the army began incremental payments from the annual rate of $540 as opposed to $500 for a midshipman at Annapolis. In either case payments to cadets and midshipmen were to commence after admission, but there was a lag in the first disbursement. Reed, *Cadet Life at West Point*, xi, and *Annual Register of the United States Naval Academy, Annapolis, Md.* (Washington, DC: Government Printing Office, 1880), 62. Given the relatively slight difference in annual pay between the two academies Clarke's decision to opt for the army rather than the navy seemingly had little to do with financial incentives.
40. Reed, *Cadet Life at West Point*, 41.

41. Reed, *Cadet Life at West Point.*, 56, and iii–iv, lists the basic checklist for the physical examination.
42. Reed, *Cadet Life at West Point*, xiii.
43. Reed, *Cadet Life at West Point*, 45–46.
44. Reed, *Cadet Life at West Point*, iv–x, outlined the questions posed on the examination of the period.
45. Reed, *Cadet Life at West Point*, 55.
46. Reed, *Cadet Life at West Point*, 56.
47. Reed, *Cadet Life at West Point*, 57.
48. PHC to Papa, June 22, 1880, Box 1, PHC Papers.

Notes to Chapter 2

1. *Annual Report of the Secretary of War 1884*, I (Washington DC: U.S. Government Printing Office, 1884), 840, hereafter cited as *ARSW* with year, volume, and date. Some seventy-two other candidates entered with Clarke's Class of 1884. List of Cadets Admitted to the United States Military Academy, S193. United States Military Academy Library Special Collections, hereafter referred to as USMA. According to "Semiannual Cadet Merit Rolls and Conduct Rolls" (Register of Merit), S198, USMA Library Special Collections, 108–109, during 1880 the gain was 98 by appointment, one by reappointment, and two for instruction, but as noted only 72 passed and were admitted but by June of 1884 only thirty-seven of that number remained at graduation in Clarke's class. Those who passed the examination but did not graduate included seven who resigned, fourteen who were discharged for deficiencies, and one who died (Julian Smith February 24, 1884). Among those who sought entry at the same time Clarke did was one other Louisiana native, Robert Layton Preston of Carrollton, who was a bit younger than Clarke at 17 years 1 month. "Semiannual Cadet Merit Rolls and Conduct Rolls," 52–53. To place these statistics in perspective between June 1871 through June 1880, 731 cadets were admitted to the Academy with 394 (53.8%) graduating and for cadets entering each September during 1871 through 1880, the so-called "Seps" (who were "candidates who for some good reason did not report in June") accounted for another 224 cadets of which 112 (50%) graduated. *ARSW, 1884* I, 80; and Reed, *Cadet Life at West Point*, 110. Finally, according to *ARSW, 1884* I, 828, there were 85 cadets accepted and

60 candidates rejected by the academic board and 4 by the medical board in 1881, whereas there were 129 admitted in 1882 versus 52 rejected for academic reasons and 3 for medical reasons. In 1883, some 141 candidates were accepted with 56 being rejected by the academic board and another 3 by the military board. This last class posed a problem in that if they tended to follow the typical ratio of admissions to graduates, there would be more cadets than vacancies in the army thereby leading to the discharge to civilian life of a number of them who would not be commissioned. *ARSW, 1884* I, 6. In fact, the Class of 1886 seventy-seven strong, was the largest number of cadets to receive their diplomas "in the first century of the Academy; nor was it until 1903, as a result of the Spanish War and the consequent enlargement of the U.S. Army and the Cadet Corps, that" their "number was exceeded." *1886–1911: In commemoration of the 25th Anniversary of Graduation of the Class of '86, U.S.M.A. West Point, June, 1911* (Philadelphia: The Holmes Press, 1911), 1.

2. Reed, *Cadet Life at West Point*, 73.
3. Reed, *Cadet Life at West Point*, 96–97. Clarke would receive sixty-three demerits for three dozen infractions of uniform regulations during the course of four years including a rakish propensity to wear his cap on the side of his head. He totaled far many more demerits (84) for being late to various formations and functions on eighty occasions. Title 102 Register of Cadet Delinquencies, Powhatan H. Clarke, USMA Library Special Collections.
4. Powhatan Clarke, "West Point Account Book, 1880–1884," Ledger Folio 17; P.H. Clarke June 5th 1880, Vol. 1 of 8, Box 2, PHC Papers.
5. Clarke, "West Point Account Book, 1880–1884," Ledger Folio 17, Vol. 1 of 8, Box 2, PHC Papers.
6. Reed, *Cadet Life at West Point*, 61. *ARSW,1884* I, 835–39, provides a complete listing of charges and related costs or fees items for cadets at the Academy with the entries in Clarke's account, which would include the services of shoe blacks, who were located in the basement of one of the barracks where cadets were to have their "shoes cleaned and polished … as often as necessary" to maintain their footgear "in proper order." Reed, *Cadet Life at West Point*, 45.
7. Habitual lateness was just one of many violations of the so-called "Blue Book" issued to all cadets, in this case produced on June 1, 1884, just a few weeks prior to Clarke's graduation. This infraction regularly marred Clarke's record, despite the clear definition of what constituted

being late for formations, and other required functions. *Orders for the U.S. Cadet Corps 1884*, 38.

8. Reed, *Cadet Life at West Point*, 76. Internal bathing facilities were limited at the Academy and according to the superintendent not sufficient for the entire corps of more than "300 strong." *ARSW, 1883* I, 191. Nonetheless, a requirement for bathing at least once a week and a written record to be kept that could not be filled out by anyone but the bather attesting to this fact was adhered to by West Point authorities. *Orders for the U.S. Cadet Corps 1884*, 16. Clarke, on more than one occasion, received demerits for non-compliance.
9. Reed, *Cadet Life at West Point*, 66. Also see Reed, *Cadet Life at West Point*, 68, for the various duties assigned to Plebes for maintaining the camp.
10. Reed, *Cadet Life at West Point*, 77. Post Orders Special Orders No. 41 June 24, 1882, read in part: "Beginning Monday, the 26th instant, and continuing until the close of the encampment. Dancing Lessons will be given to the Corps of Cadets in the fencing academy…." necessitating the presence of the officer of the guard to ensure proper conduct. *Orders for the U.S. Cadet Corps*, 24.
11. Reed, *Cadet Life at West Point*, 31–35 set forth the prescribed manner in which the room was to be maintained as does *Orders for the U.S. Cadet Corps 1884*, 12–15, which, according to the board of visitors in 1884, contained the "minute and complete" listing of the consequences, i.e. punishments, meted out for infractions. *ARSW, 1884* I, 831.
12. Reed, *Cadet Life at West Point*, 95.
13. Reed, *Cadet Life at West Point*, 88.
14. Reed, *Cadet Life at West Point*, 88–96, provides a succinct summation of the routine for the academic first year.
15. Pay and expenses from March 1 to April 30, 1883, "West Point Account Book, 1880–1884," Vol. 1 of 8, PHC Papers, indicated a charge of $2.75 for a subscription to *Le Figaro*, the oldest national daily newspaper in France, published in Paris since 1826.
16. PHC to Mother, February 19, 1882, Box 1, PHC Papers.
17. Reed, *Cadet Life at West Point*, 158, referenced how difficult it was for cadets not having the skills to perform well in drawing from being "found" deficicnt in this class and thus washed out from West Point.
18. Reed, *Cadet Life at West Point*, 156–58, provides an excellent description of riding lessons which were given during the final three years of each cadet's stay at West Point.

19. PHC to Mother (Louise Clarke) April 3, 1881, Box 1, PHC Papers.
20. Reed, *Cadet Life at West Point*, 60–61.
21. James S. Robbins, *Last in Their Class: Custer, Pickett and the Goats of West Point* (New York: Encounter Books, 2006), 188–89.
22. Class Arranged According to Merit in Drawing, Tactics, and Chemistry, January 11, 1883, 107–08; 110–112. S14 S 14, Proceedings (Staff Records), USMA Library Special Collections; and January 16, 1883, 125–6, Proceedings (Staff Records), USMA Library Special Collections, which discussed the deficiencies of Clarke and three of his classmates.
23. Clarke was assigned to the Second Class according to Merit in Drawings as determined June 9, 1883, 164–5. Proceedings (Staff Records), USMA Library Special Collections.
24. Payment to Just Bros. on June 5, 1882, "West Point Account Book, 1880–1884." Vol. 1 of 8, PCH Papers. Black Starr & Frost of New York made the Class of 1884 ring for Hutcheson Grote now in the USMA Library Special Collections, so it is possible that Clarke was purchasing a signet ring instead as indicated by a subsequent letter to his father.
25. For coverage of the graduation and Crook's address read "Off to Be Real Soldiers," (New York) *Sun*, June 15, 1884; and (New York) *Times*, June 15, 1884.Ohioan George Crook graduated from West Point in 1852 and spent considerable time thereafter as a company grade infantry officer in the West. The outbreak of the Civil War brought him temporary promotions up to the grade of major general of volunteers. On January 15, 1866, he became a major in the Third U.S. Infantry and thereafter made his way up the military ladder to major general as of April 6, 1888. He died on March 21, 1890. Crook was one of the most enthusiastic proponents for the deployment of Indian scouts. For Crook's military career relative to the post-Civil War U.S. Army in the West see Utley, *The Commanders*, 35–66. Further, Paul Magid's *George Crook: From the Redwoods to Appomattox* (Norman: University of Oklahoma Press, 2011); and *The Gray Fox: George Crook and the Indian Wars* (Norman: University of Oklahoma Press, 2015), offer valuable insights into this unconventional frontier military figure.
26. According to the U.S. Superintendent of the Census for 1890, "settlement had become so dense" in the United States "that supposedly the frontier had come to an end." From the comfort of the ivy-covered university walls this thesis seemed to ring true. For Powhatan Clarke, who reported for duty first in west Texas and later in Arizona, the wild

frontier had far from ended. Gerald D. Nash, *Creating the West: Historical Interpretations 1890–1990* (Albuquerque: University of New Mexico Press, 1991), 3.

27. Reed, *Cadet Life at West Point*, 119.
28. http://www.combat.ws/S4/MILTERMS/WP0SLANG.HTM.
29. *ARSW, 1884* I, 840.

Notes to Chapter 3

1. PHC to His Mother, October 1, 1884, Box 1, PHC Papers.
2. Powhatan Clarke, RG94, Entry 297, Box 903, 3760 ACP 1884, NARA.
3. *Official Army Register for January, 1882* (Washington, DC: Adjutant General's Officer, 1882), 365.
4. PHC to Mother, October 1, 1884, Box 1, PHC Papers.
5. John S. Billings, *Report on Hospitals with Descriptions of Military Posts* (Washington, DC: War Department Surgeon General's Office, 1870), 229. Robert M. Utley, *Fort Davis National Historic Site, Texas* (Washington, DC: National Park Service, 1965), 6–26, offers further background on the former fort now operated as a national park.
6. As summarized in Charles Reginald Shrader, gen. ed., *Reference Guide to United States Military History, 1865–1919* (New York: Sachem Publishing Associates, Inc., 1993), 5: after 1865, although the U.S. Army was responsible for "the defense of the continental United States against external attack, but other more pressing tasks took priority…, a major portion of the army occupied and maintained order in the states of the Confederacy," some federal troops remaining on duty until finally being withdrawn in 1877." But "All such missions were secondary; for 25 years after the Civil War, the main task of the army was to protect the growing settlements and migration routes west of the Mississippi River." Thus "the nation assigned" its multipurpose army "a wide range of functions." Shrader, *Reference Guide*, 26.
7. Dobak and Phillips, *Black Regulars*, 25, 56–7, 69–2, 74–7, 90–1, 96, 114, 224–5, 248, and 290n36, summarizes congressional debates and hearings relative to including blacks in the post-Civil War Regular Army.
8. Dobak and Phillips, *Black Regulars*, 3–9, and 12–16. The army by the March 3, 1869, act was to be reduced by twenty infantry regiments, this being accomplished for the most part by consolidating understrength

existing units. Thus, the four black infantry regiments were combined into two, the Thirty-eighth and the Forty-first becoming the Twenty-fourth United States Infantry while the Thirty-ninth and Fortieth were designated as the Twenty-fifth United States Infantry. William G. Mullin, *The Twenty-fourth Infantry Past and Present: A Brief History of the Regiment Compiled from Official Records, Under the Direction of the Regimental Commander* (N.P., 1923), 7. For additional background on the Tenth Cavalry during the quarter century after the Civil War's conclusion, refer to E.L.N. Glass, comp. and ed., *The History of the Tenth Cavalry 1866–1921* (Ft. Collins, CO: Old Army Press, 1972), 12–23.

9. Constance Wynn Altshuler, *Cavalry Yellow & Infantry Blue: Army Officers in Arizona Between 1851 and 1886* (Tucson: Arizona Historical Society, 1991), 146–7. William H. and Shirley A. Leckie, *Unlikely Warriors: General Benjamin Grierson and His Family* (Norman: University of Oklahoma Press, 1984) offers an in-depth look at the colonel and his extended family.
10. Elvid Hunt and Walter E. Lorence, *History of Fort Leavenworth 1827–1937* (Fort Leavenworth: The Command and General Staff School Press, 1937) provides an early history of the rare remaining ante bellum frontier post that continues as an active duty U.S. Army installation. For the difficult beginnings for the Tenth Cavalry at this garrison and its subsequent early activities in Kansas at Forts Dodge, Harker, Hays, Larned, Riley, and Wallace, consult William H. and Shirley A. Leckie, *The Buffalo Soldiers: A Narrative of the Black Cavalry on the West* (Norman: University of Oklahoma Press, 2003), 8, 13–14, 17, 20, 22, and 30–33.
11. Named in honor of Philip H. Sheridan's West Point classmate and friend, Joshua W. Sill, who was killed during the Civil War, originally known as Camp Wichita, the post was first garrisoned by four companies of the Tenth U.S. Cavalry during June 1868 under Grierson. The standard reference to the post's early history remains, Wilbur S. Nye, *Carbine and Lance: The Story of Old Fort Sill* (Norman: University of Oklahoma Press, 1937).
12. Leckie and Leckie, *The Buffalo Soldiers*, 80; 116–21; 125–40; 142–44; 158–61; 174–76; 180–95; 211–16; and 221–33.
13. Leckie and Leckie, *The Buffalo Soldiers*, 7 and 80–81.
14. Glass, *The History of the Tenth*, 20.
15. Leckie and Leckie, *The Buffalo Soldiers*, 50, 125–27; and 144–50.

16. Entries in Eric S. Johnson, comp., *No Greater Calling: A Chronological Record of Sacrifice and Heroism During the Western Indians Wars, 1865–1898* (Atglen, PA: Schiffer Military History, 2012), 298, 292–92, 302–5, and 307–317; Berndt Kühn, *Chronicles of War: Apache & Yavapai Resistance in the Southwestern United States and Northern Mexico, 1821–1937* (Tucson: Arizona Historical Society, 2014), 221–30, 232–35, and 237–240; and Gregory F. Michno, *Encyclopedia of the Indian Wars: Western Battles and Skirmishes, 1850–1890* (Missoula, MT: Mountain Press Publishing Company, 2003), 323–35, 337–38, and 359 provide highlights about the Victorio Campaign.
17. Leckie and Leckie, *The Buffalo Soldiers*, 239–46.
18. James N. Leiker, *Racial Borders: Black Soldiers Along the Rio Grande* (College Station: Texas A&M University Press, 2002); and Garna L Christian, *Black Soldiers in Jim Crow Texas 1899–1917* (College Station: Texas A&M University Press, 1995) provide the best sources analyzing the race bias and situation existing in Texas and along the border pertaining to black troops posted to the region.
19. PHC to His Mother, October 1, 1884, Box 1, PHC Papers.
20. Billings, *Report on Hospitals with Descriptions of Military Posts*, 227, published Fort Davis's medical statistics for 1868 and 1869.
21. Knight, *Life and Manners in the Frontier Army*, 128.
22. Whitman, *The Troopers*, 152; and Frances M.A. Roe, *Army Letters from an Officer's Wife, 1871–1888* (Lincoln: University of Nebraska Press, 1981), 55. The term "dog robber" also had been used for "a servant to an officer" implying "'that the man is a consumer of what daily morsels should fall' thus robbing the officer's dog of his due." Paul Dickson, *War Slang: American Fighting Words and Phrases from the Civil War to the Gulf War* (New York: Simon & Schuster, 1994), 8 and 100. Similarly, the British employed soldier-servants they often referred to as "batman, a term that derived from the French *bât*, or packsaddle." Candice Millard, *Hero of Empire: The Boer War, A Daring Escape, and the Making of Winston Churchill* (New York: Doubleday, 2016), 61.
23. PHC to His Father, October 4, 1884, Box 1, PHC Papers.
24. Coffman, *The Old Army*, 194–95, 200, 262, 324, 328–29, 331–32, 338–39, 365–69, and 374–75 provides insight into the attitude of officers towards enlisted men including blacks. Kevin Adams, *Class and Race in the Frontier Army: Military Life in the West, 1870–1890* (Norman: University of Oklahoma Press. 2009) represents an attempt to expand on this subject.

25. Lebo along with Crook, Grierson, and a host of others represented the immediate post-Appomattox officer corps, most of whom held ranks of captain and higher, and were Civil War veterans. In contrast, Clarke and Bigelow were characteristic of the next generation of those who held commissions based mainly on West Point graduates. As with many of the veterans, Lebo remained a fixture with the Tenth Cavalry until his promotion to the Sixth United States Cavalry effective July 26, 1893. After the Spanish American War, Lebo gained his silver oak leaves as a lieutenant colonel of the First U.S. Cavalry effective September 14, 1899, at which time he was sent to the Philippines. When the United States Congress expanded the army in the wake of the war which propelled the country on the international scene on February 19, 1901, Lebo became the colonel of the newly organized Fourteenth United States Cavalry. He retired on June 23, 1905, having been promoted the previous day to brigadier general, as was the policy for Civil War officers allowing them to retire at a higher grade to enhance their pensions. Long suffering with ailments, he succumbed to pneumonia on February 23, 1910. Altshuler, *Cavalry Yellow & Infantry Blue*, 199–200; Lebo Pension File, RG94 Entry 297, Box 712 ACP 3083 1876; Box 1465 ACP File 3053 1893; and Special Orders No. 174 Adjutant General's Officer, August 1, 1893, NARA.
26. PHC to His Father, October 4, 1884, Box 1, PHC Papers.
27. *Official Army Register for January, 1880* (Washington, DC: Adjutant General's Office, 1880), 280–81. Coffman, *The Old Army*, 264–66, adds details relative to pay.
28. PHC to His Father, October 4, 1884, Box 1, PHC Papers. Lieutenant John Bigelow, as second in command of Troop K, recorded in his diary on November 21, 1884, he "commanded the company" at battalion drill "Capt. Lebo not being well enough to do so." Bigelow also provided another telling detail common throughout the army of the times when junior officers received no training or experience in anything but small formations and troop movements. He confessed: "… I never saw a battalion of regular cavalry before in my life." Douglas C. McChristian, ed. and comp., *Garrison Tangles in the Friendless Tenth: The Journal of First Lieutenant John Bigelow, Jr. Fort Davis, Texas* (Bryan and Mattituck, TX: J.M. Carroll & Company, 1985),7. It is unclear whether the absence was due to illness or one of the captain's alleged drinking bouts. Thereafter Bigelow indicated he continued to take charge of both mounted and dismounted drill of the

company because "the Captain excused himself" from being present at this and all other similar functions which devolved on his first lieutenant. McChristian, *Garrison Tangles*, 11–12.

29. PHC to His Mother, November 15, 1884. PHC Papers. Presumably besides the post library other officers possessed reading material that Clarke could have borrowed. For instance Bigelow referenced in his diary such diverse titles as William Winthrop, *Digest of the Opinions of the Judge Advocate General of the Army*; William E. Birkhimer, *History Sketch of the Organization, Administration Matériel and Tactics of the Artillery, United States Army*; Helmuth Graf von Moltke, *Franco-German War of 1870–71*; Henry Drummond, *Natural Law in the Spiritual World*; George E. Pond, *The Shenandoah Valley in 1864*; and Francis Vinton Greene, *The Mississippi* (both from the "Campaigns of the Civil War" series); as well as the New York *Herald*, a subscription for this periodical probably being available through the post library. McChristian, *Garrison Tangles*, 11–12, 15, 25, 29, 31, and 34. Incidentally, Clarke did avail himself of a local Catholic priest's offer "to take lessons from him in Spanish" an invitation also extended to Bigelow as well.
30. PHC to His Mother, November 15, 1884. Box 1, PHC Papers.
31. Salient references to military justice of the era are found in Coffman, *The Old Army*, 265, 284, and 295.
32. McChristian, *Garrison Tangles*, 1.
33. McChristian, *Garrison Tangles*, 9–11 and 31.
34. PHC to His Father, November 21, 1884, Box 1, PHC Papers.
35. Shrader, *Reference Guide to United States Military History*, 26. As postulated by John M. Gates, "The Alleged Isolation of US Army Officers on the Late 19th Century," *Parameters: Journal of the U.S. Army War College* 10, no. 3 (September 1980): 33–34, "the situation reached scandalous proportions" that the testimony of one cavalry officer emphasized as he reported in the 1870s to the House Military Affairs Committee: "I am absent on sick leave; my first lieutenant on recruiting service; my second lieutenant is an aide-de-camp to General Crook; and there is not an officer on duty with the company.'" Colonel Wesley Merritt, commanding the Fifth United States Cavalry, substantiated that this was not an unusual situation when he "noted that of 12 first lieutenants, only one was present for duty with his … regiment."
36. Knight, *Life and Manners*, 112, and 123–24. Also consult Coffman, *The Old Army*, 217, 262, 292–93, and 296, on the matter of quarters.

37. PHC to His Father, November 21, 1884, Box 1, PHC Papers. Between 1867 and 1895 desertion ranged from a low of just under 5% of the total force in 1894 to a record high of just under 33% in 1871. For a succinct summary see Jack Foner, *The United States Soldier Between Two Wars: Army Life and Reforms 1865–1898* (New York: Humanities Press, 1970), 6–10; 77, 81–82, 94, 97–98, 149–151, and 222–24. Also see ibid., 30, 40, 67, and 80, relative to alcohol abuse.
38. Knight, *Life and Manners*, 5, 22–23, 93–24, and 108. Also see Coffman, *The Old Army*, 63–64, 69, 99, and 110.
39. While U.S. Army regulations provided for post schools, "Army parents agonized over the future of their school-age children" with many of them deciding to send their daughters and sons to boarding schools in the East and elsewhere. Patricia Y. Stallard, *Glittering Misery: Dependents of the Indian Fighting Army* (Fort Collins, CO: The Old Army Press, 1978), 94–95 and 98–99.
40. Steve Wilson, ed., *Child of the Fighting Tenth: On the Frontier with the Buffalo Soldiers by Forrestine C. Hooker (Oxford: Oxford University Press, 2003), 159–60.*
41. Wilson, *Child of the Fighting Tenth, 167–8.*
42. Wilson, *Child of the Fighting Tenth, 160.*
43. Quanah Parker was born around 1845 near Wichita Falls into the Kawahadi band. He died on February 23, 1911. Much has been written on this figure, but it often tends toward fanciful portrayals. To place Quanah in context consult: Pekka Hämäläinen, *Comanche Empire* (New Haven: Yale University Press, 2008).
44. Wilson, *Child of the Fighting Tenth*, 160.
45. McChristian, *Garrison Tangles*, 15–16.
46. Unless otherwise indicated, all reference to Clarke's foray with Quanah Parker and his party were drawn from PHC to His Mother, December 6, 1884, Box 1, PHC Papers.
47. Wilson, *Child of the Fighting Tenth*, 160.
48. Stallard, *Glittering Misery* ably underscores the distinction of the stratified society of a Gilded Age army.
49. The recapitulation of Christmas at Fort Davis was taken from Wilson, *Child of the Fighting Tenth*, 164–67. For context compare Ms. Cooper's experience to an overview found in Lori A. Cox-Paul and Dr. James W. Wengert, *A Frontier Christmas* (Lincoln: Nebraska State Historical Society, 1996).
50. McChristian, *Garrison Tangles*, 10 and 44n13.
51. Wilson, *Child of the Fighting Tenth*, 161.

52. Knight, *Life and Manners*, 5. Officer and chronicler Charles King described a self-promoter as a "carpet knight, ballroom soldier, or wire-puller." This veteran frontier cavalry officer railed about those who "could display brass buttons to awed young ladies." Ibid., 94–95. King contended this group relied on "friends at court" who "had more to do with a fellow's sphere of duty—very much more—than had the regimental commander or even the adjutant general." For these privileged few "an ounce of influence" proved more important than "a pound of pure record." Charles King, *A Wounded Name* (New York: Hobart, 1901), 12.
53. McChristian, *Garrison Tangles,* 23.
54. McChristian, *Garrison Tangles*, 29–30, and 54–55 n45.
55. One individual recalled Johnson was: "The most picturesque character in the regiment." The reminiscence continued that Johnson always would be cherished for his "fighting qualities with many a laugh at his eccentricities, adventures and misadventures." Glass, *History of the Tenth Cavalry*, 141. After Johnson's retirement and death, his place in history faded. Nonetheless, some of his exploits were preserved as oral history and available in Richard E. Jensen, ed., *Voices of the American West,* Volume 1: *The Indian Interviews of Eli S. Ricker, 1903–1919* and *Voices of the American West, Volume 2: The Settler and Soldier Interviews of Eli S. Ricker, 1913–1919* (Lincoln: University of Nebraska Press, 2005).
56. McChristian, *Garrison Tangles*, 27, 32, 36–38, 52–53 n37, and 55 n47.
57. PHC to His Mother, February 7, 1885, Box 1, PHC Papers. Of interest is that as early as November 8, 1884, while in Baltimore, Bigelow had heard rumblings "to the effect that the 10th Cavalry is to be moved … to the Department of Platte or to Kansas. This is no doubt to make room for some regt. with a wire pulling colonel who is coveting our good quarters and pleasant climate at Fort Davis. The quarters in the Dept. of the Platte are wretched and the climate of Dakota unpleasant for the severity of its winters." McChristian, *Garrison Tangles in the Friendless Tenth*, 5.
58. PHC to His Father, Undated Letter from Fort Davis, Texas, Box 1, PHC Papers. *Cornelius C. Smith* Jr., *Fort Huachuca: The History of a Frontier Post* (Washington: Government Printing Office, 1977) charts the establishment of this installation in 1877 and its long history, being one of the only remaining active duty U.S. Army garrisons dating from the so-called Indian Wars.
59. Coffman, *The Old Army*, 265–66.

60. McChristian, *Garrison Tangles*, 2. McChristian also pointed out: "The Tenth Cavalry seems to have had its share of internal strife, but it may have been no worse than in other regiments." Ibid., 51 n34. Frank M. Temple, "Discipline and Turmoil in the Tenth U.S, Cavalry (unpublished Mss Fort Davis National Historic Site, n.d.) delves further into this topic.
61. PHC to Father, Undated Letter from Fort Davis, Texas, Box 1, PHC Papers. With the transfer of regimental headquarters to Fort Davis in 1882, "Colonel Grierson plunged heavily into ranching" with a goal to provide for his family's future. "At one time he either owned or leased more than 45,000 acres of land in west Texas." Shirley Anne Leckie, ed., *The Colonel's Lady on the Western Frontier: The Correspondence of Alice Kirk Grierson* (Lincoln: University of Nebraska Press, 1989), 6. Once Grierson reached Arizona, he continued to spend considerable time and energy on his less than successful cattle "empire" that remained in Texas. At one point he took leave from military duties to return to his Texas livestock operations. John P. Langellier, "The Tenth U.S. Cavalry in Prescott, A.T.," *Territorial Times Prescott Arizona Corral of Westerners International*, no. 1 (November 2009): 27. Regimental quartermaster M.M. Maxon, who like William Davis married into the Grierson clan, followed the family tradition of outside private enterprise. He kept "leased grounds. His stock consisted of 869 head of goats – among them are some 300 Angoras...." Further, Maxon "bought 10 thoroughbreds for 450 dollars" evidently for speculative purposes rather than for personal use as a cavalry officer. McChristian, *Garrison Tangles*, 14.
62. McChristian, *Garrison Tangles*, 26.
63. PHC to His Mother, Undated Letter from Fort Davis, Texas, Box 1, PHC Papers. On February 14, 1885, Bigelow reiterated "the rumor that the regiment is to move to Arizona to exchange with the 3d Cavalry...." This news concerned Troop K's first sergeant who raised a practical issue: "Sir, if the troop has to move, we haven't a single packing box" to ship the unit property accumulated over a lengthy stay at Fort Davis. Bigelow retorted that nothing was official, and oddly confided to his diary" "My first sergeant is too zealous His fault though not so difficult to correct is the opposite one of indifference...." In reality Bigelow had failed to appreciate that he and the other officers should have been considering potential actions in case the speculations about a transfer were true. McChristian, *Garrison Tangles*, 34.
64. Shrader, *Reference Guide to United States Military History*, 9.

Notes to Chapter 4

1. Earle R. Forrest, *Arizona's Dark and Bloody Ground* (Caldwell, ID: The Caxton Printers, Ltd., 1936). For military organization and posts in Arizona see: Constance Wynn Altschuler *Chains of Command: Arizona and the Army, 1856–1875* (Tucson: Arizona Historical Society, 1981); and Constance Wynn Altschuler, *Starting with Defiance: Nineteenth Century Arizona Military Posts* (Tucson: Arizona Historical Society, 1983). As examples of the diversity among the so-called Apache, the grouping commonly referred to as the *Chiricahua*, a Spanish term which had been adapted from Chidikáágu consisted of several complex entities as indicated by https://en.wikipedia.org/wiki/Chiricahua. Additionally, as Timothy Braatz points out in his foreword to *All My People Were Killed: The Memoir of Mike Burns (Homothya) A Captive Indian* (Prescott, AZ: Sharlot Hall Museum, 2010), v, "the mountains of Arizona were … home to Athabaskan speakers, now called Apaches. These included Tonto, Cibecue, San Carlos, White Mountain, and Chiricuahua Apaches, but again these terms probably signify ethnicity more than political unity among people whose primary socioeconomic unit was the foraging band." Moreover, the terms were applied by outsiders rather than members of these groups. Similarly, "To U.S. citizens who entered Arizona in the nineteenth century…all mountain bands, even the Yuman speakers, were 'Apaches' of some sort. This meant that people generally referred to as Yavapai would be such as the Toklapaya branch would be became " 'Yuma Apaches' " or " 'Apache Yumas' " while their Wipukepas and Yavepes kinsmen were transformed into " 'Mohave Apaches' " or " 'Apache Mojaves" and the fourth division of the Yavapai, the Kewevkapayas were "usually 'Tonto Apaches' or simply 'Apaches.' An official government document from the 1800s, the word 'Apache' could refer to one of many Athabaskan-speaking groups or it could mean an Upland Yuman." Further "if that were not confusing enough, there actually were some mixed, bilingual bands of Tonto Apaches and Wikpukepas." Ibid., iv–v. Also compounding the perplexity was the fact that to the east other groups associated with the Apaches included the Kiowa-Apache and the Lipan, the former usually residing "in southeastern Kansas, western Oklahoma, and the north part of the Texas panhandle" while the latter group traditionally were found "to the south in Texas and northern Mexico." Moreover:

"The Jacarilla [Apache] ranged over northeastern New Mexico and southeastern Colorado…, and the Mescalero wandered through south-central New Mexico, and the Big Bend region of Texas, and northern Mexico." Gordon C. Baldwin, *The Warrior Apaches A Story of the Chiricahua and Western Apache* (Tucson: Dale Stuart King, 1965), 16. Also see C.L. Sonnichsen, *The Mescalero Apaches* (Norman: University of Oklahoma Press, 1958) for further background of the last-mentioned group.

2. Charles R. Lummis, *General Crook and the Apache Wars* (Flagstaff, AZ: Northland Press, 1985), 10.
3. Angie Debo, *Geronimo: The Man, His Time, His Place* (Norman: University of Oklahoma Press, 1976), ranks among the more important biographies of this military-religious figure, who along with Cochise became a household name. For a comparison of these two men consult Edwin R. Sweeney, *From Cochise to Geronimo: The Chiricahua Apaches, 1874–1886* (Norman: University of Oklahoma Press, 2010). Moreover, Robert M. Utley, *Geronimo* (New Haven: Yale University Press, 2012), provides a brief but highly satisfying biography. Also see an extensively illustrated publication aimed at popular readers: Bob Boze Bell, *The Illustrated Life and Times of Geronimo* (Cave Creek, AZ: Two Roads West, 2020).
4. Britton Davis, *The Truth About Geronimo* (New Haven: Yale University Press, 1929), 142. Born in Brownsville, Texas, Britton Davis graduated from West Point in June of 1881. His father remained loyal to the Union and even raised a regiment that fought for the North as well as later became governor of Texas. The younger Davis joined the Third U.S. Cavalry first in Wyoming and later in Arizona where he spent a brief period at Fort Thomas before being sent to San Carlos where he "was put in charge" of Apaches living at Turkey Creek, Geronimo numbering among them. He resigned his commission in 1886 to pursue various civilian interests including mining and ranching. Late in life he resided in San Diego where "he wrote *The Truth About Geronimo*, taking issue with pro-Miles officers" who had been publishing their accounts of the campaign. Altschuler, *Cavalry Yellow & Infantry Blue*, 94–95.
5. Wilson, *Child of the Fighting Tenth, 169–70.*
6. Wilson, *Child of the Fighting Tenth,* 170.
7. Paul H. Carlson, *"Pecos Bill": A Military Biography of William R. Shafter* (College Station: Texas A&M University Press, 1989), discusses

this complex military man's life whose career spanned from the Civil War to the Spanish American War.

8. Glass, *The History of the Tenth Cavalry*, 23–24.
9. The scattered garrisons in Arizona Territory where the Tenth first reported had varied histories. See for instance, Altshuler, *Starting with Defiance*, 9–12; 15–21; 28–32; 32–37; 54–6; and Ray Brandes, *Frontier Military Posts of Arizona* (Globe, AZ: Dale Stuart King, Publisher, 1960), 10–12: 14–20; 40–45; 49–52; 67–73; 75–80. In addition to these Tenth Cavalry haunts Clarke periodically made his way to Fort Bowie that had served as the guard of Apache Pass since 1862, and after the fort lost its usefulness was abandoned officially on October 17, 1894. Douglas C. McChristian, *Fort Bowie, Arizona: Combat Post of the Southwest, 1858–1894* (Norman: University of Oklahoma Press, 2005) traces the history of this former fort that now is a National Historic Site.

   Another southern Arizona post, Fort Huachuca, was established in 1877. It remains as the only active U.S. Army installation to survive from the Apache campaigns. For further details obtain Cornelius Cole Smith, Jr., *Fort Huachuca: The Story of a Frontier Post* (Washington, D.C.: Dept. of the Army, 1981). The post's long association with black troops is treated in Stephen D. Smith, *The African American Soldier at Fort Huachuca, Arizona, 1892–1946* (Fort Huachuca: U.S. Army, 2001). In turn, Clarke passed through Fort Lowell east of Tucson, where in 1873 it became a replacement for an earlier camp of the same name in the town. David T. Faust and Kenneth A. Randall, *Camp Lowell, and Tucson's Military Outpost 1853–1873* (Tucson: Tucson Corral of the Westerners, 2003); and David T. Faust and Kenneth A. Randall, *Life at Post: Fort Lowell, Arizona Territory 1873–1891* (Tucson: Tucson Corral of the Westerners, 2002) are recommended.
10. John P. Langellier, "Buffalo Soldiers in Big Sky Country, 1888–1898," *Montana: The Magazine of Western History* 67, no. 3 (Autumn 2017): 41–56; *Ronald G. Coleman, "The Buffalo Soldiers Guardians of the Uintah Frontier 1886–1901," Utah Historical Quarterly 67 No. 4 (Fall 1979): 421–39; Michael J. Clark, U.S. Army Pioneers: Black Soldiers in Nineteenth-century Utah (Salt Lake: Fort Douglas Military Museum, n.d.); Michael J. Clark, "A History of the Twenty-fourth United States Infantry Regiment in Utah, 1896–1900,"* (unpublished Ph.D. dissertation, University of Utah, 1979)*; and Frank N.* Schubert, "The Black Regular Army Regiments in Wyoming, 1885–1912," (unpublished

MA Thesis, University of Wyoming, 1970). Closer to the topic at hand Smith, *The African American Soldier at Fort Huachuca*; Mark F. Baumler, *The Archeology of Faraway Ranch, Arizona: Prehistoric, Historic, and 20th Century* (Tucson: Western Archeological Center and Conservation Center, 1984), provide a southern Arizona perspective.

11. Theo. F. Rodenbough and William L. Haskin, eds., *The Army of the United States Historical Sketches of Staff and Line with Portraits of Generals-in-Chief* (New York: Maynard, Merrill & Co., 1896), 296.
12. Among several sources two overviews by Paul R. and Kathleen M. Nickens particularly deserve attention: *History of the Apache Agency and Army Camp at Old San Carlos, 1873–1929* (Tucson: Tucson Corral of the Westerners, 2009), and *Old San Carlos* (Charleston, SC: Arcadia Publishing, 2008). The description of San Carlos as Clarke would have known it was taken from Owen Wister, "Specimen Jones," *Harper's New Monthly* 80, no. 530 (July 1894): 209.
13. Numerous biographies treat Crook. For useful summations see Altshuler, *Cavalry Yellow & Infantry*, 86–88; and Jerome A. Greene, "George Crook" in Hutton and Ball, *Soldiers West*. 246–72.
14. John G. Bourke, *On the Border with Crook* (New York: Charles Scribner's Sons, 1891), 464.
15. For examples of the variety of army contacts to provided hay, beef, flour, fuel and many other necessities to the military consult: Darlis A. Miller, *Soldiers and Settlers: Military Supply in the Southwest, 1861–1885* (Albuquerque: University of New Mexico Press, 1989), 4, 39–41, 64–70, 73–74, 82–83, 99–100, 122–24, 132–34, 138–43, 199–200, and 308–9.
16. Crook to Editor of Clifton *Clarion*. May 18, 1886.
17. Thrapp, *Conquest of Apacheria*, 311. Johnson, *No Greater Calling*, 340–47, places the number of officers killed in 1885 and 1886 as only two, with eleven enlisted men and three Indian scouts also dying as a result of the campaign; Kühn, *Chronicles of War* 272–83; and Michno, *Encyclopedia of the Indian Wars*, 346–48, all also attest to the reign of terror that coincided with period following this 1885 outbreak.
18. Thrapp, *Conquest of Apacheria*, 311; and Dan L. Thrapp, *Encyclopedia of Frontier Biography* 1 (Glendale, CA: Arthur H. Clark Company 1988), 262.
19. Thrapp, *Conquest of Apacheria*, 311. Captain Charles L. Cooper of the Tenth Cavalry apprehended Mangas and a pair of followers as they were making their way back to Fort Apache evidently to surrender.

Mangas would be shipped to Florida as a prisoner of war. After being relocated to Mount Vernon Barracks, Alabama he enlisted as private in Company I, Twelfth U.S. Infantry as part of a short-lived experiment to incorporate Indians into the Regular Army. After one more move, this time to Fort Sill, Oklahoma, he signed on as a member of Troop L, Seventh U.S. Cavalry as did his son, once again as part of the experimental program that ended in that year. Mangas then enlisted as an Indian scout and remained one until his death. Thrapp, *Encyclopedia of Frontier Biography* 2, 936.

20. Davis, *The Truth About Geronimo*, 143. A succinct account of the 1883 campaign appears in Dan L. Thrapp, *General Crook and the Sierra Madre Adventure* (Norman: University of Oklahoma Press, 1972).
21. Thrapp, *Conquest of Apacheria*, 311. Like Mangas, Naiche went into exile in Florida, after transfer to Mount Vernon Barracks where he enlisted in Company I, Twelfth U.S. Infantry, and at, Fort Sill, became a member of Troop L, Seventh U.S. Cavalry. After the troop disbanded, he also signed on as a scout. By 1913 he was again uprooted, in this instance to Mescalero where he died. Thrapp, *Encyclopedia of Frontier Biography* 2, 1037–8.
22. Thrapp, *Conquest of Apacheria*, 311. Numerous interesting snippets about Chihuahua, Mangas, Nana and Natchez can be found in the highly detailed Sweeney, *From Cochise to Geronimo*, in numerous references throughout the text.
23. Thrapp, *Conquest of Apacheria*, 311. As with the others Nana found himself on an eastbound train to Fort Marion, and like many of his fellows he ended his days at Fort Sill. Thrapp, *Encyclopedia of Frontier Biography* 2, 1038–9.
24. Thomas W. Dunlay, *Wolves for the Blue Soldiers: Indian Scouts and Auxiliaries with the United States Army, 1860–1890* (Lincoln: University of Nebraska Press, 1982), 43–47. For Crook's embryonic employment of scouts on the West Coast see John G. Bourke, "General Crook in Indian Country," *The Century Magazine: A Popular Quarterly* 41, no. 87 (March 1891): 644.
25. George Crook, "The Apache Problem," *Journal of the Military Service Institution of the United States* 7 No. 27 (October 1887): 262.
26. Allan Radbourne, *Mickey Free, Apache Captive, Interpreter, and Indian Scout* (Tucson: Arizona Historical Society, 2005), 6; and John Morgan Gates, "General George Crook's First Apache Campaign," *Journal of the West* 6 No. 2 (April 1967): 318.

27. Crook, "The Apache Problem:" 262.
28. Gates, "General George Crook's First Apache Campaign:" 311. Gates based his conclusions on Crook, "The Apache Problem:" 263.
29. Crook, *Resume of Operations*, 20.
30. Crook to Assistant Adjutant General, Division of the Pacific, July 7, 1885, George Crook Papers, Rutherford B. Hayes Memorial Library, Fremont, OH.
31. Wilson, *Child of the Fighting Tenth*, 175–6.
32. Wilson, *Child of the Fighting Tenth*, 175–6.
33. Altshuler, *Starting with Defiance*, 28–32.
34. Wilson, *Child of the Fighting Tenth*, 177–80.
35. Wilson, *Child of the Fighting Tenth*, 180–81.
36. Frederic Remington, "Two Gallant Young Cavalry Men," *Harper's Weekly* 34, no. 1735 (March 22, 1890): 220.
37. Wilson, *Child of the Fighting Tenth*, 181–82. For more on Captain Cooper and the deployment of his Troop I to the field read: Martyn D. Tagg, *The Camp at Bonita Cañon: A Buffalo Soldier Camp in Chiricahua National Monument, Arizona* (Tucson: Western Archeological Center and Conservation Center, 1987).
38. Wilson, *Child of the Fighting Tenth*, 182–183.
39. PHC to His Mother, June 2, 1885, Box 1, PHC Papers.
40. PHC to His Mother, June 20, 1885, Box 1, PHC Papers.
41. PHC to His Father, July 8, 1885, Box 1, PHC Papers.
42. Elizabeth Bacon Custer, *Following the Guidon* (New York: Harper & Brothers, 1890), 139.
43. PHC to His Mother, July 18, 1885, Box 1, PHC Papers.
44. Sherry L. Smith, *View from Officers' Row: Army Perceptions of Western Indians* (Tucson: University of Arizona Press, 1990), offers further insight relative to this subject.
45. While most of his methods were not new or unique "Crook's techniques of Indian warfare that became his trademarks—using pack mules, employing Indian auxiliaries, and keeping the natives on the run—marked him as a comer." In the first category his "company pack train or *atajo* (short-cut) consisted of a pack master or *patrón*, a *cargador*, or assistant pack master who had charge of deciding which mule carried specific loads, a cook, a blacksmith, ten packers, fifty mules, fourteen saddle mules and a bell mare. Emmit M. Essin, *Shavetails and Bell Sharp: The History of the Army Mule* (Lincoln: University of Nebraska Press, 1997), 94.

46. John G. Bourke, *An Apache Campaign in the Sierra Madre: An account of the Expedition in Pursuit of the Hostile Chiricahua Apaches in the Spring of 1883* (New York: C. Scribner's Sons, 1886), 40, echoed Clarke in that the captain similarly described the Apache scouts' "a loosely fitting shirt of red, white or grey stuff, generally of calico, in some gaudy figures, but not infrequently the same article of woolen raiment [*sic*] [i.e., the blue wool pullover campaign shirt] issued to white soldiers. This came down outside a pair of loose cotton drawers, reaching to the moccasins … a leather waist belt encircling the waist holds forty rounds of metallic cartridges and also keeps in place the regulation blue blouse and pantaloons…." Added detail appears in" W.E. Shipp, "Captain Crawford's Last Expedition," *Journal of the United States Cavalry Association* 5 No. 19 (December 1892): 347.
47. PHC to His Mother, August 8, 1885, Box 1; and PHC to His Mother, June 2, 1885, Box 1. PHC Papers.
48. PHC to His Mother, August 14, 1885, Box 1; and PHC to His Mother, June 2, 1885, Box 1, PHC Papers.
49. Separ (originally called Sepas) in Grant County lies in the "boot heel" of southwestern New Mexico. It served as a watering and overnight stop on the Janos Trail, a byway to carry copper ore south to smelters in Chihuahua and mining equipment along with trade goods north to the copper mines. When the railroad came through in the 1880s, it became a loading station for cattle. T. M. Pearce, ed., *New Mexico Place Names: A Geographical Dictionary* (Albuquerque: University of New Mexico Press, 1965), 153.
50. Altshuler, *Cavalry Yellow & Infantry Blue*, 99.
51. Sweeney, *From Cochise to Geronimo*, 444–45, and 581.
52. PHC to His Mother, September 2, 1885, Box 1, PHC Papers.
53. All of the quotations in the above section represent extracts from Powhatan Clarke "Pocket Journal 1," Box 6, PHC Papers.
54. Altshuler, *Starting with Defiance*, 6, notes the daily garrison ration per soldier consisted among other things of "12 ounces of pork or bacon, one pound four ounces of salt or fresh beef; one pound six ounces of soft bread or flour, or one pound of hard bread, or one pound four ounces of corn meal." Additionally, "for every hundred was added 15 pounds of beans or peas and 10 pounds of rice or hominy; 10 pounds of green coffee or eight pounds of roasted coffee, one pound eight ounces of tea; 15 pounds of sugar; four quarts of vinegar; … three pounds

twelve ounce of salt; four ounces of pepper; 30 pounds of potatoes (when practicable) and one quart of molasses."

55. Kühn, *Chronicles of War*, 279. For more on encounters during the fall and though winter of 1885 consult ibid., 279–83; Michno, *Encyclopedia of the Indian Wars*, 348; and Johnson, *No Greater Calling*, 341–43.
56. Charles M. Strauss numbered among several civilians tagging along with Crook. Born on April 15, 1840 in New York City, forty years later for health reasons he went West. Strauss settled in Tucson and secured a position of manager with the Tucson mercantile operation of L. Zacekendorf & Co. Once in town he worked to eliminate the use of the Mexico peso as currency and secured the closure of stores on Sundays. By 1883 he became sufficiently prominent to be elected mayor where among other initiatives he promoted the establishment of a public library, the building of a "well equipped and efficient fire department" and the construction of a city hall. Later he worked closely with J.S, Mansfield for the creation of the University of Arizona as well became the territorial superintendent of public instruction. He died March 13, 1892. *Arizona Enterprise*, March 17, 1892; and C.L. Sonnichsen, *Tucson: The Life and Times of an American City* (Norman: University of Oklahoma Press, 1982), 114–16.
57. John Brete Harte, "The San Carlos Indian Reservation, 1872–1886: An Administrative History" (Ph.D. diss., University of Arizona, 1972), is essential for its numerous references about Pierce and an overview of the operation of this controversial Indian reservation.
58. Paul A. Hutton, *Phil Sheridan and His Army* (Lincoln: University of Nebraska Press, 1985), remains the best single source about this influential U.S. Army officer especially his impact on Trans-Mississippi military operations.
59. Clarke's medical records indicate he had suffered from "stricture of the urethra" since 1882. By February 20, 1887, he requested a medical leave of absence from the commanding officer at Fort Grant to return to Baltimore to undergo surgery. Besides some sprains and other minor scrapes during this period the only other medical issue reported was a case of gonorrhea for which he was admitted on December 2, 1885. This led to complications of cystitis pyelitis (chronic inflammation of the bladder), possibly associated with his urethra complaint. It is interesting that the year reported for the start of the urethra problem, 1882, coincided with Clarke's furlough leave. Perhaps his sexually transmitted disease and his other medical

problem could be traced to this foray. It also should be noted that the medical report relative to gonorrhea stated he was "cured" upon release. Given the lack of effective treatment until antibiotics and other advances well after Clarke's time, this statement seems inaccurate. Clarke's medical file is found in Record Group 94, Office of the Adjutant General, Entry 297, Box 908, ACP 3760, 1884 Clarke, Powhatan, NARA.

60. Glass, *The Tenth Cavalry*, 102, indicated Troop K first had halted at "Pantana" which was a misspelling of Pantano in eastern Pima County, Arizona, near the present-day town of Vail. It had been a mail and stagecoach stop named Ciénega Station, after the nearby Ciénega Creek. Byrd Howell Granger, *Arizona's Names (X Marks the Place)* (Tucson: Falconer Publishing Company, 1983), 59–60.

Notes to Chapter 5

1. PHC to His Mother, January 2, 1886, Box 1, PHC Papers.
2. Although born in Virginia, Samuel Warren Fountain fought for the North. After the Civil War he entered West Point graduating thirty-fourth in his Class of 1870. He received his commission as a second lieutenant in the Eighth U.S. Cavalry in July of that year, rose to first lieutenant in 1878, and became a captain in 1889. On February 2, 1901, he transferred to the Ninth U.S. Cavalry as a major. Later that same year he left the cavalry to serve with the adjutant general's department. Heitman, *Historical Register and Dictionary*, 410.
3. PHC to His Father, January 23, 1886, Box 1, PHC Papers.
4. See Sidney B. Brinckerhoff, "Aftermath at Cibecue: Court Martial of the Apache Scouts, 1881," *Smoke Signal*, no. 36 (Tucson: Tucson Corral of the Westerners, 1978).
5. As one example the *Daily Tombstone Epitaph*, January 1,1886, 1, connected Governor Zulick with having mining interests in Sonora which made this economic association suspect as a conflict of interest, while the next day learning of the presence of the governor's secretary T.E. Farrish had arrived in Tucson he received a telegram from Tombstone "to explain Governor Zulick's action in the Indian and other sectional questions." Farrish replied, "The Truth will vindicate Governor Zulick in the position he had taken and other territorial questions; and this I can give you" when in Tombstone after arriving on the coming Thursday's stage. *Daily Tombstone Epitaph*, January 14, 1886, 1.

See *Daily Tombstone Epitaph*, January 1, 1886, 1, and June 22, 1886; (Tucson) *Arizona Weekly Citizen*, January 2, 1886, 3 and February 20, 1886, 2; as well as (Prescott) *Arizona Weekly Journal-Miner*, April 14, 1886, 2 and September 29, 1886, 2 for sample newspaper accounts about the territorial governor and the Geronimo campaign.

6. *Daily Tombstone Epitaph*, January 15, 1886, 3. *Daily Tombstone Epitaph*, May 18, 1886, 2, lambasted the editor of a rival newspaper editorializing "[John] Marion of the [Prescott] Courier, thinks that anyone who criticizes his pets, Crook and Zulick, is in league with the devil."
7. Don Rickey, *Forty Miles A Day: The Enlisted Soldier Fighting the Indian Wars*, (Norman: University of Oklahoma Press, 1963), 143; and Dobak and Phillips, *Black Regulars*, 62–64.
8. Rodenbough and Haskin, *The Army of the United States*, 523–24.
9. PHC to His Father, January 25, 1886, Box 1, PHC Papers.
10. Whitman, *The Troopers*, 103.
11. Remington, Frederic. "Journal of a Trip across the Continent through Arizona and Sonora Old Mexico." Robert Taft Collection. Mss Collection 975, Kansas Historical Society, Topeka, 7. (Hereafter referred to as "Remington Journal 1"). A number of newspapers in Arizona shared a negative opinion of Crawford. For examples see: (Globe) *Arizona Silver Belt*, February 21, 1885, 3, March 7, 1885, 3, and November 21, 1885, 2; (Prescott) *Weekly Arizona Miner*, February 27, 1885, 2; and (Tucson) *Arizona Weekly Citizen*, March 7, 1885, 3, December 12, 1885, 4.
12. "Remington Journal 1," 10. As one study summarized, the border between Mexico and the United States "has never known a placid year since it emerged from the Mexican War of 1848." John Myers, *The Border Wardens*, (Englewood Cliffs, NJ: Prentice-Hall, 1971), 3.
13. PHC to His Mother, February 14, 1886, Box 1, PHC Papers.
14. Born in Paris on December 18, 1865 to Alexander and Louisa Van Rensselaer, she would bear her mother's Christian name and father's surname until she married Edmund Lincoln Baylies, Jr. a graduate of Harvard School of Law. The elaborate society wedding took place on January 18, 1887 at Manhattan's St. Thomas Episcopal Church. She died on died December 1, 1945 at age 80. The difference in status and religion presented two of the obstacles that could have made Catholic middle-class Clarke's appeal as a suitor less appealing than the man she did marry. "The Baylies-Rensselaer Wedding," *New York Times*, January 19,

1887; "Mrs. Baylies Dead Helped Build the Cathedral," *New York Times*, December 2, 1945; and Cuyler Reynolds, ed., *Hudson-Mohawk Genealogical and Family Memoirs* IV (New York. Lewis Historical Publishing Company, 1911), 1819. Clarke would mention that he dined with the couple when he was in New York during 1887. Also see PHC to His Mother, May 10, 1886, Box 1,; and PHC to His Father, October 23, 1887, Box 2, PHC Papers, for further references to Louisa Van Rensselaer.

15. PHC to His Father, March 4, 1886, Box 1, PHC Papers. August V. Kautz, *Customs of the service for Officers of the Army as Derived from Law and Regulations and Practices in the Army of the United States Being Hand-Book of Military Administration for Officers of the Line. Showing the Specific Duties of Each Grade from Lowest to the Highest, Enabling Officers Promoted to a New Grade to Know What to Do, and How to Do It* (Philadelphia: J. B. Lippincott& CO., 1866) provides as excellent detailing of the many duties devolving on officers in both peace and war.
16. Hutton and Ball, *Soldiers West*, 255 and 262–63.
17. PHC to His Father, April 7, 1886, Box 1, PHC Papers. As "Remington Journal 1," 7, recognized, Maus's "story of the Crawford killing [was] variously told & questioned." For Maus's official account see *ARSW 1886* I, 155–60. Read *ARSW 1886* I, 160–64 for several more accounts in English and Spanish from other eyewitnesses. Also see the version of the incident written by one of Clarke's fellow officers, William E. Shipp, "Captain Crawford's Last Expedition," *Journal of the United States Cavalry Association* 5, no, 19 (December 1892): 343–61.
18. Dan L. Thrapp, ed., *Dateline Fort Bowie: Charles Fletcher Lummis Reports on the Apache War* (Norman: University of Oklahoma Press, 1979), 51–52; 163–70; and 194–96, provides the Mexican response, Maus's report, and Crook's views about Crawford and his final battle. Official mention of the incident read in part as follows: "In the execution of the Lieutenant General's (Sheridan) instructions to pursue, capture, or destroy the hostiles under Geronimo, a sad and unexpected encounter with a body of Mexican troops, said to have been pursuing the same object, led to the death of Captain Crawford." The report continued that on the morning of July 11, "a body of Mexican soldiers attacked Crawford's camp, wounding one of our scouts" but after about fifteen minutes the American officers succeeded in halting the fire of their command and sent Tom Horn "forward for a parley. While it was in progress, suddenly, and without warning, the Mexicans opened

fire, wounding Captain Crawford mortally and the interpreter in the arms." A series of claims from the Mexican government resulted in the matter to be handed over to the State Department. As far as the War Department was concerned "the conduct of the Mexican irregulars was utterly unjustifiable…." What was unknown was what motivated them to attack, "and how far the Mexican Government is responsible for their misconduct." Ben Perley Poore, ed., *Message of the President of the United States to the Two Houses of Congress at the Commencement of the Second Session of the Fifty-fourth Congress with Reports of the Heads of Departments and Selections from Accompanying Documents* (Washington, DC: Government Printing Office, 1886), 206–07. For samples of references in newspapers from Arizona Territory concerning Crawford's death see: (Clifton) *Clarion*, July 7, 1886, 1; (Prescott) *Arizona Weekly Journal-Miner*, February 24, 1886, 2; *Daily Tombstone*, February 22, 1886, 2, and June 26, 1886, 3; and (Tucson) *Arizona Weekly Citizen*, February 13, 1886, 3.

19. PHC to His Father, March 5, 1886, Box 1, PHC Papers.
20. Named after one of the lesser known United States presidents, Millard Fillmore Eggleston joined the Troop M, Tenth U.S. Cavalry after his graduation from West Point in 1877 ranking 61 out of 76. He served at Forts Clark, Davis and other Texas posts during which time he received his promotion to first lieutenant. Altshuler, *Cavalry Yellow & Infantry Blue*, 120.
21. PHC to His Mother, March 19, 1886, Box 1, PHC Papers.
22. It is interesting to note that while stationed at Fort Davis, Texas in 1884 John Bigelow discussed the raid with Grierson with the view of possibly publishing an account of the strike into Mississippi and Louisiana. He asked the colonel if he would assist him. Grierson said "he would think about it, that he did not like to have anything to [do] with any writing that treated at all of him." McChristian. *Garrison Tangles*, 22–23.
23. Dobak and Phillips, *Black Regulars*, 244–66, offers some insight into this complex subject and among other observations reached one very salient conclusion: "Throughout the first three decades in the regular army, black soldiers always had to satisfy two sets of criteria, the professional and racial. From the outset, they managed to meet professional standards. Prejudice, on the other hand, dogged them and their successors for generations." Dobak and Phillips, *Black Regulars*, 365–6.
24. McChristian. *Garrison Tangles*, 51, points out "that of the Tenth's officers only thirty-eight percent were graduates" of West Point while

in the Ninth U.S. Cavalry the number was a slightly higher forty percent. By way of comparison in the Fourth, Fifth, and Seventh U.S. Cavalry regiments the percentages were "sixty-three, sixty-seven and sixty-four percent, respectively." This difference may not have been the result of the propensity for West Point graduates to avoid serving with the Ninth and Tenth, but instead stemmed from the original 1866 "Congressional mandate that required black regiments .... to select the majority of their officers from recently disbanded volunteer units" or so McChristian speculated. He also indicated that like Clarke both "Mills and Bigelow apparently were concerned about the general quality of the Tenth's officers…."

25. Dobak and Phillips, *Black Regulars*, 36–38.
26. McChristian, *Garrison Tangles*, 29–30 and 54–55 n45.
27. Douglas C. McChristian, *Regular Army O! Soldiering on the Western Frontier, 1865–1891* (Norman: University of Oklahoma Press, 2017), 16–17. Also see McChristian, *Regular Army O!*, 334–35 for other accounts related to St. Patrick's Day festivities.
28. Bill Green, *The Dancing Was Lively: Fort Concho, Texas: A Social History, 1867 to 1882* (San Angelo: Fort Concho Sketches Publishing Co., 1974), 109–10 provides additional background on garrison dances relative to black troops.
29. PHC to His Father March 22, 1886, Box 1, PHC Papers.
30. In 1882, U.S. Army leaders spelled out the mission of the newly established School of Application for Infantry and Cavalry at Fort Leavenworth, Kansas. This early effort at continuing education for officers evolved into the Army's Combined Arms Center. For more on the first hundred years of this institution see; Boyd L. Dastrop, *The U.S. Army Command and General Staff College: A Centennial History* (Manhattan, KS: Sunflower University Press, 1982).
31. Here Clarke gossiped that Samuel C. Robertson, West Point Class of 1879, "must have been extravagant, probably gambled." After Robertson's death, W.T. Hornaday the chief taxidermist of the Smithsonian's and later the first director of what became the Bronx Zoo, hinted at a problem with money noting his comrade expended "more money than he could afford with the generosity of a prince," but "he had only the pay of a cavalry officer." Despite the difficulties Clarke mentioned, Robertson would be promoted to first lieutenant, published some promising articles about military subjects, and remained in service until he resigned his commission in 1893 due to

health issues and to pursue outside business opportunities. The former condition proved critical and he died soon after leaving the army. *Twenty-fifth Annual Reunion of the Association of the Graduates of the United States Military Academy at West Point, New York* (NP: Seemann & Peters Printers and Binders, 1894), 31–37. Coincidentally this same publication carried a submission about Clarke, but rather than contain the byline of a classmate, the obituary was signed, "The Tenth Cavalry." *Twenty-fifth Annual Reunion*, 19–24.

32. Many sources such as Knight, *Life and Mores*, 73 and 93; McChristian, *Garrison Tangles*, 23, 49–50 n32, 50–51 n34, and 51–52 n35; and Robert M. Utley, ed., *An Army Doctor on the Western Frontier: Journals and Letters of John Vance Lauderdale, 1864–1890* (Albuquerque: University of New Mexico Press, 2014), 182, chronicle problems found at frontier garrisons. John M. Gates, "The Alleged Isolation of US Army Officers in the Late 19th Century," *Parameters: Journal of US Army War College* 10, no. 3 (September 1980): 32–45, offers some alternative views.
33. PHC to His Mother, March 28, 1886, Box 1, PHC Papers.
34. The above references were taken from "Clarke Pocket Journal 1," April 13, 1885, Box 5, PHC Papers.
35. The above synopsis drew on Sweeney, *From Geronimo to Cochise*, 521–26. Of this debacle the (Prescott) *Arizona Weekly Journal-Miner*, April 7, 1886, 3, mocked: "A Tucson telegram of the 30th inst. Says that 'a party consisting of Gov. Zulick, U.S Marshal Meade, Gen. Ned McCook, Judge and Mrs. Barnes, Mrs. Judge Shields and representatives of the press, left the city this morning for Fort Bowie, in response to an invitation from Gen. Crook to inspect Geronimo and the captive renegades.' Geronimo had an invitation to attend the reunion, but respectfully declined."
36. PHC to His Father, April 7, 1886, Box 1, PHC Papers.
37. Distribution of troops was taken from Charles Gatewood Papers, Box 1, Folder 4, Arizona Historical Society, Tucson. During the final push, Miles fielded nearly a quarter of the U.S. Army's combat strength with no less than "forty troops of cavalry and forty-three companies of infantry" plus Indian scouts and a number of contract civilians including packers. "Taming the Savage Apache Followers of Geronimo," *Frontier Times* 1, no. 1 (October 1923): 12.
38. "Clarke Pocket Journal 1," April 15, 1885, Box 5, PHC Papers. Benson was founded in 1880 as a station along the Southern Pacific Railroad

after its arrival in Cochise County, and was named in honor of California Judge William B. Benson president of the railroad. Granger, *Arizona's Names*, 59–60. In 1874 M.W. Stewart laid out what would become Willcox in Cochise County. A half dozen years later the Southern Pacific Railroad reached the budding community and supposedly Department of Arizona Commander Orlando Willcox was aboard the first train. This event prompted the residents to change the original name of the community, which was Maley, to Willcox. Granger, *Arizona's Names*, 675–6. Fort Crittenden in Santa Cruz County was manned from 1868 through 1873, having been established near the site of the nearby ante bellum garrison Fort Buchanan. With the newer installation's discontinuance civilians remained in the area residing in a small adobe known as Casa Blanca, which was the temporary name until 1882 when Crittenden was readopted and used through 1901. Granger, *Arizona's Names*, 187.

39. Located in Santa Cruz County, the claim also was known as the Patagonia Mine. The latter name came from Sylvester Mowry, an 1852 West Point graduate, who after resigning his commission, purchased the claim from several fellow officers in 1858. The site had been worked previously but abandoned. Granger, *Arizona's Names*, 423–4. Constance Wynn Altshuler, "The Case of Sylvester Mowry," *Arizona and the West* 15, nos. 1 and 2 (Spring and Summer 1973): 63–82 and 149–74, treats the mine's colorful namesake and his claim.

40. Named after San Pedro Valley rancher David Tecumseh Harshaw, who agreed to move his stock at the request of Indian Agent Tom Jeffords. The cattleman turned miner complied, relocating to a place called Durasno by local Mexicans because of peach trees in the area. A mining camp sprang up with some stores along Harshaw Creek south of Patagonia in Santa Cruz County. By the time of Arizona statehood the community had all but disappeared. Granger, *Arizona's Names*, 291. La Moira was a small border crossing twenty-five miles south. (Prescott) *Arizona Weekly Journal-Miner*, April 7, 1886, 3.

41. For more details on the British-inspired technology read Paul J. Scheips's unpublished "The Military Heliograph and its Use in Arizona and the Southwest" (Fort Monmouth, NJ: Historical Office, U.S. Army Signal Corps, 1954); Bruno J. Rolak, "General Miles' Mirrors: The *Heliograph* in the Geronimo Campaign of 1886," *Journal of Arizona History* 16, no. 2 (Summer 1975): 145–160; Roger E. Kelly, "Talking Mirrors at Fort Bowie: Military Communication in the Southwest,"

(Chiricahua National Monument: National Park Service, 1967); William W. Neifert, "Trailing Geronimo by Heliograph," *Winners of the West* 12 No. 11 (October 1935), 1–4; and "Heliography in the Army," *Harper's Weekly* 30, no 1547 (August 14, 1886), 523.

42. The name Nogales appeared on maps as early as 1859 and supposedly was derived from two walnut trees (*los dos Nogales*) that flanked the newly established international boundary during the survey to establish the border between the United States and Mexico after the Gadsden Purchase. Granger, *Arizona's Names*, 320.

43. Enrique Ronstadt was one of four children born to Frederick August and Concepcion (Quiroga) Ronstadt. His father, a native of Hanover, Germany, spent 23 years "in the military of his adopted country, Mexico becoming a colonel of the National Guard of the state of Sonora…." He also engaged in ranching and mining. In 1882 he, his second wife and their children relocated to Tucson engaging in various business ventures such as carriage making and a hardware store as well as becoming part of the local music scene, a trait that continued for generations including the most famous of this talented family, Linda Ronstadt. Edward F. Ronstadt, ed., *Borderman: Memoirs of Federico José María Ronstadt* (Albuquerque: University of New Mexico Press, 1993, xvii, 77, 83, and 107; and MS 0695 Ronstadt Family Papers 177–1993, "Family History–Ronstadt Family Tree," Box 1 Folder 1, Arizona Historical Society, Tucson.

44. Another Santa Cruz County site, Buena Vista, was a Mexican land grant dating from 1831. It consisted of over 18,000 acres deeded to Doña Josefa Morales. Known as the Maria Santisima del Carmen Grant, its location was east of Nogales. After the Gadsden Purchase, Fred Maise and Thomas Driscoll received a portion of the lands. Granger, *Arizona's Names*, 98. Agua Zarca, Sonora, had been the site of early clashes with Mexicans and Apache during 1870. Kŭhn, *Chronicles of War*, 165 and 168.

As for the death toll one of the three men killed on April 22 was Manuel Molina. The next day a woman and boy, Guadalupe Salina and Ignacio Salina fell as victims. That same date, April 23, a pair of Mexican soldiers, Estarislao Bonilla and Francisco Grijalva were killed as was one civilian, Juan Gordon, while another civilian was wounded as a result of an ambush two miles from Casita, Sonora. Yet another man died that same day near there and on March 26 George Sheppard, Jose Maria Incland, Epifanio Murrieta, and Marcos Laguna met their end at the Buena Vista Ranch along the Santa Cruz ten miles east of Nogales while on April 26 man was killed "near the old custom house, a few miles south of Nogales (Son.)." Kŭhn, *Chronicles of War*, 286.

45. The locale of Calabasas under the name San Cayetano de Calabazas appears as early as 1701 on a map produced by the missionary-explorer Eusebio Kino. The title presumably came from the presence of gourds or melons in the area. The site lay along the Apache raiding route. Granger, *Arizona's Names*, 108–9. After the railroad arrived in the vicinity in 1882 the community was offered many amenities including the two-story Hotel Santa Rita where Clarke occasionally relaxed and used some of their stationary to write home. -Additional information is found in Sybil Ellinwood, "Calabasas," *Arizoniana* 5, no. 4 (Winter) 27–41; and Bernard L. Fontana, "Calabazas of the Rio Rico," *Smoke Signal*, no. 24 (Tucson: Tucson Corral of the Westerners, 1971). Also of note as recorded in MS 282 AHS Gatewood Collection F1, Box 1, Lebo was "at Calabasas May 13, 1886—ready to move—knows of no other Indians in vicinity except hostiles."
46. PHC to His Mother, May 10, 1886, Box 1, PHC Papers.
47. Sweeney, *From Geronimo to Cochise*, 537.
48. Kŭhn, *Chronicles of War*, 286.
49. John Bigelow, *On the Bloody Trail of Geronimo* (Tucson: Westernlore Press, 1986), viii–ix. This publication consolidates Bigelow's original serialized articles from *Outing*. The originals appeared in *Outing* as follows: (April 1886), 50–56; (May 1886), 147–56; (June 1886), 291–300; (July 1886), 416–23; (August 1886), 535–43; (September 1886), 646–52; (December 1886), 223–33; (January1887), 308–17; (February 1887), 428–40; and (March 1887), 515–25. Frederic Remington's illustrations started to appear in the Jaanury 1887 edition, and throughout the remainder of the series.
50. Bigelow, *On the Bloody Trail*, 64.
51. Bigelow, *On the Bloody Trail*, 133.
52. Bigelow, *On the Bloody Trail*, 88.
53. William H. and Shirley K. Leckie: *The Buffalo Soldiers: A Narrative of the Black Cavalry in the West* (Norman: University of Oklahoma Press, 2003), 6.
54. *Annual Report of the Adjutant-General of the State of New York for the Year 1894* III (Albany: State of New York, 1895), 924.
55. Thomas West Smith, *The Story of a Regiment: "Scott's 900" Eleventh New York Cavalry from the St. Lawrence River to the Gulf of Mexico,*

1861–1865 (Chicago: Veteran Association of the Eleventh New York Cavalry, 1897), 157.

56. Frederic Remington to Scott Turner, March 3, 1877; and undated 1877 from Highland Academy. Splete and Splete, *Frederic Remington—Selected Letters*, 14–15,
57. Peggy and Harold Samuels, *Frederic Remington: A Biography* (Garden City, New York: Doubleday & Company, Inc., 1982), 19.
58. This was a reference to Upton's *A New System of Infantry Tactics*, and his updated and revised *Infantry Tactics: Double and Single Rank*. These treatises would become virtual scripture and verse for the army during most of the last part of the Victorian era. David J. Fitzpatrick, *Emory* Upton*: Misunderstood Reformer* (Norman: University of Oklahoma Press, 2017), discusses this post-Civil War military theorist in depth.
59. Samuels, *Frederic Remington: A Biography*, 22.
60. Poultney Bigelow, "Frederic Remington: With extracts from Unpublished Letters," *The Quarterly Journal of the New York State Historical Association* 10, no. 1 (January 1929): 45. For Remington's take on his early benefactor read an instructive article titled "A Cosmopolitan—Mr. Poultney Bigelow" is found in Peggy and Harold Samuels, eds., *The Collected Writings of Frederic Remington* (New York: Castle: 1986), 205–7.
61. David McCullough, *Brave Companions: Portraits in History* (New York: Prentice Hall, 1992), 69. *Based on an historic standard of living* value of the sum of $10, 0000 in 1880 was equivalent to $242,000.00 in 2016. https://www.measuringworth.com/uscompare/relativevalue.php.
62. McCullough, *Brave Companions*, 69. Also see, Robert Taft, *Artists and Illustrators of the Old West 1850–1890* (New York: Bonanza Books, 1953), 194–211.
63. McCullough, *Brave Companions*, 70.
64. Peter Hassrick, *Frederic Remington* (New York: Harry N. Abrams, Inc., 1973), 23. This biography coupled with Hassrick's, *Frederic Remington: A Catalogue Raisonné II* (Norman: University of Oklahoma Press, 2016), rank among the best works treating this iconic artist of the American West.
65. Sandra Forty, *Remington* (Edison, NJ: Chartwell Books, Inc., 2008), 12.
66. "Remington Journal 1," 9–10.
67. Henry Ware Lawton received accolades during and after his lifetime, albeit fleeting ones. At the outbreak of the American Civil War eighteen-year-old Lawton volunteered for the Union infantry, thereby

expectantly launching a military career. The gangly 6'4" teenager rapidly rose through the ranks working his way from private to captain within a year of his enlistment. Young Lawton displayed both leadership qualities and bravery, which ultimately would be acknowledged by brevets (honorary ranks) as a major and lieutenant colonel and the Medal of Honor. Altshuler, *Cavalry Yellow & Infantry*, 198–99, Michael E. Shay, *Henry Ware Lawton: Union Infantryman, Frontier Soldier, Charismatic Warrior* (Columbia: University of Missouri Press, 2016), provides ample details about a professional soldier "who served the country nearly uninterrupted from the day he enlisted at age 18…."

68. "Remington Journal 1," 11.
69. John Alexander Carroll observed George Crook and Nelson Miles "had long been directly counterpoised as professional rivals" as well as "for fully a decade…regarded by their superiors and public alike, as America's greatest Indian fighters." These competing views gave rise to "controversy both within and outside the Army" as to which of them was superior. This duel of words and wits continued well into the twenty-first century. *Generals Crooks and Miles in Arizona: From Contemporary Accounts of Fellow Soldiers with the Original Illustrations of Frederic Remington* (Tucson: Tucson Corral of the Westerners, 1967), 114.
70. Selections from Arizona Territory newspapers indicate how local press viewed laudatory Bourke's writing negatively as they typically did when it came to Crook's use of scouts. Examples include: (Globe) *Arizona Silver Belt*, February 27, 1886, 2 and August 22, 1885, 2; *Daily Tombstone*, February 2, 1886, 2, February 5, 1886, 3, and March 18, 1886, 3; and (Tucson) *Arizona Weekly Citizen*, January 23, 1886, 4, January 30, 1886, 2, and July 17, 1886, 4.
71. "Remington Journal 1," 9. Here Remington referred to John Bourke's *An Apache Campaign in the Sierra Madre* (New York: Charles Scribner's Sons, 1886).
72. Poultney Bigelow, *Seventy Summers* 1 (New York: Longmans, Green & Co., 1925), 307.
73. "Remington Journal 1," 6.
74. "Remington Journal 1," 14.
75. When the Tenth U.S. Cavalry headed to Cuba in 1898 Givens would be mentioned by John Bigelow as "a steadying and encouraging influence upon the men" at San Juan, which contributed to his receiving a

commission as an officer to cap his career that ended in retirement in 1901. Givens died in 1907, but not before John Bigelow's unsuccessful attempt to secure recognition for the brave veteran's actions in Cuba. Givens's biographical background was taken from Record Group 94 (AGO), Entry 91a (US Army Enlistment Papers-Series One), Box 28; Entry 91b (US Army Enlistment Papers-Series Two), Box 488; Entry 501 (R&P Document File), Box 1418, File 719108 Spanish American War Commissions; Entry 522 (Carded Records-Spanish American War Volunteers) Spanish-American War Compiled Military Service Record; CMSR, Givens, William, Co E, 10th Regt US Volunteer Infantry – Colored; Entry 530 (Carded Medical record-Regulars 1894), Box 752; Entry 529 (Carded Medical record-Regulars 1884), Box 505; and Entry 25 (AGO Document File), Box 2116, File 319311; and Frank N. Schubert, *On the Trail of the Buffalo Soldier: Biographies of African Americans in the U.S. Army, 2866–1917* 1 (Wilmington, DE: Scholarly Resources, Inc., 1995), 164–5.

76. "Remington Journal 1," 14.
77. "Remington Journal 1," 17.
78. "Remington Journal 1," 14–15. Elsewhere during his early encounters with Clarke and his men Remington recorded several additional pithy details almost unknown to all but the most seasoned soldier of the era. For instance, see "Remington Journal 1," 16–18.
79. Dobak and Phillips, *Black Regulars*, 5–6, 9–10, 12–13, 40, 51, 58, 64, 81–83, 114, 125, 127, 130, 135, 141, 180, 182, 200–01, 203–04, 247, 254–56, 258–61, underscores the significance of black non-commissioned officers.
80. During the Spanish American War, Givens served in Cuba where he received a recommendation for a Certificate of Merit for leading his company in combat at Santiago, while a first sergeant. Bigelow, then a captain reported Givens exercised "a steadying and encouraging influence upon his men." *ARSW*, I, 1898, 711. The recommendation came too late, as he had already accepted a commission as second lieutenant in the Tenth Volunteer U.S. Volunteer Infantry, as one of the few black officers in this unit manned by African American enlisted personnel. When the volunteers were mustered out, he was forced to resume his rank as an enlisted man (a private) in the Tenth U.S. Cavalry. The Certificate of Merit was brought before the board, which denied the recommendation as it also did for a Medal of Honor. Givens retired in June 1901 with thirty years' service. Givens,

Williams, Composite Service Record, RG94, NARA; and Schubert, *On the Trail of the Buffalo Soldiers*, I, 164–5. Note AGO Circular No. 2, February 11, 1892 stipulated "certificates of merit should, under law, be awarded for distinguished service, whether in action or otherwise, of a valuable character to the United States as, for example, extraordinary exertion in the preservation of human life, or in the preservation of public property, or rescuing public property from destruction by fire or otherwise, or any hazardous service by which the Government is saved loss in men or material." This was the only other recognition for enlisted men save the Medal of Honor during this period.

81. Sweeney, *From Cochise to Geronimo*, 538.
82. Glass, *History of the Tenth Cavalry*, 27. For context and more background read: Jack C. Gale, "Lebo in Pursuit," *Journal of Arizona History* 21, no. 1 (Spring 1980): 1–24.
83. See for example (Tucson) *Arizona Daily Star*, May 5,1886, 1; and May 8, 1886, 4. According to enlistment papers Edward Scott was born in Danville, Kentucky, during 1857, probably to enslaved parents. On December 12, 1878, the 5' 9 ½" Scott signed on at Cincinnati, Ohio, for the first of his two five-year tours of duty. He would be listed variously as a laborer and hostler. Typical of the period, he reported to the depot at Jefferson Barracks in the St. Louis, Missouri, area as a recruit. He then was sent to Fort Lewis, Colorado, as his first post. Allan Radbourne, *Corporal Edward Scott, Frontier Cavalryman* (London: The English Westerners' Society, 2015), 1–3, which likewise contains many other well researched details about Scott and other related topics.
84. (Tucson) *Arizona Daily Star*, May 13,1886, 4, which ran as a reprint of the *Nogales Frontier* account.
85. Joseph Follis enlisted at Cincinnati on July 2, 1882. This meant he was near the end of his first enlistment when killed. Radbourne, *Corporal Edward Scott*, 35, n56.
86. Glass, *History of the Tenth Cavalry*, 24.
87. "Clarke Pocket Journal 1," May 3, 1885, Box 5, PHC Papers.
88. The Esperanza Ranch (established circa 1880) was named by the spread's owner, Bullinger, for his sister. It later became part of the New York Ranch. Granger, *Arizona Names*, 230.
89. Harry Coupland Benson had attended Kenyon College in Ohio. After receiving his A.B. and A.M. degrees this Phi Beta Kappa entered West

Point. He graduated in the class of 1882, ranking number seven of 37 cadets. He would be assigned to the First U.S. Artillery and served on Alcatraz as a second lieutenant until his transfer to the Fourth U.S. Cavalry on January 31, 1884. For further biographical information consult Altshuler, *Cavalry Yellow & Infantry Blue*, 30–31. Although more modest in length than Britton Davis's *The Truth About Geronimo*, Benson published a worthwhile recapitulation of the campaign as well. See, *A&NJ*, July 3, 1909, 1240–41. Of note, he also authored a summary of the last year of pursuing Geronimo as "The Geronimo Campaign," *A&NJ*, July 3, 1909, 1240–41.

90. PHC to His Father, May 4, 1886, Box 1, PHC Papers.
91. PHC to His Mother, May 10, 1886, Box 1, PHC Papers.
92. Scott's comment on having observed many other severely wounded men stemmed from an incident during his first enlistment. While serving in Company D, Ninth U.S. Cavalry under its commanding officer, Captain Francis Dodge, the unit was in the field. During the fall of 1879, Dodge and his men replied to a desperate call for help from a besieged column of white soldiers surrounded by Ute Indians on the White River reservation near in Colorado. The would-be rescuers also fell into the same trap. When finally reached by a second group of reinforcements Company D had thirty horses killed, four men wounded and two others killed. Radbourne, *Corporal Edward Scott*, 4–5. Adding to these casualty figures were another eleven soldiers and civilians killed and forty-three wounded from the first contingent of troops who fought the Utes. Michno, *Encyclopedia of Indian Wars*, 327.
93. Forrestine Cooper provided one of many second-hand accounts of this incident. She stated: "During the fight, Corporal Edward Scott was badly wounded and unable to escape as the Apaches, behind boulders, made him a target for their bullets as he lay help less on the ground. Then Lieutenant Clarke dashed to the side of the Negro soldier without thought of his own danger, and carried the man to a place of safety. Later a Medal of Honor was awarded him for that daring deed." Wilson, *Child of the Fighting Tenth*, 219–20.
94. *Daily Tombstone Epitaph*, May 8, 1886, 2.
95. "Remington Journal 1," 36.
96. "Remington Journal 1," 39.
97. "Our Soldiers in the Southwest," *Harper's Weekly* 30, no. 1547 (August 21, 1886): 535.

98. Harold McCracken, *Frederic Remington's Own West* (New York: Dial Press, 1960), 17–25. Unfortunately the author failed to cite where the manuscript was located and none of the obvious repositories for Remington's primary materials appear to house the original. In this version a sergeant, who may have been Givens gave: '"Dat 'ar Lieutenant Clark is a -- -- fighting man, you'd better believe." Remington also maintained that Corporal Scott, "as he lay on his cot in the Fort Huachuca hospital" recalled '"dat when he jumped fo' me as I alydar in de open, dem Injuns, dey jus' done plowed de groun' round dar, and msuer, efdat lieutenant warn't a right brave man, he'd done dusted out and lef' me as I tole him to.'" McCracken, *Frederic Remington's Own West*, 23.
99. *Arizona Daily Star* (Tucson) May 13 1886, 4.
100. McCracken, *Frederic Remington's Own West*, 23.
101. PHC to His Father, May 20, 1886, Box 1, PHC Papers. Two days earlier, Clarke, who was out with his detachment from Troop K, received a telegram from Lebo with instructions to "Have noncommissioned officer and ten men meet paymaster at Crittenden tomorrow morning sent there today. Keep sharp lookout at the passes in Patagonia Mountains. Some Indians were seen near Buena Vista yesterday evening." Telegram Lebo to Clarke, May 18, 1886, Box 1, PHC Papers. Two days later General Miles wired from Nogales telling Clarke who was at Calabasas "The first thing to do is to get information to Lebo & second to order men to occupy pass in mountains between you and Oro Blanco." Telegram Miles to Clarke, May 20, 1886, Box 5, PHC Papers.
102. An Alabaman and member of the West Point Class of 1872, Hatfield graduated a respectable twenty-seventh out of fifty-seven, He assumed command of Troop D, Fourth U.S. Cavalry with his promotion to captain occurring on November 26, 1884. Operating out of Fort Huachuca he took to the field frequently, sometimes operating under Henry Lawton. Altshuler, *Cavalry Yellow & Infantry Blue*, 160. He eventually rose to colonel in command of the newly formed Thirteenth U.S. Cavalry regiment. Thereafter he shuttled to various assignments in the Philippines, Fort Myer, Virginia, and Arizona along the border. He retired on December 9, 1914, but returned to active duty briefly during World War I "in charge of the Philadelphia recruiting district." Hatfield died on February 23, 1935, at his home in Washington, D.C. Altshuler, *Cavalry Yellow & Infantry Blue*, 160.

103. For more on the pair of Hatfield engagements see Jack C. Gale, "Hatfield Under Fire, May 15, 1886," *Journal of Arizona History* 18, no. 4 (Winter 1977): 447–68; Alan Radbourne, "Captain Hatfield and the Chiricahuas," "*Ho for the Great West !" and Other Original Papers to Mark the 25th Anniversary of the English Westerners Society* (London: English Westerners Society, 1980): 71–81; Kŭhn, *Chronicles of War*, 287; McCracken, *Frederic Remington's Own West*, 23 and 25; and "Remington Journal 1," 3, the last source recording the testimony of a Private Kelly from the Fourth U.S. Cavalry "who was in the fight" and told Remington on May 15 Hatfield's unit surprised encamped Apaches about 10 a.m. and captured a dozen ponies, a pair of mules, saddles, and camp equipage. The troopers fired a volley and saw one Indian fall from his mount. After the raid the solders found evidence "of lots of blood on the trail" but as they pursued the fleeing party and halted, the Apaches ambushed the cavalrymen while they watered their thirsty government horses. One man died (Gustave Liebernord) and Sergeant Samuel Craig received a leg wound before the troops could fall back to cover. A two-hour skirmish followed with another dead, blacksmith John Courde and another wounded non-commissioned officer, First Sergeant Samuel Adams, added to the casualty list.
104. PHC to His Father, May 21, 1886, Box 1, PHC Papers.
105. Mississippian Charles Barrows, like Clarke's father, had attended the University of Virginia. He had been dispatched from his duties at Fort Whipple to the field but not many months afterward would be transferred to Florida with the capture of Geronimo and his removal along with many of his people to Florida. (Prescott) *Arizona Weekly Journal-Miner*, September 22, 1886, 3. "First Lieut Chas C Barrows Asst Surgeon ordered to report to commanding officer St Francis Bks St Augustine Fla at Ft Marion SO 180 Division of the Atlantic," Journal of the American Medical Association 7 (November 10, 1886): 588. "Except for a brief period while serving in the army Dr. Barrows has been connected with Bellevue Hospital since 1880 when he won his appointment as interne. After his return to New York he was appointed visiting assistant gynecologist [at Cornell University] holding this position until he became visiting gynecologist in 1915. He died on January 2, 1916," *Science* 1111 (April 14, 1916): 538. In an August 13,1886, letter Clarke also told his father that Barrows was from Jacksonville, Mississippi. PHC to His Father, August 13, 1886, Box 1, PHC Papers.

106. Kŭhn, *Chronicles of War*, 290. The origin and meaning of the name Arivaca located in today's Pima County remains obscure. One suggestion was it derived from the Tohono O'Odom (Papago) *hijovajilla-for* "son of the great valley" while others contended it is the Spanish corruption of Aki mult a tham (Pima) word *Alivapk* meaning little reeds. Still one more theory says it was a local term for "rotten ground" given the marshy environment of the area. These and other explanations cannot be ascertained with certainty but at least as early as 1773 the Indian village of Aribac (or Arivaca) appeared on a map. The site had been deserted as the result of the 1750 Pima revolt, but some mining continued for more than a decade thereafter. By 1812 a petition was granted for two farming lots of the Aribac ranch. By 1835 the site again was deserted. More than three decades later Charles Poston noted he bought the claim for $10,000 with the renewal of mining underpinning community evolved including a post office that started in 1878. Granger, *Arizona's Names*, 29–30. Also see Mary Noon Kasulaitis, "The Village of Arivaca: A Short History," *Smoke Signal* no. 75 (Tucson: Tucson Corral of the Westerners, 2002).
107. Telegram Miles to Clarke, June 10, 1886, Box 1, PHC Papers.
108. Pennsylvanian William Newlin Tisdall received a commission as a second lieutenant in the First U.S. Infantry on October 24, 1861. His early duties took him to Fort Leavenworth, Kansas, but by 1863 after promotion to first lieutenant he joined his regiment in the east at the siege of Vicksburg, Mississippi and subsequently on campaign in Louisiana. After the war he remained in the First Infantry, rose to captain on January 13, 1869. He would be stationed at Fort McDowell, Arizona in late 1882 but soon moved to Fort Huachuca. Altshuler, *Cavalry Yellow & Infantry Blue*, 333, offers further informaiton.
109. PHC to His Mother, July 6, 1886, Box 1, PHC Papers.
110. Supposedly this Santa Cruz County place name came from the ore extracted at this mine containing so much silver mixed with gold the Spanish term *oroblanco* (white gold) was applied. The original operators of the mining concern included Robert Leatherwood and Charles O. Brown, both prominent southern Arizona names at the time. Its proximity to the border briefly caused some confusion that it was located in Mexico, but that proved an unfounded concern. How long the place had been exploited for its minerals is unknown, but "it is said that the location had been worked so long ago that in some places large

oak trees had grown up at the site of obviously old mining activities." Granger, *Arizona's Names*, 451.

111. William F. Nye, trans., *Sonora: Its Extent, Population, Natural Productions, Indians Tribes, Names, Mineral Lands, Etc., Etc.* (San Francisco: H.H. Bancroft and Company, 1861), 105–06 and 122.

112. Leatherwood was a native of Clay County, North Carolina, "who had saved his military cap and uniform and wore them on great occasions." He was born to William and Elizabeth (Nelson) on June 21, 1844, as one of eight children. During the Civil War Leatherwood enlisted as a private in Company I, Thirty-ninth Regiment of Georgia Volunteers ("Gilmore Tigers II"). During the battle of Chattanooga, Tennessee, he became a Union prisoner of war. Leatherwood came to Tucson in 1869, establishing a stables "at the corner of Church and Pennington, where the southwest corner of the old presidio stood." This 5 feet 5 inch 130 pound transplanted Southerner was known for his "valor and grit." He promoted the Southern Pacific Railroad being routed through town, taking office as mayor on January1, 1880, just in time to head up a major celebration of the railroad's arrival. Likewise he championed retaining the capital in Tucson, and establishing the University of Arizona there, the former effort failing with Phoenix being named the new seat of territorial government. Leatherwood served as a Tucson city councilman, two-time legislator, Pima County sheriff, county treasurer, mined in the Santa Catalina Mountains, helped form the Masonic lodge in 1875, and organized as well as served as captain of the Tucson Rangers. Leatherwood died on April 4, 1920. Sonnichsen, *Tucson: The Life and Times of an American City*, 102–3; and Mss 1475 Biofiles, Leatherwood, Robert Nelson, Box 73, Arizona Historical Society, Tucson.

113. James Finley recorded Trinidad Berdine's statement which indicated that while her brother-in-law was away with a vaquero, the Apaches came to the ranch. Hearing their dog bark, Mrs. Peck said, "'Trinie look out and see what the dog is barking at.' I ran out to see, and saw an Apache...." Trinidad called to her older sister who "ran out of the house with her baby in her arms. The Apache shot and killed them both." She thought there were thirty or forty in the main party with "a fat old man, short and thick-set and big cheeked" apparently in command, but then they split up into smaller groups as Clarke had feared. They made their way to the Pajarito Mountains and from there continued southwest remaining constantly on the move Gatewood Collection, MS 282, Folder 15, Box 1, Arizona Historical Society, Tucson.

114. Sweeney, *From Cochise to Geronimo*, 537–8, concluded that a young Apache with a command of English introduced Peck to Geronimo. In turn, Geronimo called Peck "Mangus Coloradas (Red Sleeves), for he was wearing red flannel underwear under his shirt, which he had rolled up above his elbow." In this version of the story Geronimo thought Peck " 'was a good man' so he spared his life. They stripped him to his underwear and took his boots. Only Geronimo knows why he let him go – perhaps because he was unarmed, perhaps because he knew what it was like to lose a family, or perhaps because Peck's red sleeves reminded him, nostalgically, of times with Mangas Coloradas."
115. PHC to His Father, July16, 1886, Box 1, PHC Papers.
116. PHC to His Father, August 13, 1886, PHC Papers.
117. Schubert, *On the Trail of the Buffalo Soldier* I, 435. This same source noted that Turner received s promotion to corporal on September 28, 1895, and was stationed at Fort Custer, Montana at least as early as 1897. Seven years earlier he had been cited for "conspicuous bravery against Apaches" at Salt River, Arizona. He would accompany the regiment to Cuba as did First Sergeant Givens as a member of Troop K in 1898.
118. For an overview of this complex subject consult Evelyn Hu-DeHat, *Yaqui Resistance and Survival: The Struggle for Land and Autonomy 1821–1910* (Madison, WI: The University of Wisconsin Press, 2016). Also of note, Frederic Remington shared sympathy with the Yaquis and a similar disdain for Mexican officials as indicated in several articles in *Harper's Weekly* such as: "The Uprising in Chihuahua" (May 6, 1898); "The Rebellion in Northern Mexico" (December 30, 1893); and "Uprising of the Yaqui Indians" (August 29, 1896) all reprinted in Samuels and Samuels, *The Collected Writings of Frederic Remington*, 102–03; 122–23; 234–35. The first two articles likewise reference the killing of Emmet Crawford.
119. PHC to His Mother, September 12 and 13, 1886, Box 1, PHC Papers.
120. Thrapp, *Conquest of Apacheria*, 350–363, briefly treats the final events leading up to Geronimo's exchange at Skeleton Canyon with Miles and his removal with many followers to Fort Marion, Florida.
121. Kŭhn, *Chronicles of War*, 292–309, charts many lesser incidents with Indians that continued to plague the peace in Arizona from 1886 through as late as 1937!
122. Clarke's choice of the term Sepoy to apply to Indian Scouts is a curious one. Adopted in the eighteenth century by the East India Company for

locals serving as military forces in the Subcontinent, the word evolved and took on various connotations, not the least of which was the 1857 rebellion against the British that became synonymous with duplicity. With few exceptions the scouts maintained a steadfast loyalty when they enlisted. For more on the rebellion and the Sepoys read: Jill C. Bender, *The 1857 Indian Uprising and the British Empire* (Cambridge: Cambridge University Press, 2016).

A series of telegrams outline Clarke's brief second assignment as an officer in charge of Apache scouts beginning on June 22, 1886. At that time the department acting assistant adjutant general contacted him from Willcox while the lieutenant was Calabasas. He was directed to "Make out the necessary enlistment papers in triplicate for … scouts dated June 1st, 1886. On July 9, 1886 the same officer, who was at Fort Bowie at that point, informed Clarke that the quartermaster department would pay the scouts "$5 payment due regular pay and forty cents per day for horses" the standard rate permitted for private mounts. This detail approached a rapid end when on August 26 word came that "Orders were sent you by mail yesterday to march" his scouts to Fort Lowell for mustering out of service. "According to a wire on September 1, he was authorized to travel by rail to Tucson and he was instructed to proceed to Calabasas were he would be furnished transportation." In conjunction with the disbandment of the scout detail on Clarke received a series of orders from September 9 through 12 requiring him to "bring in all your ordnance stores and turn over to C.O. Ft Huachuca" and when a delay in heading to Tucson occurred told him to "send for more rations and keep your men there until the paymaster arrives has been ordered to pay you on 12th at Calabasas." A September 11 message further confirmed that the paymaster would "leave on twelfth for Calabasas" and asked that he have rolls with the names of his scouts in "readiness…." Finally, by September 24, 1886 departmental headquarters released Clarke for his return to Fort Grant. Telegrams June 22, space here July 9, August 26, September 1, September 9 through 12, and September 24, 1886, Box 1, PHC Papers.

123. "Extract from General Miles' Annual Report Received Sept. 28, 1886," *ARSW 1886*, I, 167, printed this report and added a mention of the death of the Pecks as well as the 200 mile pursuit by Lebo's troopers.
124. PHC to His Father, October 6, 1886, Box 1, PHC Papers.
125. Oliver Otis Howard, who had been a previous commander of the Department of Arizona, began military life when he entered West

Point as a cadet on September 1, 1850, graduating on July 1, 1854, with a commission as a second lieutenant of ordnance. Arsenal duties followed until being posted as chief of ordnance in Florida against the Seminoles in 1857. A long and distinguished career followed. He died at age 76 on November 29, 1909. George W. Cullum, *Biographical Register of the Officers and Graduates of the United States Military Academy Since Its Establishment in 1804 to 1890 I–VI* (West Point: Association of Graduates, U.S. Military Academy, 1890), I, 576; IV, 94; and V, 82.

126. PHC to His Mother November 29, 1886, Box 1, PHC Papers.
127. During the post-Civil War, recognition of a deficiency in marksmanship at last prompted army officials to concede that a program needed to be developed to address this critical shortcoming. By the 1880s a series of initiatives had grown ranging from post shooting ranges to departmental and even national competitions to improve the heretofore nearly neglected foundation for combat. William K. Emerson, *Marksmanship in the Army: A History of Medals, Shooting Programs, and Training* (Norman: University of Oklahoma Press, 2004) provides an overview of the evolution of this program.
128. PHC to His Father, December 5, 1886, Box 1, PHC Papers.
129. Faust and Randall, *Life at Post*, 71.
130. PHC to His Father, December 5, 1886, Box 1, PHC Papers.
131. PHC to His Father, December 14, 1886, Box 1, PHC Papers.
132. Clarke actually meant Dr. Charles Borrows and corrected himself later in his December 14 letter. In turn, Egan had met Clarke the previous year as did Barrows. Born in Ireland Peter Ralph Egan received his appointment as an assistant surgeon (first lieutenant) from New York on May 23, 1882; his promotion to captain assistant surgeon came on May 23, 1887. He served as a major with volunteers from June 4, 1898 through March 22, 1899 when he was honorably discharged, and received his promotion to major as a surgeon in the Regular Army on February 2, 1900. During the 1880s, Egan served variously at Forts Bowie, Huachuca, and Lowell. This graduate of the Medical Department of Columbia College, New York, died on October 1, 1923, at age 68. Powell, *List of Offices of the United States Army*, 298; Heitman, *Historical Register* I, 399; and http://ahsl.arizona.edu/spec-coll/personal-names/egan-peter-ralph...
133. As a matter of fact, Kennedy, a native of Ireland, served as a first lieutenant in Company I of the First California Volunteer Cavalry. He rose

to captain after only two weeks service at Tubac in 1864, the site of a former eighteenth century Spanish outpost. He remained in Arizona until ordered for mustering out on May 22, 1866. While his volunteer service ended there, Kennedy managed to secure a slot as the first lieutenant of Company G, Tenth U.S. Cavalry as it formed up at Fort Leavenworth, Kansas, in 1867. Three years later he had become a captain and company commander, which eventually led him back to Arizona when the regiment deployed there. Kennedy remained with the Tenth until promotion to major as of January 1, 1892. He resided in Los Angeles until his death on October 7, 1907. Altshuler, *Cavalry Yellow & Infantry Blue*, 189.

Regarding Tubac, the origin of the name remains obscure but it is certain that as early as 1741 the Spanish had arrived at the place where there were numerous adjacent Indian communities. By 1752 the Spanish established a presidio there to protect the region, and one of its commanders Juan Bautista de Anza achieved considerable note. More than a century later the place had been long abandoned, but all that changed when hundreds of miners poured into the area after the land became United States territory in 1856 with the completion of the Gadsden Purchase. Deserted once more with the outbreak of the Civil War, people again began to filter back during the following decade with a town site being laid out in 1878. Granger, *Arizona's Names*, 629–30.

134. Forrestine Cooper held a higher opinion of Mills, but her views stemmed from a different perspective as the child of a senior officer rather than a subordinate like Clarke. See Wilson, *Child of the Fighting Tenth*, 125, 160–61,170–71, and 251–52.
135. Merritt Barber was born on July 31, 1838. in Vermont. During the Civil War he enlisted as a private in Company E in his home state's Tenth Infantry on June 2, 1862 After the war he secured a commission in the peacetime army and moved up the military ladder, where for a brief time he served as a brigadier general of volunteers but within months retired on June 20, 1901. Barber died on April 19, 1906, at 67 years of age. Heitman, *Historical Register* I, 190; and https://www.findagrave.com/memorial/15916163/merritt-barber.
136. Smith, born on January 13, 1860, in Harrisonville, Missouri, was one of a pair of 1883 graduates, who like Clarke and Hughes from the following year, had been assigned to the Tenth U.S. Cavalry. Unlike Clarke and Hughes, however, who ranked last and second to last in the Class of 1884, Smith graduated a respectable twenty-seven out of

fifty-two. He did have another similarity with these two officers in that he started his active duty at Fort Davis, Texas, but only remained there for approximately two weeks when he was sent to Camp Rice. When the Tenth made its way to Arizona, Smith bounced from Forts Verde, Apache, and Grant and was in the field, and did a stint on special duty at the headquarters Department of Arizona. He went with the regiment to Cuba, where during the battle at Santiago on July 1, 1898, Smith, while commanding and leading his troop, was killed in the assault at age 38 afterwards being laid to rest at Arlington National Cemetery. Cullum, *Biographical Register of the Officers and Graduates of the United States Military Academy*, III, 37; and V, 377.

137. PHC to His Mother, December 16, 1886 Box 1, PHC Papers.
138. PHC to His Mother, December 29, 1886, Box 1, PHC Papers.
139. As published in Hassrick, *Frederic Remington: A Catalogue Raisonne II*, 106.

Notes to Chapter 6

1. Republished from the New York *Times* in the St. John, Arizona *Herald*, November 22, 1888; and Altshuler, *Starting with Defiance*, 7.
2. Faust and Randall, *Life at Post*, 71.
3. PHC to His Mother, January 19, 1887, Box 2, PHC Papers.
4. Examples of courts martial on which Clarke served included September 3, 1888, *A&NJ*; September 8, 1888, 27; November 1, 1888 *Arizona Weekly Citizen* (Tucson) November 3, 1888, 3; and June 25, 1888 *ANJ* June 30, 1888. 975. Faust and Randall, *Life at Post*, 76–78, summarizes the courts-martial process.
5. PHC to His Mother, January 30, 1887, Box 2, PHC Papers.
6. Faust and Randall, *Life at Post*, 93.
7. As indicated by the map accompanying Henry P. Walker and Don Bufkin, *Historical Atlas of Arizona*, 2nd ed. (Norman: University of Oklahoma Press, 1986), 37, a half dozen military installations in Arizona closed and by "1920 Fort Huachuca was the only active regular army post in Arizona."
8. Here Clarke also reflected the fact that "well after the turn-of-the-century, the senior officers of the Army were Civil War veterans. Most of these men were technically competent but generally set in their ways. As a group, they were also remarkably long-lived and thus impeded advancement of their juniors. Consequently, officers who entered service after

the Civil War have very limited prospects. Interested in their profession and the Army as an institution, this course of junior officers promoted professional development and a number of reforms that transformed the Army after 1898," changes that Clarke would not live to see. Shrader, *Reference Guide to United States Military History*, 12.

9. Hutton and Ball, *Soldiers West*, 308.
10. McChristian, *Garrison Tangles*, 27.
11. PHC to His Mother, February 3, 1887, Box 2, PHC Papers.
12. One example of money changing hands for a swap between regiments with the understanding that an extra monetary incentive would be required if the transaction meant service in a black regiment was an advertisement that appeared in *ANJ*, January 21, 1871, 364, which read: "LIBERAL INDUCEMENTS OFFERED BY A captain of colored infantry for transfer with a captain of a white regiment in either arm of service. Address stating terms. 'T.G. 8.'"
13. Arthur M. Schlesinger, Jr., *The Almanac of American History* (New York: Barnes and Noble Books, 1993), 319 and 363–64.
14. Schlesinger, *The Almanac of American History*, 360–61.
15. Matloff, *American Military History*, 318. The concept of concentration appeared as early as mid-1880s, while Lieutenant General William T. Sherman still commanded the U.S. Army. See for example *ARSW*, 1886, I, 5, which read in part: "by the abandonment of small, unimportant, and inconvenient posts now occupied for shelter merely, and by concentrating the troops in larger numbers at these new and other important places, it is hoped that good results will be obtained, not only in their discipline, but in reduced cost of maintaining them." Efforts to achieve the consolidation and closure of military posts gained momentum under Sherman's successors, such as Major General John Schofield who in 1888 wrote: "Substantial progress is being made toward a solution of the great Indian problem. Danger of savage warfare is continually diminishing, and the time is not very distant when, it may be hoped, that danger may disappear. But for the present and near future increased vigilance, caution, and preparation are and will be necessary, for the reason that the rich settlements now surrounding the Indian reservations render possible greater destruction of life and property in a few days than was formerly possible during a long period of hostilities. Hence the military posts, on and near the great Indian reservations, should be strengthened, while smaller ones, no longer necessary, should be broken up. Considerable

appropriations of money will yet be required to carry out this policy. But the wisdom and ultimate economy of the policy are manifest, and it has already received the sanction of Congress as well as that of the Executive. I recommend that liberal appropriations be made to complete the work so well begun." *ARSW*, 1888, I, 69

16. PHC to His Mother, March 2, 1887, Box 2, PHC Papers.
17. To date the only piece of correspondence from Remington to Clarke (which as noted he always spelled as Clark) and vice versa written prior to November 1887 was dated in August and sent to Clarke in North Haley, Quebec, indicating the lieutenant was well enough to travel to Canada yet stated he was not sufficiently healed to return to duty at Fort Grant. Frederic Remington to Powhatan Clark[e], August 6, 1887, Box 7, PHC Papers.
18. Powhatan PHC to His Father, March 13, 1887, Box 2, PHC Papers; and Altschuler, *Cavalry Yellow & Infantry Blue*, 240–41.
19. *ARSW, 1887*, I, 159.
20. *ARSW, 1887*, I, 159.
21. RG 94, Office of the Adjutant General, Entry 297, Box 908, ACP 3760, 1884 Clarke, Powhatan, NARA.
22. PHC to His Father, May 23, 1887, Box 2, PHC Papers.
23. PHC to His Father, June 1, 1887, PHC Papers.
24. PHC to His Father, June 2, 1887, PHC Papers.
25. PHC to His Mother, June 14, 1887, PHC Papers.
26. Frederic Remington to Powhatan Clark[e], undated, Box 7, PHC Papers.
27. See for instance: "The extension of leave on account of sickness granted 2d Lieut. Powhatan H. Clarke is further extended three days on account of sickness." (S. O., October 18. H. Q. A.). *A&NJ*, October 22, 1887, 242.
28. Among his excursions was one to West Point. "USMA Lieut. Powhatan Clarke 10th Cavalry dropped into see his friends last Sunday." *ANJ*, September 17, 1887, 143, as well as a visit to St. Louis. PHC to His Father, October 22, 1887, Box 2, PHC Papers.
29. PHC to His Mother, October 26, 1887, Box 2, PHC Papers.
30. Powhatan Clarke, "A Hot Trail," *Cosmopolitan Magazine* 16, no. 6 (October 1894): 716.
31. PHC to His Mother, October 31, 1887, Box 2, PHC Papers.
32. Established in 1826 Jefferson Barracks was one of the earliest U.S. Army installations established in the Trans-Mississippi West. After the Civil War Jefferson Barracks became the recruit depot that funneled

replacements to posts in the various western territories and states. Marc E. Kollbaum, *Gateway to the West: The History of Jefferson Barracks from 1826–1894* (St. Louis: Friends of Jefferson Barracks, 2001).

33. As quoted in McChristian, *Regular Army O!*, 421.
34. *A&NJ*, February 14, 1887, 576.
35. Coffman, *The Old Army*, 282. Also see Nelson Appleton Miles, *Personal Recollections of General Nelson A. Miles Embracing a Brief View of the Civil War, or from New England to the Golden Gate: and the Story of his Indian Campaigns, with Comments on the Exploration, Development and Progress of Our Western Empire* (Chicago: Werner, 1897), 533–44 for more on Miles's approach to training after the Geronimo Campaign.
36. PHC to His Father, November 7, 1887 Box 2, PHC Papers.
37. Bear Springs and the Gila Valley, also known as Safford Valley, are in Graham County. Granger, *Arizona Place Names*, 53 and 260.
38. PHC to His Mother, November 12, 1887, Box 2, PHC Papers.
39. PHC to His Mother, November 13, 1887, Box 2, PHC Papers.
40. Stallard, *Glittering Misery*, 94–95; and 98–99.
41. Frederic Remington to Powhatan Clark[e], November 3, 1887, Box 7, PHC Papers. Again, drawing on an anonymous writer, who was a fellow which officer commanding black troops he remarked having learned to take "all prejudices, remarks, slurs, etc., good humoredly." *A&NJ*, February 14, 1887, 576. Perhaps Clarke developed s similar thick skin in this regard.
42. Frederic Remington to Powhatan Clark[e], [December ?] 10, 1887, Box 7, PHC Papers.
43. Schlesinger, *The Almanac of American History*, 354 and 355–56. Ultimately Republican Benjamin Harrison would oppose Grover Cleveland and return a GOP Civil War veteran as commander in chief.
44. Clarke had indicated Remington's letters frequently mentioned "his friend Redwood also an artist but this correspondence has disappeared." PHC to His Mother, March 2, 1887, Box 2, PHC Papers.
45. PHC to His Father, December 2, 1887, Box 2, PHC Papers.
46. PHC to Mother, December 3, 1887, Box 2, PHC Papers. Given that Clarke seems to have been interested in an Episcopalian, Louisa Van Rensselaer, views on religion and marriage, a topic that became increasingly important to him, differed from his mother's stricter criteria for marriage within the Catholic faith.
47. PHC to His Mother, December 16, 1887, Box 2, PHC Papers.

Notes to Chapter 7

1. Knight, *Life and Manners in the Frontier Army*, 163.
2. Frederic Remington to Clark[e], January 3, 1888, Box 7, PHC Papers.
3. In fact, Remington had written and illustrated "Coursing Rabbits on the Plains," *Outing* (May 1887), 111 and 113, based on this pastime Clarke had shared with the artist previously.
4. PHC to His Mother, January 12, 1888, Box 2, PHC Papers.
5. The new colonel would not arrive for some time. This meant that from December 2, 1888 through August 20, 1890, Grierson's second in command, Lieutenant Colonel George C. Hunt, headed the regiment until Colonel J.K. Mizner replaced him. Glass, *The Tenth Cavalry*, 28 and 94. Mizner did not join the regiment immediately because as onc report indicated "Colonel J.K. Mizner, Tenth US Cavalry, who has been in Europe on leave, will go to Fort Apache, A. T., on his return, to take command of the post and his regiment." (Santa Fe) *Daily New Mexican*, May 21, 1890, 1.
6. PHC to His Mother, February 7, 1888, Box 2, PHC Papers.
7. PHC to His Father, February 25, 1888, Box 2, PHC Papers. Tres Alamos began in the late 1700s when farmers from Tucson presidio raised crops at the site along the San Pedro River. Spanish military protection failed to keep the area safe from Apache raids. Because of the threat abandonment followed, but in 1867 the U.S, Army established a picket post there with an officer and ten men. A decade became a crossroads for stage lines with stations on both sides of the San Pedro under Thomas Dunbar. Granger, *Arizona's Names*, 626.
8. PHC to His Father, February 27, 1888, Box 2, PHC Papers. Dr. G. King, who as early as 1876 lived at this steaming water source near Willcox, gave the name to Hooker's Hot Springs in Cochise County in honor of Henry C. Hooker, owner of the Sierra Bonita Ranch was nearby and Forrestine Cooper's father in law. Indians killed King "a mysterious person who lived in seclusion" in 1884. Granger, *Arizona's Names*, 304; and Frances E. Quebbeman, *Medicine in Territorial Arizona* (Phoenix: Arizona Historical Foundation, 1966), 352.
9. Born in Maine to a Scottish father and Irish mother, Thomas Jerome Dunbar arrived in the Tres Alamos and Tombstone during the 1870s. The oldest of three siblings in July 1874, Dunbar along with A. A. and Caroline Wilt bought the Cienaga Stage Station from James Sylvester Douglass for $1,500. (Tucson) *Arizona Citizen*, July 11, 1874; and

Pima County Deed Record Entry 2: 505–507.Thomas and his wife Agnes along with their firstborn son, Edward William (1871–1915), also ranched along the San Pedro River. Later, he persuaded one of his younger brothers, John Orlando Dunbar (1853–1923) to travel from Colorado to this often precarious "graveyard of the San Pedro." Thomas eventually presided over one of the largest ranches in the region located northeast of Benson.

Also see *Arizona Weekly Enterprise*, August 6, 1887, 2; *Daily Tombstone Epitaph*, May 5, 1887, 1; *Daily Tombstone Epitaph*, March 11, 1887, 1; Chuck Hornung, *Wyatt Earp's Cow-boy Campaign: The Bloody Restoration of Law and Order Along the Mexican Border, 1881* (Jefferson, NC: McFarland & Company, Inc., 2016), 26; Richard J. Hinton, *The Hand-Book to Arizona: Its Resources, History, Towns, Mines, Ruins, and Scenery* (San Francisco: Payot, Upham & Co., 1878), ix; and *Cochise County Legacy Project Treasurer's Office History 1881–2016* (https://www.cochise.az.gov/sites/default/.../Treasurers OfficeLegacyProject-History.pdf).

10. *A&NJ*, January 14, 1888, 487, reprints the proposed legislation that never was enacted.
11. Frederic Remington to Clark[e], March 13, 1888, Box 7, PHC Papers. Elsewhere Remington referred to Kemble as "the nigger artist" in that this author often depicted African Americans in his work. Frederic Remington to Cleark [*sic*], May 3, 1888, Box 7, PHC Papers.
12. PHC to His Father, March 24, 1888, Box 2, PHC Papers.
13. Frederic Remington to Powhatan Clark(e), April 3, 1888, Box 7, PHC Papers. For the complete text of this and all correspondence between Remington and Clarke consult: Splete and Splete, *Frederic Remington—Selected Letters*, 41–51; 61–67; 70–75; 87–93; 95–106; 111–29; 142–46; 150–51 159–66; 168–75.
14. Here Remington used an archaic phrase for horse soldier (dragoon) as did fellow illustrator, predecessor, and in some ways rival, Rufus Zogbaum for the title of his book, *Horse, Foot, and Dragoons* (New York: Harpers & Brother, 1887) contrasted British, French, German, and U.S. troops with a narrative based on travel and study in Europe and the West. Taft, *Artists and Illustrators of the Old West*, 183–93; 347; 351; and 359 provides brief information about this now nearly forgotten but formerly well-known illustrator. Fortunately, a detailed albeit unpublished biography exists by Janet Howard Ruhnke, "Impressions from Sketchpad and Notebook:

A Biographical View of Rufus Fairchild Zogbaum" (MA Thesis, University of San Diego, 1976).

15. Frederic Remington to Powhatan Clark(e), April 11, 1888, Box 7, PHC Papers.
16. Kathryn Kalinak, *How the West Was Sung: Music in the Westerns of John Ford* (Berkeley: University of California Press, 2007), 192 and 231 n46.
17. Tom Phillips, "Sobriquet: A Chronological Commentary on the Name 'Buffalo Soldier,'" *The Journal of America's Military Past* 35 No. 2 (Spring/Summer 2010): 5–30, provides an exhaustive study of the term and its malleable meaning. Also so Frank N. Schubert, "Buffalo Soldiers: Myth and Reality," *Army History: The Professional Bulletin of Army History* (Spring 2001): 13–18.
18. PHC to His Father, May 4, 1888, Box 2, PHC Papers. Before being sent out on what may have been a punitive assignment, Clarke along with almost every officer at Fort Grant sat on a series of courts martial on May 2., 1888. *A&NJ*, June 30, 1888, 975.
19. Founded by a decedent of eighteenth-century Tucson presidial soldier Antonio Campo Soza, El Rancho de los Sosa was located just southeast of Redington on the east bank of San Pedro. The family resided there from the late 1870s and grew such crops as "alfalfa, corn, wheat, barley, lentils, peanuts, peas, yams, and garbanzos" plus tried tobacco. Patricia Preciado Martin, comp., *Beloved Land: An Oral History of Mexican Americans in Southern Arizona* (Tucson: University of Arizona Press, 2004), 41 and 44; and Soza Family Collection, MS 0750, Box 1, Folder 12. Arizona Historical Society, Tucson.
20. These remarks appeared in a few pages interleafed with PHC to His Mother, January 12, 1889, Box 2, PHC Papers, contain no opening page or pages, but because of the mention of Smither's retirement, which took place during May 1888, along with Clarke's brief posting away from Fort Grant and return in time for Remington to join him that June the date of this partial letter placed it in May of 1888.
21. Frederic Remington to Powhatan Clark(e), May 18, 1888, Box 7, PHC Papers.
22. PHC to His Mother, May 21, 1888, Box 2, PHC Papers.
23. Martha Summerhayes, *Vanished Arizona: Recollections of Army Life* (Philadelphia: J.B. Lippincott Co., 1908), 9. In a June 14 letter from Fort Grant Remington informed his wife Eva he had arrived safely. In gratitude he told her: "We can never do enough for Clark [sic] should

he come East." He then let her know he would leave on a scout with Clarke soon, which meant being out of contact over the next two or three weeks. Splete and Splete, *Frederic Remington: Selected Letters*, 56. Remington's impressions of the trip are found in a pocket journal in marked "House Book," MS Collection 975, Kansas Historical Society, Topeka. This second pocket journal, as was the case for the one from 1886, is un-paginated. Page numbers in the forthcoming notes represent the sequence in which they appear after the first few leafs had been removed. Also note, despite the positive pronouncement about black soldiers, Remington was not color blind as another journal entry caustically indicated: "I witnessed an exhibition of American greatness today—a group—a Chinaman Apache negro soldier and white man." "House Book.," 11. What he seemingly failed to realize or most certainly did not appreciate was the diversity that existed in the West by the late 1800s.

24. "House Book," 2–3.
25. "House Book," 3–4.
26. "House Book," 4.
27. Patricia Stallard, ed., *Fanny Dunbar Corbusier: Recollections of Her Army Life, 1869–1908* (Norman: University of Oklahoma Press, 2003), 147. An interview with her youngest son "Willie" collaborates these statements. See Corbusier, William T. Interview October 1968, AV0060 RR, Arizona Historical Society, Tucson.
28. "House Book," 4.
29. "House Book," 6.
30. Fred to My Dear Little Gal, Fort Grant, Sunday [June 17, 1888], Frederic Remington Art Museum.
31. "House Book," 5.
32. "House Book," 6. Apparently Remington also accepted the conventional wisdom that black soldiers had to be led by white officers, maintaining the latter group "must be paternal with these people at all times." "House Book," 10.
33. "House Book," 7.
34. "House Book," 7–8.
35. Dobak and Phillips, *The Black Regulars*, 58; and Langellier, *Fighting for Uncle Sam*, 132–33.
36. "House Book," 4 and 9–10.
37. "House Book," 10.
38. "House Book," 12–13.

39. "House Book," 14.
40. "House Book," 16.
41. "House Book," 17. On this same page Remington jotted down "10th Nubian Horse" a term that he would resurrect later.
42. See Frederic Remington to Eva Remington, Fort Grant, June 22, 1888, the original of which is in the Frederic Remington Art Museum, and a transcript of which appears in Splete, *Frederic Remington-Selected Letters*, 56–59, for his departure from Arizona with "blistered face" and a loss of twenty pounds. For details about other aspects of his trip to Texas and a mention of moving on to Fort Sill at the beginning of June read, ibid., 59–60.
43. Stallard, *Fanny Dunbar Corbusier*, 150. Also see *A&NJ*, September 15, 1888, 42. The article also listed among those present "were Lieut. -Col. Pearson, 24th Inf.; Colonel and Mrs. Mills, Tenth. Cavalry; Mrs. Viele, wife of Captain Viele, and sister, Miss E. Munroe; Mrs. Beck, wife of Captain Beck, and daughter, Miss Mamie Beck; Dr. and Mrs. Corbusier, Lieutenant and Mrs. Keene, Mr. and Mrs. John H. Norton, Mrs. Ducat, wife of Lieut. A. C. Ducat; Lieutenants James Watson, Hardeman, Albright, Johnson, Hall, Finley, Clarke and Dade, Dr. Johnson, Mr. Sheen and Mr. Claude Corbusier."
44. Frederic Remington to Powhatan Clark(e), September 11, 1888, Box 7, PHC Papers.
45. PHC to His Mother, October 18, 1888, Box 2, PHC Papers.
46. Blaine Peterson. Lamb, "Jewish Pioneers in Arizona, 1850–1920" (unpublished Ph.D. Dissertation, Arizona State University, 1982), provides additional details on this topic.
47. PHC to His Mother, October 25, 1888, Box 2, PHC Papers.
48. Frederic Remington to Powhatan Clark(e), October 25, 1888, Box 7, PHC Papers.
49. According to Peter Hassrick: "We do not have enough information to determine whether *The Alert* is the painting to which he referred, but we suspect so. The central figure may have been adapted from his *Sketch of a U. S. Cavalryman Made in Arizona* (cat. no. 208)." http://remington.centerofthewest.org/artworks/viewprivate/209.
50. *A&NJ*, November 10, 1888, 207.
51. PHC to His Father, November 9, 1888, Box 2, PHC Papers.
52. A white trooper with the Sixth U.S. Cavalry recorded his first hand impressions of Willcox as a "roaring frontier town. The dance hall was in full swing. Some of the soldiers had considerable 'tarantula juice'

under their belts and were in high spirits. The gambling tables were in high swing.... At one 'stud-horse poker' table I saw Chinamen, cowpunchers, Mexicans, Indians, colored troopers and men from my own troop, all taking a chance." It seemed that when it came to money the only color that matter was green. Anton Mazzanovich, *Trailing Geronimo* (Hollywood, CA: Privately Printed, 1931), 179–80.

53. Radbourne, *Mickey Free*, 193.
54. Dan L. Thrapp, *Al Sieber: Chief of Scouts* (Norman: University of Oklahoma Press, 1964), 324, contains a list of the many names associated with the Apache Kid as well as provides a biography of German born Sieber. For additional information on the Apache Kid see: Phyllis de la Garza, *The Apache Kid* (Tucson: Westernlore Press, 1995); Jess G. Hayes, *Apache Vengeance* (Albuquerque: University of New Mexico Press, 1954); Charles W. McKanna, Jr., *Renegade of Renegades: Court-Martial of Apache Kid* (Lubbock: Texas Tech University Press, 2009).
55. Radbourne, *Mickey Free*, 193.
56. Burns, *All My People Were Killed*, 40.
57. Radbourne, *Mickey Free*, 193.
58. Burns, *All My People Were Killed*, 40.
59. Consult De la Garza, *The Apache Kid*, 41–65; and McKanna, *Renegade of Renegades*, 82–144, for the court martial and appeal process.
60. For examples read: (Clifton)*Clarion*, November 14, 1889, 3; (Mineral Park) *Mohave County Miner*, November 17, 1888, 2; (Florence) *Arizona Weekly Enterprise*. November 17, 188, 3; and (Globe) *Silver Belt*, November 17, 1888, 4.
61. Renaud appears in the *Official Register of the United States. Consisting of a List of Officers and Employees in the Civil, Military and Naval Service on the First of 1889, Together with a List of Vessels Belong to the United States* (Washington, DC: Government Printing Office, 1889), 282, as a U.S. Army quartermaster agent at Benson. At various times he also carried on mercantile operations, served as president of the Tombstone Dragoon Mining and Smelting Company founded in 1902 and had a livestock brand registered to him. *The Copper Handbook: A Manual of the Copper Industry of the World* (Houghton: MI: Horace J. Stevens, 1907) 7, 569–70; and *Brands and Marks of Cattle, Horses, Sheep Goats and Hogs as They Appear in the Office of the Live Stock Sanitary Board of Arizona at Phoenix, Arizona* (Phoenix: Livestock Sanitary Board of Arizona, 1908), 270.

62. The year before Clarke and his men nearly took part in a shootout with cattlemen from the Chiricahua Cattle Company the body of a murdered white soldier named Drake was found at the unoccupied Sulphur Spring ranch house of this same outfit. No clues existed as to the perpetrator or perpetrators who killed Drake, a military mail carrier between Forts Bowie and Huachuca. His corpse was found about a hundred yards from the ranch house with two bullet holes in the head, and another in the hip. "He was also robbed of his fire arms, money, blankets, etc." The paper went on to say "The murdered man is highly spoken of by none other than Mr. C. M. Renaud, 'who knew him well.'" (Tucson) *Weekly Citizen* October 8, 1887, 4.
63. Besides Arizona such racial tensions existed elsewhere including in Texas as underscored by Dobak and Phillips, *The Black Regulars*, 236–42.
64. Edward Arhelger Collection, MS1475, Box 4, 6, Arizona Historical Society, Tucson. Probably civilians in Arizona preferred other musical diversions from the black troops for their benefit such as "The minstrel performance, by members of the 10th Cavalry, at the Rink on Thursday night, attracted one of the finest audiences seen in Globe for some time, and the entertainment was very fair" (Globe) *Arizona Silver Belt*, December 22, 1888.
65. Frederic Remington to Clark(e), December 27, 1888, Box 7, PHC Papers. A brief reference to this incident indicated "The sergeant, who was shot by the negro soldier brought to Tucson last week and discharged for want of jurisdiction by U.S. courts, is recovering." *Arizona Weekly Citizen* December 29, 1888, 3.
66. Samuel and Samuels, *Frederic Remington—Selected Writings*, 66 concluded this illustration was published as one in Remington's article "Skirmish Drill of the New York State National Guard," *Harper's Weekly*, August 4, 1888. A number of details in the image of a New York guardsman's uniform and the uniform depicted in *Taps* make it unlikely that the above statement in *Frederic Remington—Selected Writings* is correct.
67. *A&NJ*, November 10, 1888, 207.
68. PHC to His Father, December 30, 1888, Box 2, PHC Papers.
69. PHC to His Father, January 9, 1889, Box 2, PHC Papers. Towering more than 10,000 feet in the background of Fort Grant, the Graham Mountains or Mount Graham was mentioned by army explorers in the 1840s and the 1850s. "As for whom it was name, no one can say

definitely." Other 19th century writers frequently called to peak and range "Sierra Bonita." Barnes, *Arizona Place Names*, 134–35.

70. (Globe) *Arizona Silver Belt*, December 22, 1888, 1.
71. PHC to His Mother, January 21, 1889, Box 2, PHC Papers.
72. For more on this complex and sometimes contentious officer consult Donald D. Connelly, *John M. Schofield and the Politics of Generalship* (Chapel Hill University of North Carolina Press, 2006).
73. Connelly, *John M. Schofield*, 417 n 25.
74. In 1888, when Nelson A. Miles moved on to San Francisco as commander of the Division of the Pacific while Headquarters of the Army General Orders No. 97 assigned Grierson command the Department of Arizona. By Orders No. 51 of December 1, 1888 from the Headquarters of the Tenth Cavalry the latter announced relinquishment of command of the regiment which he did after twenty-two years with the unit. He expressed his "deepest regret at being thus separated" from a military organization that had "been in the field and at the most isolated posts on the frontier; always in the vanguard of civilization and in contact with the most warlike and savage Indians…"Until August of 1890 the regiment's lieutenant colonel, George C. Hunt, commanded the Tenth. Glass, *The History of the Tenth Cavalry*, 28.
75. PHC to His Father, January 25, 1889, Box 2, PHC Papers.
76. Examples are found in Dobak and Phillips, *Black Regulars*, 18–19.
77. PHC to His Mother, February 8, 1889, Box 2, PHC Papers.
78. Son of a Mexican American War and Civil War veteran, William H. McKittrick (1862–1939) married Shafter's daughter Mary. He became one of the founders of the Arizona Cattlemen's Association, for which he served as president at one point. He had both ranching and oil interests in the Willcox area. During the Spanish American War McKittrick served on his father in law's staff in Cuba. Richard Schaus Collection, FM MSS 6, AHS (Tempe); and *Arizona Cattlelog* (May 1969), 37–38.
79. PHC to His Mother, February 19, 1889, Box 2, PHC Papers.
80. For examples of Clarke's persistent efforts from 1886 through 1889 to obtain a year's detached duty to study in France, including a letter of support from his father see: RG 94, Entry, 29, Box 908, 760 ACP 188, Clarke, Powhatan, 54; 82–88; 94, 96–97; 157; 160–64; 175–77; 181, 213–14; and 217. NARA.
81. In due course, Clarke's received a letter from the Headquarters of the Army Adjutant General's Office while he was on leave with family at

Harley, Canada, stating that the lieutenant's request "to be absent from his regiment "for one year for the purpose of attending the Cavalry School at Saumur, France, has been disapproved. Thomas Ward, Acting Adjutant General to 2d Lieut. Powhatan H. Clarke, August 21, 1889, Box 2, PHC Papers.

82. *A&NJ*, April 13, 1889, 659. The same page indicated "there is an unusual season of enjoyment for the young people of Apache as several young ladies, from their homes in civilization, have honored our garrison with their presence. The Misses Darst from St. Louis, and their cousin, Miss Green, are guests of Major and Mrs. McClellan. Miss Davis, niece of Capt. Wm. H. Davis, is visiting his family here, and Miss Roberta Latham, daughter of Col. R. B. Latham of Lincoln. Illinois, accompanied her cousins, Mrs. Wm. H. Beck and Miss Beck, wife and daughter of Capt. Beck, 10th Cavalry on their return to Fort Apache, where she expected to spend the summer." Adding to the list of women visiting their military family members was "Miss Johnson, sister of Lieut. Carter Johnson,10th Cavalry, has arrived in Apache, and welcomed as a member of our social circle. Mrs. Davis, widow of General Jeff. C. Davis, is a guest of her brother-in-law, Capt. Wm. H. Davis, and his wife" so the Davis household had a pair of guests under their roof. It may have been some if not all of these "young ladies spending a season with relatives" were among those "usually husband hunting" as Oliver Knight commented in his *Life and Manners of the Frontier Army*, 138. A.G. Bracket, "Our Frontier Forts," (Chicago) *Times*, September 13, 1897, 14, made a similar reference to the season when army posts became marketplaces for perspective brides. One of the entourage managed to do just that because Mary Louise Darst, one of the temporary members of the McClellans' household, would wed Second Lieutenant William Harvey Smith, the officer Clarke claimed was reputed to be the handsomest in the army. Altshuler, *Cavalry Yellow & Infantry Blue*, 311.
83. Frederic Remington to Clark[e], March 14, 1889, Box 7, PHC Papers.
84. Frederic Remington to Clark[e], April 2, 1889, Box 7, PHC Papers.
85. Clarke had mentioned a medical problem in an earlier letter to his mother. He began to pursue a sick leave of absence to treat "retinitis of the right eye" which Fort Thomas's post surgeon William Johnson diagnosed might spread to the left eye and extend to the optic nerve. He recommended a specialist and a change of climate "to prevent permanent disability." The process to obtain permission for Clarke to

travel to the East began April 14, 1889 and finally after working its way through the army bureaucracy received approval from the secretary of war on May, 18, 1889. RG 94, Entry, 29, Box 908, 760 ACP 188, Clarke, Powhatan, 181–84, NARA.

86. Frederic Remington to Clark[e], April 15, 1889, Box 7, PHC Papers.
87. Larry Ball, *Ambush at Bloody Run* (Tucson: Arizona Historical Society, 2000), 5. This monograph is a must to in order to understand this complex footnote in Southwestern history that "had developed political overtones almost from the start" along with racist and religious implications "plus personal animosities between court officials and attorneys…." Ball, *Ambush at Bloody Run*, 87.
88. Wham recommended Brown and Mays for Medals of Honor. On February 1, 1890, Secretary of War Redfield Proctor approved Wham's request along with the remainder of the detail receiving Certificates of Merit for their actions. Ball, *Ambush at Bloody Run*, 174–75.
89. Captain Thomas Lebo to Lt. Clarke 10th Cav, May 13, 1889, Box 2, PHC Papers.
90. Captain Thomas Lebo to Lt. Clarke 10th Cav May 14, 1889, Box 2, PHC Papers.
91. Captain Thomas Lebo to Lt. Clarke 10th Cav May 20, 1889, Box 2, Powhatan H. PHC Papers. Established late in the Civil War by General Orders No. 12, May 1, 1864, the post located two and a half miles south of the Gila River received its name from Arizona's first territorial governor, John Noble Goodwin. The post's purpose was to serve as an operational "base for a campaign against the Apaches." After the Civil War Regular Army troops arrived taking up station in May 1866. Sometime thereafter the location of the first garrison to a spot several miles west occurred and shortly thereafter the designation of the post changed from fort to camp. The need for the outpost declined to the degree that gradual abandonment began in 1870. The last troops departed on March 14, 1871. Some of the adobes remained intact however and in 1879 the commander of Fort Thomas instructed that blocks be "hauled from the ruins of Goodwin to use in building quarters on his post." Atshuler, *Starting with Defiance*, 27–28; and Brandes, *Frontier Military Posts of Arizona*, 32–33.
92. The leave began on May31 and lasted through September 30, 1889. RG 94, Entry, 29, Box 908, 760 ACP 1884, Clarke, Powhatan, 17. NARA.
93. PHC to His Mother, Undated letter written from St. Luke's Hospital, approximately June 13, 1889, Box 2, PHC Papers.

94. According to the *A&NJ*, May 25, 1889, 79, "LIEUTENANT P. H. CLARKE, 10th U. S. Cavalry, of San Carlos, will go abroad shortly for the summer, returning in September." In order to visit Canada, he had to gain permission from the War Department which he did in early July. *A&NJ*, July 20, 1889, 959.
95. *A&NJ*, September 8, 1889, 84 mentioned Clarke was at the U.S. Military Academy "for a few days' visiting." The same report mentioned the seemingly never present with the Tenth Cavalry, First Lieutenant. John Bigelow:, Jr., was "at his father's residence, the 'Squirrels'."
96. (Tucson) *Arizona Weekly Citizen*, November 3, 1888, 3.
97. Dr. Powhatan Clarke to His Son, November 8, 1889, Box 2, PHC Papers.
98. Frederic Remington to Clark[e], October 25, 1888, Box 7, PHC Papers. Because Clarke most likely have seen Remington on his leave from May through September 1889, he could have received the promised water color and sent the painting to his parents. If so, the piece is either a watercolor of a saber wielding buffalo soldier on horseback which is in the Missouri Historical Society's, or the piece has been lost.
99. Frederic Remington to Clark[e], December 1, 1889, Box 7, PHC Papers.
100. PHC to His Father, December 21, 1889, Box 2, PHC Papers.
101. Edward Arthur Dolph, *"Sound Off" Soldier Songs from Yankee Doddle to Parley Voo* (New York: Cosmopolitan Book Corporation, 1929), 563–66. For some of the other military tunes and their associated backgrounds which are used as chapter headings such as: *Army Blue* ("We'll bid farewell to 'Cadet Gray,' And don the 'Army Blue'"); *Dixie*; *Old Arizona Again*; *Dragoon Bold*; *Regular Army, O!* one of the choruses being: "We went to Arizona for to fight the Indians there"); *Girl I Left Behind*; and *Fiddler's Green*, see Dolph, *"Sound Off,"* 6–9; 25–26; 238–41; 456; 507–09; 552–54; and 576–70.
102. Whitman, *The Troopers*, 65.
103. For more on this high ranking German general officer consult Max Von Versen, *Reisen in Amerika Und Der SudamerikanischeKreig* (Breslau, Germany: M. Malzer, 1872); and Werthern, Alfred Hermann Thilo, Freiherr von. *General von Versen: Ein Militärisches Zeit und Lebensbild. Aus Hinterlassenen Briefen und Aufzeichnungen Zusammengestellt*. Berlin: E.S. Mittler, 1898.
104. Wilson, *Child of the Fighting Tenth*, 220–22.

Notes to Chapter 8

1. Frederic Remington to Clark[e], January 9, 1890, Box 7, PHC Papers.
2. Utley, *The Commanders*, 117.
3. Frederic Remington to Clark[e], January 30, 1890, Box 7, PHC Papers.
4. PHC to His Mother, February 14, 1890, Box 2, PHC Papers.
5. James Clemens's wife, the former Elizabeth Brown Mullanphy, also was from one of the oldest families in English speaking St. Louis. "The Family of James Clemens of Buffalo Township, Washington County, Pa." http://chartiers.com/raybell/1981-clemens2.html..
6. PHC to His Mother, January 18, 1890, Box 2, PHC Papers. In part this letter appears to be Clarke's response to mother's correspondence from the previous week. See, Louise PHC to His Son, January 10, 1890, Box 2, PHC Papers.
7. PHC to His Mother, January 27, 1890, Box 2, PHC Papers.
8. Dr. Powhatan Clarke to His Son, February 20, 1890, Box 2, PHC Papers.
9. PHC to His Mother, January 27, 1890, Box 2, PHC Papers.
10. Dr. Powhatan PHC to His Son, February 20, 1890, Box 2, PHC Papers.
11. Frederic Remington to Clark[e], March 5, 1890, Box 7, PHC Papers.
12. Frederic Remington to Clark[e], March (c. 30), 1890, Box 7, PHC Papers.
13. Named after Benjamin Wingate, a Union officer who died of wounds received at the at the Battle of Valverde in 1862, Fort Wingate, New Mexico was established by executive order dated February 18, 1870, preserving 100 square miles from the public domain in in McKinley County. In 1881 another executive order added 30 more square miles for the purpose of supplying the post with timber and other necessities. Ultimately the Atchison, Topeka & Santa Fe Railroad served the post. *United States Military Reservations*, 253–54. Also see *History of Fort Wingate Depot, Fort Fauntleroy and Lyon*, https://www.ftwingate.org/docs/pub/History_FortWingate.pdf.
14. Glass, *The Tenth Cavalry*, 28.
15. PHC to His Mother, January 18, 1890, Box 2, PHC Papers.
16. Kühn, *Chronicles of War*, 296.Interestingly, Reynold's successes had placed an advertisement much earlier related to this matter which offered: "REWARD! I will pay a liberal reward for the return of the watch word by Sheriff Glenn Reynolds at the time he was killed by Indian convicts, near Riverside, on the second inst. The watch case is

of heavy gold, and handsomely chase, and engraved on the front and outside with the letters "G. R." in monogram. On the inside of the case, both front and back, the full name, "Glenn Reynolds," was engraved. Attached to the watch was a massive gold chain of block links. Any information that will lead to the recovery of either or both will be paid for by me. Jerry Ryan. Sheriff, Gila County, – Globe. November 16." (Globe) *Arizona Silver Belt*, March 1, 1890, 3.

17. Kühn, *Chronicles of War*, 297; and *A&NJ*, April 5, 1890, 599. The son of a Russian father and German mother, as a youth Kosterlitzsky lived in both countries. He would attend military school in St. Petersburg, Russia. Afterwards he spent a brief time with the Russian Navy from which he deserted during a cruise which put into Cabello, Venezuela. He made his way north to Mexico where in the 1870s he joined the army of that nation. See Thrapp, *Frontier Biography*, 795–96; and Cornelius C. Smith, Jr., *Emilio Kosterlitzsky: Eagle of Sonora and the Southwest Border* (Glendale, CA: Arthur H. Clark Co., 1970).
18. Hayes, *Apache Vengeance*, 162–63.
19. Kühn, *Chronicles of War*, 297.
20. (New York) *Herald*, May 12, 1892, 5. As an example of Clarke's dedication to improve his troops' performance as horsemen he struggled "with Lebo to get more drill" time, but the captain tended to take a laissez faire attitude toward his junior lieutenant's urgings. PHC to His Mother, January 27, 1890, Box 2, PHC Papers.
21. Kühn, *Chronicles of War*, 297. Little is known of George Roggenstroh other than a mention that he was a cattleman who bought livestock in Willcox. (Florence) *Arizona Weekly Enterprise*, July 26, 1890, 1.
22. (Tucson) *El Fronterizo*, March 15, 1890, 1. This same issue carried several other fairly lengthy articles related to the subject including opposition in Mexico to a plan to bring Geronimo and many other Apaches to Fort Sill, Indian Territory from their imprisonment far to the east.
23. (Tucson) *Arizona Weekly Citizen*, March 15, 1890, 1.
24. As Timothy Braatz pointed out in the Foreword to Burns, *All My People Were Killed*, ii–iii, there were four peoples that made up the group now generally referred to as Yavapai. These were the Kewevkapaya, Tolkapaya, Wipukpaya, and Yavape,
25. Sweeny, *From Cochise to Geronimo*, 268.
26. (Globe) *Arizona Silver Belt*, March, 15, 1890, 3.

27. (Florence) *Arizona Weekly Enterprise*, March 15, 1890, 2. Also see (St. Johns) *Herald*, March 20, 1890, 2; and *A&NJ*, March 15, 1890, 543.
28. Downey and Jacobsen, *Red Bluecoats*, 167. Sadly, the last observation about loving liquor may have proven Rowdy's downfall. While he had been praised for "faithfulness, zeal, and bulldog tenacity" such admirable qualities did not prevent him from being gunned down on March 31, 1893, when in a saloon near Fort Grant the intoxicated scout "decided to 'clean out' the place, As he ran around with a cocked Winchester … the bartender killed him with a blast from his shotgun." Phyliss de la Garza, *The Apache Kid* (Tucson: Westernlore Press, 1996), 182, n9.
29. (Globe) *Arizona Silver Belt*, March 29, 1890, 3.
30. Johnson, *No Greater Calling*, 358. McBryar is of particular note because of his association with Troop K of the Tenth U.S. Cavalry. Frank N. Schubert, *Black Valor: Buffalo Soldiers and the Medal of Honor, 1870–1898* (Wilmington, DE: Scholarly Resources Inc., 1997), 101–15; 150, 155, 158, 161, 166–67, outlines the career of this dedicated professional. Also read *Arizona Silver Belt*, June 21, 1890, 3, which indicated the presentation of the Medal of Honor to Rowdy on the parade ground at Fort Grant and the bestowal of brevet ranks of captain and first lieutenant on Watson and Clarke respectively, at the same ceremony. Brevet rank, from the French *brevis* or brief, "meant a temporary rank higher than an officer's nominal link as it appeared on the seniority list," but he was not to enjoy the "'command, pay and emolument'" of such rank. Whitman, *The Troopers*, 122–23. The confusing custom ultimately gave way to other means to recognize service such as various medals for valor, campaigns, and similar reasons that began to appear in the early Twentieth Century. In addition, the system brevets, given in the absence of medals because only the Medal of Honor existed prior to 1905, "became so confusing that the War Department issued orders to abolish the practice, but officers continued to be addressed by their brevets…." Utley, *The Commanders*, 4.
31. Schubert, *Black Valor*, 106, 194 n 11, and 195 n12.
32. Grierson also must have been pleased of a mention in the Santa Fe *Daily New Mexican*, March 22, 1890, 4, that he was the commander officer for Watson and Clarke and made it appear that their colonel deserved some credit for the success of his two subordinates.
33. *ARSW 1890* I, 167. Also, for a synopsis of the operation and Grierson's comments consult *A&NJ*, April 5, 1890, 599. Also note, both officers wrote of this firefight. The first, which received considerable assistance

from Frederic Remington, was Powhatan Clarke, "A Hot Trail," *Cosmopolitan Magazine* 16, no. 6 (October 1894): 706–16; and James W. Watson, "Scouting in Arizona," *Journal of the U.S. Cavalry Association* 10 (June 1897): 128–134. Curiously, Remington's own attempt to narrate the tale of what happened to the Kid's group, "How an Apache War Was Won," remained unpublished in his lifetime. McCracken, *Frederic Remington's Own West*, 49–61. In the story he mentions only Watson. In turn, Watson and Clarke do not mention McBryar by name although they refer to Rowdy.

34. *A&NJ*, March 15, 1890, 542.This was for a department wide heliograph practice that is detailed in William J. Volkmar, *Report of the Practice of the Heliograph System, Department of Arizona in May1890* (Washington, DC: Office of the Chief of Signal Corps, 1890).
35. PHC to His Father, March 16, 1890, Box 2, PHC Papers.
36. Dr. Powhatan Clarke to His Son, March 26, 1890, Box 2, PHC Papers.
37. Dr. Powhatan Clarke to His Son, April 1, 1890, Box 2, PHC Papers.
38. PHC to His Mother, April 5, 1890, Box 2, PHC Papers.
39. Louise Clarke to Her Son, April 5, 1890, Box 2, PHC Papers.
40. Frederic Remington to Clark[e], April 9, 1890, Box 7, PHC Papers.
41. PHC to His Mother, April 10, 1890, Box 2, PHC Papers.
42. General Orders No. 100, Adjutant General's Officer, December 17, 1891.
43. In this scheme Clarke hoped the former Elizabeth Brown Harney, daughter of noted and recently deceased General William S. Harney would pave the way for a French assignment. Powhatan's mother had attended school with Miss Harney as young students in Paris. They were distantly connected by marriage and "intimate friends." Miss Harney had married a French army officer, Baron de Noue of Paris, and when he died, she would marry another officer, the Baron de Este. (New York) *Sun*, January 6, 1890, 2. Given these connections Clarke was not off the mark in his supposition that the widowed Baroness de Noue might be of assistance.
44. Dr. Powhatan Clarke to His Son, May 14, 1890, Box 2, PHC Papers.
45. "P.H. Clarke, Lieut. 10th Cav. Please Return," Journal, May (no date), 1890, Box 5, PHC Papers. As to the reference to some of the Wham payroll perpetrators it seems that some of them had not abandoned their larcenous ways. For instance, "Lyman and Ed Follett were convicted of cattle stealing in the District Court and Solomonville the last week, and sentenced to two years each in the Territorial prison. They have

made an appeal to the Supreme Court, and in the meantime are out on bail." (Tucson) *Arizona Weekly Citizen*, May 31, 1890, 4. Although Clarke may have been incorrect about Gilbert and Wilfred Webb being involved in cattle theft, the pair have to post a "$500 bond each to appear and answer to the grand jury of Graham County upon the charge of defrauding School District Number Six of $160." (Globe) *Arizona Silver Belt*, June 7, 1890, 2.

46. Ash Creek is approximately seven and half miles northwest of Mount Graham and Fort Thomas. Granger, *Arizona Names*, 34.
47. "P.H. Clarke, Lieut. 10th Cav. Please Return," Journal, May 17–19, 1890, Box 5, PHC Papers.
48. "P.H. Clarke, Lieut. 10th Cav. Please Return," Journal, June 20,1890, Box 5, PHC Papers.
49. Eva Remington to Clarke, May 24, 1890, Box 7, PHC Papers.
50. Frederic Remington to Clark[e], June 5, 1890, Box 7, PHC Papers.
51. Dr. Powhatan Clarke to His Son, June 2, 1890, Box 2, PHC Papers.
52. (Tombstone) *Epitaph*, May 31, 1890, 3.
53. (Globe) *Arizona Silver Belt*, June 21, 1890, 3.
54. PHC to His Father, June 30, 1890, Box 2, PHC Papers.
55. Altshuler, *Starting with Defiance*, 9, refers to a description of an army inspector of Fort Apache.
56. "P.H. Clarke, Lieut. 10th Cav. Please Return," Journal, June 21, 1890, Box 5, PHC Papers. According to the Florence *Arizona Weekly Enterprise*, July 12, 1890, 3, Clarke had gathered thirty scouts.
57. "P.H. Clarke, Lieut. 10th Cav. Please Return," Journal, July 3–6, 1890, Box 5, PHC Papers. Cedar Springs in Graham County was headquarters for the Norton & Stewart Cattle Co. It was there on October 2, 1882 that an engagement between troops versus Natchez, Juh and others who had fled San Carlos. The site also was known as "Battleground" because of this fight. Granger, *Arizona's Names*, 132.11
58. PHC to His Father, July 5, 1890, Box 2, PHC Papers.
59. "P.H. Clarke, Lieut. 10th Cav. Please Return," Journal, July 7, 1890, Box 5, PHC Papers.
60. Form Number One War Department Signal Service USA United States Telegraphy July 17, 1890 Department Headquarters to Lieut. P.H. Clarke, July 17, 1890, Box 5, PHC Papers. The same telegram authorized Clarke while his "command is maintained at its present strength equal to a company of scouts … to hire one civilian packer at $50 per month and report his name an appointment to chief quartermaster." Extract copy

endorsement of communication to Second Lieut. P.H. Clarke 10th cavalry commanding detachment 10th Cavalry and Indian scouts from Headquarters the Division of the Pacific July 14, 1890, referred this an action to the commander of the Department of Arizona with the instructions that "the Mexican who sold liquor two scouts should be presented in accordance with law by command of Maj. Gen. Miles."

61. Form Number One War Department Signal Service USA United States Telegraphy W.E. Ewell to Lieut. Clarke July 8, 1890, Box 5, PHC Papers, in which he asked from Willcox: "Shall I remain here or come to Bowie tomorrow"? Likewise, Clarke learned at that time that Lieutenant Stockle was to be "assigned to outfit" and would join them at Fort Bowie. Department of Arizona Assistant Adjutant General Volkmar.to Commanding Officer Fort Apache, July 7, 1890, ibid., indicated that Lieutenant Stockle was to report to "Clarke for duty with his detachment at Ft. Bowie or such other place" as Clarke transmitted via telegraph. Form Number One War Department Signal Service USA United States Telegraphy Lieutenant Stockle to Lieutenant Clarke, July 9, 1890, read: "Will start to Bowie July 16." Evidently Stockle had delayed in deploying from Fort Apache as he was supposed to have left on June 11. Form Number One War Department Signal Service USA United States Telegraphy Carter Johnson to P.H. Clarke, July 10, 1890, Box 5, PHC Papers.
62. Troops from Fort Bowie used nearby Pinery Canyon in Cochise County as a source of timber. For a brief period, it served as the agency for the Chiricahua Apaches. A stream of the same name flows through the canyon. Graham, *Arizona's Names*, 485–86.
63. The foregoing was extracted from: "P.H. Clarke, Lieut. 10th Cav. Please Return," Journal, July 8–12, 1890, Box 5, PHC Papers.
64. Form Number One War Department Signal Service USA United States Telegraphy Carter Johnson to P.H. Clarke, July 10, 1890, Box 5, PHC Papers.
65. Form Number One War Department Signal Service USA United States Telegraphy James Watson to P.H. Clarke, July 11, 1890, Box 5, PHC Papers.
66. (Globe) *Arizona Silver Belt*, May8.10, 1890, 2. For further information see Kühn, *Chronicles of War*, 292, 296; 299; 300–01; 303; and 305–06; Radbourne, *Mickey Free*, 202–03' and Allan Radbourne, "In Pursuit of Ma-say: Lieutenant River's Report," English Westerners' *Tally Sheet* 47 (Spring 2001): 33–38.

67. (Globe) *Arizona Silver Belt*, May 10, 1890, 2.
68. (Globe) *Arizona Silver Belt*, April 5, 1890,3; and June 7, 1890, 2.
69. In the early 1870s, when General George Stoneman recommended closure of several military posts in Arizona Territory, which would have resulted in a severe economic impact on a wide array of contractors who supplies these garrisons with nearly everything they needed to operate, locals strongly opposed the plan. See John P. Langellier, "Camp Grant Affair, 1871: Milestone in Federal Indian Policy?" *Military History of Texas and the Southwest* 15 No. 2 (1979): 17–30.
70. Form Number One War Department Signal Service USA United States Telegraph Carter Johnson to P.H Clarke, July 12, 1890, Box 5, PHC Papers.
71. Guadalupe Cañon in Cochise County offered a natural smuggling route in the 1870s and 1880s for Mexican and American rustler, as well as a prime site for Apache attacks. Granger, *Arizona's Names*, 280
72. Cloverdale in Hidalgo County lies just east of the Arizona-New Mexico line and above the Mexican border. A man named Bob Anderson founded a community there in the early 1890s. The place was so named because of the grass covering the area. Pearce, *New Mexico Place Names*, 37.
73. Animas, New Mexico, in Hidalgo County took its name from the Spanish for "departed souls." A Mexican community started here in 1843 but this had been the previous site of an Indian village. Pearce, *New Mexico Place Names*, 8.
74. The foregoing was extracted from: "P.H. Clarke, Lieut. 10th Cav. Please Return," Journal, July 13–14, 1890, Box 5, PHC Papers.
75. John Horton Slaughter, like Clarke was a Louisiana native who headed west, in his case with the family who settled in Texas. At an early age he became a cowboy working with his father Ben Slaughter. During the Civil War he served as a Confederate soldier followed by a stint with the Texas Rangers. In the 18709s he moved to New Mexico and by the next decade was off to Arizona where he resided in Tombstone for a short while before purchasing the San Bernardino Ranch in 1884. Two years later he was elected Sherriff of Cochise County. By 1907 he became of member of the territorial legislature. Slaughter died in 1922 and according to one biographer "will long be remembered." Thrapp, *Encyclopedia of Frontier Biography*, II, 320–21. The standard biography remains Allen A. Erwin, *The Southwest of John Horton*

Slaughter (Glendale, CA: Arthur H. Clark Co., 1965). As for their ranch, it became the headquarters of a cattle empire. Ann E. Huston, "San Bernardino Ranch/John H. Slaughter Ranch," (February 1986) National Register of Historic Places Inventory-Nomination Form; and Mary Whatley Clarke, *The Slaughter Ranches and Their Makers* (Austin: Jenkins Publishing Co., 1979).

76. (Florence) *Arizona Weekly Enterprise*, July 19, 1890, 3.
77. Form Number 1 War Department Signal Service Telegram July 7, 1890; and Form Number One War Department Signal Service, July 9, 1890, updated Clarke that Stockle would arrive in July 16, Box 5, PHC Papers.
78. Form Numbcr One War Department Signal Service, July 8, 1890, Box 5, PHC Papers, queried "is there a chance to get a good pony about Bowie for Stockle?"
79. Form Number One War Department Signal Service, from Headquarters Department of Arizona, Los Angeles, California to Lieut. Clarke 10th Cavalry Fort Bowie A.T, July 8, 1890, Box 5, PHC Papers.
80. General Crook had banned the making of this "Apache intoxicant" but old customs died hard, plus there were other options for spirits beside ones produced by the Apaches themselves. Porter, *Paper Medicine Man*, 168.
81. The foregoing was extracted from: "P.H. Clarke, Lieut. 10'th Cav. Please Return," Journal, July 20, 1890, Box 5, PHC Papers. As Clarke stated on July 17, Carter Johnson's roving command engaged with about five Apaches some thirty-five miles northeast from San Carlos near Gila Peak and Ash Creek. Johnson's force killed Pash-ten-tah (aka Bach-e-on-al) and wounded Say-es, whom they took prisoner. Another Apache who escaped during the firefight, Curley, surrender the following day. Slowly the Kid's accomplices and others who had bolted the reservation were being eliminated. Kühn, *Chronicles of War*, 299. According to the Florence *Arizona Weekly Enterprise*, August 23, 1890, 3, Deputy Sheriff Peter R. Young with a guard of a dozen troops under Lieut. R.E.L. Michie "accompanied the officer and prisoner [Say-es] from San Carlos to Florence. It was there that Say-es "confessed that he held Sheriff Reynolds while Kid shot him, but it is believed that he was the one that did the shooting."

    (Florence) *Arizona Weekly Enterprise*, July 21, 1890, ibid. (Tombstone) *Epitaph*., March 20, 1892, 6, recorded "Brannock Riggs one of the earliest pioneers in Sulphur Valley." On September 19, 1887 the

Sulphur Springs Valley commenced its rodeo at his ranch. (Florence) *Arizona Weekly Enterprise*, September 10, 1887, 2.

82. The foregoing was extracted from: "P.H. Clarke, Lieut. 10'th Cav. Please Return," Journal, July 22–24, 1890 Box 5, PHC Papers.
83. PHC to His Father, July 26, 1890, Box 2, PHC Papers.
84. Telegram to 2nd Lieut. P.H. Clarke, 10th Cavalry, Fort Bowie, Arizona from Assistant Adjutant General Department of Arizona, July 2, 1890, Box 5, PHC Papers.
85. Translation special correspondence from Governor of the State of Sonora to Brig. Gen. B.H. Grierson, July 4, 1890, Box 5, PHC Papers.
86. Letter from Headquarters Division of the Pacific San Francisco California to Commanding General Department of Arizona, July 7, 1890, Box 5, PHC Papers.
87. "P.H. Clarke, Lieut. 10th Cav. Please Return," Journal, July 28, 1890, Box 5, PHC Papers. PHC to His Father, July 26, 1890, Box 2, PHC Papers.
88. At this same time the Florence *Arizona Weekly Enterprise*, August 2, 1890, 1, reported "Lieut. [Carl] Reichmann and detachment [Twenty-fourth U.S. Infantry], who were sent out from San Carlos on the 18th inst, to investigate the shooting of the Apache squaw, about ten miles south of Globe, scouted the country for several miles around where the deed was committed, without getting any clue to the perpetrator. The Indians who reported the shooting alleged that it was the work of Masse, the lone Chiricahua renegade." In related article carried in that same issue Captain Francis Pierce's replacement as San Carlos agent, Captain J. D. Bullis, "stopped over here [Willcox] Monday night on his return to the agency from Tucson. In conversation with the writer, Captain Bullis stated that the recent killing of one of the Kid's band of renegade Apaches and the surrender of two others, left only seven hostile four men, two women and a boy off the reservation, and he is confident these will soon be captured. We sincerely hope the Captain is correct as to the small number of the renegades, and that his confidence in their capture will not prove a delusion."
89. "P.H. Clarke, Lieut. 10th Cav. Please Return," Journal, August 1–5, 1890, Box 5, PHC Papers.
90. "P.H. Clarke, Lieut. 10th Cav. Please Return," Journal, August 6, 1890, Box 5, PHC Papers. Thomas Darlington was born in Brooklyn, New York on September 24, 1858. Following three years' scientific and engineering courses at the University of the City of New York he

graduated, then took another path by entering the College of Physicians and Surgeons, New York, from which he was graduated as M.D. in 1880. He engaged in the practice of medicine at Newark, N. J., for two years, holding several hospital appointments. In 1882 he located at Kingsbridge, N. Y., and practiced there until 1904, except for two years spent in Arizona, where he was surgeon to several mining companies. *Columbia Alumni News* 37 (October 1945): 26; and *Columbia University College of Physicians and Surgeons* (New York: Bradstreet Press, 1891), 118. Dr. Darlington would be recorded as starting his practice in Cochise County as of April 8, 1889. The practice was in Bisbee in the main from 1889 to 1892 and he periodically jointly performed surgery with Doctor Goodfellow. Quebbeman, *Medicine in Territorial Arizona*, 337; (Tombstone) *Daily Epitaph*, August 24, 1889, 3; ibid., August 25, 1889; ibid., November 8, 1889, 3; (Tombstone) *Daily Prospector*, December 3, 1890, 1; and ibid., July 2, 1890. As Clarke stated the doctor's wife died in Bisbee on June 15. (Tombstone) *Epitaph*, June 21, 1890, 3.

91. To supplement doctors who held commissions, the army hired civilian physicians under contract. These temporary medicos "might be expected to be of two types. The first of these were Civil War veterans who accepted assignments to … remote areas." Additionally, there was a second type consisting mainly of "the young graduate from a medical school who signed on … in hope of eventually obtaining a permanent army commission." Quebbeman, *Medicine in Territorial Arizona*, 63–64,
92. Frederic Remington to Clark[e], August 7, 1890, Box 7, PHC Papers.
93. For Clarke's first in-print theoretical military piece see: Powhatan H. Clarke, Lieutenant Tenth Cavalry, "Revolvers and Revolver Practice," *Journal of the United State Cavalry Association*. III (1890): 222–25. Interestingly another one of Clarke's comrades in Arizona provided an article to the same issue, which was only the third year of the periodical and the organization, of which Clarke was a charter member. Clarke's fellow Tenth Cavalry second lieutenant also provided and article for this addition. See William H. Smith Second Lieutenant Tenth Cavalry "Post Instruction," *Journal of the United State Cavalry Association*. III (1890): 25–33.
94. Irish born Austin Henely immigrated with his family to the United States where they settled on a farm in Easton, Pennsylvania. Late in the Civil War he enlisted in the Eleventh U.S Infantry and became the

quartermaster sergeant. He subsequently attended the United States Military Academy graduating in 1872 as number 34 of his class of 57. His first assignment was as a second lieutenant with the Sixth U.S. Cavalry, which brought him to Kansas, but by 1875 he moved with his regiment to Arizona, in his case to Camp Bowie. Using that post as his base of operations, Henely spent considerable time in the field on scouting expeditions. In December 1876 he received his promotion to first lieutenant. Henely also would be stationed at Camps Apache and Verde, but as in the past often was away for garrison in command of Indian scouts in southern Arizona. A flash flood on July 11, 1878, near Camp Supply caught him unawares. He drowned despite efforts of his comrade, Lieutenant John Rucker, as Clarke noted, attempting to save his fellow officer.

Rucker, too, perished in the torrential waters. Son of a general, and great-grandson of the officer who established Fort Dearborn at Chicago in 1803, Rucker carried on the family tradition by being commissioned a second lieutenant in the Sixth U.S. Cavalry in 1872. Prior to that he had attended West Point for two years before becoming an officer. It seems his connection with Philip Sheridan, another fact reported by Clarke, helped him to obtain direct entry into the officer corps. He would be assigned to Company M of the Sixth Cavalry at Camp Grant, Arizona, in 1875. By 1876 he also led an Indian scout company and actively campaigned. "Local opinion held that Tony Rucker was the best Apache fighter since Gen. George Crook." As noted, when he tried to rescue his friend Henely he was swept away. As a consequence of his bravery the site of this tragic accident, Camp Supply, thereafter became known as Camp J. A. Rucker. Altshuler, *Cavalry Yellow & Infantry Blue*, 164 and 289.

As for Camp J.A. Rucker, short-lived installation located approximately forty-two miles south of Fort Bowie was established on April 29, 1878 as Camp Supply. On October 11, 1878, the post was renamed Camp Rucker. It became a picket post on November 5, 1880, and a bit later would be abandoned although served as the occasional site for patrols in the area to camp and also the location of a heliograph station. Altshuler, *Starting with Defiance*, 51.

95. Louis Craft, *Gatewood & Geronimo* (Albuquerque: University of New Mexico Press, 2000), offers details this dedicated officer's career.
96. Stein's Pass through the Peloncillo Mountains in Hidalgo County, New Mexico was named after United States Army Major Enoch Steen,

who camped nearby in 1856, during an exploration of the recently acquired Gadsden Purchase. Robert Hixson Julyan, *The Place Names of New Mexico*, 2nd ed. (Albuquerque: University of New Mexico Press, 1998), 341–42.

97. PHC to His Mother, August 20, 1890, Box 2, PHC Papers. PHC to His Father, July 26, 1890, Box 2, PHC Papers.
98. (Tombstone) *Daily Prospector*, September 13, 1890, 4.
99. "P.H. Clarke, Lieut. 10th Cav. Please Return," Journal, August 15–20, 1890, Box 5, PHC Papers. The (Lordsburg) *Western Liberal*, August 22, 1890, 2, reported that "The Copper Dick mine below Hachita shut down on account of the Indian outbreak." The article went on to say "a cowboy named Andy Riley" that some Apaches had left the reservation, stole horses at the Rail N ranch on the Gila and went south along the Stein's peak range." Earlier at the opening of the story, Keyes received considerable approbation along with Second Lieutenant Herbert Whipple. Both officers took a hard line against the Apaches which endeared them to many frontiersmen.
100. As reported in several papers "Lieutenant Clarke intends to make Rucker canon the headquarters for his command of Indian scouts. (Globe) *Arizona Silver Belt*, September 6, 1890, 1; (Florence) *Arizona Weekly Enterprise*, September 6, 1890, 1; and (Tucson) *Arizona Weekly Citizen*, September 6, 1890. 4. The (Florence) *Arizona Weekly Enterprise*, September 6, 1890, 4 further reported that Clarke recently went through "Stein's Pass bound for Hachita." The article exaggerated that he had about fifty scouts with him.
101. Simon Cienaga (St. Simon's sink) is located in the south-central part of Hidalgo County, New Mexico. Pearce, *New Mexico Place Names*, 148. Splitting into small units made some sense but could have a negative impact as one story carried in a few papers at this time disclosed. According to the *John's Herald*, August 21, 1890, titled "Take no Chance" a resident of Horseshoe by the name of Col. Wiggins "was sitting upon his porch viewing the beauties of nature. Suddenly there came over the knoll three or four Apaches." In fear he "lost time in getting inside the house for his rifle, and as he said afterwards, 'I never slipped a cartridge into my gun quicker in my life.'" Getting ready to fire when "the colonel poked the rifle out of the door...at the nearest Indian he was met with the salutation of 'bueno Apache.'" The mantra of the frontiersman that "The only good Apaches … were the proverbial dead ones," came to mind and "he thought he had better begin

shooting, and not run any chances." So, with that "he pulled down his gun and just as he was going to press the trigger there rode over the knoll behind the Indians a buffalo soldier." These "Apaches were scouts and he did not fire." After that nearly deadly episode, "He advised the sergeant in change of the detachment to ride ahead of the scouts when approaching a house…."

102. PHC to His Mother, September 6, 1890 (Stein's Pass, New Mexico) Box, 2, PHC Papers.
103. Frederic Remington to Clark[e], September 1, 1890, Box 7, PHC Papers.
104. The black and white version of the "Arrival of the Courier" appeared in the *The Century Monthly Magazine* (March 1891), 660, as one of the illustrations for John Bourke's article "General Crook in Indian Country." Likewise, the rendering was a painting and was Remington's practical approach to making his work as profitable as possible.
105. In addition to a painting, Remington used Clarke's photograph for a montage that appeared in "Skirmish Line Target Practice in the Regular Army," *Harper's Weekly* (October 26, 1889): 862.
106. Portions of the foregoing also were drawn from "P.H. Clarke, Lieut. 10th Cav. Please Return," Journal, August 24-Spetember 10, 1890, Box 5, PHC Papers. A few days later he recorded related that while in Willcox awaiting Major Wham's arrival "with paycheck" the lost camera had not been returned so he "sent to Remington for another camera." He added that unlike other outings his scouts "do not get drunk this trip."
107. PHC to Frederic Remington, September 13, 1890, Box 7, PHC Papers.
108. The (Florence) *Arizona Weekly Enterprise*, September 20, 1890, 4, substantiated the fact that "Lieutenant P.H. Clarke, with his command of nine Colored troops and twenty three Indian scouts, arrived here Monday from Fort Bowie, and on Tuesday went to Dragoon on a scouting expedition. From the Dragoon the lieutenant expected to return to Rucker Canon. He had just returned from a, scouting trip to the Stein's Peak country, but saw no Indian signs. He is confident that if he ever strikes the trail of the Kid his White Mountain scouts will run him to earth. Lieutenant Stockle is with Lieutenant Clarke, being second in command."
109. Frederic Remington to Clark[e], September 13, 1890, Box 7, PHC Papers.
110. Frederic Remington to Clark[e], October 1, 1890, Box 7, PHC Papers.

111. "P.H. Clarke, Lieut. 10th Cav. Please Return," Journal, October 5, 1890, Box 5, PHC Papers.
112. "P.H. Clarke, Lieut. 10th Cav. Please Return," Journal October 8, 1890, Box 5, PHC Papers.
113. In an article with the headline "White Liquor" and carried by a few papers reported "the arrival today from Sonora for horse load of the mescal which was drawn up in front of the custom house in Tombstone." The shipment came "from Mescal Ranch just below the San Bernardino Ranch" of Clarke's libations. While the liquor was manufactured and sold in Sonora for a dollar a gallon in Mexican money" it was higher north of the border because of "a duty of two dollars a gallon on this side in American money." (Tucson) *Arizona Weekly Citizen*, August 30, 1890.
114. As an example of the income that could be made by the government this import, the new Nogales bonded warehouse's first shipment was "1000 gallons of mescal" or twice that amount in duties payable to Uncle Sam. Similarly, at about the same time, "the total amount of duty to be paid on the mescal brought up…to Tombstone is in round figures, $600." (Tombstone) *Daily Prospector*, August 18, 1890; and ibid., August 2, 1890, 4. Illegal cross-border trade went far beyond bootleg, and had long precedents as summarized in George T. Díaz, *Border Contraband: A History of Smuggling Across the Rio Grande* (Austin: University of Texas Press, 2015).
115. "P.H. Clarke, Lieut. 10th Cav. Please Return," Journal, October 8–9, 1890, Box 5, PHC Papers. For a synopsis of Ewell's colorful career with an emphasis on Arizona consult Altshuler, *Cavalry Yellow & Infantry Blue*, 125.
116. It was because of the twin culprits—*tiswin* or *tulpai* and violence—that George Crook attempted to ban the concoction of this home brew. Sweeney, *From Cochise to Geronimo*, 21, 25–26, 56, 118, 371, 373, 382, 285–86, 397, 400, 485, 532, and 632 n27., charts in some detail the deadly role played by alcohol among the Apaches, including the Indian scouts.
117. "P.H. Clarke, Lieut. 10th Cav. Please Return," Journal, October 10 1890, Box 5, PHC Papers. While Clarke had not ascertained the source of the high-octane mescal, previously he had learned through Corporal William Ewell that two members of his command, Private Frederick Wilson and another trooper named Walker, had been selling beer to Indians. September 13, 1890, ibid. Consequently, some of Clarke's

own troopers might have provided the mescal to the scouts, or just as likely Foster or one of his crew would have had no compunction about doing so.

118. The "Apache Kid" had been captured and almost executed by the no-nonsense Emilio Kosterlitzky after his troops had a firefight with some of Crawford's errant scouts. Arguably this was one of a chain of incidents that led to Crawford's death at the hands of Mexican troops. de Garza, *The Apache Kid*, 23–24.
119. PHC to Frederic Remington, Undated Letter (probably October 9, 1890), Box 7, PHC Papers. Interestingly, a marked-up letter to Clarke's mother dated November 1, 1890, on the same subject, recounts many of the details of the roundup and mescal drinking episode and is found in the Frederic Remington Art Museum. Perhaps in anticipation of receiving photographs from Clarke, Remington kept this correspondence for future reference as a source for a possible article that never materialized.
120. For a far more accurate summary of the Lincoln County War than Jim Porter's version, consult Robert M. Utley, Billy the Kid: A Short and Violent Life (Lincoln: University of Nebraska Press, 1991).
121. "P.H. Clarke, Lieut. 10th Cav. Please Return," Journal, October 12 and 17, 1890, Box 5, PHC Papers.
122. PHC to Frederic Remington, October 24, 1890, Box 7, PHC Papers.
123. (Globe) *Arizona Silver Belt*, October 18, 1890, 2 mentions McCook's was taking a six-week tour of the Department of Arizona posts and added that he favored removal of the Apaches to the East, a stance that bought him stock among many readers in the territory.
124. In his journal for October 28 he proclaimed: "McCook wants to know who this young Clarke is thinks he will clip his wings." "P.H. Clarke, Lieut. 10th Cav. Please Return," Journal, October 28, 1890, Box 5, PHC Papers.
125. "P.H. Clarke, Lieut. 10th Cav. Please Return," Journal, October 28, 1890, Box 5, PHC Papers, Clarke also mentioned Irwin being McCook's selection for Clarke's new immediate superior.
126. The above information was taken from. "P.H. Clarke, Lieut. 10th Cav. Please Return," Journal, October 17–27, 1890, Box 5, PHC Papers.
127. The above excerpts were taken from "P.H. Clarke, Lieut. 10th Cav. Please Return," Journal, October 28–30, 1890, Box 5, PHC Papers.
128. Richard Bailowitz and Hank Brodkin, *Finding Butterflies in Arizona: A Guide to the Best Sites* (Boulder, CO: Johnson Books, 2007), 68.

129. Even as Clarke and his men came in for one of many breaks from the field one paper reported: "Troops have been scouring the country for the renegade and his gang of cutthroats, and it is only a question of time when they will be run in. In all there are 11 Indians at large, who are wanted by the authorities." (Phoenix) *Arizona Republican*, November 12, 1890, 4.
130. "P.H. Clarke, Lieut. 10th Cav. Please Return," Journal, October 20-November 28, 1890, Box 5, PHC Papers. Further the (Florence) *Arizona Weekly Enterprise*, December 6, 1890, 3, reported: "Lieut. P. H. Clarke, with his Indian command, stopped here a few hours Tuesday, en route from Fort Bowie to Fort Grant to attend the Thanksgiving festivities at the latter place, which will be conducted on a grand scale. The following morning an ambulance load of ladies and officers arrived from the same post, proceeding in the afternoon to Grant. They anticipate a royal time."
131. "P.H. Clarke, Lieut. 10th Cav. Please Return," Journal, November 1-November 30, 1890, Box 5, PHC Papers.
132. Frederic Remington to Powhatan Clark[e], November 12, 1890, Box 7, PHC Papers.
133. With George Crook's death in the spring of 1890 Nelson Miles received his promoted to major general on March 21, 1890, and took over Crook's command of the Division of the Missouri. Miles barely was situated at his headquarters in Chicago "when troubling reports came from the Sioux reservation in Dakota. A new religion had taken hold." The movement began by "Nevada Paiute, the Dance religion south the return of the old free life by nonviolent means." Once the preaching reached the Dakotas, however, the message morphed. The situation began to take a dangerous turn. Hutton and Ball, *Soldiers West*, 353. Before it did so Miles headed to the area, and Remington readily responded to the general's invitation to take a trip to the region. From this outing Remington produced "Chasing a Major General," *Harper's Weekly* 34 (December 6, 1890), 946–47; and "Indians as Irregular Cavalry, ibid. 34 (December 27, 1890), 1001 and 1004–6.
134. Major Marcus A. Reno had been the next senior officer in of the Seventh U.S. Cavalry, when Custer and the regiment faced its ordeal at the Little Bighorn. To combat charges that he acted in a cowardly manner he called for a court of inquiry which officially cleared his name, but nevertheless his reputation remained besmirched in many circles. For a biography see Ronald H. Nichols, *In Custer's Shadow: Major Marcus*

Reno (Norman: University of Oklahoma Press, 2000). As an aside, in Remington's behest, Clarke had contacted the U.S. Army's Adjutant General's Office with an inquiry about certain details related to sabers, Springfield carbines, campaign hats, and lists of engagements in the West including Washita and perhaps Little Bighorn. Such information stemmed from Remington's efforts to achieve a certain degree of accuracy in his work. See, Adjutant General's Office to Second Lieutenant Powhatan Clarke, February 27, 1890, in the collections of the Frederic Remington Art Museum.

135. The slang term "coffee cooler" even appeared in a line of an old army tune, *O'Reilly's Gone to Hell*, that dated to at least the 1880s. The song charted the woes of a drink-plagued sergeant, who after stealing a government blanket and "shoved it for a dollar and invested that in beer" [selling it for money to buy la drink] assaulted "a coffee cooler because he said he'd tell." Dolph, *Sound Off*, 56; and Rickey, *Forty Miles a Day*, 191.
136. PHC to His Mother, December, 19, 1890, Box 2, PHC Papers. In "P.H. Clarke, Lieut. 10th Cav. Please Return," Journal, December 28, 1890-January 3, 1891, Box 5, PHC Papers, he recorded a similar bit of information appears, stating: "Two men killed by Apaches in Guadalupe Cañon. Mr. Hickey before the corner's jury Orders to reform the detachment 20 men and ten scouts."
137. Kühn, *Chronicles of War*, 299. Also see (Tucson) *Arizona Weekly Citizen* (December 20, 1890), 3.
138. (Tombstone) *Daily Prospector* (January 19, 1891), 4.
139. The foregoing information was based on "P.H. Clarke, Lieut. 10th Cav. Please Return," Journal, December 6–28, 1890, Box 5, PHC Papers.
140. Both McChristian, *Garrison Tangles*; and Robert M. Utley, *An Army Doctor on the Western Frontier*, provides additional insights into this typical state of affairs at frontier forts.
141. "P.H. Clarke, Lieut. 10th Cav. Please Return," Journal, December 29–31, 1890, Box 5, PHC Papers.
142. The foregoing was based on "P.H. Clarke, Lieut. 10th Cav. Please Return," Journal, December 28, 1890, Box 5, PHC Papers.
143. "P.H. Clarke, Lieut. 10th Cav. Please Return," Journal, January 1–3, 1890, Box 5, PHC Papers.
144. "P.H. Clarke, Lieut. 10th Cav. Please Return," Journal, January 4–13, 1891, Box 5. PHC Papers.

145. Professor of journalism Elmo Scott Watson wrote *The Last of the Indian Wars, 1890–91: A Study of Newspaper Jingoism* (Minneapolis: University of Minnesota, 1943) proposing that Wounded Knee completed the press' quarter of a century exploitation of the Indian wars that began with coverage of the Red Cloud's War of 1866–67. Watson argued that "the coverage of the 'hostilities' of 1890–91 foreshadowed 'yellow journalism' that was soon to stampede the nation in a real war" in 1898.
146. "P.H. Clarke, Lieut. 10th Cav. Please Return," Journal, January 14, 1891, Box 5, PHC Papers.
147. (Tombstone) *Epitaph*, January 11, 1891, 1.
148. P.H. Clarke, Lieut. 10th Cav. Please Return" Journal, January 14, 1891, Box 5, PHC Papers; and Kühn, *Chronicles of War*, 299.
149. (Tombstone) *Daily Prospector*, January 17, 1891, 4.
150. "P.H. Clarke, Lieut. 10th Cav. Please Return," Journal, January 15, 1891, Box 5, PHC Papers.
151. "P.H. Clarke, Lieut. 10th Cav. Please Return," Journal, January 20, 1891, Box 5, PHC Papers. Kühn, *Chronicles of War*, 330, declared "The camp had been permanently occupied for a year." In contrast the St. Johns *Herald*, February 19, 1891, 2, summarized Clarke's report to Brigadier General McCook indicated "the captured camp gave evidence of having been occupied for months and a large number of blankets, provisions and cooking utensils were captured. Apparently, the Indians saved only their guns and ammunition." The article further stated Clarke's "scouts had identified the man they fired upon as Masai." Finally, the matter of fact reporting allowed that the patrol had "followed the trail for a week over the roughest section of Arizona. Most of the time it was so rough that his men could not ride their horses, and two of his troopers lost their horses, which rolled down precipices." Also see (Tombstone) *Epitaph*, February 8, 1891, 3.
152. (Tombstone) *Daily Prospector*, January 21, 1891, 4. The article reappeared in the St. John's *Herald*, February 5, 1891, 2; and (Tombstone) *Epitaph*, January 25, 1891, 5. Further there were other military men besides Clarke who were belittled by the press. Just as Crook became a target late in his Arizona tenure others replaced him such as in the instance of "the residents of the lower Sulphur Spring valley" who looked with suspicion on a "report made by Lieut, Hornbrook to the commander of the department, General McCook." The young officer and his patrol had been mobilized after the murderers of Bridges and

Robinson only followed for eighteen miles over a three-day period. Despite the slow pace supposedly "the trail was fresh when they left it and the next day or the fourth day … they went to a mescal ranch before returning and got pretty well full with mescal juice, after which they came up to Hall's ranch and camped." Looking for fuel the scout "used up his fence posts and adobe molds to build a fire, with which to cook." Because of such behavior the article contended, "The troops are getting to be looked upon down there as more-of a menace than the hostiles." (Tombstone) *Daily Prospector*, January 22, 1891, 1.

153. Despite carrying the Los Angeles story without comment the (Tombstone) *Daily Prospector*, January 23, 1891, 4, countered in one of its own stories that the man who brought the news from Smith's ranch of the killing there by Apaches states that there were five Indians in the party. Lieut. Clark [sic] says in his report that there were but three.
154. "There are many persons who believe that the Scouts killed Smith in the Chiricahua mountains; there is a peculiar look to the affair which should be ventilated." (Tombstone) *Epitaph*, January 25, 1891, 7.
155. Eva Remington to LT. Powhatan Clarke, January 20, 1891, Box 7, PHC Papers.
156. Frederic Remington to LT. Powhatan Clark[e], January 27, 1891, Box 7, PHC Papers. Remington's perspective on Wounded Knee appears in "The Sioux Outbreak in South Dakota," *Harper's Weekly* 35 (January 31, 1891): 57–62.
157. As with the Tenth U.S. Cavalry the Ninth U.S. Cavalry was established by "An Act to increase and fix the military peace establishment of the United States" approved on July 28, 1866. Two dozen years later Troops D, F, I, and K under Major Guy V. Henry, Sr. were sent to the Pine Ridge reservation where on December 30, 1890 they were engaged in two combat operations against the Sioux. Rodenbaugh and Haskin, *The Army of the United States*, 280–86. Charles L. Kenner, *Buffalo Soldiers and Officers of the Ninth Cavalry, 1867–1898* (Norman: University of Oklahoma Press, 1999), explores the history of this other buffalo soldier regiment.
158. Remington's admiration for Nelson Miles seemed to be a mutual one given that the general invited the artist and his wife to Mexico. The couple joined him during March of 1891, even as Clarke was wrapping up his last duties in Arizona never to return. Linking up with Miles in Chicago, they accompanied the general on a private railway coach

to Mexico where "they met President Diaz and attended a dance at the American ministry." When they returned, Remington provided *Harper's Weekly* with his illustrated account, "General Miles's Review of the Mexican Army" that would appear in the July 4, 1891, issue. Splete and Splete, *Frederic Remington—Selected Letters*, 113.It may not be coincidental that Powhatan Clarke's Medal of Honor process received support from Miles as a result of the urging of both Fred and Eva Remington while on this junket because the approval for this award for valor came soon after the Mexico tour as indicated in Chapter 9 which follows.

159. "P.H. Clarke, Lieut. 10th Cav. Please Return," Journal, January 24, 1891, Box 5, PHC Papers.
160. Kühn, *Chronicles of War*, 300–07, charts numerous other raids and other incidents in Arizona and New Mexico through the early twentieth century.

Notes to Chapter 9

1. J.K. Mizner to Adjutant General of the Army from Headquarters 10th U.S. Cavalry Fort Grant, Arizona Territory February 5, 1891 transmitted Regimental Orders No. 4 Appointing Second Lieutenant Powhatan H. Clarke as adjutant "vice First Lieutenant T. W. Jones, promoted and relieved as adjutant…. The regimental commander, congratulates Captain Jones upon his well-deserved promotion, after 18 years of arduous service with the regiment, and takes this occasion to express a full recognition of his valuable services in the office as regimental adjutant, and to testify publicly to Captain Jones's zeal, ability, and untiring devotion in the performance of every duty."
2. J.K. Mizner to Doctor Powhatan Clarke, February 6, 1891, Box 2, PHC Papers.
3. All information related to the Medal of Honor process initiated by Colonel Mizner and approved by the Secretary of War was based on RG94, Office of the Adjutant General, Entry 25a, Box 15, File 2690, Personnel Records Department-1891, Clarke Meda1, NARA. Late that same year Clarke would be commended in General Orders No. 100 AGO December 17, 1891 "For prompt and indefatigable pursuit of a party of Apache Indian murderers, and for conspicuous gallantry in the successful encountered with them March 7, on the Salt River, Ariz. March 2 to 7, 1890." NARA, RG94, Office of the Adjutant General,

Entry 25a, Box 15, File 2690, Personnel Records Department-1891, Clarke Medal.

4. *Medal of Honor Recipients 1863–1973* (Washington, DC: U.S. Government Printing Office, 1973), 284.
5. Special Orders No. 41, February 20, 1891, War Department, A.G.O. Also see: (Washington, DC) *Evening Star*, February 26, 1891, 7. "The following-named officers will report to the examining board convened at the Presidio of San Francisco for examination for promotion: Second Lieut. John A. Perry, Tenth Infantry; Second Lieut. Jas. B. Hughes, Tenth Cavalry; Second Lieut. Powhatan H. Clarke, Tenth Cavalry; Second Lieut. John P. Finley, Nineteenth Infantry."
6. General Orders No. 19, War Department, Adjutant General's Office, March 11, 1891.
7. For representative correspondence relative to Clarke's efforts to be posted to the French cavalry school Powhatan Clarke to the Adjutant General of the Army, September 26, 1886 with endorsements; Adjutant General of the Army to Powhatan Clarke, November 10, 1886 with endorsements; Adjutant General of the Army to Powhatan Clarke, November 18, 1888: and Adjutant General of the Army to Honorable William O. Ross, December 1, 1886. NARA, RG94, Office of the Adjutant General, Entry 29, Box 908, File 3760 ACP 1884.
8. (Washington, DC) *Sunday Herald and Weekly National Intelligencer*, March 8, 1891, 7, indicated "Second Lieut. Powhatan H. Clarke, Tenth Cavalry, has been ordered to this city to report to the Secretary of War for Instructions." Coincidentally on that same date the paper reported: "The President has directed the transfer of the military reservation of Fort Lowell, Ariz., to the Interior Department for disposition under the law."
9. Brigadier General Kelton to Mr. Clarke, March 4, 1891, Box 2, NARA, RG94, Office of the Adjutant General, Entry 25a, Box 15, File 2690, Personnel Records Department-1891, Clarke Medal.
10. On March 21 the Acting Secretary personally approved this request to the Secretary of State for "Lieutenant Clarke" who was to be "ordered abroad under a detail to 'obtain military information.'" NARA, RG94, Entry 29, Box 908, File 3760 ACP 1884.
11. Clarke scurried to obtain a passport as he did on March 19, 1891, asking for this document "for the purpose of traveling abroad." On March 21 the Acting Secretary personally approved this request to the Secretary of State for "Lieutenant Clarke" who was to be "ordered abroad under a detail to 'obtain military information.'" Ibid.

12. Passenger List French Mail Steamer *Champagne*, April 4, 1891, New York to Le Havre France, Box 2, PHC Papers.
13. PHC to His Mother, April 16, 1891, Box 2, PHC Papers.
14. PHC to His Mother, April 22, 1891, PHC Papers. Powhatan provided Elsie with a similar description the nest day. PHC to Elsie Clemens, April 23, 1891, PHC Papers.
15. PHC to His Mother, August 28, 1891, Box 2, PHC Papers.
16. PHC to Elsie Clemens February 3, 1892, Box 3, PHC Papers.
17. PHC to Elsie Clemens, March 23, 1892, Box 3, PHC Papers.
18. Frederic Remington to Clark[e], Early May 1891, Box 7, PHC Papers.
19. In 1895, Remington similarly cheered: "I think I smell war in the air" to a fellow martial enthusiast Owen Wister. Ben Merchant Vorpahl, *My Dear Wister: The Frederic Remington—Owen Wister Letters* (Palo Alto, CA: The American West Publishing Company, 1972), 217. Remington and Wister were but two of an influential group of powerful Easterners such as Theodore Roosevelt, Henry Cabot Lodge was joined by Californian William Randolph Hearst, who shared similar views not only about the virtues of trial by combat as the test of an individual and of a nation, but also the glories of the West, racial superiority of white men especially Americans, and many other manly Victorian "virtues" as treated in Evan Thomas, *The War Lovers: Roosevelt, Lodge, Hearts, and the Rush to Empire, 1898* (New York: Little, Brown and Company, 2010); and Christine Bold, *The Frontier Club: Popular Westerns and Cultural Power, 1880–1924* (New York: Oxford University Press, 2013).
20. Frederic Remington to Clark[e], Box 7, PHC Papers.
21. See Frederic Remington, "Training Cavalry Horses to Jump Obstacles," *Harper's Weekly* (September 19, 1891): 709–10. Remington's montage of nine vignettes featuring Tenth Cavalry troopers mentioned Clarke and Smith.
22. PHC to Elsie Clemens, December 25, 1891Box 2, PHC Papers. The bride was Agnes Foy's half-sister.
23. (St. Louis) *Republic*, June 4, 1891, 16.
24. See Boxes 2 and 3, PHC Papers, for scores of Clarke's letters to Elsie Clemens, although her responses have disappeared.
25. PHC to His Mother, July 21, 1891, PHC Papers.
26. PHC to His Father Undated 1891, Box 2, PHC Papers.
27. PHC to Elsie Clemens October 9, 1891, Box 2, PHC Papers. A pair of titles, William Manchester, *The Arms of Krupp, 1587–1968* (Boston:

Little Brown, 1968). Barbara Wertheim Tuchman, *The Guns of August* (New York: Macmillan, 1962), offer provocative insight into the Krupp complex and its pivotal place in European military history.

28. PHC to His Cousin Laura, June 10, 1891, Box 2, PHC Papers. Elsewhere he added:" I am quite homesick and very much annoyed for fear that I will not be put back into my old regiment for nearly all interests I have in life is in it." PHC to Elsie Clemens, June 10, 1891, Box 2, PHC Papers.
29. PHC to His Mother, September 6, 1891, Box 2, PHC Papers.
30. PHC to His Mother, Undated c. June 10, 1891, Box 2, PHC Papers.
31. PHC to Elsie Clemens, July 10, 1891, Box 2, PHC Papers. Graduating in 1860 from West Point, Merritt entered the Second U.S. Dragoons after his commissioning. Merritt would be posted to the frontier, but the Civil War brought him East again where from 1861 through 1865 he gained acclaim as "one of the 'boy wonders' of the war" jumping from captain to brigadier general, which although unusual was not unique in that George Custer and one other Union officer shared this distinction as would John J. Pershing in a later generation.

    He remained in service after Appomattox, actively campaigning in the West followed by appointment as superintendent of his alma mater. Boatner, *Civil War Dictionary*, 544–45.
32. Frederic Remington to Clark[e], October 14, 1891, Box 7, PHC Papers.
33. Mrs. Louise Clarke to Powhatan Clarke, October 18, 1891, Box 2, Powhatan H. PHC Papers.
34. PHC to Elsie Clemens, December 4, 1891, Box 2, PHC Papers.
35. PHC to Elsie Clemens, December 23, 1891; and PHC to Elsie Clemens, December 29, 1891; PHC to Elsie Clemens, December 25, 1891, Box 2; and PH to Elsie Clemens, January 2, 1892, Box 3, PHC Papers.
36. Frederic Remington to Clark[e], Undated (c. February 1892), Box 7, PHC Papers.
37. Special Orders No. 49, Headquarters of the Army Adjutant General's Office Washington, DC, February 29, 1892 directed "First Lieutenant Powhatan H. Clarke, 10th Cavalry, now serving by authority of the War Department with the German Army" to prepare for his return to the United States" where he was to "report in person to the Secretary of War, not later than May 21, 1892."
38. PHC to Elsie Clemens, April 4, 1892, Box 3, PHC Papers. As to professional publications Clarke mentioned: "I have been driving this little quill all day making a little article for the Military Service Journal all

for fame, and because I had to give vent to my ideas." He realized the piece would be push back from what he had to say as it would make "all the staff people red-hot but that is one way I have of getting warm." PHC to Elsie Clemens, January 13, 1892, Box 2, PHC Papers. "Having nothing else to do," he next sent "a clipping of an answer I wrote" in response to an "enthusiastic article by one of our young infantry lieutenants"to whom Clarke would respond. He feared his views, which ran counter to those of the infantryman, prompted Clarke to predict "the man won't like me and will think me sarcastic but he did tell us poor hard-working cavalryman as much that we all knew." PHC to Elsie Clemens, January 16, 1892, Box 3, PHC Papers.

39. PHC to Elsie Clemens, March 20 1892; and March 31, 1892, Box 3, PHC Papers.
40. PHC to Elsie Clemens, May 4, 1892, Box 3, PHC Papers.
41. PHC to Elsie Clemens, May 12, 1892, Box 3, PHC Papers.
42. General von Versen died on October 8, 1893, just a few months after Clarke. See (Kansas City, MO) *Times*, October 9, 1893, 2, which read: "A telegram to General D. M. Frost from Berlin, Germany, today announced the death there General Maximilian von Versen of the Sixth Corps of the German cavalry. Von Versen was quite well known in St. Louis he was the son-in-law of James Clemens, Jr. as is general Frost. The wedding of Miss Clemens to General von Versen twenty-two years ago, being one of the most notable society events in the history of St. Louis. General von Versen was one of the most noted men in the Prussian army during the Franco Prussian war and was on the staff of Emperor William. His son afterwards became a page of the old Emperor and his daughter, a beautiful girl, was married just a week ago to one of the young Count von Arnim."
43. (Alexandria, D.C.) *Gazette*, June 16, 1892, 2; and *A&NJ*, August 27, 1892, 10. Also see: "Leave for four months, to take effect May 28, 1892, is granted 1st Lieut. Powhatan H. Clarke, 10th Cav., and he is authorized to go beyond sea (S. O., May 18. H. Q. A.)" *A&NJ*, May 21, 1892, 674; and "Announcement is made that Lieut. Powhatan H. Clarke, 10th U. S. Cav., will be married in June to Miss Clemens, of St. Louis." Ibid *A&NJ*, May 21, 1892, 678; and "Announcements are out for the marriage of Elizabeth Clemens, of St. Louis, to Lieut. Powhatan H. Clarke, 10th Cav., which will take place at St. Francis Xavier's Church June 15. Canada is the object-point for the honeymoon. They will be 'at home' to their friends at Fort Custer, Mont.

After Oct. 1." Ibid., June 11, 1892, 731. Also see (St. Louis) *Special Telegram*, June 14, 1892, mentioned Slocum and Walsh: (St. Louis) *Post Dispatch*, June 15, 1892, 1; (St. Louis) *Post Dispatch*, June 15, 1892, 1; and Elsie Clemens Clarke to Her Mother, June 17, 1892, Box 3, PHC Papers. Established the year after its namesake's "last stand." Fort Custer stood near today's Hardin, Montana. The post served as an operational base to watch over the Cheyenne and Crow people. For more on the garrison's history consult Richard Upton, comp. and ed., *Fort Custer on the Big Horn, 1877–1898: Its History and Personalities as Told and Pictured by its Contemporaries* (Glendale, CA: A.H. Clark Co., 1973).

44. Font: Not bold "Extract from a personal letter to the chief of military or information division from Hatley, Province of Québec August 12, 1892 I forward here in the last of my reports now that I am out of the Bureau of military information I had to worry you with questions, but if you can, please let me know if it is the intention of the department for me to go to Custer at expiration of leave, and if they intend to kick me in Washington, how long it will be before I can get off, as I want to get to my regiment for many reasons. Yours, Powhatan H. Clarke." NARA, RG94, Entry 29, Box 908, File 3760 ACP 1884, Clarke. In reply Special Orders No. 200 Headquarters the Army, Adjutant General's Office, Washington, DC. August 25, 1892 extract one confirmed Clarke was "relieved from further duty in the city, to take effect at the expiration of his present leave of absence, and will then proceed to his troop. The traveling enjoined is necessary for the public service. By command of Major General Schofield: R. Williams adjutant general." Ibid. Also see: *A&NJ*, August 2, 1892, 10, "Lieut. P. H. Clarke, 10th Cavalry, is relieved from further duty in Washington at the expiration of the present leave, and is ordered to join his troop." An outside source thought Clarke's overseas duty merited another posting. According to *A&NJ*, June 25, 1892, 761, "The Kansas City Times suggests that on his return from Germany, Lieut. Powhatan H. Clarke, 10th U. S. Cavalry, be assigned to duty at the Infantry and Cavalry School so that the information gathered by him may be disseminated among a large number of officers of his branch of the service."
45. Elsie Clemens Clarke to Her Mother, September 22, 1892, Box 3, PHC Papers.
46. Elsie Clemens Clarke to Her Mother, September 30, 1892, Box 3, Box 3, PHC Papers. For comparative information several sources may

be consulted such as: Stallard, *Glittering Misery*; Anne Brunner Eales, *Army Wives on the American Frontier: Living By the Bugles* (Boulder, CO: Johnson Books, 1996); and Summerhayes, *Vanished Arizona*.

47. Elsie Clemens Clarke to Her Mother, October 6, 1892, Box 3, PHC Papers. A letter sent the next day revealed another detail in that Elsie received a $105 allowance from her mother in September. Elsie Clemens Clarke to Her Mother, October 7, 1892, Box 3, PHC Papers. It appears that this subsidy, which probably derived from her father's estate, continued thereby expanded the Clarke household monthly income by nearly ten percent. Another reference to an allowance appears in Elsie Clemens Clarke to Her Mother, December 5, 1892, Box 3. PHC Papers.
48. Theo A. Bingham to Secretary of War, No. 163 Legation of the United States of America Berlin, Germany, July 25, 1892, NARA, RG94, Entry 29, Box 908, File 3760 ACP 1884, Clarke.
49. Proctor wrote: "I hear from Adj. Gen. Williams very strong commendation of your reports, but he fears that there is some 'criticism of the service generally' – he does not say what service – that makes it impractical to publish them 'by authority.' He suggests that you make application for a return of the reports with permission to publish extracts in the service journals, the original papers to be returned to his office." Redfield Proctor to Lieut. Powhatan Clarke, May 11, 1893, Box 3, PHC Papers.
50. (New York) *Herald Tribune*, May 7, 1893, 13.
51. Wesley Merritt Commander Department of Dakota to General Thomas W. Vincent Assistant Adjutant General, U.S. Army, May 22, 1893, NARA, RG94, Entry 297 Box 908 3760 ACP Clarke.

Notes to Epilogue

1. Asst. Surgeon P.R. Egan to Surgeon General of the U.S. Army, July 21, 1893, NARA, RG94, Entry 297, Box 908, 3760 ACP, Clarke.
2. Lieutenant Colonel D. Perry, 10 U.S. Cavalry to Adjutant General of the U.S. Army, Fort Custer, July 22, 1893, NARA, RG94, Entry 297, Box 908, 3760 ACP, Clarke.
3. Frederic Remington to Mrs. Powhatan Clark[e], July 24, 1893, Box 7, PHC Papers. For scores of other examples of letters of condolence, review Box 3, PHC Papers; and *A&NJ*, September 16, 1893, 63, from Lieutenant-Colonel Count von Itzenplitz, the commander of the hussar regiment in which Clarke served.

4. William H. Smith to Dr. Powhatan Clarke, July 22, 1893, PHC Papers. For later recollections made in relation to Clarke's death see: W.T. Johnson to Adjutant General of the U.S. Army, November 5, 1896; and William H. Smith to Commissioner of Pensions, November 10, 1896, NARA, RG94, Entry 297, Box 908, 3760 ACP, Clarke,

   Coincidently South Carolinian Leighton Finley, a Princeton graduate, who joined the Tenth U.S. Cavalry on November 11, 1879, also died at Fort Custer. A few months before Clarke's drowning, Finley was drilling his company. During the course of the training "one of the troop horses became unmanageable and ran against Finley's horse, breaking its neck and killing it instantly. Finley fell under the dead horse, which crushed his leg. When the "fractures failed to heal, and after months of suffering he was taken to St. Luke's Hospital, St. Paul, Minne." for surgery, but complications must have occurred. Finley died on February 12, 1894. In the aftermath "complaints about his treatment reached the War Dept." with the subsequent investigation reaching an ambivalent conclusion that while the Fort Custer surgeon could not be faulted, "he was guilty of an 'error of judgment.'" Altschuler, *Cavalry Yellow & Infantry Blue*, 130–31.
5. Further this same obituary "related of the late Lieut. Powhatan H. Clarke 10th U. S. Cav. that while at North Hatley, Canada, in the summer of 1890, his sail-boat capsized. He did not lose his nerve, but being unable to right the boat, coolly struck out for the shore, and when he arrived the lighted pipe which was in his mouth at the time of the accident was still burning and he was coolly puffing away." One of the earliest mentions of Clarke's drowning appeared in ibid., August 5, 1893, 827. For examples of other obituaries see: (Baltimore) *Sun*, August 1, 1893: (Cincinnati, OH) *Democrat Watchman*, July 28,1893; (Grand Rapids, WI) *Wood County Reporter*, August 10, 1893, 7; (Helena, MT) *Independent*, July 29, 1893, Morning Edition;(Mineral Point, WI) *Iowa County Democrat*, August 11, 1893, 6; (Salt Lake) *Herald*, July 26, 1893, 3; (St. Paul) *Daily Globe*, July 23, 1893, 6; (Santa Fe) *Daily New Mexican*, July 24, 1893; (Tucson) *Arizona Weekly Citizen*, August 26, 1893, 1; (Washington, DC) *Evening Star*, July 24, 1893, 1, and July 29, 1893, 6; (Washington, DC) *National Tribune*, August 3, 1893, 8;*West Point Class Bulletin 1893*, 5–6; and Scrapbook, Box 6, PHC Papers. Besides memorials and recording Clarke's death, he also received mention because of the vacancy he left in the regiment. This meant Second Lieutenant

William Hay of the Third U.S. Cavalry moved up to first lieutenant to fill Clarke's slot in the Tenth. Other changes within the regiment that took place during the same period was Captain Thomas Lebo's advancement to major with the retirement of T. C. Tupper, Sixth U.S. Cavalry thereby moving First Lieutenant R. D. Read, Jr., to backfill Lebo, and Second Lieutenant J. E Noland took Read's place as first lieutenant. Former Clarke comrade Captain Kelly became a major as well, which gave John Bigelow his captaincy. *AN&J*, July 29, 1893, 811; and August 5, 1893, 826. On a more routine matter First Lieut. William H. Smith doubled as regimental adjutant plus was detailed as judge advocate "at Fort Custer. Mont., vice 1st Lieut. Powhatan H. Clarke deceased." *AN&J*, August 26, 1893, 2. Thus the dominos toppled with Clarke's departure in this seniority-based system.

6. *Harper's Weekly* (August 12, 1893), 763. The term had come into common usage to describe a valiant military figure and was said to have been applied first to the Chevalier de Bayard (c. 1500).
7. *A&NJ*, Supplement, 1893, 3, mentioned Clarke's brevet for first lieutenant "for Indian service" while *A&NJ* (April 28, 1894), 608, reiterated that "2d Lieut. Powhatan H. Clarke, 10th Cav. (since deceased)," had been recognized "for gallant service in action against Indians near Salt River, Ariz., March 7, 1890, in the Penito Mountains, Mex., May 3, 1886." Similar posthumous commendations "for services in campaign with hostile Indians" mention his receiving the Medal of Honor "for gallantry in action against hostile Apaches in the Penito Mountains, Mexico May 3, 1886 rushing forward to rescue a soldier who was severely wounded and lay disabled exposed to enemy's fire, and carrying him to a place of safety, while serving as second lieutenant, 10th cavalry" appear in NARA, RG94, Adjutant General's Office, Entry 29, Box 908, File 3760 ACP 1884. As an aside, *A&NJ*, December 10, 1893, 317, printed the names of all U.S. Army officers who likewise were members of the Sons of the American Revolution, the late Powhatan Clarke being listed among them.
8. *A&NJ*, (May 11, 1895), 605 and 613. *The West Point Class* Bulletin 1884 for 1914, 2 republished the Tenth Cavalry Officers' Club official thanks that first appeared in *The Army and Navy Journal*. Evidently the painting eventually would be sent to the Army and Navy Club in New York City, but today its whereabouts are unknown. One writer presumed it was a painting by Frederic Remington, but because it showed "Lieutenant

Clarke carrying the negro trooper on his shoulder against the pathway of fire" it must have been the piece provided by T.H. Lambert. (Marion, KY) *Crittenden Record-Press*, August 16, 1917, 2.

9. One obituary led off with the title "Modern Knight Errant. The Chivalrous and Daring Spirit of Lieut. Clarke," a stirring description which may have pleased him. (Washington, DC) *Post*, July 24 or 31, 1893, Scrapbook, Box 6, PHC Papers.
10. Frederic Remington, "Two Gallant Young Cavalry Men," *Harper's Weekly* 34, no. 1735 (March 22, 1890): 220.
11. According to the (Los Angeles) *Herald*, December 15, 1894, 10, "A distinguished party of tourists from St. Louis arrived at the Westminster [California] last evening. The party consists of Mrs. H. I. Clemens and daughter; Mrs. Powhatan H. Clarke and maid and Powhatan H. Clarke, Jr. They will winter in Southern California and for a time will be guests of Cave Couts, at the celebrated Guajome ranch, in San Diego county." Incidentally, Couts had been an officer who came to California with U.S. troops during the Mexican War. It seems seeking warmer vacation locales continued at least one other time when Elsie, her son and sister visited Daytona, Florida, staying at the Palmetto. (Daytona) *Daily News*, March 20, 1909, 3.
12. For more on Powhatan James Hughes Clarke and World War I see: "Notebook of Powhatan H Clarke, Jr., While Cadet at School of Military Aviation University of Illinois, 1917," Box 6, PHC Papers; and http://missourioverthere.org/explore/collections/clarke-powhatan-papers/.
13. (Marion, KY) *Crittenden Record-Press*, August 16, 1917, 2; (Doniphan, MO) Ripley County Democrat, August 17, 1917, 2; (Tallulah, LA), Madison Journal, August 18, 1917, 8; (Meade, KS) *Meade County News*, August 23, 1917, 6; (Bismarck, ND) Tribune, August 28, 1917, 2; (Wahpeton, ND) Times, August 30, 1917, 2; and (St. Joseph, LA) *Tensas Gazette*, August 31, 1917, 6.
14. Clarke, Powhatan Hughes (1893–1920), Saint Louis University Libraries Special Collections: Archives and Manuscripts. For further information on his papers see: http://archon.slu.edu/?p=creators/creator&id=17.
15. Clarke's "Hot Trail" drafted while in Germany, and which Remington instructed his friend to revise without success, was not the only posthumous article penned by a Tenth Cavalry officer that reached a popular audience in 1894. As with Clarke, Remington provided illustrations for *Harper's Weekly*, in this case for the October 13, 1894,

issue, "Private Myers' First Scout." The piece was the work of an eyewitness and was revealed as "a true account of the outbreak of Geronimo's band of Chiricahua Apaches, of the pursuit and of a sharp fight with the Indians, in which the U. S. troops were delivered from an almost desperate predicament by a vigorous counter attack." But what is especially interesting about the article is the evidence which it supplies, mainly by the modest way in which the services of the 'junior lieutenant' who used the nom de plume of "Lewis Ferguson" was in reality Leighton Finley. The fact that this tale had "been written by the gallant officer who has just died," and appeared in print "after his death" revealed that during this engagement Finley "displayed exceptional bravery, being the first to reach the top of the canyon and the intrenchments of the Indian" a fact not known to most before reaching print. *A&NJ*, October 20, 1894, 114.

16. Frederic Remington to Dr. Clarke, October 3, 1893, Box 7, PHC Papers.
17. As David McCullough suggests, Wister pioneered literature that took "the cowboy seriously," to the extent that this noteworthy historian viewed Wister, Remington, and Roosevelt as the "three Eastern contemporaries of 'good background'—who in their efforts to catch 'the living breathing end' of the frontier produced what in large measure remains the popular vision of the 'real West.'" McCullough, *Brave Companions*, 633.
18. German-born Charles (Carl) Schreyvogle struggled to achieve success and make a living as an artist. That situation quickly changed "when Remington died in 1909, Schreyvogle wore the mantle of premier Western artist for the brief remainder of his life." Michael David Zellman, comp. *American Art Analog* (New York: Chelsea House Publishers in association with American Art Analog, 1986), 557. For more details see James David Horan, *The Life and Art of Charles Schreyvogle, Painter-Historian of the Indian-fighting Army of the American West* (New York, Crown Publishers, 1969).
19. As previously noted, Dippie, "'A Very Good Friend to the Army ...,'" 99–118, ably summarizes the important contribution Remington made in capturing and establishing the image of the U.S. Army in the post-Civil War American West.
20. Irene Schubert and Frank N. Schubert, *On the Trail of the Buffalo Soldiers* I, 164–5. Also see William B. Gatewood, Jr., *Smoked Yankees and the Struggle for Empire: Letters from Negro Soldiers, 1898–02* (Urbana: University of Illinois, Press, 1971), 58.

21. Givens's biographical background was taken from NARA Record Group 94 (AGO), Entry 91a (US Army Enlistment Papers-Series One), Box 28; Entry 91b (US Army Enlistment Papers-Series Two), Box 488; Entry 501 (R&P Document File), Box 1418, File 719108 Spanish American War Commissions; Entry 522 (Carded Records-Spanish American War Volunteers) Spanish-American War Compiled Military Service Record; CMSR, Givens, William, Co E, 10th Regt US Volunteer Infantry – Colored; Entry 530 (Carded Medical record-Regulars 1894), Box 752; Entry 529 (Carded Medical record-regulars 1884), Box 505; and Entry 25 (AGO Document File), Box 2116, File 319311; and Frank N. Schubert, *On the Trail of the Buffalo Soldier: Biographies of African Americans in the Army, 1866–1917* I (Wilmington, DE: Scholarly Resources, Inc., 1995), 164–5. Also see William B. Gatewood, Jr., *Smoked Yankees and the Struggle for Empire: Letters from Negro Soldiers, 1898–1902* (Urbana: University of Illinois, Press, 1971), 58. "First Sergeant Givens was ever at his post exercising a steady influence on the men, and conducting himself like the thorough soldier which I had long known him to be,"133. Ibid., 51, 64, 96, 112, 135, 163 likewise makes reference to Givens. As indicated, Givens would he promoted to second lieutenant in a so-called Immune regiment comprised in the main of African Americans. Gatewood, *Smoked Yankees*, 166–67. Givens returned to Tenth but having lost his first sergeant's position due to temporary promotion returned to the ranks as a corporal in Troop K. For more on Givens and black regulars in the Spanish American War read: John Bigelow, *Reminiscences of the Santiago Campaign* (New York: Harper, 1899); Herschel V. Cashin, *Under Fire with the Tenth Cavalry* (Niwot: University Press of Colorado, 1993); Jerome Tuccille, *The Roughest Riders: The Untold Story of the Black Soldiers in the Spanish-American War* (Chicago Review Press, 2015); Edward Van Zile-Scott. *Unwept, Unhonored, Unsung: Black American Soldiers & the Spanish American War* (Montgomery, AL: The Black Belt Press, 1995).
22. Altschuler, *Cavalry Yellow & Infantry Blue*, 32–33.
23. Altschuler, *Cavalry Yellow & Infantry Blue*, 199–200.
24. For Shipp's public post mortem defense of Clarke read *A&NJ*, August 19, 1893, 25.
25. Altschuler, *Cavalry Yellow & Infantry Blue*, 301.
26. Altschuler, *Cavalry Yellow & Infantry Blue*, 309.
27. "The Silver Star Medal had its beginnings in World War I. An Act of Congress of July 9, 1918, authorized the wearing by Army personnel

of a small star…." The device came to be called "the 'citation star,' the award was made retroactive, so that all those coted for gallantry as far back as the Spanish American War, were eligible to wear it." Kerrigan, *American War Medals and Decorations*, 24.

28. Altschuler, *Cavalry Yellow & Infantry Blue*, 171–2; and Cullum, *Register of Officers and Graduates of the United States Military Academy*, VI-A, 390
29. Andrew Carroll, *My Fellow Soldiers: General John Pershing and the Americans Who Helped Win the Great War* (New York: Penguin Press, 2017), 185. Donald Smyth, *Guerrilla Warrior: The Early Life of John J. Pershing* (New York: Charles Scribner's Sons, 1973), 44, and 295 n77, indicated that the nickname "Black Jack" began while Pershing served as a tactical officer at West Point, and stemmed from his unpopularity among the cadets there. Pershing accepted this was the source of the sobriquet's origin, but one of this boyhood friends contended it had been used long before that when Pershing before entering the Military Academy "'taught an unexpired term of the colored school at Laclede…."

    Supposedly "Pershing's own thoughts about African Americans were complicated and inconsistent. 'My attitude toward the Negroes was one that of one brought up among them….'" As a teacher with black students in a Missouri public school he maintained: "'I have always felt kindly and sympathetically toward them and knew that fairness and due consideration of their welfare would make the same appeal to them as to any other body of men.'" Smyth, *Guerrilla Warrior*, 39.
30. This quote was in reference to a young World War I officer, George Redwood, who had been cast in a similar mold to Clarke and carried in (Baltimore) *Sun*, March 30, 1918.
31. Colonel Theodore Lyman referring to Abraham Lincoln as quoted in Burke Davis, *To Appomattox: Nine April Days 1865* (New York: Rinehart & Company, Inc., 1959), 26.

Bibliography

Manuscript Sources

Arizona Historical Society. Tempe.
Schaus, Richard. Collection FM Mss 6.
Arizona Historical Society. Tucson.
Arhelger, Edward. Box 4. Mss 1475.
Corbusier, William T. Oral History Interview, 1968. Sound Cassette. AV0060 RR.
Gatewood, Charles. Box 1. Mss 282.
Leatherwood, Robert Nelson. Biofiles. Mss 1475.
Soza Family. Box 1. Mss 0750.
Wardwell, William Lanterman. Letters 1880–1888. Box 1. Mss 1074.
Rutherford B. Hayes Memorial Library. Fremont, OH.
George Crook Papers.
Kansas Historical Society. Topeka.
Remington, Frederic. "House Book." Robert Taft Collection. Mss Collection 975
————. "Journal of a Trip across the Continent through Arizona and Sonora Old Mexico."
Robert Taft Collection. Mss Collection 975.
Louisiana State University Libraries, Baton Rouge.
Boyd Estate. Oral History Interview, 1971. Sound Cassette (45 minutes). L:4700.0041, Mss. 4700.004.
Clarke (Powhatan) Diary. Mss. 893.
Missouri Historical Society, St Louis.
Powhatan H. Clarke Papers, Collection No. A0293. Boxes 1–7.
National Archives and Records Administration, Washington, DC.
Record Group 94, Records of the Office of the Adjutant General
Christopher Smith Collection
F.L. Palmer Scrapbook 1909–1920.
United States Military Academy Library, Special Collections. West Point, NY.
John Bigelow Diary. Bigelow Papers.
Letters Sent. S 2.
Proceedings (Staff Records). S14.
Delinquency Classifications. S100.
Register of Cadet Delinquencies. S102.
Name and Subject Indexes to S167. S166.

Post Orders. Special Orders. S167.
Regulations of the United States Military Academy. S178.
List of Cadets Admitted to the United States Military Academy. S193.
Semiannual Cadet Merit Rolls and Conduct Rolls (Register of Merit). S198.
University of Arizona Libraries. Special Collections. Tucson.
Leighton Finely Collection. AZ005.

Government Documents

Annual Report of the Adjutant-General of the State of New York for the Year 1894. Albany: State of New York, 1895.

Annual Report of the Superintendent of the United States Military Academy, 1882. Washington, DC: War Department, 1882.

Annual Report of the Visitors of the United States Military Academy Made to the Secretary of War, 1880. Washington, DC: War Department, 1880.

Annual Report of the Visitors of the United States Military Academy Made to the Secretary of War, 1881. Washington, DC: War Department, 1881.

Annual Reports of the Secretary of War I. Washington DC: U.S. Government Printing Office, 1880–1893.

Billings, John S. *Report on Hospitals with Descriptions of Military Posts*. Washington, DC: War Department Surgeon General's Office, 1870.

Brands and Marks of Cattle, Horses, Sheep Goats and Hogs As They Appear in the Office of the Live Stock Sanitary Board of Arizona at Phoenix, Arizona. Phoenix: Livestock Sanitary Board of Arizona, 1908.

Heitman, Francis B. *Historical Register and Dictionary of the United States Army*. Washington, DC: U.S. Government Printing, Office, 1903.

Medal of Honor Recipients 1863–1973. Washington, DC: U.S. Government Printing Office, 1973.

Official Army Register for January, 1880. Washington, DC: Adjutant General's Office, 1880.

Official Army Register for January, 1882. Washington, DC: Adjutant General's Office, 1882.

Official Army Register for January 1890. Washington, DC: United States Adjutant-General's Office, 1890.

Official Register of the United States. Consisting of a List of Officers and Employees in the Civil, Military and Naval Service on the First of July, 1889, Together with a List of Vessels Belonging to the United States. Washington, DC: Government Printing Office, 1889.

Poore, Ben Perley, ed. *Message of the President of the United States to the Two Houses of Congress at the Commencement of the Second Session of the Fifty-fourth Congress with Reports of the Heads of Departments and Selections from Accompanying Documents*. Washington, DC: Government Printing Office, 1886.

Volkmar, William J. *Report of the Practice of the Heliograph System, Department of Arizona in May 1890*. Washington, DC: Office of the Chief of Signal Corps, 1890.

Winthrop, William. *Digest of the Opinions of the Judge Advocate General of the Army*. Washington, Government Printing Office, 1866.

Books

Adams, Kevin. *Class and Race in the Frontier Army: Military Life in the West, 1870–1890*. Norman: University of Oklahoma Press, 2009.

Altshuler, Constance Wynn. *Cavalry Yellow and Infantry Blue: Army Officers in Arizona Between 1851 and 1886*. Tucson: Arizona Historical Society, 1991.

———. *Chains of Command: Arizona and the Army, 1856–1875*. Tucson: Arizona Historical Society, 1981.

———. *Starting with Defiance: Nineteenth Century Arizona Military Posts*. Tucson: Arizona Historical Society, 1983.

Bailowitz, Richard, and Hank Brodkin. *Finding Butterflies in Arizona: A Guide to the Best Sites*. Boulder, CO: Johnson Books, 2007.

Baldwin, Gordon C. *The Warrior Apaches: A Story of the Chiricahua and Western Apache*. Tucson: Dale Stuart King, 1965.

Ball, Larry. *Ambush at Bloody Run*. Tucson: Arizona Historical Society, 2000.

Baumler, Mark F. *The Archeology of Faraway Ranch, Arizona: Prehistoric, Historic, and 20th Century*. Tucson: Western Archeological Center and Conservation Center, 1984.

Bell, Bob Boze. *The Illustrated Life and Times of Geronimo*. Cave Creek, AZ: Two Roads West, 2020

Bender, Jill C. The 1857 Indian Uprising and the British Empire. *Cambridge: Cambridge University Press, 2016.*

Bigelow, John. *Reminiscences of the Santiago Campaign*. New York: Harpers, 1899.

Bigelow, Poultney. *Seventy Summers*. New York: Longmans, Green & Co., 1925.

Birkhimer, William E. *Historical Sketch of the Organization, Administration Matériel and Tactics of the Artillery, United States Army*. Washington, DC: J.J. Chapman, Agent, 1884.

Boatner III, Mark Mayo. *The Civil War Dictionary*. New York: David McKay Company, Inc., 1959.

Bold, Christine. *The Frontier Club: Popular Westerns and Cultural Power, 1880–1924*. New York: Oxford University Press, 2013.

Bourke, John G. *An Apache Campaign in the Sierra Madre: An Account of the Expedition in Pursuit of the Hostile Chiricahua Apaches in the Spring of 1883*. New York: C. Scribner's Sons, 1886.

————. *On the Border with Crook*. New York: Charles Scribner's Sons, 1891.

Brandes, Ray. *Frontier Military Posts of Arizona*. Globe, AZ: Dale Stuart King, Publisher, 1960.

Brinckerhoff, Sidney B. *Aftermath at Cibecue: Court Martial of the Apache Scouts, 1881*. Tucson: Tucson Corral of the Westerners, 1978.

Carlson. Paul H. *"Pecos Bill": A Military Biography of William R. Shafter*. College Station: Texas A&M University Press, 1989.

Carroll, Andrew. *My Fellow Soldiers: General John Pershing and the Americans Who Helped Win the Great War*. New York: Penguin Press, 2017.

Carroll, John Alexander. *Generals Crook and Miles in Arizona: From Contemporary Accounts of Fellow Soldiers with the Original Illustrations of Frederic Remington*. Tucson: Tucson Corral of the Westerners, 1967.

Cashin, Herschel V. *Under Fire with the Tenth Cavalry*. Niwot: University Press of Colorado, 1993.

The Centennial of the United States Military Academy at West Point, New York, 1802–1902. 2 vols. Washington, DC: U.S. Government Printing Office, 1904.

Clark, Michael J. U.S. Army Pioneers: Black Soldiers in Nineteenth-century Utah. Salt Lake: Fort Douglas Military Museum, N.D.

Clarke, Mary Whatley. *The Slaughter Ranches and Their Makers*. Austin: Jenkins Publishing Co., 1979.

Coffman, Edward M. *The Old Army: A Portrait of the American Army in Peacetime 1784–1898*. New York and Oxford: Oxford University Press, 1986.

Columbia University College of Physicians and Surgeons. New York: Bradstreet Press, 1891.

Connelly, Donald D. *John M. Schofield and the Politics of Generalship*. Chapel Hill: University of North Carolina Press, 2006.

Copper Handbook: A Manual of the Copper Industry of the World. Houghton: MI: Horace J. Stevens, 1907.

Corbusier, William T. *Verde to San Carlos: Recollections of a Famous Army Surgeon and His Observant Family on the Western Frontier 1869–1886*. Tucson: Dale Stuart King, 1971.

Christian, Garna L. *Black Soldiers in Jim Crow Texas*. College Station: Texas A&M University Press, 1995.

Cullum, George W. *Biographical Register of Officers and Graduates of the US Military Academy at West Point, New York Since Its Establishment in 1804 to 1890*. Vols. 1–6. West Point, NY: Association of Graduates, U.S. Military Academy, 1890–1920.

Custer, Elizabeth Bacon. *Following the Guidon*. New York: Harper & Brothers, 1890.

Dastrop, Boyd L. *The U.S. Army Command and General Staff College: A Centennial History*. Manhattan, KS: Sunflower University Press, 1982.

Davis, Britton. *The Truth About Geronimo*. New Haven: Yale University Press, 1929.

Davis, Burke. *To Appomattox: Nine April Days 1865*. New York: Rinehart & Company, Inc., 1959.

Debo, Angie. *Geronimo: The Man, His Time, His Place*. Norman: University of Oklahoma Press, 1976.

de la Garza, Phyllis. *The Apache Kid*. Tucson: Westernlore Press, 1995.

Dickson, Paul. *War Slang: American Fighting Words and Phrases from the Civil War to the Gulf War*. New York: Simon & Schuster, 1994.

Díaz, George T. *Border Contraband: A History of Smuggling Across the Rio Grande*. Austin: University of Texas Press, 2015.

Dinges, Bruce J., and Shirley A. Leckie. eds. *A Just and Righteous Cause: Benjamin H. Grierson's Civil War Memoir*. Carbondale: Southern Illinois University Press, 2008.

Dippie, Brian W. *The Frederic Remington Art Museum Collection*. Ogdensburg, NY: Frederic Remington Art Museum, 2001.

Dobak, William A., and Thomas D. Phillips. *The Black Regulars, 1866–1898*. Norman: University of Oklahoma Press, 2001.

Dolph, Edward Arthur. *"Sound Off": Soldier Songs from Yankee Doddle to Parley Voo*. New York: Cosmopolitan Book Corporation, 1929.

Drummond, Henry. *Natural Law in the Spiritual World*. New York: J. Pott & Co., 1884.

Dunlay, Thomas W. *Wolves for the Blue Soldiers: Indian Scouts and Auxiliaries with the United States Army, 1860–1890*. Lincoln: University of Nebraska Press, 1982.

Eales, Anne Brunner. *Army Wives on the American Frontier: Living by the Bugles*. Boulder: Johnson Books, 1996.

1886–1911: In Commemoration of the 25th Anniversary of Graduation of the Class of '86, U.S.M.A. West Point, June, 1911. Philadelphia: The Holmes Press, 1911.

Erwin, Allen A. *The Southwest of John Horton Slaughter*. Glendale, CA: Arthur H. Clark Co., 1965.

Essin, Emmett M. *Shavetails and Bell Sharps: The History of the Army Mule*. Lincoln: University of Nebraska Press, 1997.

Emerson, William K. *Marksmanship in the Army: A History of Medals, Shooting Programs, and Training*. Norman: University of Oklahoma Press, 2004.

Faust, David T., and Kenneth A. Randall. *Camp Lowell, and Tucson's Military Outpost 1853–1873*. Tucson: Tucson Corral of the Westerners, 2003.

————. *Life at Post: Fort Lowell, Arizona Territory 1873–1891*. Tucson: Tucson Corral of the Westerners, 2002.

Fitzpatrick, David J. *Upton: Misunderstood Reformer*. Norman: University of Oklahoma Press, 2017.

Fontana, Bernard L. *Calabazas of the Rio Rico*. Tucson: Tucson Corral of the Westerners, 1971.

Forrest, Earle R. *Arizona's Dark and Bloody Ground*. Caldwell, ID: The Caxton printers, Ltd., 1936.

Forty, Sandra. *Remington*. Edison, NJ: Chartwell Books, Inc., 2008.

Gatewood, William B., Jr. *Smoked Yankees and the Struggle for Empire: Letters from Negro Soldiers, 1898–1902*. Urbana: University Illinois Press, 1971.

Gladstone, William A. *United States Colored Troops, 1863–1867*. Gettysburg: Thomas Publications, 1990.

Glasrud, Bruce A., and Michael N. Searles, eds. *Buffalo Soldiers in the West: A Black Soldiers Anthology*. College Station: Texas A&M University Press, 1984.

Glass, E.L.N., comp. and ed. *The History of the Tenth Cavalry 186–1921*. Ft. Collins, CO: Old Army Press, 1972.

Granger, Byrd Howell. *Arizona's Names (X Marks the Place)*. Tucson; Falconer Publishing Company, 1983.

Grant, Ulysses S.*U.S. Grant Papers: The Papers of Ulysses S. Grant, 1866*. Vol. 16. Carbondale: Southern Illinois University Press, 1988.

Green, Bill. *The Dancing Was Lively: Fort Concho, Texas: A Social History, 1867 to 1882*. San Angelo: Fort Concho Sketches Publishing Co., 1974.

Greene, Jerome A. *American Carnage: Wounded Knee, 1890*. Norman: University of Oklahoma Press, 2014.

Hämäläinen, Pekka. *The Comanche Empire*. New Haven: Yale University Press, 2008.

Hassrick, Peter H. *Frederic Remington: A Catalogue Raisonné II*. Norman: University of Oklahoma Press, 2016.

———. *Frederic Remington Paintings, Drawings, and Sculpture in the Amon Carter Museum and The Sid Richardson Foundation Collection*. New York: Harry N. Abrams, Inc., 1973.

Heitman, Francis B. *Historical Register of the Officers of the Continental Army During the War of the Revolution, April, 1775 to December, 1783*. Vol. 1. Washington, DC: W.H. Lowdermilk & Co., 1893.

Hinton, Richard J. *The Hand-Book to Arizona: Its Resources, History, Towns, Mines, Ruins, and Scenery*. San Francisco: Payot, Upham & Co., 1878.

"Ho for the Great West!" and Other Original Papers to Mark the 25th Anniversary of the English Westerners Society. London: English Westerners Society, 1980.

Horan, James David. *The Life and Art of Charles Schreyvogel, Painter-Historian of the Indian-fighting Army of the American West*. New York, Crown Publishers, 1969.

Hornung, Chuck. *Wyatt Earp's Cow-boy Campaign: The Bloody Restoration of Law and Order Along the Mexican Border, 1881*. Jefferson, NC: McFarland & Company, Inc., Publishers, 2016.

Hu-DeHat, Evelyn. *Yaqui Resistance and Survival: The Struggle for Land and Autonomy 1821–1910*. Madison, WI: The University of Wisconsin Press, 2016.

Hunt, Elvid, and Walter E. Lorence. *History of Fort Leavenworth 1827–1937*. Fort Leavenworth: The Command and General Staff School Press, 1937.

Hunter, J. Marvin, ed. *Nine Years Among the Indians 1870–1879: The Story of the Captivity and Life of a Texan Among the Indians Herman Lehmann*. Albuquerque: University of New Mexico Press, 1993.

Hutton, Paul Andrew. *The Apache Wars: The Hunt for Geronimo, the Apache Kid, and the Captive Boy Who Started the Longest War in American History*. New York: Crown, 2016.

———. *Phil Sheridan and His Army*. Lincoln: University of Nebraska Press, 1985.

———. and Durwood Ball, eds. *Soldiers West: Biographies from the Military Frontier*. Norman: University of Oklahoma Press, 2009.

Jensen, Richard E., ed. V*oices of the American West, Volume 1: The Indian Interviews of Eli S. Ricker, 1903–1919 and* Voices *of the American West, Volume 2: The Settler and Soldier Interviews of Eli S. Ricker, 1913–1919.* Lincoln: *University of Nebraska Press, 2005.*

Johnson, Eric S., comp, and ed. *No Greater Calling: A Chronological Record of Sacrifice and Heroism During the Western Indians Wars, 1865–1898.* Atglen, PA: Schiffer Military History, 2012.

Joslin, Christina. *Fort Bayard: A Post on the Apache Frontier*. N.P.: Privately published, 2004.

Julyan, Robert Hixson. *The Place Names of New Mexico*. 2nd ed. Albuquerque: University of New Mexico Press, 1998.

Kalinak, Kathryn. *How the West Was Sung: Music in the Westerns of John Ford*. Berkeley: University of California Press, 2007.

Kasulaitis, Mary Noon. *The Village of Arivaca: A Short History*. Tucson: Tucson Corral of the Westerners, 2002.

Kautz, August V. *Customs of the service for Officers of the Army as Derived from Law and Regulations and Practised in the Army of the United States Being Hand-Book of Military Administration for Officers of the Line. Showing the Specific Duties of Each Grade from Lowest to the Highest, Enabling Officers Promoted to a New Grade to Know What to Do, and How to Do It*. Philadelphia: J. B. Lippincott & CO., 1866.

Kenner, Charles L. *Buffalo Soldiers and Officers of the Ninth Cavalry, 1867–1898*. Norman: University of Oklahoma Press, 1999.

Kerrigan, Evans E. *American War Medals and Decorations: Newly Revised and Expanded*. New York: The Viking Press, 1971.

Kimmel, Michael. *Manhood in America: A Cultural History*. New York: The Free Press, 1996.

Knight, Oliver. *Life and Manners in the Frontier Army*. Norman: University of Oklahoma Press, 1978.

Kühn, Berndt. *Chronicles of War: Apache and Yavapai Residence in the Southwestern United States and Northern Mexico, 1821–1937*. Tucson: Arizona Historical Society, 2014.

Kupke, William, comp. *Fort Bayard's Military Period: 1866–1899*. Fort Bayard: Fort Bayard Historical Preservation Society, 2011.

Langellier, John P., ed. *All My People Were Killed: The Memoir of Mike Burns (Homothya) A Captive Indian*. Prescott, AZ: Sharlot Hall Museum, 2010.

———. *Fighting for Uncle Sam: Buffalo Soldiers in the Frontier Army*. Atglen, PA: Schiffer Publishing, 2016.

Leckie, Shirley Anne, ed. *The Colonel's Lady on the Western Frontier: The Correspondence of Alice Kirk Grierson*. Lincoln: University of Nebraska Press, 1989.

Leckie, William H., and Shirley A. Leckie. *The Buffalo Soldiers: A Narrative of the Black Cavalry on the West*. Norman: University of Oklahoma Press, 2003.

————. *Unlikely Warriors: General Benjamin Grierson and His Family*. Norman: University of Oklahoma Press, 1984.

Leiker, James N. *Racial Borders: Black Soldiers Along the Rio Grande*. College Station: Texas A&M University Press, 1995.

Lummis, Charles R. *General Crook and the Apache Wars*. Flagstaff: Northland Press, 1985.

McChristian, Douglas C. *Fort Bowie, Arizona: Combat Post of the Southwest, 1858–1894*. Norman: University of Oklahoma Press, 2005.

————. ed. and comp. *Garrison Tangles in the Friendless Tenth: The Journal of First Lieutenant John Bigelow, Jr. Fort Davis, Texas*. Bryan and Mattituck, TX: J.M. Carroll Company, 1985.

————. *Regular Army O! Soldiering on the Western Frontier, 1865–1891*. Norman: University of Oklahoma Press, 2017.

McCracken, Harold. *Frederic Remington's Own West*. New York: Dial Press, 1960.

McCullough, David. *Brave Companions: Portraits in History*. New York: Prentice Hall, 1992.

Magid, Paul. George Crook: From the Redwoods to Appomattox. Norman: University of Oklahoma Press, 2011.

————. *The Gray Fox: George Crook and the Indian Wars*. Norman: University of Oklahoma Press, 2015.

Mails, Thomas. *The People Called Apache*. New York: BDD Illustrated Books, 1993.

Manchester, William. *The Arms of Krupp, 1587–1968*. Boston: Little Brown, 1968.

Marszalek, Jr. John F. *Court-Martial: A Black Man in America*. New York: Charles Scribner's Sons, 1972.

Martin, Patricia Preciado, comp. *Beloved Land: An Oral History of Mexican Americans in Southern Arizona*. Tucson: University of Arizona Press, 200

Matloff, Maurice. *American Military History*. Washington, DC: Office of the Chief of Military History United States Army, 1960.

Mazzanovich, Anton. *Trailing Geronimo*. Hollywood, CA: Privately Printed, 1931.

Medal of Honor Recipients 1863–1973. Washington, DC: U.S. Government Printing Office, 1973.

Michno, Gregory F. *Encyclopedia of the Indian Wars: Western Battles and Skirmishes, 1850–1890*. Missoula, MT: Mountain Press Publishing Company, 2003.

Miles, Nelson A. *Personal Observations and Recollections of General Nelson A. Miles Embracing a Brief View of the Civil War, or, From New England to the Golden Gate: and the Story of his Indian Campaigns, with Comments on the Exploration, Development and Progress of our Great Western Empire*. Chicago: Werner, 1896.

Millard, Candice. *Hero of Empire: The Boer War, A Daring Escape, and the Making of Winston Churchill*. New York: Doubleday, 2016.

Miller, Darlis A. *Soldiers and Settlers: Military Supply in the Southwest, 1861–1885*. Albuquerque: University of New Mexico Press, 1989.

Mills, Anson. *My Story*. Washington, D.C.: The Author, 1918.

Mullin, William G. *The Twenty-fourth Infantry Past and Present: A Brief History of the Regiment Compiled from Official Records, Under the Direction of the Regimental Commander*. N.P., 1923.

Myers, John. *The Border Wardens*. Englewood, NJ: Prentice-Hall, 1971.

Nash, Gerald D. *Creating the West: Historical Interpretations 1890–1990*. Albuquerque: University of New Mexico Press, 1991.

Nickens, Paul R., and Kathleen M. Nickens. *History of the Apache Agency and Army Camp at Old San Carlos, 1873–1929*. Tucson: Tucson Corral of the Westerners, 2009.

————. *Old San Carlos*. Charleston, SC: Arcadia Publishing, 2008.

Nye, Wilber S. *Carbine and Lance: The Story of Old Fort Sill*. Norman, University of Oklahoma Press, 1937.

Nye, William F., trans. *Sonora: Its Extent, Population, Natural Productions, Indians Tribes, Names, Mineral Lands, Etc., Etc*. San Francisco: H.H. Bancroft and Company, 1861.

Paul, R. Eli, ed. *The Frontier Army: Echoes from Dakota and the West*. Pierre: South Dakota Historical Society Press, 2019.

Pearce, T. M., ed. *New Mexico Place Names: A Geographical Dictionary*. Albuquerque: University of New Mexico Press, 1965.

Pond, George E. *The Shenandoah Valley in 1864*. New York, C. Scribner's Sons, c1885.

Quebbeman, Frances E. *Medicine in Territorial Arizona*. Phoenix: Arizona Historical Foundation, 1966.

Radbourne, Allan. *Corporal Edward Scott, Frontier Cavalryman*. London: The English Westerners' Society, 2015.

Radbourne, Allan. *Mickey Free: Apache Captive, Interpreter, and Indian Scout*. Tucson: Arizona Historical Society, 2005.

Reed, Hugh T. *Cadet Life at West Point*. Chicago: Hugh T. Reed, 1896.

Reynolds, Cuyler, ed. *Hudson-Mohawk Genealogical and Family Memoirs*. Vol. 4. New York. Lewis Historical Publishing Company, 1911.

Rickey, Jr., Don. *Forty Miles a Day on Beans and Hay: The Enlisted Soldier Fighting the Indian Wars*. Norman: University of Oklahoma Press, 1963.

Robbins, James S. *Last in Their Class: Custer, Pickett and the Goats of West Point*. New York: Encounter Books, 2006.

Rodenbough, Theo. F., and William L. Haskin, eds. *The Army of the United States: Historical Sketches of Staff and Line with Portraits of Generals-in Chief*. New York: Maynard, Merrill, & Co., 1896.

Roe, Frances M.A. *Army Letters from an Officer's Wife, 1871–1888*. Lincoln: University of Nebraska Press, 1981.

Ronstadt, Edward F., ed. *Borderman: Memoirs of Federico José María Ronstadt*. Albuquerque: University of New Mexico Press, 1993.

Rush, Nixon O. *Remington and Owen Wister: The Story of a Friendship, 1893–1909*. Tallahassee: Privately Printed, 1961.

Samuels, Peggy, and Harold Samuels. *Frederic Remington: A Biography*. Garden City, New York: Doubleday & Company, Inc., 1982.

————, eds. *The Collected Writings of Frederic Remington*. New York: Castle, 1986.

Schlesinger, Jr., Arthur M. *The Almanac of American History*. New York: Barnes and Noble Books, 1993.

Schubert, Frank N. *On the Trail of the Buffalo Soldier: Biographies of African Americans in the U.S. Army, 1866–1917*, I. Wilmington, DE: Scholarly Resources, Inc., 1995.

————. *Black Valor: Buffalo Soldiers and the Medal of Honor, 1870–1898*. Wilmington, DE: Scholarly Resources Inc., 1997.

Schubert, Irene, and Frank N. Schubert. *On the Trail of the Buffalo Soldier II*. Lanham, MD: Scarecrow Press, Inc. 2004.

Shay, Michael E. *Henry Ware Lawton: Union Infantryman, Frontier Soldier, Charismatic Warrior*. Columbia: University of Missouri Press, 2016.

Shellum, Brian G. *Black Cadet in a White Bastion: Charles Young at West Point*. Lincoln: University of Nebraska Press, 2006.

Shrader, Reginald, gen. ed. *Reference Guide to United States Military History, 1865–1919*. New York: Sachem Publishing Associates, Inc., 1993.

Smith, Sherry L. *The View from Officers' Row: Army Perceptions of Western Indians*. Tucson: University of Arizona Press, 1990.

Smith, Stephen D. *The African American Soldier at Fort Huachuca, Arizona, 1892–1946*. Fort Huachuca: U.S. Army, 2001.

Smith, Thomas West. *The Story of a Regiment: "Scott's 900" Eleventh New York Cavalry from the St. Lawrence River to the Gulf of Mexico, 1861–1865*. Chicago: Veteran Association of the Eleventh New York Cavalry, 1897.

Sonnischsen, C.L. *Tucson: The Life and Times of an American City*. Norman: University of Oklahoma Press, 1982.

Splete, Allen P., and Marilyn D. Splete, eds. *Frederic Remington—Selected Letters*. New York: Abbeville Press, 1988.

Stallard, Patricia Y., ed. *Fanny Dunbar Corbusier: Recollections of Her Army Life, 1869–1908*. Norman: University of Oklahoma Press, 2003.

————. *Glittering Misery: Dependents of the Indian Fighting Army*. Fort Collins, CO: The Old Army Press, 1978.

Stiles, T.J. *Custer's Trials: A Life on the Frontier of America*. New York: Alfred A. Knopf, 2015.

Summerhayes, Martha. *Vanished Arizona: Recollections of Army Life*. Philadelphia: J.B. Lippincott Co., 1908.

Sweeney, Edwin R. *From Cochise to Geronimo: The Chiricahua Apaches, 1874–1886*. Norman: University of Oklahoma Press, 2010.

Taft, Robert. *Artists and Illustrators of the Old West 1850–1890*. New York: Bonanza Books, 1953.

Tagg, Martyn D. *The Camp at Bonita Cañon: A Buffalo Soldier Camp in Chiricahua National Monument, Arizona*. Tucson: Western Archeological Center and Conservation Center, 1987.

Thomas, Evan. *The War Lovers: Roosevelt, Lodge, Hearst, and the Rush to Empire, 1898*. New York: Little, Brown and Company, 2010.

Thrapp, Dan L. *Al Sieber: Chief of Scouts*. Norman: University of Oklahoma Press, 1964.

————. *Conquest of Apacheria*. Norman: University of Oklahoma Press, 1967.

————. *Encyclopedia of Frontier Biography*. 4 vols. Glendale, CA: Arthur H. Clark Company, 1988.

————, ed., *Dateline Fort Bowie: Charles Fletcher Lummis Reports on the Apache War*. Norman: University of Oklahoma Press, 1979.

————. *General Crook and the Sierra Madre Adventure*. Norman: University of Oklahoma Press, 1972.

Tuccille, Jerome. *The Roughest Riders: The Untold Story of the Black Soldiers in the Spanish-American War*. Chicago Review Press, 2015.

Twenty-fifth Annual Reunion of the Association of the Graduates of the United States Military Academy at West Point, New York. NP: Seemann & Peters Printers and Binders, 1894.

Upton, Emory. *The Armies of Asia and Europe. Embracing Official Reports on the Armies of Japan, China, India, Persia, Italy, Russia, Austria, Germany, France, and England. Accompanied by Letters Descriptive of a Journey from Japan to the Caucasus*. New York: D. Appleton & Co., 1878.

————. *Military Policy of the United States Army*. Washington, DC: Government Printing Office, 1904.

————. *A New System of Infantry Tactics, Double and Single Rank Adapted to American Topography and Improved Fire-Arms*. New York: D. Appleton & Co., 1868.

Upton, Richard, comp. and ed. *Fort Custer on the Big Horn, 1877–1898: Its History and Personalities as Told and Pictured by its Contemporaries*. Glendale, CA: A.H. Clark Co., 1973.

Utley, Robert M., ed. *An Army Doctor on the Western Frontier: Journals and Letters of John Vance Lauderdale, 1864–1890*. Albuquerque: University of New Mexico Press, 2014.

————. *Billy the Kid: A Short and Violent Life*. Lincoln: University of Nebraska Press, 1991.

————. *Cavalier in Buckskin: George Custer and the Western Military Frontier*. Norman: University of Oklahoma Press, 1988.

————. *The Commanders: Civil War Generals Who Shaped the American West*. Norman: University of Oklahoma Press, 2018.

————. *Fort Davis National Historic Site, Texas*. Washington, DC: National Park Service, 1965.

————. *Geronimo*. New Haven: Yale University Press, 2012.

Van Zile-Scott, Edward. *Unwept, Unhonored, Unsung: Black American Soldiers and the Spanish American War*. Montgomery, AL: The Black Belt Press, 1995.

von Versen, Maximilian. *Reisen in Amerika Und Der Sudamerikanische Kreig*. Breslau, Germany: M. Malzer, 1872.

Vorpahl, Ben Merchant. *My Dear Wister: The Frederic Remington—Owen Wister Letters*. Palo Alto, CA: The American West Publishing Company, 1972.

Walker, Henry P., and Don Bufkin. *Historical Atlas of Arizona*. 2nd ed. Norman: University of Oklahoma Press, 1986.

Werthern, Alfred Hermann Thilo, Freiherr von. *General von Versen: Ein Militärisches Zeit und Lebensbild. Aus Hinterlassenen Briefen und Aufzeichnungen Zusammengestellt*. Berlin: E.S. Mittler, 1898.

Whitman, S.E. *The Troopers: An Informal History of the Plains Cavalry, 1865–1890*. New York: Hastings House Publishers, 1962.

Wilson, Steve, ed. *Child of the Fighting Tenth: On the Frontier with the Buffalo Soldiers by Forrestine C. Hooker*. Oxford: Oxford University Press, 2003.

Winters, John D. *The Civil War in Louisiana*. Baton Rouge: Louisiana State University Press, 1963.

Woodard, Arthur, ed. *On the Bloody Trail of Geronimo: Lt. John Bigelow, Jr*. Tucson: Westernlore Press, 1986.

Wooster, Robert, ed. *Soldier, Surgeon, Scholar: The Memoirs of William Henry Corbusier 1844–1930*. Norman: University of Oklahoma Press, 2003.

Zellman, Michael David. Comp. *American Art Analog*. New York: Chelsea House Publishers in association with American Art Analog, 1986.

Zogbaum, Rufus. *Horse, Foot, and Dragoons*. New York: Harpers & Brother, 1887.

Articles

Altshuler, Constance Wynn. "The Case of Sylvester Mowry." *Arizona and the West* 15, nos. 1 and 2 (Spring and Summer 1973): 63–82 and 149–74.

Arizona Cattlelog (May 1969): 37–38.

Bigelow, John. *Outing*: *An Illustrated Magazine of Recreation*. (April 1886): 50–56; (May 1886): 147–56; (June 1886): 291–300; (July 1886): 416–23; (August 1886): 535–43; (September 1886): 646–52; (December 1886): 223–33; (January1887): 308–17; (February 1887): 428–40; and (March 1887): 515–25.

Bigelow, Poultney. "Frederic Remington: With Extracts from Unpublished Letters." *The Quarterly Journal of the New York State Historical Association* 10, no. 1 (January 1929): 45–52

Bourke, John G. "General Crook in Indian Country." *The Century Magazine: A Popular Quarterly* 41, no. 87 (March 1891): 644.

Clarke, Powhatan H. "Characteristic Sketches of the German Army." *Harper's Weekly* 37 (May 20, 1893): 479–81.

————. "A Hot Trail." *Cosmopolitan Magazine* 16 (October 1894): 706–16.

————. "The Military Riding School of Germany." *Harper's Weekly* 35 (November 14, 1891): 893.

Clarke, Powhatan H. “Revolvers and Revolver Practice.” *Journal of the United States Cavalry Association* 3 (1890): 222–25.

Columbia Alumni News 37 (October 1945): 26.

Coleman, Ronald G. *“The Buffalo Soldiers Guardians of the Uintah Frontier 1886–1901.” Utah Historical Quarterly* 47, no. 4 (Fall 1979): 421–39.

Crook, George. “The Apache Problem.” *Journal of the Military Service Institution of the United States* 7, no. 27 (October 1887): 257–269.

Diab, Jamil, “Philip Cassadore: Apache Singer and Lecturer.” *Indians Illustrated* 1, no. 7 (September 1968): 7–9.

Ellinwood, Sybil. “Calabasas,” *Arizoniana* 5, no. 4 (Winter): 27–41

Gale, Jack C. “Hatfield Under Fire, May 15, 1886.” *Journal of Arizona History* 18, no. 4 (Winter 1977): 447–68.

————. Lebo in Pursuit.” *Journal of Arizona History* 21, no 1 (Spring 1980): 1–24.

Gates, John M. “The Alleged Isolation of U.S. Army Officers on the Late 19th Century.” *Parameters*, no. 10 (September 1980): 32–45.

————. “General George Crook’s First Apache Campaign.” *Journal of the West* 6, no. 2 (April 1967): 310–18.

“Heliography in the Army.” *Harper’s Weekly* 30 (August 14, 1886), 523.

Journal of the American Medical Association 7 (November 10, 1886): 588.

Langellier, John P. “Buffalo Soldiers in Big Sky Country, 1888–1898.” *Montana: The Magazine of Western History* 67, no. 3 (Autumn 2017): 41–56.

———— . “Camp Grant Affair, 1891: Milestone in Federal Indian Policy?” *Military History of Texas and the Southwest* 15, no. 2 (1979): 17–30.

————. “The Tenth U.S. Cavalry in Prescott, A.T.” *Territorial Times Prescott Arizona Corral of Westerners International*, no. 1 (November 2009): 22–29.

Lovell, Margaretta M. “Dashing for America: Frederic Remington, National Myths, and Art Historical Narratives.” *The Journal of the Association of Historians of American Art* (Fall 2015): 1–20.

The Military Surgeon: Journal of the Association of Military Surgeons of the United States (1907): 79.

Neifert, William W. “Trailing Geronimo by Heliograph.” *Winners of the West* 12 No. 11 (October 1935): 1–4.

“Our Soldiers in the Southwest.” *Harper’s Weekly* 30 (August 21, 1886): 535.

Phillips, Tom. “Sobriquet: A Chronological Commentary on the Name ‘Buffalo Soldier.’” *The Journal of America’s Military Past* 35, no. 2 (Spring/Summer 2010): 5–30.

Radbourne, Allan. "Captain Hatfield and the Chiricahuas," in "*Ho for the Great West!" and Other Original Papers to Mark the 25th Anniversary of the English Westerners Society*. London: English Westerners Society, 1980: 71–81.

————. "In Pursuit of Ma-say: Lieutenant River's Report." English Westerners' *Tally Sheet* 47 (Spring 2001): 33–38.

Remington, Frederic. "A Scout with the Buffalo Soldiers." *Century* 37 (April 1889): 899–912.

————. "Chasing a Major General." *Harper's Weekly* 34 (December 6, 1890): 946–47.

————. "General Miles's Review of the Mexican Army." *Harper's Weekly* 35 (July 4, 1891): 495.

————. "Indians as Irregular Cavalry." *Harper's Weekly* 34 (December 27, 1890): 1001 and 1004–6.

————. "Lt. Johnson and the 10th U.S. Cavalry in Arizona." *Harper's Weekly* 32 (December 22, 1888): 989.

————. "Massai's Crooked Trail." *Harper's Monthly* 96 (January 1898): 240–46.

————. "Skirmish Line Target Practice in the Regular Army." *Harper's Weekly* 33 (October 26, 1889): 862.

————. "The Sioux Outbreak in South Dakota." *Harper's Weekly* 35 (January 31, 1891): 57–62.

————. "Training Cavalry Horses to Jump Obstacles." *Harper's Weekly* 35 (September 19, 1891): 709–10.

————. "Two Gallant Young Cavalry Men." *Harper's Weekly* 35 (March 22, 1890): 220.

Rolak, Bruno J. "General Miles' Mirrors: The *Heliograph* in the Geronimo Campaign of 1886." *Journal of Arizona History* 16, no. 2 (Summer 1975): 145–160.

Schubert, Frank N. "Buffalo Soldiers: Myth and Reality." *Army History: The Professional Bulletin of Army History* (Spring 2001): 13–18.

Science 1111 (April 14, 1916): 538.

Shipp, W.E. "Captain Crawford's Last Expedition." *Journal of the United States Cavalry Association* 5, no. 19 (December 1892): 343–61.

"Taming the Savage Apache Followers of Geronimo." *Frontier Times* 1, no. 1 (October 1923): 12.

Watson, James W. "Scouting in Arizona." *Journal of the U.S. Cavalry Association* 10 (June 1897): 128–134.

Wister, Owen. "Specimen Jones." *Harper's New Monthly* 89 (July 1894): 204–16.

Newspapers

Anderson Court House (SC) *Intelligencer*
Arizola (AZ) *The Oasis*
Army and Navy Journal
Baltimore Sun
Boston Herald
Boston Post
Chicago Times
Clifton Clarion
Daily Tombstone Epitaph
Florence Arizona Enterprise
Globe Arizona Silver Belt
Jasper (IN) *Weekly Courier*
Kansas City (MO) *Times*
Kingston (NM) *Sierra County Advocate*
L'Anse Sentinel (MI)
London Standard
Lordsburg Western Liberal
Mineral Park (AZ) *Mohave County Miner*
The Nation: A Weekly Journal Devoted to Politics, Literature Science, Drama, Music, Art, Finance
New York Herald
New York Sun
New York Times
New York Herald,
Omaha Daily Bee
Opelousas (LA) St. Landry Democrat
Phoenix Arizona Republican
Pittsburg Dispatch
Prescott Weekly Arizona Miner
St. Johns (AZ) *Herald*
St. Louis Republic
St. Paul Daily Globe
Santa Fe Daily New Mexican
Shreveport Times
Springfield Illinois Record
Tucson Arizona Daily Star
Tucson Arizona Weekly Citizen

Prescott Arizona Weekly Journal-Miner
Vancouver Independent
Washington, DC Evening Star
Washington, DC National Tribune
Washington, DC Sunday Herald and Weekly National Intelligencer
Watertown (NY) *Daily Times*

Unpublished Materials

Lamb, Blaine Peterson. "Jewish Pioneers in Arizona, 1850–1920." Ph.D. Dissertation. Arizona State University, 1982. Tempe.

Phillips, Thomas D. Undated notes from a public lecture.

Ruhnke, Janet Howard. "Impressions from Sketchpad and Notebook: A Biographical View of Rufus Fairchild Zogbaum." MA Thesis, University of San Diego, 1976

Scheips, Paul J. "The Military Heliograph and its Use in Arizona and the Southwest." Fort Monmouth, NJ: Historical Office, U.S. Army Signal Corps, 1954.

Schubert, *Frank N.* "The Black Regular Army Regiments in Wyoming, 1885–1912." Master's Thesis, University of Wyoming, Laramie, 1970.

Electronic Sources

"Henry Boyce." *Biographical Directory of Federal Judges*. Washington, DC: Federal Judicial Center. www.fjc.gov/history/judges/bouyce-henry.

"Powhatan Clarke 19 Sep. 1837-A5 Apr. 1917," *Students of the University of Virginia, 1825–1872*. www.uvastudents.wordpress.com/2012/11/18/powhatan-clarke-19-sep-1837-25-apr-1917.

Covington, Jr., Robert R. Chaplain (MAJ), "Army Chaplains for the Corps of Cadets: An Inquiry." 1Research Paper Presented to The United States Army Chaplain School Fort Hamilton, New York 11252. May 11, 1973. https://archive.org/stream/armychaplainsfor00covi/armychaplainsfor00covi_djvu.txt.

Gates, John M. *The U.S. Army and Irregular Warfare*. Wooster, OH: The College of Wooster, 1998. http://discover.wooster.edu/jgates/progressives-in-uniform.

History of Fort Wingate Depot, Fort Fauntleroy and Lyon. https://www.ftwingate.org/ docs/ pub/History_FortWingate.pdf.

Jamison. Tommy. "'Looks Like a Chilean War': The Baltimore Incident as Counterfactual Exercise." http://cimsec.org/looks-like-a-chilean-war-the-baltimore-incident-as-counterfactual-exercise/1936.

www.arlingtoncemetery.net/jamescre.htm.

www.chartiers.com/raybell/1981-clemens2.html.

www.combat.ws/S4/MILTERMS/WP0SLANG.HTM.

www.findagrave.com/ memorial/5844313.

www.findagrave.com/memorial/15916163.

www.flickr.com/photos/ fredericremington/5042136001.

www.internment.net/data/us/ca/sanfran/sfnat/san-francisco-national-cemetery-records-st-sz.htm.

www.measuringworth.com/uscompare/relaticvevalue.php.

www.umd.edu/history-andmission/timeline.

Index

A

B

C

E

F

I

J

K

L

M

N

O

P

Q

R

S

U

V

W

Y

Z